KING SOLOMON'S CHILDREN

MORE WILDSIDE CLASSICS

Dacobra, or The White Priests of Ahriman, by Harris Burland
The Nabob, by Alphonse Daudet
Out of the Wreck, by Captain A. E. Dingle
The Elm-Tree on the Mall, by Anatole France
The Lance of Kanana, by Harry W. French
Amazon Nights, by Arthur O. Friel
Caught in the Net, by Emile Gaboriau
The Gentle Grafter, by O. Henry
Raffles, by E. W. Hornung
Gates of Empire, by Robert E. Howard
Tom Brown's School Days, by Thomas Hughes
The Opium Ship, by H. Bedford Jones
The Miracles of Antichrist, by Selma Lagerlof
Arsène Lupin, by Maurice LeBlanc
A Phantom Lover, by Vernon Lee
The Iron Heel, by Jack London
The Witness for the Defence, by A.E.W. Mason
The Spider Strain and Other Tales, by Johnston McCulley
Tales of Thubway Tham, by Johnston McCulley
The Prince of Graustark, by George McCutcheon
Bull-Dog Drummond, by Cyril McNeile
The Moon Pool, by A. Merritt
The Red House Mystery, by A. A. Milne
Blix, by Frank Norris
Wings over Tomorrow, by Philip Francis Nowlan
The Devil's Paw, by E. Phillips Oppenheim
Satan's Daughter and Other Tales, by E. Hoffmann Price
The Insidious Dr. Fu Manchu, by Sax Rohmer
Mauprat, by George Sand
The Slayer and Other Tales, by H. de Vere Stacpoole
Penrod (Gordon Grant Illustrated Edition), by Booth Tarkington
The Gilded Age, by Mark Twain
The Blockade Runners, by Jules Verne
The Gadfly, by E.L. Voynich

Please see www.wildsidepress.com for a complete list!

KING SOLOMON'S CHILDREN

Some Parodies

of H. Rider Haggard

Edited by

R. Reginald
and
Douglas Melville

WILDSIDE PRESS

For George and Dany Slusser,
this little bit of She and Allan

KING SOLOMON'S CHILDREN

Introduction Copyright © 1978 by R. Reginald. All rights reserved

This edition published in 2006 by Wildside Press, LLC.
www.wildsidepress.com

CONTENTS

[Biron, Henry Chartres], Hyder Ragged, pseud.,
KING SOLOMON'S WIVES; Or, The Phantom Mines, London, 1887

[De Morgan, John], KING SOLOMON'S TREASURES by the Author of "He," "It," "Pa," "Ma," etc., New York, [1887]

[De Morgan, John], "BESS," A COMPANION TO "JESS," by the Author of "King Solomon's Wives," "King Solomon's Treasures," "He," "It," etc., etc., New York, 1887

KING SOLOMON'S WIVES;

OR,

THE PHANTOM MINES.

[Henry Chartres Biron]
Hyer Ragged, pseud.

THE GREAT KING TWOSH AND HIS COURT: A SNEEZE AND ITS CONSEQUENCES.
[Page 58.

KING SOLOMON'S WIVES;

OR,

THE PHANTOM MINES.

BY HYDER RAGGED.

WITH NUMEROUS ILLUSTRATIONS.

LONDON:
VIZETELLY & CO., 42 *CATHERINE STREET, STRAND.*
1887.

GLASGOW:
C. L. WRIGHT,
PRINTER.

CONTENTS.

	PAGE
INTRODUCTION, ...	9

CHAPTER I.
MY PLAN OF THE CAMPAIGN—I MEET SIR HARRY—THE VOYAGE OUT, ... 13

CHAPTER II.
PREPARATIONS FOR OUR JOURNEY—UMBUGS ENTERS OUR SERVICE—UNHAPPY ENDS OF BOSS AND JOSS—OUR START, ... 26

CHAPTER III.
OUR JOURNEY ACROSS THE GREAT DESERT—STARVATION—THIRST—THE GIRAFFE—THE BUFFALO—THE BEAR, 36

CHAPTER IV.
WE FIND KING SOLOMON'S ROAD—THE SAVAGES FIND US—RECEPTION BY NATIVES AND JOURNEY TO THE GREAT KING TWOSH, ... 46

CHAPTER V.
WE ENTER IPECACUANHA LAND—OUR RECEPTION BY TWOSH THE KING, ... 56

CONTENTS.

CHAPTER VI.

THE WITCH HUNT—THE ECLIPSE—ITS EFFECT ON TWOSH THE KING—REMARKABLE CONDUCT OF UMBUGS—SAVED! SAVED! 67

CHAPTER VII.

THE BATTLE—THE CHARGE OF THE BLUES—CONFESSIONS OF TWOSH, ... 79

CHAPTER VIII.

THE TREASURES OF KING SOLOMON, ... 92

CHAPTER IX.

WE FIND SIR HARRY'S BROTHER—SUPPRESSED EMOTION OF SIR HARRY—SCANDAL IN HIGH LIFE—INTERVENTION OF A GREAT PERSONAGE, . . . 104

CHAPTER X.

AN OLD FRIEND—OUR DEPARTURE—OUR ARRIVAL IN ENGLAND—ENTHUSIASTIC RECEPTION, . . . 113

INTRODUCTION.

NOW that this book is printed, and about to be given to the world, the question will perhaps arise— Why do I write it? Captious people may suggest—For reasons not unconnected with the paltry pence which its sale may produce. Such suggestions I repel with scorn. My reason—I give it without hesitation—is this: To prove my veracity. The one quality for which my family has always been noted is its unswerving veracity. A Quarterman's word has always been as good as his bond. I have never heard our greatest enemy

—and we have enemies, what great family has not?—suggest that the one was worth more than the other.

Now, the scepticism with which my tales of adventure have hitherto been received has been a constant source of annoyance to me, especially as I have no intention of going into the wholesale kettle trade, so I determined to take the step of appealing to the credulity of the public in print. The public, I have observed from long experience, will swallow most things in print, and anything, however outrageous, if only it deals with savages and appears within measurable distance of Christmas. Perhaps I may be forgiven for adding that our family is one of the oldest in Ireland, and that my initial A. does not stand for Ananias—a popular idea which has caused me much annoyance.

There are many things connected with my journey which I could dwell upon at length:— The indigent fawners of Ipecacuanha Land; How we won the great battle of Unlimited Loo. (They would go on the king of trumps unguarded, with five players!) Want of space, and not imagination, as some insinuate, is the sole reason I do not. As for my literary style, I do not think that needs any apology. For years I have borrowed a *Sporting Times* every Saturday, and what would Sunday be without its *Referee?* So if any one says, after this, that my style is not pure, or my wit is lacking in refinement, you will know what to think of him.

When I told Sir Harry and Captain Noegood, R.H.M., that I was writing this book, their advice was: "Pitch it strong, Ananias" (a playful way of addressing me they have. It probably led to the error about my name), and I have endeavoured to carry out their advice to the best of my ability. *Aprôpos* I might quote a proverb of Ipecacuanha Land, but as it is quite pointless in the original, and slightly improper in English, I will forbear.

A. QUARTERMAN.

KING SOLOMON'S WIVES;

OR,

THE PHANTOM MINES.

CHAPTER I.

MY PLAN OF THE CAMPAIGN—I MEET SIR HARRY—
THE VOYAGE OUT.

TALES of mysterious adventure have always been my delight. Having come to the conclusion,* from a careful perusal of some of the more recent of these histories, that the

---

* *Note by* EDITOR: Why, you have only just begun!
Note by ME: Am I writing this book, or you?
Note by EDITOR: Very sorry; only my fun.
Note by ME: It may be your idea of fun; it is not mine. Don't let it occur again.

present race of savages is of a peculiarly confiding nature, the time seemed all fitting for a visit to their midst. Why should not I, A. Quarterman, venture on a personally-conducted tour in search of treasure, which there seems to be lying about to a considerable extent just now?* Though no boaster, I may say for an expedition of this character I was suited above my fellows. My life has been adventurous from my cradle. During a brief career as an Irish M.P. of Nationalist leanings I lost a limb. My constituents, with the wild justice of revenge, mistook me for a land-grabber and shot me in the legs—the right one. The American funds supplied me with a cork substitute.

The affair, published in the *Benighted Irishman* as an incident of the campaign, proved a great success. Our receipts doubled within the week. How well I remember the parish priest presenting me with the leg, and saying as he did so with a humour racy of the soil:

---

* *Note by* EDITOR : Is not this sentence rather ambiguous?
Note by ME : Not a bit—one of my pet passages.

"Ye have stood for Cork for some time, me boy, now cork shall stand for you."

Dear chap, I wonder what, or whom, he is doing now!

In addition to this advantage, I have been bald for years, and have allowed Art to step in to Nature's aid (as the advertisement beautifully puts it) in the form of a wig. Any one who pretends to any knowledge of the savage mind will see at a glance what weapons we had here, what a wealth of resource to fall back upon in the case of any encounter with the aborigines. Of course, I bought an eye-glass. Oddly enough, I never could hold it properly in my eye. Eventually, I gave it to Umbugs— but I am anticipating.

The idea of fitting myself with a complete set of false teeth did occur to me, but I abandoned it on account of the expense. However, I took a few easy lessons in legerdemain to keep up, if necessary, the character of magician, which I understand the simple child of the desert ascribes to one on the smallest provocation.

After making all my arrangements, I had to account for my absence to my wife, for I am a family man. To soften the shock of my departure, I adopted a *ruse* for which I hope I may be forgiven. I stated I had been summoned to serve on a special jury in the great *cause célèbre* of "Dash *v.* Dash and Dash and several others" before Mr. Justice Tub, in the High Courts of Justice. My wife was loth to let me leave her; and I only got away in the end on faithfully promising to take down all the suppressed evidence in short hand. She bore, as I heard afterwards, the separation with an equanimity which proved her a worthy mate of a great traveller.

The reader may ask, Was I going alone on this great enterprise, to seek single-handed for the treasures of King Solomon? for such I do not now mind admitting was the desperate nature of my quest.

No, no, not such a juggins* was A. Quarter-

---

* A term much in vogue among the bloods of Ipecacuanha Land, signifying "a man of little experience." We should say "fool" or "silly fellow."

man. In all these adventures, in the interests of veracity one of the party must be killed at *least*.

If he is lucky enough to escape the hot pot, he may meet his end at the hands—that is the feet—of a rogue elephant, or swell visibly and die in great agony from a poisoned arrow. Possibly he may be thrown into the crater of a volcano by the local priest to appease the gods, or be let down gently in a rough and tumble with a jaguar, but killed he must be. It was clear if I went alone I must die in the interests of truth.

In spite of my abstract love of veracity I must say I did not like the idea. I did not feel prepared to make this sacrifice in the cause of *Truth*, possibly it was *World*ly in me to prefer *Life;* still, *Society*, even *Modern Society*, has its charms, and the view I have always taken of existence has been a roseate, not to say a *Pink 'un*. To expect me to leave this *Vanity Fair* so soon was to ask me for too great a sacrifice, and one which I felt but little disposed to make entirely off my own *Bat*. So I determined to give myself a chance at short odds by surrounding

B

myself with some trusty companions on my voyage out.

Sir Harry and Captain Noegood, late of R. H. M., were my fellow travellers. Their acquaintance I made in the following manner: When we had been some days at sea I appeared at dinner for the first time. Sir Harry and Captain Noegood were opposite me. The Captain and I got on to sporting stories; I led off with my famous Tiger story. (It is a good one, though I say it who should not.) The Captain promptly trumped it with an anecdote about an anaconda. "Ah!" remarked some one, "Quarterman is the chap for snake stories, he is such an agreeable rattle."

Sir Harry, who had sat quite quiet through the first three courses, at the mention of snakes opened his mouth and started—for the leeward port-hole —returning somewhat pale.

"Excuse me," he said.

"Not at all," I replied.

Speaking in a husky voice, he asked:

"Is your name Quarterman?"

I said it was.

THE VOYAGE OUT: A LURCH TO LEEWARD.

He muttered into his beard. A nasty trick I never could cure him of.

During dinner Sir Harry made no further remark, except to refuse, with some asperity, a lobster *mayonnaise*, obviously tinned. After dinner he came up and asked me if I would come into his cabin and smoke a pipe. I accepted his invitation, but noticed he did not indulge in the fragrant herb himself.*

Sir Harry looked like a Dane, and was certainly stout; as he put it, he had a fine presence. I think I have mentioned his habit of muttering in his beard. Captain Noegood was a half-pay Captain, late of H.M. Royal Horse Marines, and always wore dress clothes in the evening, a circumstance which—(but I am anticipating).

In the smoking-room I told them the story of Don Noséy. How he had left Notatall a few years back to search for the visionary treasures of the Great King. How, long after, he staggered

---

* *Note by* EDITOR : Good.

back, a strong man broken-down, and died in my arms; babbling of a strange land where striped giraffes sported with spotted elephants, and crying for "wiskaye" (a drug of great potency, only known in these distant regions, from which he had escaped to die).

Sir Harry was visibly affected. Throwing a broiled bone at my head (an old Danish custom—blood will show—strange, but true), he asked in a quivering voice:

"Have you ever been at Wotabanga?"

I had. I could not deny it.

"You met my brother?" he continued. "My elder brother," he said, with a sigh which betrayed the warm heart which beat under that Danish exterior. "Years ago, in a moment of temporary but unpardonable irritation, I kicked him down the front staircase. He left the country somewhat hurriedly in a bath chair, and has not been heard of since. The title and estates I have assumed; but does he live?" Here he sighed again.

My generous nature was touched. "We will

seek him together," I cried, "on our way to the boundless treasures."

"Done with you," said Sir Harry, "and Noegood shall come, too."

I hesitated.

"You are not half a man," he said.

"Quarterman is my name," was my dignified reproof.

"I was wrong; your pardon!"

"Granted. But there is one question I must ask before admitting Captain Noegood as a partner in our enterprise."

"Just so," said Sir Harry; "only fair."

I looked at Noegood and asked him: "Have you false teeth?" He turned pale. "Have you false teeth?" I repeated sternly, "and will they work with a snap?"

"I have; they will!" he cried, and leaning his head on the table, burst into bitter tears.

It turned out I had unwittingly alluded to a painful incident in the gallant Captain's career. One of the smartest officers in the Royal Horse Marines (whose confiding nature, he afterwards told me, was grossly exaggerated), he had been retired on half-pay. The First Lord at the time had been reading the subject of *Mayhem* in a second-hand copy of "The Student's Blackstone," which he had borrowed from his secretary, and discovered that a front tooth was a fighting member. A man of action, he insisted at once on all the officers in Her Majesty's Navy being examined by a dentist. Noegood, who had not had a tooth in his head for years, procured a perfect set, regardless of expense. It was of no avail. He was compulsorily retired, and the Admiralty deducted the price of the set (they had been obtained on credit) from his first year's pension.

"He shall come," I decided. At this he brisked up.

"Had that Don Noséy anything to leave?" he asked.

"He made me his heir," I answered. "I paid legacy duty on two unreceipted bills, a county court summons, and this strange document." Here I showed them the document*

---
* See folding plate facing Chapter I.

which Don Noséy had brought back from his fatal journey.

We joined hands, and spent the rest of the night in endeavouring to decipher what we hoped would prove the sure, the *Bradshaw Guide* of our great expedition.

CHAPTER II.

PREPARATIONS FOR OUR JOURNEY—UMBUGS ENTERS OUR SERVICE—UNHAPPY ENDS OF BOSS AND JOSS—OUR START.

THE remainder of our voyage passed very quickly, as our time was fully occupied in discussing our plans. We soon came to terms. Of course the treasure hunt was my own venture, but the elder brother was an extra. After a little explanation Sir Harry quite saw this, and fell in with my suggestion of £5 down and expenses. It was agreed that any treasure we found should be divided equally. If our expedition proved the success we hoped it would, we determined to work the affair as a limited liability company. It was understood I was to have the refusal of the post of secretary, as being to a great extent the originator of the scheme. We decided, after some consultation, on taking no firearms. Armed as we were, they would be quite superfluous, besides which, I never was much of a marksman. Of course Sir Harry and Captain Noegood might be dead shots, but they agreed with me on this point with suspicious alacrity.

On reaching Notatall we landed in a surf-boat. On the way to the shore Sir Harry insisted on finishing a case of champagne, which had been sent out as a present to the Governor, on the ground that he hated waste, and that the bottles were sure to get broken on passing the bar—" a thing," he added, "I never once did without taking a drink." Sir Harry seemed a sensible sort of chap.

On landing, our baggage was taken up the town in a " calêga," which is not unlike a Cuban "volanté," but which could not possibly be mistaken for a Victoria hansom. As for our weapons of defence, I cannot do better than put down here a list of those we finally selected.

Catalogued briefly, they were as follows :—

1. My wig and cork-leg (with patent spring).
2. My eye-glass (subsequently given to Umbugs).
3. Captain Noegood's teeth.
4. One big bag of buns (of which more anon).
5. One pocket almanac.

This was our total armament. To conciliate the natives we included in our baggage:

1. The complete insignia of the Primrose League.
2. A portrait of Mrs. Langtry in the act of preferring Pears' Soap to any other. Bought a bargain from the interior of a Peckham 'bus.
3. One tall hat, white with black band; one rabbit to be brought out of ditto; one omelette to be cooked in ditto; a disappearing lady; three thimbles and a pea.

Besides these, one big bag (extra size) for diamonds, to be given us by the savage king, and treasure generally. As provender we provided one Strasbourg pie, a tin of dog biscuits (for our native retinue) and a dozen of old brandy.

DEATH OF BOSS.

Mem. by ARTIST: I have made the elephant sit upon him, as it is more funny.
Mem. by ME: Stick to the text. Remember this is a serious book, and don't sacrifice *Truth* to *Fun*.

Our *entourage* consisted of two natives and Umbugs. The two natives I may dispose of at once, and save the reader a lot of bother. We had to engage them to be killed on the way and provide incident. We called them Boss and Joss—I do not know why, unless from the fact that these happened to be their names.

Poor Boss! his was a sad end. A wild elephant trod on him inadvertently. He was frightfully crushed. The intelligent beast was much upset at the *contretémps*—a pure accident —and showed very good feeling at the funeral. Joss had his head bitten off by a lion. He was certainly unfortunate. The lion happened to be an animal of ambitious mind, and was desirous of obtaining a berth as a performing lion in a travelling circus, with a tamer interviewed in the *Pall Mall*. He must have worked hard at it, for he was *letter* perfect, except in the one scene, where the tamer puts his head in the mouth of the king of beasts. This situation the latter would rehearse with Joss. To this day I believe he only forgot his part, and meant poor Joss no ill. He seemed to *feel* it almost as much as the elephant, and—indeed he seemed aware it was the least he could do—spared us all anxiety about the funeral.

Umbugs was a man of very different stamp. He was a magnificent Zulu. Reserved until he came out of his shell, he might have seemed too large to be a good native, and though of superb courage was never a roysterer. Before consenting to enter our service he asked where we were bound for. On being told, he gave a wild laugh. We asked what this meant. In answer he made a reply we could not quite catch, but which sounded something like—

"No matter! a time will come."

This rather bored us. He also annoyed Sir Harry by calling him Incubus and Jumbo (the same thing in different tongues). Poor Sir Harry, I think I mentioned, had a presence.

Then he cried:

"I like pale faces, I will come with you, I know their ways, I have seen their cities. After an ephemeral success as corner man in a wandering troupe of Christy Minstrels, did I not perform as one of a Zulu family in the palace of ten thousand lights? Do I not still correspond with a black-eyed houri who kept a scent stall?" (Here he sighed.)

Captain Noegood was touched.

"I like your looks," said Sir Harry, who had decided on taking Umbugs' remarks as a compliment. "We will engage you."

"Thanks you, White Elephant," said Umbugs.

This was carrying a joke too far. Sir Harry frowned, and looked a Dane all over. The Captain and I would not encourage Umbugs. On the whole I am not sorry we engaged him. He seemed a strong beast, and if he became troublesome we could always lose him in the desert.

The day is fixed for our departure. Sir Harry prepares for the journey by teaching Umbugs double dummy, with the help of some popular manuals of the game of short whist. When I remonstrate with him on the ground that I never heard of travellers playing double dummy in a desert, he asks somewhat tartly:

"What are we to do in the evenings?" and

goes on to say: "If we meet the savages, don't you know, the Clay and Cavendish will come in handy for the pipe of peace."

Umbugs laughs; he is becoming quite a sycophant. If Sir Harry is going to turn everything into ridicule, we had better give the whole thing up. When he is not playing double dummy, he takes the air on a tricycle.

We have one great disappointment. At the last moment our disappearing lady threw up her engagement and declined to come. Most annoying, as I cannot get the hat trick to go quite smoothly. Captain Noegood is quite upset. Perhaps it is as well, these sailors are so susceptible. If we were not so pressed for time we might get an injunction from the Vice Chancellor.

By the way, I hope these treasures are all right. Curiously enough, every one here seems to know the legend, and is immensely interested on hearing that we are going in search of them. We are quite the lions of the place. But these natives show their interest in such an odd way. I was chatting on the subject to-day with six of the most intelligent. They all made guttural sounds, and put one finger on the side of the nose. I am told it is a custom of the country, and I make every allowance, but I find it rather irritating.

At last we are off. The entire town turns out to see the start. The church-bells ring and the bands are playing. Preparations are being made for fireworks in the evening and general rejoicings. Very gratifying.

Captain Noegood arrives at the trysting place in a hansom. He won't walk a yard further than he can help. These sailors are so lazy. He arrives rather late, as he sat up all night pressing his dress clothes and oiling the snap of his teeth.

Sir Harry rides up on a tricycle which he has chartered by the hour. He is so pleased with it that he decides, just before starting, to buy the machine on the hire system, and ride across the desert on it. The natives are delighted. Umbugs leads the way, and at last we are started on the great journey which was to end so strangely for us all.

CHAPTER III.

OUR JOURNEY ACROSS THE GREAT DESERT—STARVATION—THIRST—THE GIRAFFE—THE BUFFALO—THE BEAR.

FOR days our journey resolves itself into a sort of go-as-you-please contest across the desert, with no gate-money and a very vague prospect of prizes.

Noegood is not a good walker. About once every ten minutes he says, "if it is very much further he really must go back in a cab."

Our native contingent are much pleased with Sir Harry's tricycle. It leads to unpleasantness in the end. Sir Harry is so selfish. Noegood suggests his giving him a lift. Sir Harry answers tetchily that it's not a sociable, but offers to sublet it at the usual rate per hour. Noegood refuses in a huff. He tells me in confidence that he never thought much of "Wheelers," and as to Sir Harry, if he goes on like this it would do him good to send him to Coventry. "And the machine too," I suggest. It had suffered a good deal over the hills.

In the evening Captain Noegood dresses for dinner. Sir Harry wins at double dummy from Umbugs.

We suffer a good deal from insects, especially owning to the frequent presence of the dreadful "Tsetse" fly. Umbugs reassures us by saying its bite is fatal to everything except donkeys.

"Lucky for you chappies," observes Noegood.

Sir Harry and I ignore him, it is the only way.

In killing these insects with the flat palm the natives display great dexterity, but poor Joss presumed upon his position in selecting Sir Harry's waistcoat for the feat. He said it saved his life, but our cycling friend did not like it.

After about a week of this I find the following entries in my diary:

Monday.

Tired out. Food, too, running very short. We have come down to our last dog biscuit. Sir Harry says fasting is all very well, but he prefers doing it on salt-fish and plenty of pancakes, but then he is so greedy. Captain Noegood says if one must fast, give him a first-floor room in a hotel with a large plate for collections. Visitors give what they please.

This scarcity of provisions is really becoming serious. We dine off the covering of the Strasbourg pie. The natives eye Sir Harry curiously. Noegood dresses for dinner and wears a white waistcoat. More double dummy between Sir Harry and Umbugs. The latter, who is becoming quite a proficient, wants to scalp his dummy for not seeing his call for trumps. Sir Harry pacifies him.

Tuesday.

Finished all our provisions. We all have robust appetites.

What is to be done? Captain Noegood says, Why not eat the entries in my diary? I find he means "ongtrays." These sailors are such funny dogs.

In spite of my entreaties, they will breakfast off the rabbit which I was keeping for my hat trick. Very annoying, just as I was getting it to go so well. Still, it barely goes round. Things are becoming serious. We all take in our clothes. Umbugs tightens his belt—it is his clothes.

We are saved, and by Noegood. The gallant captain met a giraffe and wrung its neck, after a spirited contest. "It was neck or nothing," he says quaintly.

Here occurs the lamented death of Boss.

Captain Noegood dresses for dinner, and leaving off his white waistcoat, wears a black tie. We dine off the giraffe and finish the old brandy. We make quite a night of it. After dinner they would have speeches. When "The Queen" had been drunk in silence, Captain Noegood insists on proposing "The Ladies."

Here the diary becomes somewhat illegible.

Wednesday.

Have we been saved from starvation only to die of thirst? I may here note a curious effect produced by the rarified air of the desert—our heads feel twice their natural size. Sir Harry says giraffe never did agree with him.

Noegood suffers least, as he takes the precaution of rising early and drinking the dew* collected with great difficulty for our morning bath. We stagger on through the weary day. Sir Harry becomes misanthropical. Noegood calls him "stout and bitter," which does not improve matters.

Here occurred the sad demise of Joss.

---

* *Note by* ME: "Mountain dew" was a weakness of Noegood's.

Noegood dresses under a cypress tree, and wears crape round his sleeve. Umbugs remarks pleasantly that if we do not find water before to-morrow we shall all be corpses. Umbugs is becoming a bore.

Sir Harry is too upset to play double dummy; he asks to be buried quietly. No cards.

Thursday.

Saved! saved! Umbugs is an ass. We find drink, and plenty of it, just below the great Sherbet Mountain, but only just in time. "If I had not got it just then," says Noegood, "I should have left this party and gone over to the majority—a 'split' in time saves nine." We refresh and congratulate each other on our escape.

Sir Harry and Umbugs return to double dummy. They are quite inveterate. Sir Harry promises to propose Umbugs for the Portland on his return. Umbugs is much flattered.

By the way, poor Sir Harry had a narrow

shave later on in the day. A wild buffalo chased him on his tricycle. Noegood was delighted. Sir Harry held his own very fairly on the flat, but on coming to a hill, abandoned the tricycle and took to a tree. The infuriated beast attacked the tricycle wildly, and perished miserably in the machinery. "A close thing," said Sir Harry, sliding down his tree, "he very nearly laid another buffer low," pointing to the mangled remains of the bull. The carcase came in very well for lunch, but the tricycle was never fit for anything afterwards, and we had, much to Sir Harry's regret, to leave it behind.

At lunch, we had a curious adventure. We selected a cool-looking cave for the meal, and were just enjoying a post-prandial cigarette with our coffee, when we became aware of a presence, a black, awful presence, with a gleaming eye.*

---

* *Note by* CAPT. NOEGOOD : "And claws ; you did not get them, *I did.*"

SIR HARRY HAS A NARROW SHAVE.

Our nerves were not very strong; we had never really got over that giraffe dinner. When we had written to the *Field* our time for the mile "sprint"—it did beat record, but that is neither here nor there—we made up our minds it could only be a bear.

"I must go back," suddenly cried Sir Harry.

"Why?" said Noegood, who had got off badly at the start, and did not see it.

"Possibly that thing may be my brother," was the rejoinder, "he was always such a bear."

A grisly jest, we all agreed. The bear, however, proved excellent eating—(my buns finished him, I had concealed them for this emergency)—and Noegood carefully potted his grease for future use. These sailors think so much of their personal appearance.

A strange thing now happened—one indeed of the strangest of our many strange adventures,

CHAPTER IV.

WE FIND KING SOLOMON'S ROAD—THE SAVAGES FIND US—RECEPTION BY NATIVES AND JOURNEY TO THE GREAT KING TWOSH.

O my readers I may explain I have here dropped the diary, as the incidents which follow require accurately telling. We suddenly came upon what in this country would be called a sign-post. On the sign-post was the inscription:

☞ *To King Solomon's Road, 1 Mile.*
Nearest Route to the Treasures.

Breathless with excitement—that is, Noegood and myself, with Sir Harry it was chronic ever since the tricycle accident—we hurried on. At last we came to a broad turnpike road. Its name (we noticed it on a lamp-post) was *King Solomon's Road, S.W.* We could say nothing; we were almost lost in wonderment. As for the road, I never saw engineering work like it. Straight ahead it tunnelled through the solid rock. The metropolitan subway at South Kensington is child's play to it. On entering the tunnel we noticed its sides were covered with strange devices of female figures. Underneath those quaint designs were inscriptions in the native tongue. Some of these, with Umbugs' aid, we succeeded in deciphering. Freely translated, they ran as follows:—

KING SOLOMON'S TREASURES.

GREAT ATTRACTION! SPECIAL HOLIDAY PROGRAMME!
Bullock Waggons run every half hour for the convenience of Visitors from the Suburbs.
NO NEW THING UNDER THE SUN?
NONSENSE!!!
SEE KING SOLOMON'S TREASURES!

These devices, we afterwards learnt, were called "Postâhs" in the native vernacular.

We were almost dumb with emotion. Had we at last obtained our goal after so many tries? Had we been saved from hunger and thirst only to make our success at last still more striking? These conundrums were never destined to be answered. I am thinking of getting up a competition in the advertisement columns of the daily press for the three best solutions. Umbugs was just giving them up, when we were surrounded by a party of savages. Captain Noegood, who was making his evening toilet, and struggling with his single stud (a large cat's-eye—he says a family heirloom; but I have seen one very like it in the Burlington Arcade marked "1s. 6d., a bargain!"), was much put out at the interruption.

The savages were led by a youth who answered to the name of Scraggi. He made a wild shot at us with a spear and missed badly. "Nil spear random," said a wily savage, touching his elbow. He looked an old soldier. His name we afterwards learnt was Fairdooes. The savages held a brief consultation, apparently divided in opinion as to whether we should afford

SOBRAGGI MAKES A WILD SHOT WITH A SPEAR.

more fun by being flayed alive, or as the subjects of a spear contest with five-yards rise. The old grim savage inclined to the flaying process, but Scraggi, who, I fancy, had a point or two the better of him at the game, preferred the more sporting event.

Sir Harry met the situation by looking like a Dane. The savages did not care, in spite of the prevalence of lions in the vicinity, and said so boldly, in their uncouth tongue. But what was I doing the while? Did I quail? not I. Had I not my wig and leg (with patent spring)? Had not Noegood his teeth? Where was the eye-glass lent to Umbugs?

"We will give them a wigging," I cried, hastily dancing on my peruke, and unscrewing my cork leg* I waved it defiantly in the air. Noegood backed me up like a man. He snapped

---

Note by EDITOR: Something wrong in the engraving. Quarterman has a wooden leg, not a cork one. How's this?

Note by ME: Artist would draw a wooden one; said it was funnier. Perhaps Quarterman economised by using a substitute for the superior article over the desert.

Note by EDITOR: Across the desert I should have thought he would put his best leg forward. But no matter.

his teeth, and as a last resource took out his glass eye. (For days I had my suspicions, but he always denied it with warmth. These sailors are so vain.) As for Umbugs, he nearly put his eye out in the effort to secure his eye-glass in its place. Poor fellow, it was screwed in his left eye quite tight, and turned out to be quite superfluous after all, indeed a glass too much.

Our readers have guessed the result, of course. Did not Fairdooes grovel on the ground and invoke the aid of the Great Spirit? Was not Scraggi limp with terror, and though dumb with apprehension, did not his teeth chatter? Did not his followers rush headlong in a wave of panic? Were A. Quarterman a romancer, a holder of the great iron pot, as the Ipecacuanha idiom quaintly has it, I could descant for pages on the effect this demonstration of ours produced; but a Quarterman is truthful or nothing, and stern veracity bids me confess they did nothing of the kind. Scraggi barely smiled, and Fairdooes yawned behind his hand. As for their rank and file, less *blasé*, they went into a roar.

"No," said Fairdooes, with a weary look about the eyes, "it won't do; it is really too old. The first few we caught at this kind of thing caused us some surprise; then it amused us; but now it has got into the Society papers, and the game is played out."

"Stay!" said Scraggi. "Have the pale faces—who come from over the sea" (as if we had never got over the crossing), "who roar out thunder and slay from afar—the death-dealing tubes with which the great medicine men spread their lightning and make their enemies as is a sieve?"

This I could not stand.

"Hang it all," I said. "You call our business with the wig and teeth old (I don't believe the leg has ever been done before), and want the old death-dealing tube swindle! Why, it's as old as Robinson Crusoe. No savage with a grain of self-respect could stand it any longer. I had not the face to try it on you; besides which, Sir Harry, if he does look like a Dane, could not hit a haystack sitting to save his life. As for me, I have been nervous with firearms from a boy; and

Noegood there, he is a naval officer, and knows from professional experience far too much about guns to stand behind one when it goes off."

I was wrong to give way like this, but I was sorely tried, and, as it turned out, it saved our lives.

"The bald-headed old fox," said the old savage called Fairdooes (a nice way to speak of me!), "talks wisdom; he has been merciful in his weakness, and spared us the death-dealing tubes. Shall we not be merciful in our strength and spare their lives? Still, we will rifle their pockets." They did not find much.

"We will take them," continued Fairdooes, "to Twosh, the great king; the bald fox, also the fat Jumbo, likewise the black dog (meaning Umbugs), not forgetting the dusty swallow with one tail."

(A reference to Noegood's coat, not in the best of taste. It had certainly suffered on the journey, but why draw public attention to it like this?)

Sir Harry was so used to being called Jumbo by this time that for once he quite forgot to look like a Dane. As for Umbugs, he was so used to being called anything, especially by Noegood—

these sailors will use such language—that black dog was rather a compliment than otherwise.

Before we started Fairdooes said, "Allow me," with a wave of his hand: "Pale faces, Scraggi; Scraggi, Pale faces. Scraggi, son of Twosh, the King of Ipecacuanha Land, husband of a thousand wives" (Noegood looked interested, Sir Harry quailed), "terror of his tradesmen, Prince of the Blackguards, the (usually) black-eyed. I am Fairdooes," he concluded, after this outburst.

We bowed our acknowledgments, and commenced the march along the road, through the confines of Ipecacuanha Land, to the palace of the great King Twosh.

CHAPTER V.

WE ENTER IPECACUANHA LAND—OUR RECEPTION BY TWOSH THE KING.

IT will not be necessary for me to detail the incidents of our journey.

We passed several bands of natives who were travelling in the same direction as ourselves. Noegood was much struck by the women, who, as he said, for a native race are exceedingly handsome. What surprised me most was the superb air of disdain with which they eyed us, though I am bound to say Noegood's dress clothes surprised them into betraying a little interest. They could not have shown greater self-possession if they had been the *habituées* of a fashionable drawing-room, as, indeed, from the scantiness of their attire, might have been the case.

Fairdooes put us up for the night in a very decent hut.

"A little food shall be brought you," he suggested. "Two or three oxen, a few sheep," he added, diffidently.

"This is how I like to be treated," said Sir Harry, "they are going to serve us well."

When the savages found we ate and drank like other people, only rather more so—that is Sir Harry—we got on much better together; their opinion of us seemed to improve. We insisted on Fairdooes and Scraggi joining us, and kept it up quite late. They were much puzzled at our smoking. Scraggi would have been wiser not to have tried that cigar. I warned him, but he would do it. When we awoke the next morning it was to find the sun high in the heavens.

Fairdooes, who had been up for hours, found us in bed. He announced that Twosh the king would give us audience.

Sir Harry answers rudely that he is not going to hurry himself for Twosh or any other beastly savage, and desires to be called again in two hours' time.

Somehow or other we don't feel up to much breakfast, but after a pipe we feel better and declare ourselves ready to face Twosh himself. Fairdooes led the way, and after a short walk we are ushered into the great presence.

Twosh was an enormous man, nearly as large as Sir Harry, and with perhaps the most repulsive face ever seen. He looked every inch, and there were a great many of them, a savage king. He was made up very carefully for the part. His whole expression was cruel and sensual to a degree. I only discovered later how under that mask of savagery lurked—but I am anticipating. Twosh the king did not display much interest in us. Fairdooes introduced us. Scraggi had not yet recovered the effects of the cigar.

"I suppose they are from the stars," said Twosh, with an air of unmistakable *ennui*.

"'Pon my word," said Fairdooes, "I did not think it worth an inquiry. I took it for granted, but perhaps as a matter of form——"

"They look like a strolling company," said Twosh, yawning.

"No, sire," I said, "for we are all stars. The great king in his wisdom has guessed the place from whence we came."

"For heaven's sake," whispered Sir Harry, hurriedly, "think of what you are saying. Don't put that in his head; he will be putting on the black cap in a minute!"

Taking no notice of the interruption, I continued:

"We do come from the stars; our address is on the bottles. Three star Martel is our constellation." I had kept a few of the empty ones. One can never tell what may come useful on these occasions.

Noegood's dress coat here caught Twosh's eye.

"Who is he that hath two eyes in his head and one in his 'Tûm Tûm?'" (a native expression for the third button of the waistcoat).

This was Noegood's single cat's-eye.

"Hang it," said Noegood. "None of your chaff; it's a very good stud."

We trembled at this outburst. What its consequence might have been, who can tell? Luckily at this point one of Twosh's guards sneezed.

"Bless you!" said Twosh; then suddenly recollecting that he was a savage potentate, he turned on his heel in a paroxysm of rage, and he cried, in a voice hoarse with passion:

"What! Will you dishonour your father in the eyes of strangers who come from the stars? I'll show you if I am to be sneezed at."

"It was by chance, O son of cow," was the low reply.

"Oh! I'm a son of cow now, am I? I'll heifer word with you."

When the remains of the sneezer had been removed in a waste paper basket, Twosh turned to us and said, in a mild tone:

"You will come to our annual witch hunt this day week?"

We replied we should be only too pleased.

"It is not bad fun sometimes," said he in a deprecating manner. "I'll see you have a good place."

Here Twosh signified our audience was at an end, and withdrew, entering his hut in a curiously dejected manner.

The most interesting event which calls for notice in the next few days is a tremendous row between Scraggi and Noegood.

At the Hall of Varieties, one of the favourite places of amusement in the ———, Noegood would encore Scraggi's particular friend in the most marked manner, and insisted on taking her out to supper after the performance. Fullarder was a nice girl, for such was her name, but what could it end in but a row? These sailors have no discretion where a petticoat is concerned—indeed, in this affair Noegood had not even that excuse, for Fullarder's costume was scanty. Scraggi got the worst of it, and did not take it well. He retired to put on a clean collar muttering, "Wait for the witch hunt." What can he mean?

The Society papers are full of the "fracas," as they call it. Twosh, who in private life is a stickler for the proprieties, is furious.

On inquiry I have found out all about the witch hunt. It seems to be an interesting ceremony. Umbugs is my informant; he keeps us posted in all the news, and seems to know his way about here wonderfully. Still, I fear we must get rid of him soon; he is becoming proud, and declined the other day to varnish Sir Harry's boots.

The ceremony of the witch hunt, as explained to me by Umbugs, seems to be this :—

In theory, the witch hunters scent out the evil doers, those who are ill disposed towards Twosh, or who have killed too many mothers-in-law lately, and they are put out of the way for their country's good.

In practice, what happens is this :—Twosh keeps a list of all those to whom he owes money, and stands in with the witch finders. They, instructed by Twosh, denounce them all as witches. The witches are first killed, and then boiled.

"But," I asked, "if this obtains, why does anyone lend money to Twosh?" Umbugs smiled in a pitying manner.

"Little do you reck of the wiles of the great king; he also keeps a list of all who have refused to lend him money. These are first boiled, and then killed!"

As regards ourselves, it turns out that Twosh's plan is this—Scraggi put him up to it—to get us on his list, have us denounced, including Umbugs, as witches, and put us comfortably out of the way. Such was the fiendish plan, devised by the ingenuity of Scraggi. He never did like us; I fear he harboured animosity about that cigar. Scraggi, with Noegood removed from the path, hopes to regain Fullarder's affections. Poor Noegood, though his feelings might be at boiling point, as a rival—to put it vulgarly—would have gone to pot.

On hearing of this plot against our lives, Sir Harry revokes at double dummy. Noegood becomes very profane, but declares nothing will induce him to give up his "tart." What this means,

I do not know. It is an Ipecacuanha expression, which Noegood has picked up. No one will tell me its meaning; they seem afraid to explain. Noegood is also depressed at having to wear dress clothes all day (they won't let him take them off), "like a beastly waiter," as he says.

In vain we rack our brains for a plan to circumvent our enemies. Noegood suggests several, the most feasible being to get Twosh to cash a cheque, and so have an interest in keeping us alive. This is ingenious in itself, but depends too much for its success on the credulity of Twosh. I suggest several plans, but feel they are not of much use.

"I have it!" suddenly cries Sir Harry. "'Eclipse first, the rest nowhere.' Here is the plan to save us."

We were dumbfounded at his ingenuity.

"You have an almanac, Quarterman?" Of course I had.

"Where is the use," he continued, " of travelling in savage climes if one cannot get up an eclipse to order? Just see if there is not one about due."

I hurriedly turned over the pages of the almanac (how lucky that I had brought one !), and, oddly enough, at the *exact time* the witches' hunt was announced to commence, we found the sun would be eclipsed. Saved! saved!!

Our course was now clear. We must wait in patience for the witch hunt, and frighten old Twosh out of his life with the eclipse, then make our own terms—none too cheap—and depart in triumph. As for the treasure, I had had about enough of treasure-seeking. Besides, we are not going to let old Twosh off any too easily.

Umbugs seems strangely excited at our plan. I cannot quite make him out; his conduct has been very odd the last few days. In one day I caught him three times throwing off his girdle (very embarrassing, as he hardly wears anything else), and saying, striking an attitude as he does so—" At last the time has come, I am the rightful something or other," I could not quite make out what.

When I remonstrate with him on this extraordinary behaviour he laughs shrilly, "He! he!" and says he is recalling the days of "Auld lang syne."

He is degenerating into a sort of Merry Andrew. We must certainly get rid of him.

Noegood is enthusiastic about the eclipse, he thinks he sees his way to settling Scraggi's pretensions for ever. I am not quite so sanguine. Those savages do not seem up to the Christmas book form—still I hope there will be no hitch about the eclipse.

CHAPTER VI.

THE WITCH HUNT—THE ECLIPSE—ITS EFFECT ON TWOSH THE KING—REMARKABLE CONDUCT OF UMBUGS—SAVED! SAVED!

HE few days remaining before the witch hunt we spent in resting and talking over the situation, which was sufficiently exciting. On the morning of the day itself, Noegood devoted all his time to preparing a glossary of nautical expressions suitable for use on the occasion of an eclipse. "It will make the thing go better," he explains. So engrossed is he that he actually forgot Fullarder for the moment. Sir Harry practises his most Danish expression.

Just after we had finished dinner, Fairdooes arrived clad in full war toggery, and accompanied by a guard of twenty men to escort us to the performances. He very thoughtfully provides us with three suits of black armour for the night, at what *he* calls a nominal charge.

"Well," said Sir Harry, as he struggled into his several sizes too small, "we must expect to be black-mailed." Mine was a shocking fit, so was Noegood's, who said he really could not be seen in such a thing, and wore his suit under his dress clothes. On arriving at the great kraal where we had previously been interviewed by the king we found the seats very fairly occupied. Curiously enough, in the front rows there seemed plenty of room. In the front row of all, where Twosh had very kindly kept seats for us, there was scarcely any one. I suppose they do not wish to intrude on our privacy. Those savages, simple children of the desert though they be, have sometimes wonderful tact. So unassuming is their demeanour that each one tries to thrust his neighbour into a more prominent place than himself. How different from an English mob bent upon pleasure! That is our great fault as a nation. We are so selfish.

At last a small party enter the royal box. We make out Twosh and Scraggi. They seem in high spirits. Scraggi points at us and laughs. "You wonder why we laugh," shouts Twosh, waving his spear; "it's because we *assegai*."

After the overture, composed of the popular airs of the day, in which all the audience join, the performance opens. I may here mention that the leading witch hunter was Gargle, a lady of uncertain age to a century or two, and with one eye, which she kept well on us. She bore us no goodwill owing to an unfortunate mistake of Sir Harry's. He took her for a monkey when first they met, and offered her nuts. She had a fit in consequence, and never forgave this slur on her personal attractions.

The eyes of the entire audience were centred on her movements. There was a breathless silence. A pin, had such things been invented in

Ipecacuanha Land, might have been heard to drop. Suddenly, with a wild shriek she spun into the air, and waltzing round hissed forth:

"Ho! ho! I'll show them who's *which!*"

The utmost agitation prevailed. In the excitement of the moment, every one tried to get behind some one else; and a well-known bill discounter hid himself under his seat. Sir Harry could hardly keep his place, so anxious was he to go and see what time the carriages were ordered for.

"Sit still," I implored him; "our lives may depend upon it."

When three money-lenders, the court tailor, and a sheriff's officer had been dropped in the cauldron, Gargle fixed her eye steadily on Sir Harry, and began to waltz towards us.

Twosh clapped loudly, and Scraggi nearly fell off his seat with delight. At last she made a dead point at us. It was obviously a put up thing.

"Brava! brava!" cried Twosh from his throne. "You must die at once."

THE WITCH HUNT.

"Why-O-king?" I asked, in my agitation running the words into one.

"Woking comes after," he explained, "but you must die, it is the 9th rule of the game; besides," he continued, with a nasty chuckle, "if you lose your lives you can star one."

Here he beckoned to the executioners to advance, and added in a gentle tone:

"Boiling is a quick death; they say the lobsters rather like it."

The executioners, who had just been taking a short rest, received their cue from Twosh, and advanced towards the spot. Now or never was the time for my hazard.

"Hold!" I cried, "you shall yet be baulked. Though an easy shot you will break down, Attempt to run in and we will put out the sun and plunge the table land in darkness."

Our great *coup* was played. A groan arose from the onlookers. Twosh the king gave a wild yell of anguish and fell off his throne and lay moaning piteously in the dust.

"Oh, spare me that! spare me that! be

merciful! Anything—anything but that ancient fraud!" he just found strength to gasp.

His agony moved me, but I was firm.

"I am sorry for you, Twosh," I said; "you have not treated us well, still I am sorry for you. You can't think it gives me any pleasure to rake up this venerable device again; but there is no help for it; it must be done. You see this is a story of adventures among savages, and we have reached a point where the public expect an eclipse. They will have it; it's not my fault."

Twosh's form quivered convulsively on the ground.

"Well, look here," I said, "I do not want to be hard on you. The public expects an eclipse, and won't be disappointed; but I'll tell you what I'll do: put off the whole show for six months and I'll make it the moon this time."

Twosh, with a great effort of will, dragged himself from his recumbent position to the steps of the throne, and clinging to them for support, made answer in a dull, mechanical voice:

"Sooner, ay sooner than submit to another

eclipse at the hands of the strangers who come from the stars, will I leave this throne, never to return. My land, my wives" (I thought of Mrs. Quarterman and blushed), " my people, take them all. Do what you will with them. I will flee, a homeless wanderer upon the face of the earth. I will take a cheap ticket to England, where the sun never shines, and the thing can't be done—if only, only you will be merciful and spare me this."

I could hardly speak from emotion. His frenzy was painful to witness.

"We will! You shall!" cried a strong voice at my elbow, and Umbugs strode into the arena with my eye-glass firmly fixed in his eye, and throwing off his girdle, he cried in a loud voice:

"Ha! ha! the time has come at last. I am Umbugs, the rightful king of Ipecacuanha Land. Please observe the mark; without this none are genuine."

"You are! you are!" cried Fairdooes, raising his spear; "have I not taken him across my knee as a boy? Shall I strike less hard now for him and freedom?"

The excitement was tremendous. Twosh did not like it at first, but Umbugs had the army with him to a man. They had not forgotten the fate of the sneezer, and they all suffered from chronic influenza. Umbugs told me afterwards that such was the state of terrorism they lived in, that all their spare pay was spent in Alkaram.

Umbugs mounted the throne amidst acclamations. Fairdooes, who had egged him on to throw over the hard yoke of Twosh's rule, came in for quite an ovation.

It is very lucky that I did not discharge Umbugs from our service, and I do not regret, as things have turned out, having promised him a present at Christmas.

Sir Harry looked a little uneasy as he remembered double dummy, and thought of the possibility of future witch hunts, but Noegood was delighted, and went to look for Fullarder.

The almanac was wrong, which was fortunate for Umbugs; as, if the eclipse had come on after all, Twosh, who was rather annoyed at being taken up so quickly, would have cried off the bargain.

Umbugs occupied the throne with much dignity, though his crown was a little too large, and surveyed the scene with an easy grace, as if he had never varnished boots in his life. Twosh, who began to think he had made rather an ass of himself, had still a card to play.

When the enthusiasm had subsided, and a deaf man in the gallery, who had totally misunderstood the situation, and would go on demanding " Three cheers for Twosh!" had been ejected, Twosh advanced towards the throne and made a low obeisance.

"Has thy servant leave to speak?"

"By all means," said Umbugs, with affability.

"Well, look here," continued Twosh, "as a savage king I can't give the whole thing up without a fight."

"No, no!" said Umbugs, "certainly not. Who will you take on?"

"Jumbo for choice," said Twosh.

"Capital," said Umbugs, who never quite hit it off with Sir Harry. Was it the double dummy or the boots? "I'll see fair play."

The effect of all this on poor Sir Harry was dreadful; he quailed visibly, and for days was unable to look like a Dane. It was no good, try as he would, he could not get out of it.

"Queensberry rules?" said Umbugs.

"Of course," said Twosh.

Umbugs was delighted at the idea, and evinced the greatest interest in the whole matter.

"A good fight, and no quarter man, shall be our motto," he said, jestingly, to Sir Harry, who smiled a sickly smile.

The stakes were deposited with the editor of the local sporting paper and a day was fixed. I wonder how it will end? As it was getting late, we made our salaam to Umbugs, which he scarcely acknowledged—I hope his position is not spoiling him—and withdrew to our hut. Sir Harry was dreadfully low spirited and declined to be cheered up.

CHAPTER VII.

THE BATTLE—THE CHARGE OF THE BLUES—CONFESSIONS OF TWOSH.

IR HARRY, perhaps I wronged him, is quite brightening up. He has been in strict training for days. Noegood does his best to keep up Sir Harry's spirits by constantly humming to him the national war anthem of the country. It is a wild, barbaric air, with a very stirring chorus, which the natives always sing as they advance to battle. The words are very curious, written by the court laureate. They tell how one Tômm Kinns, a native of Beth Nalgréne, a savage and outlying district, did fall on and beat in hot blood a fellow savage upon some trivial pretext.

The chorus roughly translated runs somewhat as follows:—

> " Two lovely black eyes,
> Oh, what a surprise ! "

Though in English it is impossible to give any idea of the fire of the original.

I shall scarcely be believed when I say so popular is the air that if a party of natives are gathered together, they will often repeat the chorus for hours at a time with the utmost contentment, and require no other form of entertainment.

To our civilised minds such simplicity seems incredible, yet any traveller in the neighbourhood would corroborate me in this statement.

The contemplated set-to between Twosh and Sir Harry excites much interest in sporting circles. At first Twosh is made a warm favourite, but Sir Harry's training affects the market and he comes up to short odds. Twosh's partisans are trying to hedge their money. Twosh does not stand his preparation well, he declines to train but has a box every evening at the " Varieties." Still he carries my money; I have not much faith in Sir Harry.

The details of the fight cause us great anxiety. Umbugs says very fairly he cannot appear in the matter openly. Several places have been suggested as the field of battle, but have to be abandoned at the last moment owing to the police getting wind of them. Sir Harry professes to be annoyed at this, and says he can't think how these things get about. I fear we shall have to cross the water after all to bring it off. This would interfere sadly with Sir Harry's training, as he is such a bad sailor.

At last a place has been selected where we shall be free from interference. The venue—it is an open secret—is fixed in the private park of a popular nobleman of sporting proclivities. The police have been drawn off on a false scent by a rumour spread by Scraggi that a body of Socialists had resolved to attend church with the object of encoring the commination service. All is now arranged. Still, the very strictest secrecy has to be observed.

On the morning of the fight, Twosh leaves in a furniture van driven by Scraggi. Sir Harry, who has just been reading his "Pickwick" in the Jubilee edition, prefers a pianoforte "without works," and breathes through the legs, which are hollow. We arrive on the ground all safe, but Sir Harry is rather short of breath. Twosh is somewhat late, as he had to make a detour to avoid suspicion. Umbugs is not here, which seems odd after the interest he displayed in the proceedings. Perhaps he thinks it more judicious not to be mixed up in the matter.

Noegood is Sir Harry's second. Twosh is looked after by Scraggi. I am appointed timekeeper and referee.

Noegood is actually here without Fullarder. She wanted to come, but he would not bring her, on the ground that a prize fight was a degrading spectacle, and would do her no good.

The ring is roped off; the betting at the start

TWOSH COMES A NASTY ONE ON HIS KNOWLEDGE BOX.

is quoted at 7 to 4, Twosh taken and wanted. All being ready, Twosh and Sir Harry advance into the middle of the ring and shake hands.

The fight begins.

After a little preliminary sparring, Twosh makes a rush at Sir Harry and fobs with his right. Sir Harry fibs neatly with his left, and throws himself flat on the ground; Twosh falls over him, and pitches violently on his head.

"Time, gentlemen, time," cries Noegood; "end of first round." Sir Harry firm at 7 to 4.

Twosh seems much shaken. As the official report puts it—"he came a nasty one on his knowledge box."

I must try and get out on Sir Harry. But what is this I see advancing over the brow of the hill? Can it be—it is, it is—the famous Blues! This splendid force, the pride and glory of Ipecacuanha Land, advances shoulder to shoulder at a brisk double. They come on in their striking uniform—in highlows and helmets, and white Berlin gloves, their buttons gleaming in the sun, waving their "Trunshons" (a kind of staff) the while. Anon there rises from the serried phalanx a murmur, as the whispering of the sea, and we hear strange cries of:

"I nose yer." "Come, move on there." "Ah! would you?" "What, agen!"

We were taken before Umbugs, who said that in the whole of his experience he had never seen a worse case, and had no alternative but to fine all concerned five shillings each, with the option of being skinned alive, and costs. The "Inspectre," that is, the leader of the Blues, was presented with ten shillings from the poor box, as a reward for his dashing behaviour. On the whole, I was rather well out of it, as I had backed Twosh, and he fell rather a nasty one on his head.

Sir Harry has just told me that, bearing no animosity towards Twosh, he had thought it best to give information to the police, but asks me to keep it quiet. This is why he was so cheerful, I suppose! As he seems to have a good deal of pocket money just now, I rather suspect he stood in with Umbugs, and divided the fines. The leading daily journal came out with a scathing article, headed "Latter-Day Pugilism," and what it calls "this disreputable attempt to revive the worst traditions of the ring."

After this adventure, we settled down to our ordinary routine life in Ipecacuanha Land. Sir Harry is reduced to practising the "Great Vienna Coup" by himself. Umbugs is as proud of double dummy as ever, but says four by honours against him five times in six hands is too much. He makes no reflections on any one, but declines to play for the present. Umbugs is very pleased with me, as I invested him with the insignia of a knight-harbinger of the Primrose League, and promised on the payment of the usual fees to advance him to the higher grades. I fear Twosh is a little bit jealous. The way Noegood and Fullarder are going on is perfectly ridiculous. I gave Scraggi my—that is Pears'—portrait of Mrs. Langtry; he is quite consoled and tells me in confidence Fullarder squints. Poor old Twosh comes out very well on acquaintance. He is not half a bad chap when you know him, though I must admit you have got to know him first.

Talking to me one day in confidence, he said:

"Though it may surprise you, Quarterman, my boy, I was not altogether sorry to give up my throne to Umbugs. It's hard work always to be laying foundation-stones and opening shows, and a thankless task, too. Then the trouble and anxiety it gave me to keep up my character consistently as a savage potentate no one can ever fathom. Personally I would not hurt a fly, and have always, under an assumed name, subscribed to the 'Society for the Prevention of Cruelty to Animals,' but what could I do? I was not my own master. It was my *rôle* to be bloodthirsty, and bloodthirsty I had to be. I had to go on committing atrocities, no one regretting them more than myself, as if I revelled in the acts. There was no escape for me. The agony those witch hunts used to cause me no one would believe, and I can assure you when my forty-third wife died, and all her male relatives were tortured to death, as is the rule in the Royal House, it hardly caused me any gratification. Then look at my personal appearance," he said, "did you ever see such a guy?"

I had to admit it was odd; still beauty is only skin deep, I suggested, to comfort him.

"That is all very fine," he remarked, "it used not to matter. My royal position used to cover all deficiencies, but now I am no longer king, no woman will look at me with this face, and yet, let me tell you, though you may not believe it, I was not half a bad-looking chap once." (Here he sighed.) "Of course this would not do. I had to disfigure myself. They said I did not look sensual enough. I bought a nose machine, and took lessons in grimacing from a low comedian. You see the result."

"Ah!" he continued, "it's a thankless life is a savage king's, to say nothing of never being able to talk like a Christian, but having to twaddle on about pale faces and Great Spirits, besides having to live in a kraal, which is generally draughty and always uncomfortable. Ah! how often have I thought, on looking down on the trembling throng around my throne, you little reck how glad the haughty Twosh would be to change places with even the humblest of his subjects."

The topic seemed to pain him, so I turned the conversation; but I have often thought since how little the world knows of its greatest men; how great and small, alike the sport of circumstances, are all liable to be misjudged.

I have commenced my conjuring tricks. They are very popular, especially the three thimbles and a pea. Umbugs, who has quite given up double dummy, cannot have enough of the game. I wonder if his paper is all right? Twosh takes to the conjuring wonderfully, and for a small honorarium (he is rather pressed for ready-money since his retirement) does the confederate in the gallery, and asks, "Where is the sunflower?" in the hat trick. This always brings down the house. They can't make it out.

One day Sir Harry, whose time—now there is no more double dummy—hangs rather heavy on his hands, reminds me we have done nothing up to the present towards searching for the treasure.

"Surely," he says, "now Umbugs is king, and

Twosh is with us, the time has come for finding this treasure with their assistance!"

It does seem a good opportunity. I suggest it to Noegood, who says he will come if Fullarder is one of the party. He is really quite infatuated. Umbugs, I find, is delighted with the idea, and, like the good fellow I always thought him, says:

"Let's go to-morrow; I will show you the way and stand the lunch."

Are we, after all, on the eve of a great discovery, to make us rich beyond the dreams of Sam Lewis? Who can tell!

CHAPTER VIII.

THE TREASURES OF KING SOLOMON.

N the next day we start for the treasures. Umbugs is more than kind, and insists on coming to show us the way. The distance is not great, but Sir Harry insists on being carried on a litter, so as to husband his strength. Besides, as he says, we must have something to bring the treasures back in. On arriving at the doors, we pay a shilling each at the turnstile (through which only one person can pass at a time), and enter. We proceed along a passage wide enough to admit of two walking abreast, and rather dark; but soon the passage becomes lighter, and in another minute we stand in perhaps the most magnificent cave ever seen. But its size was the least of the wonders of the place, for running in rows adown its length were gigantic pillars of what looked like ice, but were in reality huge stalagmites. The cave is certainly splendid, but we did not come all this way to see stalagmites and stalactites, at least Sir Harry did not, and he says so audibly. The Captain and Fullarder are too well occupied to grumble at anything. Interested in geology though I am. I rather back up Sir Harry in this view.

"What!" says Umbugs; "do you desire to explore the hidden mysteries of the cave and brave its unknown perils? In your heart of hearts are ye prepared to enter the Chamber of Horrors?"

We were not going to be frightened, so we all said "yes," though we did not quite like it. Noegood, who had seen the " Salon Parisien," said he would go first. "Art thou coming, Fullarder?" he inquired tenderly, but his accent was dreadful; he would try and speak the native language.

"I fear, my lord," said the girl timidly.

"Then give me the luncheon basket," was the hasty answer. These sailors are so practical.

"Nay, my lord," was the rejoinder, "whither thou goest, there will I go also."

Noegood did not seem altogether to like this; however, he now announced his intention of showing the way. Umbugs drew his attention to the following notice on the wall:

"N.B.—IMPORTANT NOTICE AND WARNING.

"*It is suggested that none but strong-nerved persons inspect this Exhibit.*"

We still declined to be frightened.

"Then," observed Umbugs, "it will be sixpence extra including catalogue."

On the payment of this he grinned, and said, "This way, gentlemen; straight on."

We peered before us, but there was nothing but the solid rock. Noegood looked relieved.

"Do not jest with us," I said, sternly.

"I am only going to take a rise out of it," said

Umbugs, pointing to a mass of rock. " Can any gentleman oblige me with a penny? "

We managed this amongst us.

"Observe, I drop it in the slot and the machinery works."

As we looked again we saw a mass of stone slowly rising from the floor and vanishing into the rock above. The mass was about the size of a large door, and must have weighed nearly as much as Sir Harry. At last the great stone raised itself, and a dark hole showed in its place.

"Walk up, gentlemen, walk up," said Umbugs; " behold the treasures of the Great King!"

Thus adjured, we entered and found ourselves in a gloomy apartment, which had been hollowed out of the mountain. This apartment was not nearly so well lighted as the ante-cave, and at the first glance all I could make out was a stone table of great length with an enormous white pyramid at its head, and life-sized figures all round it. At last my eyes grew accustomed to the light, and I saw what these things were. I admit, if Sir Harry had not caught me firmly by the collar, in about five seconds I should have been out of that cave, never to return.

As for Noegood, he swore—feebly for him—and Fullarder seized the opportunity of fainting in his arms. Only Umbugs chuckled loud and long. The sight was a ghastly one.

"What are those things?" said Noegood, pointing to the white company round the table. "And what on earth is that thing?" said Sir Harry, pointing to the white pyramid which looked as if it were crusted with snow.

At last our eyes made out the awful spectacle before us.

Around the table were *the effigies of King Solomon's seven hundred Wives and three hundred* —— (But stay! This is a book by a family man for family men. I must be discreet.)

The vague white form at the head of the table turned out to be an enormous pile of seven hundred wedding cakes arranged in the form of a pyramid. Above it was a scroll with an inscription in large letters. Sir Harry, who was a

KING SOLOMON'S SEVEN HUNDRED WIVES AND THREE HUNDRED——.

scholar, having been rusticated from Camford with great *éclat*, translated it for our benefit as follows :—

"Extract from an unpublished volume of King Solomon's Proverbs.

"What treasure hath man like a good wife and plenty of her?"

These figures, some of great beauty (Which? the wives'? or ——; wild horses should not tear it from me), had become petrified from the constant droppings from the roof. The same process had welded the cakes into a solid cube.

"As if they had not been dropt on to often enough during life," says Noegood, who was beginning to recover from his alarm. These sailors are so irreverent.

Umbugs by this time had left us on the ground that he had an important engagement, which had hitherto slipped his memory.

"Well," said Sir Harry, "I call this a sell. Here have we come all this way, and gone through so much, to see a lot of figures, when for a little extra expense we could have done Madame

Tussaud's, and had Napoleon's tooth-brush thrown in for the money."

Noegood seemed much interested in the specimens, greatly to Fullarder's disgust. Forgetting for the moment that Umbugs had left us, I turned hastily round and cried: " Where are the treasures ? "

I heard a hoarse laugh, and looking in the direction saw that the door had descended.

" Where are the treasures ? " echoed a voice— Umbugs', without doubt. It sounded rather fluty under the door. "Aren't seven hundred enough, to say nothing of the three hundred ——— ? "

"Umbugs," I interrupted, hastily, "I implore you! Remember this is a book by a family man for family men. Above all things, let us be discreet. Think of the young person of fifteen. No scandal about King Solomon."

Now, I never could see any fun in practical joking. "Come," I said, "a joke is a joke; but let us out."

"Not if I nosit," was the reply, an idiom of the country, implying a humorous negative. Sir Harry and Noegood were furious.

"Open the door!" they cried.

"I am really very sorry," said Umbugs. "I am afraid it is impossible. You see it will only work with pennies, and I haven't got any more."

"Do it with a bit of slate," suggested Noegood.

"Any one seen tampering with the machinery is liable to a fine of £10 on conviction," was the stern rejoinder.

We saw it all now. That beast Umbugs had planned this snare for us from the first. It was just the sort of thing he would think funny.

"Do you mean to leave us here to die?" I asked.

"Well, that was my idea," he replied. "How does it strike you?"

At this we gave up all hope.

Umbugs seemed to think it the best joke in the world.

Sir Harry said, "Well, let's have some lunch; it is no good wasting that, whatever happens." He offered to divide it, but we had none of us any appetite. His never failed him.

"Stay!" said Umbugs at last. "I do not

want to be hard on the pale faces." (we were pale enough, and no mistake), "who come from the stars. Have ye with you the paper ye hold of Umbugs, the great king, which ye have won with devious wiles at the wondrous double dummy, and the mystic thimbles, and the esoteric pea?"

We consulted. It was robbery, but it might save our lives.

Sir Harry had three I.O.U.'s The first, for a tame elephant suitable for performance in a hippodrome. The other two, for a one-eyed tiger, sightly damaged, and the reversion of an interest in a learned pig. I, too, had various stamped papers, not unconnected with our little amusements. These we handed under the door in solemn silence.

"Have the pale faces," continued Umbugs, "the dials which tell the time, no man knows how?"

This was extortion, but we had no choice. Sir Harry had to hand over the family turnip. It got a little injured in transit. My watch, or its ticket, the same thing, passed under the door with less difficulty. Noegood's was only a Waterbury. Those sailors are so lucky.

"Any small change?" asked the mercenary beast. I say it advisedly.

Fourpence halfpenny in bronze was all we could manage.

"Aha!" now cried Umbugs, "I have the talisman which opens the solid rock," and we heard a penny (*our* penny) drop in the slot, and the door suddenly began to raise itself. It worked on some simple balance principle. As it opened we saw Umbugs surrounded by his guard.

Our return was somewhat humiliating. I find this entry in my diary:

"No more treasure seeking for us."

Signed: A. QUARTERMAN.
SIR HARRY.
CAPT. NOEGOOD, *late of* R.H.M.
FULLARDER. *Her* + *mark.*

CHAPTER IX.

WE FIND SIR HARRY'S BROTHER—SUPPRESSED EMOTION OF SIR HARRY—SCANDAL IN HIGH LIFE—INTERVENTION OF A GREAT PERSONAGE.

FTER our expedition in search of the treasures of the Great King, which had ended so ignominiously, lite at Ipecacuanha Land became very tedious. Umbugs turned sulky because we would not play except for ready-money, which he had not got. Was it likely, after the way he had treated us? As for Twosh he is getting too sharp, and finds out all my tricks. The only one who is contented is Noegood, who goes on shamefully with Fullarder.

We were bored to death one rainy day, when Sir Harry startled us by saying:

"There is nothing doing. Why should not we go and look for my brother?"

In the excitement of our adventures I had forgotten all about his brother, and so I firmly believe had Sir Harry himself.

"Do you mean it?" I asked.

"Certainly," he said.

I was very annoyed, and did not conceal it.

"Look here," I said, "this is too bad. Here have I got to my last chapter but one, and you suddenly spring your long-lost brother on me. He cannot be worked in now, I cannot spare the space. You should have thought of it before; it can't be done now."

Sir Harry looked like a Dane as he answered:

"I have come here to find my brother, and find him I must, alive or dead."

"Hang it," I exclaimed, "do you expect me to write another volume to find your beastly brother? It is too much to expect; it is not reasonable."

"You can do it shortly," said Sir Harry, in a conciliatory manner.

"Shortly! Why, look at the adventures he will have had."

"Break his leg," said Sir Harry, "do not mind my feelings"—he cannot have had many then—"but find him, there's a good chap, if it's only in a foot-note, it will make the thing so complete."

For the sake of peace and quietness I consented. I am always too good-natured. People know it, and take advantage of my weakness.

So we started on our wild goose chase, except that Sir Harry's brother, though from all accounts a goose, seemed to be far too great a duffer ever to have been wild.

Now I come to perhaps the strangest thing in all this strange business, and one which shows how wonderfully things can be brought about by a writer of Romance who knows his work.

We had hardly got well out of the suburbs when we came upon a small hut. Through the window we saw a white man, clothed in skins, standing with his back to the fire smoking a cheroot. Quelling his emotion with the suppressed force of a Stoic—(it was wonderful how he did it, a stray onlooker would never have suspected his delight)—Sir Harry put his head in at the window and said :

"Hullo! you here! You are my long-lost brother."

The man in the skins nearly jumped out of them with surprise, and on recognising his brother sat down somewhat abruptly.

"Did not you steal that quotation from 'Box and Cox?'" he said, in a querulous tone.

Ignoring the insinuation, Sir Harry added:

"Forgive me. Our parting was rather strained."

"I was," said his brother; "it hurt me very much."

"Still, forgive me," said Sir Harry; "I loved you all the time."

"It was all very well to dissemble your love, but why did you kick me downstairs?"

"Come," said Sir Harry, triumphantly, "that's older than 'Box and Cox' anyhow. But I was wrong, I admit it. I should have dropped him over the bannisters," he muttered in his beard.

"I have been here a long time," said his brother. "The fact is—a most awkward thing—I broke my leg."

"Any danger?" asked Sir Harry, anxiously.

"No, no; not now."

"Ah," said Sir Harry, concealing his delight at this bulletin, with a great effort. It was wonderful how he did it. "We will take you back."

Thus were the brothers reconciled.

The next question was how to get away from Ipecacuanha Land. Umbugs said we were such good company he could not spare us. Of course, this is very flattering, but is rather a nuisance under the circumstances.

Twosh comes to our rescue. To begin with, he has found out all our tricks, and thinks, with us out of the way, he might start on his own account and make a good thing of it. Ever since his abdication he has been very much out at elbows.

Then Scraggi has been causing him great anxiety; he has returned to Fullarder after all,

SCRAGGI PROPOSES TO MISS FULLARDER.

and urges his suit with renewed ardour. Poor Noegood is too infatuated to notice anything. It is becoming quite a scandal. People are beginning to talk; at last the papers get hold of it, and the most enterprising of the evening journals comes out with a paragraph headed " Scandal in Court Circles," and stating that Scraggi had offered Fullarder marriage. Poor old Twosh came to me in a frightful state.

" This must be stopped at all hazards," he said, with almost tears in his eyes. " I could never give my consent to such a match. Noegood must marry Fullarder—he has compromised her already—and then you must all leave at once and take her with you."

"But Umbugs!" I suggested.

" Oh, I'll make it all right with him."

I mentioned this scheme to Sir Harry, who was delighted. His brother did not count. Somehow or other Noegood did not quite seem to see it.

" I cannot marry a black," he complained. " To use the language of hyperbole, in which all these good people delight: The sun, that's me, cannot mate with the darkness, nor the white with the black. Fullarder would be the first to see this."

"Why not?" I said, "it's all prejudice. 'You shall take some savage woman; she shall rear your dusky race.'"

"That's all dooced fine," says Noegood, "but this is not 'Locksley Hall,' this is 'Sixty Years After.' *Nous avong changee tout cela.*" These sailors are such linguists.

Still I explained that it was our only chance of getting away, and that Noegood personally had to choose between "a cycle of Cathay" unwedded, and "fifty years of Europe" with Fullarder's company.

At last we talked him over, and he consented, though with great reluctance. But how are we to get away? Dare we tempt again the perils of the desert, and endeavour to find our way once more to Notatall? We all agreed this was out of the question, especially Sir Harry, who had fallen into arrears with the tricycle man, long before the machine came to grief.

CHAPTER X.

AN OLD FRIEND—OUR DEPARTURE—OUR ARRIVAL IN ENGLAND—ENTHUSIASTIC RECEPTION.

E sleep over this momentous question. Next day rather a curious thing happened. Who should arrive but my dear old friend Dr. Carlyon in a balloon.

"Hallo!" I said, "there's some mistake here, this is not Phantom Land. You've got into the wrong book."

"The covers are so alike," he complained, with an air of annoyance.

"Well, you are looking very well," I added; "where have you been all this while?"

"Oh!" he said; "I've had great fun. I fell over the biggest waterfall in South America and discovered a new city. Writing my name on all the principal monuments was not bad, but you should have seen my fight with a cockiolly bird* in mid-air from my balloon. You would have enjoyed that; I have not had such a holiday for years."

"What brings you here?" I asked.

"Well, before taking my vacation I heard from your wife you were somewhere in this direction, and I thought I would look you up on my way home." (I had written to my wife on getting safely away to acquaint her with my destination.) Carlyon here anchored his balloon and slid down the rope to the ground.

"Well, I am very glad to see you, anyhow," I was just saying when we were interrupted by the appearance of Umbugs and his retinue, who advanced in a menacing attitude.

"What are we to do?" said Carlyon.

An idea struck me.

---

* *Note by* EDITOR : Isn't this libellous ? Ask counsel.

"You came in the moon, don't you see? That will make it all right."

"Rather thin, isn't it?" said he; "those savages know such a lot now-a-days."

"You have found out that, have you?"

"Awful," he said; "it comes of educating the lower orders. Still, perhaps they don't know Jules Verne. We will try it."

We did. It was a great success. Umbugs was distinctly puzzled. We are saved; he had not read Jules Verne.

"Oh, that is the moon, is it?" he said, pointing to the balloon, "well, I don't think much of it. Stay," he added, with a cunning smile. "If that is the moon, he," pointing to Carlyon, "is the man in the moon!"

"Of course," I said, "the thing's obvious."

"Then," said Umbugs—dropping into metaphor, as is their tiresome custom on the least provocation, "hath not he brought in the bag of fuscy hue, the spor of the Oof-bird, the wealth-giving fowl, in whose track lie riches, and of whom the snarer is fortunate among the sons of men?"

Carlyon looked grave. He never had a sixpence to bless himself with in his life.

"No," I said, "you see how he has come; he has neither money nor expectations, he is an aer-o'-naught."

When I explained this *jeu de mot* Umbugs was delighted. It led to trouble in the sequel, as he would repeat it as his own. They are not a humorous people, and several leading men lost their lives for not laughing at the right moment.

This put matters on a more pleasant footing, and when I had introduced Carlyon to Umbugs, they got on famously together, and in a minute or two were talking as if they had known one another all their lives. Dr Carlyon solved our great difficulty as to our departure.

"Why not come in my balloon?" he suggested next day when we were discussing the subject. "There's lots of room."

"Well," I said, "that's all very fine, but how is the balloon to get back?" for I did not fancy roaming vaguely through space for an indefinite time.

"I will explain," he said. "For years I have been one of the leading members of the Royal Aeronautical Society, and have studied the subject of balloon navigation in all its bearings carefully. Scientists have failed to hit the right nail on the head; in fact, they have gone on the wrong tack altogether. They say, and truly, you can't control the air currents. I do not try to, I only ascend in a dead calm."

"Then, how do you move?" I asked.

"I don't move. I stand still."

"Progression a little slow," I suggested.

"Not a bit," he continued; "I do not move, but the world does."

A light dawned on me.

"The world, as you are perhaps aware, revolves on its own axis once in the day. What do I do? I ascend in a dead calm. By a scientific process which it would be tedious to explain here—indeed, as I propose reading a paper on it to the Society, when I return, it would be unnecessary—I keep my balloon absolutely immovable. By a simple method of reckoning which I need not trouble you with—in fact, I doubt your understanding it—I discover when London, by a process of revolution, lies directly under the base of the car. Then we descend, and there you are in twenty-four hours, or perhaps less."

The plan was stupendous. Such a journey would prove a fitting end to such an expedition as ours had proved. Our departure was soon arranged. Umbugs, though sorry to lose us, let himself be persuaded by Twosh. Still, a slight difficulty arose about Fullarder. Umbugs, to our horror, refused to let us go unless she were married first, in the interests of propriety. Sir Harry came to the rescue here.

"We must start at once," he said, "as I must be back for the Cup Day at Ascot, and we could not get the banns out in time."

Noegood backs him up, and remembers that he promised his mother never to be married in a Registrar's Office. So the marriage is postponed, much to Fullarder's disappointment, until we reach our native country.

Our leave-taking was very sad. Umbugs was

inconsolable. Twosh bore up wonderfully; but Scraggi seemed to feel Fullarder's loss immensely. A Royal mandate has been issued setting forth that any one mentioning either of our names would be tortured to death. This, we are told, is an African method of showing intense respect. Of course, it may be so.

Just before the start, Umbugs approached Noegood, and said:

"Shall the black antelope who weds with the pale face, whose eye flashes and whose teeth gnash, leave her land portionless?"

Noegood looked delighted, and evidently thought Umbugs was going to do something handsome.

"I will not offer her the jewels of my country; though fit to bedeck a savage bride, they would ill suit the maiden a pale face honours with his love. No, for her I have reserved this great honour: she shall wear the priceless gems you have brought from your land beyond the sea. What have we that can compare with such as these?" Here Umbugs invested her with the complete insignia of the Primrose League. He had advanced through all the grades by this time.

Fullarder was delighted, but Noegood's language was awful.

Sir Harry's brother would come with us. No one wanted him and Sir Harry tried hard to persuade him to stay, and stalk lions by himself, by pointing out, "what fun you could have, if you went alone and didn't take firearms." His brother, however, could not be brought to see it.

Our balloon trip was a great success. Fullarder enjoyed it immensely, though she thought it rather flighty.

Dr. Carlyon shaped his course beautifully, though perhaps it was a pity that we should have descended in Rotten Row, in the middle of the Church Parade. It was the height of the season too, the Sunday between the Derby and Ascot. The police are so officious, though, perhaps, our appearance was hardly *de rigueur*. Sir Harry's costume had shrunk from exposure, and was very tight. His brother wore his skins, but poor Fullarder had not much beyond her Primrose

OUR ARRIVAL IN ENGLAND BY BALLOON.

adornments. As for me, I had been clothed just before leaving with a coating of tar, and decorated with feathers interspersed with rare art. At some distance it had the appearance of a tightly-fitting suit of dress clothes. They would do it, though I begged them not to bother. It is a ceremony of the country reserved exclusively for distinguished strangers on their departure.

Noegood was, perhaps, the most striking figure of us all. True, he had his dress clothes, but they were considerably out of repair. In the place of his glass eye (he had lent it to Twosh, and could never get it back again) he utilised his cat's-eye solitaire, which had certainly an unique effect. On the whole our arrival was almost worthy of the sensation it created.

We managed to pacify the crowd by informing them that this was only our method of celebrating the Jubilee year of Her Gracious Majesty's reign.

Sir Harry offered us lunch at any of his clubs; Noegood selected the "Blucher," as he said, now the new rooms were open, we can take Fullarder there.

Here, as I have nothing more to say, I may bring this history to a close.

My wife received me rather coolly, but has consented to defer judgment until my book is produced, enabling me to account for my absence.

Sir Harry had to drop the title, but kept the estates. His brother is at present detained in a private lunatic asylum. He brought it on himself; he would talk about his adventures. One day he did so at dinner, when by the merest accident two doctors had dropped in to take pot-luck with Sir Harry, as I still call him. The certificate was signed over the second bottle of port, and the patient was removed the next day.

The bills for strait-waistcoats are a great tax on Sir Harry, who manages the estates, and takes the profits.

Noegood would not marry Fullarder after all. These sailors are so fickle. She sued him for breach of promise and got heavy damages. On the strength of these she came out as a star actress, and is, I hear, a great success in America.

Dr. Carlyon was unanimously elected president of the Royal Aeronautical Society, and expects with confidence a knighthood before the year is finished.

C. L. WRIGHT, PRINTER, GLASGOW.

KING SOLOMON'S TREASURES

BY THE AUTHOR OF
"HE," "IT," "PA," "MA," ETC.

[John De Morgan]

NEW YORK
INTERNATIONAL BOOK COMPANY
310-318 Sixth Avenue

KING SOLOMON'S TREASURES

BY THE AUTHOR OF "HE," "IT," "PA," "MA," ETC.

INTRODUCTION.

IF ever a man felt weary of life, I was that one. I had lost all interest in politics, art, science and fashionable gossip. I had, like the wise King of Israel, tried about

RUINS OF KING SOLOMON'S ARCH.

everything, and resolved that all was vanity and vexation of spirit. If only some one could find a new pleasure, an excitement which had not palled on me, I would welcome him as my dearest friend.

I was positively weary, and yet most men envied me.

Let me explain.

I, Arthur Montmorency, called Monty in short by my most intimate friends, had the misfortune to be left an orphan when I had reached the immature age of sixteen.

My guardians, good, kind old fellows they were, sent me to college, saw that I had plenty of pocket money, paid all my bills and troubled themselves no further about me.

When I reached the age of twenty-one, I was no longer an infant in the eye of the law, but a man, so had to fulfill a man's duty.

My guardians appointed a meeting, at which I found my father's old family lawyer, pompous and erect, with a face like parchment, and a mouth framed like the legal phraseology to which he was so accustomed—hard and stern.

When the customary handshakings had been gone through, the lawyer cleared his throat, and taking up a package of papers tied round several times with red tape, began slowly to untie the knots.

This was the work of some minutes, but at last it was accomplished and then opening the top document—of course a parchment one—he said:

"Mr. Arthur Montmorency, I was your respected father's attorney at law and general legal adviser——" he paused for effect, evidently desirous of impressing on my mind his great importance.

The words he had uttered were much in the tone a judge uses when sentencing a man to death. As I did not doubt Mr. Elmore's assertion, I made no reply, but waited for him to continue, which he did in a few moments.

"Since his lamented decease I have acted for the estate, and your most worthy guardians. It is now my duty to inform you that the property left by your paternal ancestor has by judicious management"—another pause—"judicious management, I repeat, considerably increased in value, so that now you find yourself at the age of your majority with an accumulated cash balance of nearly fifty thousand pounds—let me be correct——" Mr. Elmore raised his eyeglass, looked at the document he held in his hand, and then clearing his voice again, said:

"Ah, yes, just so; to be exact the amount in actual cash at the bank is forty-nine thousand eight hundred and ninety-seven pounds ten shillings and sixpence. From lands and houses your income from this time out will be equal to five thousand pounds sterling a year."

Much more was said, but as the subject is of no general interest I leave the lawyer's presence and dry legal facts, and proceed with my story.

Six years have elapsed since then, therefore I am twenty-seven years of age, and weary of life.

My wealth gave me an *entree* into the best families. Mothers with marriageable daughters invited me to balls and *soirees*, garden parties, and *conversaziones*. Young ladies of an uncertain age, but who retained a most miraculous appearance of youth, perhaps by the aid of certain compounds known to science, smiled on me and appeared happiest when by my side; altogether I was a pet of society.

I found no pleasure there. I tried hunting, fishing, shooting, but soon got weary of them all. I purchased some racers, won the Derby, and added a St. Leger cup to my collection. I did Paris and Rome; saw the Alps and climbed the Matterhorn, tried rouge et noir at Monaco, and spent a few thousands at Wiesbaden and Baden-Baden.

All was vanity, and I was now once again at my chambers in the Albany, heartily sick and tired of everything. While I was in this peculiar frame of mind, the door was opened quite suddenly, and handsome, dashing Jack O'Brien rushed up to me, put out his hand, and then drew back:

"Got the blues, eh?"

"Yes."

"Bad?"

"Look here, Jack, I am tired of life. I want a new sensation, or I shall die!"

"Try hunting."

"I am tired of it."

"Go to Norway, and fish."

"Been there, and found it tame and monotonous."

"Then get married."

"No, thank you, Jack; better death than that. I am sick of the scheming manners of the giggling, simpering girls, and a single man I shall remain."

"Then I don't know what to recommend, unless you go with me."

"Where to?"

"Africa," answered Jack O'Brien, as coolly as though he had mentioned the next street, or St. James' Park.

"Africa?" I exclaimed, "and what are you going to do there?"

"See, Monty, you know I am poor; well, I have the 'rale ould Oirish blood in me,' and have been going the pace, so that now I have only five hundred pounds left.

If I stay here, that will last me perhaps two months, and then I shall be dead broke."

"Well, what can you do in Africa?"

"Hunt the lion and elephant, and fraternize with the natives."

"But, O'Brien, that will take money; besides, you cannot live there always."

"No—that's so; but I shall not come back unless I am wealthy. Will you join me?"

"No." I answered shortly, for I saw no pleasure in the proposition.

"Think again, Monty; there will be loads of excitement and danger. Think what it will be when, having fired your last cartridge, you are pursued by a real, roaring lion, and know you are growing tired; your legs begin to tremble, your eyes get dim, and your brain grows dizzy, but there close behind you is the lion, getting more savage every minute You take a wild glance back and its hot breath reaches you, the creature's eyes seem to burn into your very soul, and you give yourself up for lost, when aid arrives. Wouldn't there be excitement for you?"

O'Brien had told his story well, and worked up the excitement with so much dramatic power that I had actually grown interested.

He was wise enough to leave me at that moment.

An hour later I had sent a messenger to Jack's chambers to ask when he was starting. That brought the Irish "good fellow" round to the Albany, and before we parted I had agreed to go with him, but on these conditions: I was to pay the entire expenses, the small remnant of his fortune was to be carefully invested until his return. For a long time he fought against this idea, but I was inexorable, and he had to consent.

That was how I came to go to Africa. The journey saved my life, and from the day I became the comrade of Jack O'Brien I have never felt *ennui*. To occupy my spare time, and thinking the adventures would be of interest to others, I jotted down the principal things which happened, and afterward molded them into readable shape.

CHAPTER I.
O'BRIEN'S STORY.

WHEN I had fully made up my mind to accompany Jack O'Brien on his hunting expedition to Africa, I felt for the first time that life might have charms. I was sick of the shams of society, and the more I penetrated beneath the surface, the more heartily I detested the subterfuges and hypocrisies of English high-life.

KING SOLOMON'S TREASURES.

"Society! O what a hideous sham,
Is veiled and masked beneath that specious name!
Society! its mission is to damn,
To curse, and blight; to burn with withering flame
All that is worthiest in us—to cram
The world with polished hypocrites, who claim
To sin, of right—Society has said it—
And think their crimes are greatly to their credit.
What worships rank and makes a god of gold?
What turns fair women into painted frights?
What tempts to vice and villainy untold?
And claims from all of us its devilish rites?
What prompts ambition, base and uncontrolled?
What never on the side of mercy fights!
What causes sin in horrible variety?
Mostly, the demon that we call Society."

Amid the savages of Africa I knew I should be free from sham and hypocrisy; therefore I felt almost as great an enthusiasm as did my friend Jack.

I have not fairly introduced Jack to my readers yet, so had better do so at once. I need scarcely say that O'Brien was an Irishman. His father was a small landholder in that unhappy country, but as he had the blood of the Irish kings in his veins he was desirous that his son should have a liberal education, so Jack was sent to England, and graduated with me from Caius College, Cambridge.

O'Brien was to enter one of the learned professions, but he was too gay and rollicking for the priesthood, too light-hearted and full of mischief for medicine, and far too fickle to achieve success at the bar; so he tried horse-racing, shooting, and hunting for amusements, and cards, billiards, and betting as a means of keeping up his income, with the inevitable result—loss and financial disaster. His father died, and various usurers, who had very kindly loaned money to happy, careless, thoughtless Jack, seized the property to settle certain *post-obits* they held, and the young squire found himself landless and with only a bare thousand in hard cash. This had decreased to five hundred when Jack proposed the trip to Africa.

Shall I describe O'Brien? Imagine a man with shoulders as broad as Hercules, muscles as strong, and limbs as well formed as the fabled giant, and you can form some conception of honest Jack.

His height was six feet in his stockings, and he was physically well developed and strong. I was a good contrast to him, for my height was only five feet four, and my chest measure just under thirty-four inches, but I was tough and wiry and knew I could stand a good deal of knocking about.

We formed, therefore, an excellent working pair. As to looks—even if it be thought I am egotistic, I admit—we were both good-looking, and, of course, our manners polished.

All the details of the journey I left to O'Brien, and contented myself in looking after outfits and securing letters of credit on various houses in case of need. In addition, I supplied myself with a good sum in hard cash, feeling that an occasion for it might arise.

Two days before we were to sail I received a note from O'Brien which perplexed me, and added to my excitement. It was brought by special messenger, and read as follows:

"DEAR MONTY,—I have deceived you. If you can forgive me, come around to-night, and I will explain.
"Your repentant
"JACK."

What did he mean? Had he made away with the money I had given him? If so, all right. I could stand it. Was he not going to Africa? Even that did not disturb me, for I had experienced a new sensation which was worth more than what I had expended.

I rather liked mystery; it gave a zest to life. Therefore, when I found myself puzzling over the strange, brief note, I found my blood coursing faster and more freely through my veins, and I was happy.

Nay more, I never remember experiencing curiosity before, but now I was really and truly impatient for evening's shadows to gather and twilight to usher in the time of meeting with my mysterious friend.

Just as the clock struck eight, I was knocking at the door of Jack O'Brien's chambers, and heard the hearty "come in" given as a response.

As I entered, there was Jack with his shirt-sleeves rolled up, trying to pack a lot of things, useful and useless, into a small portmanteau.

He was evidently going on a journey, but where?

"Well, old boy, so you forgive me?" he said, cheerily.

"Yes, even without knowing what I am forgiving."

"Good old soul."

"Now cease your mystery and tell me the story of your deception."

"I will; but promise—but there, I will not ask any pledge, but will tell you right off. Take a smoke——" and Jack handed me a box of cigars of the most expensive brand, just like Jack, everything must be of the very best and costliest.

"When I had lighted the cigar, he followed my example.

"I have often thought that tobacco is a great peacemaker. The Indians smoke the pipe of peace, and bury the hatchet; the savages of Africa, as I learned later, will never injure a man with whom they have smoked. So as Jack and I smoked, and the clouds which ascended mingled together, so our souls went out to each other, and we were more than ever chums.

"Now for the deception, Jack," I said. "Are you not going to Africa?"

"Yes, of course," was his reply.

"Well, then—but there, tell your own story in your own way."

"I will, Monty, but I said my object was sport."

"What then?"

"That is not my only object. I seek wealth—wealth! The very thought of it makes me dream that the whole earth is one gigantic lump of gold, that the stars are glittering gems and that the sun itself is but an enormous diamond."

I looked at my friend, thinking he must be insane, but he was calm and unruffled, so I waited, and after a short silence, he continued:

"What would you say if I could tell you of a place where we can get enough gold to build a mansion, every wall of which shall be of solid metal, the window and door frames of the finest ivory, and instead of glass, we would have the light strike through millions of diamonds?"

"Great Cæsar!" I exclaimed; "let me get some ice for your fevered brain."

"I knew that is what you would think, but do you believe I am sitting here and talking to you?"

"Certainly."

"Then I am as positive I can and will find the wealth, if I live."

"Jack O'Brien!" I said, "if you value my friendship, don't fool with me, but tell me what you mean, and although I don't want any of the wealth, if the search for it is to be exciting, I will join you, but I must know more about your craze."

"Then you shall, but the story is a long one."

"I am all attention—go on."

O'Brien walked about for a few minutes uneasily and then settled down on the chair again, and commenced to make apologies.

"You may laugh at my story, but to me it is a reality."

"Tell it, man, for I am all impatience."

"Then here goes. You must know that my mother was a seeress or clairvoyant—not that she exercised her power outside of our family circle, but all who were admitted into its fold had ample proof that she could see more than was visible to human eyes. So convinced was I of the truth of her visions, that while others laughed and scoffed at the so-called supernatural, I quietly investigated. She died, and for several years I ceased all my experiments and inquiries concerning the matter. A few months ago, I was walking home from a party, cooling my hot head by the side of the Serpentine in Hyde Park, when I saw my mother."

"But she has been dead several years," I interrupted.

"I know it," he continued, "but I saw her walking or gliding toward me. I seemed certain it was my mother returned to life, so I spoke to her, but, instead of answering, she turned her back on me and walked away. I followed, but soon lost sight of her."

"Too much champagne, Jack," I again interrupted.

"Think what you like, Monty, but listen to my story."

"Go on, old boy; I am all attention."

"I wandered about until nearly nine o'clock—I left the party at five—and then I went home; I threw myself on my bed, dressed as I was. I had not been asleep long before I dreamed I again saw my mother, and this time she spoke to me. 'Do as I direct,' she said, 'and you shall be the wealthiest of all the O'Briens and the Murdochs.' She was a Murdoch, so I am of a royal line on both sides of the house," continued Jack, with just a shade of pride in his manner.

"I awoke from my sleep, and for the rest of the day was uneasy and restless. That night I wandered about the park, thinking that I should again see my mother's spirit, but she did not appear.

"I was miserable and unmanned; nothing seemed to interest me. I tried the gaming table, but lost every time. I made a heavy book on the Derby, and came out, by hedging, just by the skin of my teeth. Several weeks passed, but I saw no more of the specter. I went to a medium, but came away disgusted; and so things went on for two months, when, as I was walking down Oxford Street, I saw the well-known figure just in front of me. I tried to overtake it, but the faster I walked the greater was its speed, until I found, with all my exertions, the same distance between us was maintained.

"When the figure reached Wardour Street it turned sharply round the corner, and moved rapidly down the street devoted to artificial antiquities, *bric-a-brac* and old-fashioned furniture.

"I followed, and saw it enter a store. When I arrived at the door I found the place locked, by means of a padlock on the outside; and yet I could have declared positively that the tempting figure which I had pursued really entered. I shaded my eyes and looked through the glass door, when I beheld the form and face of my mother standing by the side of an old escritoire or cabinet.

"The moment I caught sight of the face, it vanished. I waited about Wardour Street all day, but the store remained closed, and I could not obtain the address of its proprietor. I saw no more of the specter.

"Every day I spent in the street, and every night I dreamt about the cabinet until I became almost a monomaniac on the subject and determined to buy it no matter what the cost might be. Another month passed away and then I learned that the proprietor of the antiquities had been sick, and that now he was dead.

"The good will of the business had been sold and the stock was to be disposed of at auction.

"I obtained a catalogue, and saw that the escritoire numbered 'Lot 171' was supposed to have been made in the reign of Queen Elizabeth and had belonged to Sir Walter Raleigh. I went to the auctioneer and tried to buy Lot 171 privately, but to my dismay, was told that it was not for sale except at auction, and that it was expected the article would fetch as much as any three other articles in the store.

"The day of sale came and I was there eager for the auction to commence.

"The auctioneer felt his importance and expatiated at length on every article to be sold. I made two or three bids, more for the sake of appearing to be a buyer of general goods rather than an expectant purchaser of the escritoire. I began to think the auctioneer would never reach the article I so much coveted, but just as the evening began to draw on apace, the lot was reached. At that moment I saw my mother's face peering over the escritoire.

"'This article,' said the auctioneer, 'was made by order of good Queen Bess, and by her given to Sir Walter Raleigh, the gent who discovered tobacco and other good things. What shall I say for this article? Will any one bid a thousand pounds?'

"I was staggered. I did not possess that amount. I waited, and no one made such a bid. At last a little, old man, as antiquated as most of the furniture, offered fifty pounds, I made it fifty-five. I will not weary you, Monty, by going through all the bids, suffice it to say that whenever I stopped bidding, I saw my mother as though urging me to purchase the piece of furniture. At last I made a bid of one hundred and forty pounds, and with the customary 'Going! going!' and a long pause—'gone!' I was declared

14   KING SOLOMON'S TREASURES.

the purchaser of Lot 171. I got the desk home, and there it is."

Jack pointed to the old-fashioned desk, which I wouldn't have given a ten-pound note for, and a flush of pleasure passed over his face.

"What has this story to do with our trip to Africa?" I asked, and then continued: "It only seems to me to illustrate the old proverb—a fool and his money, etc."

"Wait, old boy, until you hear all, and you will see that it was a wise purchase, even though I sold it for firewood to-morrow."

I was still more mystified and impatient, though I confess I began to have serious doubts about the sanity of my friend.

CHAPTER II.
"LOT 171."

"WHEN I had got the desk to my chambers," continued O'Brien. "I began to wonder what good it was to me. I was half inclined to believe with you that my wits had gone wool-gathering—in other words, that I had thrown away good money for a useless piece of old furniture.

"I opened the desk, and found evidences of great age; so, although it may never have been in the possession of the great Raleigh, it was ancient, and therefore valuable.

"I looked in all the drawers—why, I cannot tell, except that I was curious to examine my purchase thoroughly. Of course, every drawer was empty, and although I had no right to feel disappointed, I did so, for a feeling that some treasure might be contained in its drawers had somehow got possession of my mind. I had been careful to get a receipt from the auctioneer, which my little knowledge of the law enabled me to draw up, whereby I purchased not only the desk, its closets, drawers, and all other appurtenances, but everything contained therein at the time of the sale.

"'It's all yours,' said the auctioneer, as he read over the receipt, and laughed at the exactness of the phraseology 'and good-luck go with it, for old Gabriel,' the late owner, ' only paid forty pounds for it.'

The executors of the dead man's estate had, therefore, made a good profit out of the desk. That night it was quite a long time before I could fall asleep. When I did so, I thought I saw some one seated at the desk and examining carefully a number of papers. I sat up in bed—at least, so my dream ran—for the escritoire was in my sleeping-room, and watched.

"The papers looked old and as antiquated as the desk.

The figure was that of a man, and as he tied up the documents he placed them back in the desk with a sigh, closed the front and disappeared. For three nights I dreamed the same dream, and then I could stand it no longer, but determined to search whether there were any secret drawers or receptacles, even if I had to smash the costly piece of furniture to find out. After several hours' diligent search, I discovered a space at the back of the drawers, and found the secret spring. When the back of the drawers came out, I saw a quantity of papers which will make our fortune."

I was now very much interested in O'Brien's story, and began to believe that after all there might be something in his visions and dreams.

"Did you read the papers?" I asked.

"Of course I did, and so shall you."

With that he left me, and presently returned with an armful of parchments and rolls of paper.

"Great Cæsar!" I exclaimed, "did you find all those in the escritoire?"

"Yes, but some of them I cannot read," was his answer.

He untied a piece of ribbon and opened out a yellow, musty sheet of paper, so old that it looked as if it would fall to pieces in our hands. The writing was scarcely legible, but Jack had read it so often that it was comparatively easy to decipher with his assistance. This is what we made out:

"And they came to Ophir and fetched from thence golde foure hundrede and twenty talentes and brought them to King Solomon."

The writing was ancient and the style of spelling would show the date to have been about the end of the sixteenth century.

As Jack unrolled another paper, I began to wonder what they all meant, for I had no inkling of O'Brien's new ideas.

On the second paper, some questions were asked.

"Where was Ophir?" and then some writing had been obliterated by lapse of time, but we were able to read another sentence further down—"Did they get all the golde?"

Jack sat down and looked at me quizzically.

"Now, Monty, don't you see what I am driving at?"

"No, I cannot say that I do. I am dense and ignorant on the matter."

"Then, old fellow, I will enlighten you. Solomon had immense treasures, and I am after them."

"You are crazy."

"Perhaps so, but wait a bit before you condemn. I have

been studying the life of Solomon, and think I can locate his great treasure store. You admit that the old king was the richest in the world?"

"Yes."

"Read the Bible and you will find he had six hundred three score and six talents of gold brought him every year.*

That was equal to over four and a half million pounds sterling. What did he do with it every year? Why, he built storehouses in different parts of his kingdom and placed there the bars of gold and of silver, of diamonds and precious stones. I am on the track of the biggest of these storehouses, which is in the land of Ophir."

"How do you know?"

"These papers tell me so; besides, the man who wrote these drew a map showing just how to get to Ophir and find the storehouse."

"Where is the map?"

"It is here, but you must not be too impatient. I want you to reason out these things as you go along. If we find Ophir, we shall know where so much gold came from, even if we don't get the storehouse. Is it likely that all the gold has been exhausted? Think of the poor implements they had for getting at the metal in those days. If, then, the gold mines are not exhausted, why shouldn't we make a good dig out of them? Then, my boy, only think, gold can never be destroyed. Melt it, and it is still gold; so, if these forty or fifty million pounds' worth of gold taken to Solomon could never be destroyed, where are they? All the gold we are using now is modern. There are rich fields in Ophir yet."

O'Brien spoke so earnestly and convincingly that I felt there was a good foundation for his reasoning, and as the night was pretty far spent, I left him; but, before doing so, said that I would follow his lead, and if we never found King Solomon's treasures, at least we should have plenty of adventures.

The next day, although very busy in arranging for our journey, we spent another hour in looking over some more of the documents found in the wonderful escritoire.

On one document we found some peculiar entries, which we were not able to understand. On one was the following:

"* * * yn Jawan * *
Blemmyes."

This was a puzzler, and neither Jack nor myself could unravel its meaning. In a more modern writing, the ink being considerably darker, we found on another parchment:

* 1 Kings x. 14.

"Bewar the Blemmyes with one eye on crossing to Mer! They will sink the boat and feed upon the crew."

"That looks lively," I said.

"Yes," answered Jack: "but you wanted excitement, and if we meet with any cannibals you are sure to get as much as your heart desires."

"All right," was my reply. "I am in for any adventure which promises plenty of sport."

The next paper Jack opened was covered with writing, but only two or three words were legible. These were:

"Makeda," "Menilek," and the letters and figures: "L 24 E., L 17 N."

"There now, you see where we have to strike for, don't you?" said Jack, as triumphantly as if he had the fortune already within his reach.

"I'm blest if I do," was my response. "You had better explain."

"So I will. Now Makeda was Solomon's wife."

"How do you know?"

"Bother take you! Let me tell my story. I said Makeda was Solomon's wife, and Menilek was her son. The figures mean east longitude 24, latitude 17 north. Now look at your map and that should bring us in Africa."

"Very well, one place will suit me as well as another. Go on. What other clew have you got?"

"Here is the best of all," answered Jack, hugging close to him a very dirty paper; on it was inscribed:

"When thou reachest the point to cross ——," this word was illegible, "take care of the Blemmyes and the Troglodytes, for they are to be feared; but go on thy way till the great head shaped like unto a man shall be before thee, and then thy ——" here followed a line entirely obliterated. The next line read: "The great god nolds the key of the golde chamber."

"How can that guide you?" I asked, for I was very dense on matters of the kind.

"Really, Monty, are you only joking? But I guess you are sincere, and therefore I will tell you that when we get to the latitude and longitude, we will keep our eyes open for the statue of some god, and will also beware of the Troglodytes, or dwellers in caverns, for that is what the word means."

"See here, Jack, I leave all to you, and if you say it is right, count me in with you."

"Be ready, my boy, then, for seven o'clock in the morning, and we will be off to the land of the vast treasures."

So we separated for the night, and I for once felt that a

new life was before me. My *ennui* had gone, and a healthy invigoration had taken its place.

Whatever might be the result of our expedition, life would be of greater value to me.

All night I tossed about uneasily, and when morning came I was as feverish and excited as a child over a new toy, or a young girl on the morning of her wedding.

CHAPTER III.
THE VOYAGE.

WE left London for Southampton, and were soon on board the palatial steamer De Lesseps, bound for Alexandria. A very jolly lot of passengers were on board, and the time passed very pleasantly.

As we passed Gibraltar, a fresh face appeared on deck, and the warm blood rushed through my veins with alarming rapidity.

It was a face which, once seen, would never be forgotten. It is scarcely necessary to say that it was that of a lady.

She was of exquisite beauty, both in face and form, and looked as cultured as the rarest gem of the hothouse. Her age was hard to tell; but, judging from appearances, I should certainly have declared she had not reached her twentieth year. She had a transparent, colorless skin; her eyes were Oriental in their deep rich blue, and looked very large in her delicate face. Eyes which at times would dance with merriment, and again could penetrate into the inmost soul of man. Her mouth was so admirably shaped, and was so near perfection, that it looked only made to kiss, while when her lips parted teeth of pearly whiteness and exquisite shape only added to her beauty; her form was perfect, and of extreme gracefulness. There was a queenly air about her which stamped her as a being above the ordinary. Who could see her without at once surrendering his heart to her keeping?

I could not, and yet half a dozen hours before I was ready to declare that there was not a woman on earth who could make my heart beat quicker.

Who was she?

Jack had asked me that question, so he said, half a dozen times, but I had never heard him.

No one seemed to know her, and, to all appearance, she was traveling alone, and yet that could not be, for surely some parent or guardian would accompany her on her long journey.

I was growing interested. Why had she not appeared

before? Could it be that she had been a victim of *mal de mer*, and so compelled to keep her stateroom?

O'Brien declared he was going to get an introduction, but how?

"Goodness only knows! but I shall, never fear," was his answer.

I almost hated him, for jealousy had taken possession of my whole being.

How absurd it seemed, when I thought it over, to be jealous about a girl whose very name I did not know.

When she was absent I felt mad with myself, but the moment the *frou-frou* of her dress passed over the carpet of the saloon my heart throbbed, and my nerves were so thrilled that I was nearly beside myself with the passion of love.

Jack was on deck smoking, while I was deep in the mysteries of Egyptian geography in the saloon.

I had grown weary with reading, and was thinking over the story told on the fragmentary documents found in the escritoire, and had unconsciously uttered my thoughts aloud.

"What the dickens does Blemmyes mean?" I said in a half whisper. I imagined I was alone, but no sooner had I uttered the words than a voice sweet as a seraphim's breath said:

"Don't you know?"

I turned, and standing close to me was my divinity.

I rose to my feet, and tried to stammer forth an apology for uttering my thoughts in an audible voice, but my tongue seemed too large for my mouth, and I could not speak. I was conscious, also, that my face was crimson and my hair was bathed in perspiration.

The lovely girl laughed, and yet so prettily that, though I knew it was at my confusion, I liked her all the better for it.

"Don't apologize," she said sweetly. "You know on board ship we are all one family."

"Thank you," I said, foolishly.

"I think you said you wondered what Blemmyes meant?"

"Yes," I stammered out.

"I can tell you."

"You?"

"Yes; is there anything strange in that?"

"Forgive me!"

She laughed again, and her beautiful teeth looked like a row of the most exquisite pearls. She had taken a seat by the table, and I followed so excellent an example.

"If I tell you," she said, "will you tell me why you wished to know?"

"With the profoundest pleasure." I answered.

"Then imagine yourself a scholar and I your teacher," she said; and I felt that paradise itself was opening to me. What would I not give if Jack could see us? "Blemmyes," she said, "is an Ethiopian word, and means hideous men."

"Hideous men!" I echoed.

"Yes; a race of men supposed to possess only one eye in the center of the forehead, to have a nose very like the trunk of an elephant, and a few other extraordinary facial peculiarities."

Was she making fun of me? I could hardly think so, and yet how absurd her answer seemed to be.

"Surely there are no such people?" I said.

"Indeed! Really, then, you are the teacher and I the scholar. Now I always thought that history told the truth."

"And does history speak of such people?"

"I will tell you all I know. When I was young, quite young I mean, I had a nurse, a good faithful creature she was, and she told me that where she came from there were many of these Blemmyes, and she was so frightened of them that when she got a chance she ran away from home."

"And where was her home?"

"Ah! that I cannot tell you; but she was an Ithiopjawan."

"Excuse me—what?"

"An Ethiopian," she answered, and a smile was plainly discernible on her pretty lips.

"But you did not say that before," I hinted.

"Didn't I? Well, perhaps I said Ithiopjawan."

"Yes; would you think I was taking too great a liberty if I asked you to spell it?"

"Is it not a teacher's place to do so? Now repeat after me 'Ith.'" and then she spelled out the word very slowly. When she had finished, she was bubbling over with merriment, and rushed from the saloon, I felt sure, to indulge in a good laugh at my expense.

I went on deck in search of O'Brien, and found him curled up on a coil of rope, deep in the contemplation of a meerschaum he was trying to color.

"Jack, old boy, I have found out what the Blemmyes are."

"The deuce you have!" he exclaimed excitedly.

"Yes;" and then I told him. His face was a sight for an artist to caricature as he listened, for his mouth opened wide, and his eyes were like saucers.

"Tell me," I said, " wasn't one of the words which we could not understand spelt jawan?"

"Yes! What of it?"

"What was the whole sentence?"

"I forget, but I'll come down and find the paper."

O'Brien brought the tin box in which he had stored the papers, and opened the documents which had been a mystery to us. It read:

"* * * yn Jawan * *
Blemmyes."

"Shall I translate it?"

"Can you?"

"I will try. The crosses I don't understand but the other words I take it to mean 'In Ethiopia there are the hideous men.'"

"I wonder," said Jack, "if the drawing of a carved head is the portrait of one of them?"

"What portrait? you never showed me any."

"Then I will."

After searching for some time he came across a modern piece of paper, inclosed in which was a torn pen and ink sketch of a rockery on which appeared a human face.

The face was not that of a Blemmye, for it had two eyes, whereas the creatures described by my divinity had but one.

"Tell me how you got your information," said Jack after we had looked over some more of the documents.

"I got it from—— But hush—here she comes."

Jack raised his head and saw the queen-like girl approach.

She was more lovely than ever, and I felt proud to think I had made her acquaintance, although I did not know her name.

She bowed with a charming grace as she passed us, and then seated herself at the piano, but instead of playing, only amused herself by turning over the music.

The captain, a jolly, fatherly man, entered, and going up to her, said in a low tone: "Nyassa, won't you play?" Then, as an afterthought, he looked round and saw us. "Ah, O'Brien," he said, "come here, you young dog, and I'll introduce you."

It was O'Brien again, I thought. He was always the favored one; but I had one advantage—I had already conversed with her.

Jack was on his feet in an instant, and I was about to retain my seat, when old Captain Godfrey laughed heartily.

"Jealous, are you? or don't you crave the honor of an introduction as well?"

I muttered something, and with O'Brien went to the piano.

PAPER WITH SKETCH OF ROCKERY.

The formal introduction was then gone through, and we learned that the young lady was under the guardianship of the captain as far as Alexandria, and that her name was Nyassa Balkis.

What a peculiar cognomen! and yet, as pronounced by the captain, who was an Oriental scholar, it was most musical.

While Nyassa was playing—Jack, of course, leaning over her shoulder—the captain became quite confidential.

"That is a most remarkable girl," he commenced.

"She is a most lovely one," was my response.

"True; and she is as good as she is beautiful. She is a queen by hereditary right, and a native of Egypt."

"She does not look so."

"What? not a queen?"

"Yes, she does look every inch a queen," I responded; "but she appears more like a European than an Egyptian."

"She is partly English," was the captain's reply, "for her mother was a native of Devonshire, but her father was the lineal descendant of one of the oldest royal houses of Africa. I knew Mr. Balkis well, long before he married Nyassa's mother, and a fine fellow he was—God rest his soul! Many a yarn he told me of his ancestors and their warlike doings, and I never dreamed of doubting his statements."

"Have you any objection to telling me something of his ancestry?"

"Not the slightest, for I have taken quite a fancy to you and O'Brien. He can trace his genealogy back to Ikon-Amlek, whose surname was Balkis, and who, in the year 1300 became king of that expanse of territory called the Soudan, Ethiopia and Abysinnia. The family reigned for four hundred years, when a revolution took place, and the Balkis family was driven into exile. That girl is the last of the royal house."

"And her father?" I asked.

"Is dead. Nyassa was sent when quite young to be educated in England, and while her mother was on a visit to her daughter, old Balkis was suddenly summoned home. In other words, he was stricken down with cholera, and in less than twenty-four hours was dead. When the faithful wife heard the news, she was so prostrated with grief that within a month she had followed her husband, and Nyassa was left an orphan at the age of fifteen. She is now of age, and is on her way to her guardians in Alexandria to take possession of the great wealth left her by her father. My daughter was at the same school with her, and is now her traveling companion."

"Your daughter?" I said, inquiringly

"Yes; but poor Emily has been sick ever since we left Southampton, and I don't think you have seen her."

"Pardon my curiosity, Captain Gordon, but the lady's guardians—do they—I mean, are they in Alexandria?"

I was getting confused, as usual, whenever Nyassa was either near or being talked about.

"Her guardians are myself, a banker in Alexandria, and her mother's brother, a Devonshire squire."

"Thanks, captain. I have been highly interested, for I never saw so much loveliness in my life as she possesses."

"Looks as though O'Brien thought the same thing, eh?"

I looked across and saw Jack in earnest conversation with Nyassa, and all the furies of jealousy took possession of my soul.

To my suspicious mind it seemed that her cheeks flushed and her dark eyes flashed with pleasure as he spoke to her in his honeyed tones.

Should I warn her against him? For Jack was a born flirt and lady killer.

What business was it of mine? I thought a moment later. Surely O'Brien had as much right to enjoy a pleasant hour as any one else?

Besides, in a few days more we should lose sight of Nyassa, and most probably never see her again. She was old enough to take care of herself, and was not the captain her guardian?

I wondered if Jack had confided to her the object of our journey? He looked so entranced that it would not have surprised me if he had told her all about his wonderful visions and strange purchase.

Nyassa was the only lady on board who could sing, so her voice was often heard, to the great delight of all, for it was like herself—simply perfect. She looked at times the Egyptian queen, while again her moods would change, and as she sang some pretty English ballad, she was sweet simplicity itself.

To our great delight, Jack and I were the most favored ones; and after that first evening she divided her attentions very fairly between us, so that neither had any cause for jealousy.

I often referred to the captain's story, and she laughingly said that it might be true, but she cared not, she would rather be a village maiden than the proudest queen, and as for riches, if all King Solomon's treasures were placed at her feet, she would throw them all into the water if their acceptance meant the giving up of her freedom.

When we were nearing our journey's end by the De Lesseps, and within sight of land, I learned from Nyassa that her stay in Egypt would most probably extend to several months, but she hoped to return to England within a year.

The temptation to throw up my share in Jack's expedition and stay near my divinity was strong in my mind. I felt how sweet it would be to remain near her presence, to see her at times, to watch the window of her room and know that she was only separated by the thin glass, to guard her from danger and follow her in her walks even if not allowed to speak with her. My dreams were of her, and I saw myself often in England asking her guardians for her hand, receiving from them the transfer of their guardianship, and then my dreams would become one long ecstasy as I clasped her in my arms, my own wife, Nyassa.

A week before I was sneering at woman's love—a few days ago I had declared that no one ever lived that could cause me the slightest tremor of emotion, and now after but a few hours in the presence of this Egyptian of whom I knew so little, I felt that she " was the ocean to the river of my thoughts," and that in future I could have no " breath, no being, but in hers."

This passionate frenzy held me in its power, and I then felt that nothing on earth could ever give me happiness without the companionship of Nyassa.

CHAPTER IV.
ALONG THE NILE.

WE were in the harbor of Alexandria, and all was confusion and excitement. Friends became reunited and business men were animated with ambitious hopes as the anchor was dropped and the good ship floated peacefully at her dock.

Nyassa Balkis was still on board; her guardian, the Alexandrian banker, had not yet made his appearance.

Perhaps he was unaware of the great beauty of his ward, and looking upon her as an ordinary being did not trouble himself to hurry about meeting her.

Captain Gordon brought Nyassa and his daughter Emily, a sweet little country primrose, to us and confided them to our care,

"Now, young fellows," he said in his usual jovial, rollickway when in good humor, "now, young fellows, I confide to you all my treasures. Take care of them, and don't part with them unless I give the word of command."

We accepted the position with pleasure, and I could not help whispering to Nyassa, who fell to my lot, that I hoped Captain Gordon would not give the order of separation for the next fifty years.

Was it imagination, or did the color rise to her face?

She laughed, and replied that she should be sorry to sit in that saloon for so long a time.

I was on the verge of saying something more pointed, and most likely committing myself, when Captain Gordon's voice was heard in loud conversation with another.

The voices grew nearer, and in a few moments Nyassa

was clasped in the arms of a tall, long-bearded man, who bore the well-known name of Emil Novarro, of the world-wide famed Banking-house of Novarro, Groschen & Company.

So this was Nyassa's guardian. It was a strange coincidence, for not only had I some letters of credit on his house, but had a personal introduction to the banker himself.

When Mr. Navarro had got through his warm welcoming of his ward, we were introduced to him, and I said I should do myself the honor of calling on him the next day.

"Next fiddlesticks!" the old gentleman said, excitedly. "You must come now, and while you stay in Alexandria you will make a mortal enemy of Emil Novarro if you stay a day anywhere but at my house."

Should I accept the invitation? I looked at Nyassa and plainly read my answer in the glance of her eyes.

So Jack and I followed the banker and ladies to the palatial residence on the Grand Square.

We had only thought of staying a few days in Alexandria to prepare our outfit, but the welcome we had received, and the pleasant company gathered at the banker's residence, caused our stay to be prolonged for nearly a month.

We had decided our course of action. We would take the rail to Cairo, where we would charter a boat and engage a crew which should take us up the Nile as far as we wished to go.

Novarro heard of our intention, though he had no idea of our object, and invited himself with Nyassa and Miss Gordon as a guest as far as Girjeh, where Nyassa had property. The pleasure was all on our side, and when Cairo was reached I took care to find a boat which should be a credit to my ancestral wealth, and at the same time fitting for a queen.

When Jack saw it, he grew purple in the face.

"This will never do; how the deuce can we go exploring in this palace?" he exclaimed.

I was angry, and for the first time reminded him that it was my money which paid for it.

"Don't I know it?" he said, sharply. "Confound your money; it is going to spoil our search."

When, however, O'Brien saw the grateful glance of Nyassa's eyes as she saw the luxurious room set apart for her and Emily Gordon, Jack was as enthusiastic as I was.

We formed a merry party up the Nile, Nyassa taking with her a guitar and Emily a harp, while Jack played the flute exquisitely, so we had plenty of music.

How quickly the time passed, for the pleasant company made the journey most enjoyable. Had we taken the ordinary dahabeah from Cairo we should have been harassed with the many rules and regulations in force, and but scant opportunity would have been provided for intercourse with the ladies.

The dahabeah we had chartered was furnished very handsomely, though not to be compared with the far-famed barge of Cleopatra, which

". . . Like a burnished throne
Burned on the waters; the poop was beaten gold;
Purple the sails, and so perfumed that
The winds were lovesick with them; the oars were silver,
Which, to the tune of flutes, kept stroke."

But ours was far more beautiful than the ordinary Nile boat.

The dahabeahs are long and shapely. About half the vessel is occupied with a windowed structure containing a saloon and cabins, with an awning on its roof, shading an agreeable lounge. The other half is filled with seats for the rowers, and the kitchen, which is usually between the masts and the end of the boat. The Egyptian rowers could not pull a stroke unless they were either singing or listening to music. They intone an interminable chant, the favorite one running on in this fashion for hours together:

"I wish I was at Osiott,
Oh, Allah! oh, my prophet!
Then I'd buy a new felt cap,
Oh, Allah! oh, my prophet!
The wind is blowing very strong,
Oh, Allah! oh, my prophet!"

And so on, introducing everything they wished to converse about in the chant.

The river's banks were full of interest to us, and as Mr. Novarro had lived in Egypt for many years he was able to point out the places so famed in the history of the far past.

The Pyramids and fabled monuments, the tombs of Beni Hassan, and other objects of historic interest are passed, and the modern city of Siout reached.

We had traveled over two hundred and fifty miles from Cairo, but were not weary of the journey, for we were ready constantly to exclaim:

"Ever charming, ever new,
When will the landscape tire the view?"

At Siout we left our dahabeah and spent a couple of days in the town.

There was but little of interest to be seen, so we again set our sail, the rowers started their song, and we proceeded up the river a distance of eighty-eight miles, until we disembarked at Girjeh.

Here we were to leave the ladies and their guardian, and our hardships and adventures to commence.

I did a costly but sensible thing at Girjeh, for I transferred the dahabeah to Mr. Novarro and chartered a smaller one, more nearly resembling a kyas or freight boat, for ourselves. For over a week we stayed at Girjeh, and even then found it difficult to tear ourselves away from Nyassa and her companion.

Bidding us God-speed on our journey, the stately Egyptian waved her handkerchief as our boat left the bank of the river, and we proceeded on our way.

"That girl will influence my whole life," I said to O'Brien, when a wind of the river hid the fair girls from our view.

"Hard hit, eh?" laughed O'Brien.

"Yes, Jack, and only for the sake of our expected adventures I would offer her my hand."

A shade passed over O'Brien's handsome features, and I thought the struggle in his breast was a severe one.

He turned away and watched the sailors rowing, and then as if with sudden impulse came to where I was standing and asked:

"Do you love Nyassa?"

"I do, Jack, above everything."

He sighed, and then with an emotion which I did not think him capable of feeling, he almost groaned, "So do I."

"Then I have no chance," I said, for I never believed I could find favor in preference to handsome Jack O'Brien.

"Have you spoken?" I asked, after a pause.

"No; have you?"

"No, Jack, for I know not what may befall me."

"Monty, it is unfortunate we both love the same lady, but will you do me a favor?"

"Anything, Jack, right heartily."

"Then, if we ever return and have plenty of treasure to take back with us, and should find Nyassa unmarried and heartwhole, will you give me an equal chance, and let her own heart decide between us."

"Gladly, but why qualify it by speaking of the treasure?"

"I should never ask her while I am poor."

"Stuff and nonsense, Jack; Nyassa is not the girl to refuse a poor man. She would marry the very poorest if she loved him, but if she did not love, all the treasures of Solomon would not tempt her."

He grasped my hand fervently, and lighted his pipe, by which I knew he desired a quiet meditation.

I left him, and going up to one of the rowers, asked him for his oar. I took his seat and exercised my muscles for a spell, but soon relinquished the work and went into the cabin for my rifle.

I called O'Brien's attention to a sand bank on our left which was literally covered with crocodiles. These strange Nile natives looked like trunks of trees lying ready for shipment. They had no fear of our dahabeah until we were within twenty or thirty yards of them, when they slowly crept into the water; all excepting one, an immense fellow who lazily lagged behind, and looked as if he would be well pleased to make a meal of the dainty portions of one of us. I raised my rifle and an instant later the fine fellow dropped dead, for the bullet struck him in the brain.

Three of the boatmen, who had never before heard a rifle at such close quarters, dropped into the body of the boat, and refused to rise until I assured them that there would be no more reports. Crocodile heads of enormous size were on all sides, and Jack was equally successful with his first shot at a genuine Nile crocodile. The natives were now delighted at the thought of our success, and one fellow whom I mistrusted very much was eager to own a rifle. He had been one of those who had fallen in the body of the boat at the first shot, but had very quickly recovered from his fright. He was so persistent that I thought I would teach him a lesson. I had with me an immense gun, which was almost as formidable as a cannon, and was made as an experiment in heavy caliber rifles, but proved a failure through its great power of kicking.

This gun I loaded, taking care to put in an extra charge; but no ball, for I had a fear and mistrust of the man.

I showed him how to pull the trigger.

Tetelar, as the boatman was called, raised the gun to his shoulder and stood on the seat to take better aim at a fine crocodile basking in the sunshine on the bank.

He pulled the trigger and a loud report startled the animal, but it did more, for I looked for Tetelar and found him spluttering about in the water and chased by a young crocodile, who evidently was in search of a good dinner.

We pulled the man into the boat, and he swore by Allah and his prophet that never more would he try to shoot with the white man's magic tube.

His shoulder was bruised with the concussion, and it taught him and his friends a lesson, for not one of them ever after suggested trying to use the white man's weapon.

When we arrived at Korosko, in latitude twenty-two degrees forty-four minutes, we had been on the water one month since leaving Cairo, including the rests at Siout and Girjeh.

At Korosko, there being a great feast of some kind going

on, we gave our men the chance of leaving the boat and joining in the devotions of their brethren.

All but two accepted the holiday, but these two sullen, silent men positively and even rudely refused our offer.

There was something strange about them and I questioned one closely but could only obtain monosyllabic replies to my interrogatories.

Jack and I determined to watch them, and wished that we had another white man with us.

It had been our intention to go on shore, but neither would leave the boat in the care of the sullen fellows.

CHAPTER V.
UP THE NILE.

THE time had come when it was necessary to find out the most likely route to take. I had trusted implicitly to Jack, and was still ready to do so, but there is a feeling that in enterprises of the kind there should be no conflict of ideas.

The same thought seemed to strike O'Brien, for, without any suggestion from me, he fetched his tin treasure chest, and we sat down to examine again its strange documents.

"We are going right, Monty," O'Brien said, in opening conversation as to our route.

"What makes you think so?"

"If wrong my mother would have appeared to me."

"Really, Jack, honestly, can you expect any one in the nineteenth century to believe that?"

"Why not? Tell me if you can, how to account for my purchase of the escritoire, explain the way I found out the secret receptacle."

"It may appear difficult to account for everything mysterious, but believe me, Jack, we must exhaust all the laws of nature before we have any right to seek beyond the grave for the *modus operandi* of what we fail to understand."

"I agree with you to a certain extent, but why should not those who have lived before, still feel an interest in our welfare?"

"So perhaps they do."

"I know what you would say. Your argument would be that while they feel an interest and watch our every action, they are powerless to interfere."

"That is so."

"Is not that the very refinement of cruelty? A mother sees her child in danger, would it not be anguish to her if she were restrained from assisting it and so saving its life?"

"Yes, Jack, but you destroy your own argument, for the child is not saved, the family sometimes is ruined, the loved one injured, and yet as you say the ones gone before see and know all."

"The injury takes place because we refuse to accept the message or warning. If you had been in my place you would not have risked so much money on an old and almost useless piece of furniture."

"No, that I should not."

"One day," continued Jack, "I was fully determined to join a party at Yarmouth, who were going out fishing. My mother appeared to me, and, by motions, warned me not to go. I obeyed her warning and, most likely, saved my life, for the boat was caught in a sudden squall and was capsized; two of my companions were never again seen."

"There are strange things in nature, I admit; but what have they to do with King Solomon's treasures?" I asked, almost petulantly, for I knew I was getting the worst of the argument.

"Everything! My mother led me to the store and pointed out the desk I was to purchase. I obeyed. The specter of an old man showed me the secret receptacle, and next day I found it just as it had been shown me. Do you think now I am to be deserted? No, Monty; I have a firm, abiding faith in the Unseen, and be sure that if we follow our guides we shall make no mistake."

"Then I must follow you, for I confess I have no such guides to aid me in my every-day life."

"Perhaps you have not sought for them?"

"Why should I? If the Unseen wish to aid me they will come to me."

"Indeed! then send a telegram to your friends in England, for the unseen electricity is here just as well as at the telegraph offices. If you wish to use any power you must go the right way to work and secure the proper instruments and conditions."

"It's all beyond me, Jack, so let us resume our conversation about old Solomon's treasures. What's that?" I exclaimed, as I glanced quickly at the curtains which divided the saloon from the sleeping berths.

"I saw nothing. What was it?"

"I am getting superstitious, for I could have sworn I saw a bright, flashing human eye staring at me through the tinted covering."

"Imagination," answered Jack at once.

"More likely Achmet," I replied.

I went outside and found Achmet and his fellow boatmen apparently sound asleep at the opposite end of the boat.

The suspicion that these fellows were spying on us could not be driven from my mind, and I determined that if I again saw the eye I would fire my revolver and settle the point at once.

When I returned Jack had spread open the map which I had not before troubled to look at.

If it was, as he believed, the way to the great storehouse, then it would be very valuable to us.

The original was very ancient, the writing very pale through lapse of years, and some of the words had the appearance of having been written over again.

"Now look at this map*, Monty, and see what you can make of it."

"I confess if that is all there is to guide us, we stand a poor chance of finding the treasures."

"I differ with you, and I will read the map as I understand it."

"Yes, do so."

"'Ye great water' is either a broad river or an inland sea. To me it looks very like the Red Sea. 'Ye river' has the exact route taken by the Nile, if so, we have arrived at the commencement of the curve into which apparently flows a small stream. This river or stream we have to follow until we reach Mer. On our way we shall meet with the Blemmyes and Troglodytes; this is what the other document told us."

"If I remember rightly," I said, "Mer was the treasure cave."

"One of them, but there are evidently several, for here is another plan or map which I found, but which is so vague that I am afraid it is of but little value."

Jack then produced what was evidently a more modern copy of a plan or map, although the copy must have been two or three hundred years old to judge by its color and appearance generally.

"I fancy that when we get to this place called Mer, we have to go fifty leagues further into the desert and to some mountains," I said, after I had examined the new map carefully. "But what do those archways mean?"

Jack's speech was interrupted by a report from my revolver, for I had again seen the eye and fired at it.

A howl of pain was heard, and we both hurried out just in time to see Achmet climbing off the roof of our tented boat, and holding his hand to his head.

Fortunately for the spy, my bullet had only caused a flesh-wound across his forehead.

* See frontispiece.

This we quickly dressed, and then I asked him what he meant by spying on us.

In his own language, a variety of Nubian, he replied that he had overheard us talking of the land beyond the Blemmye Country, and as he wanted to go there he had sought an engagement.

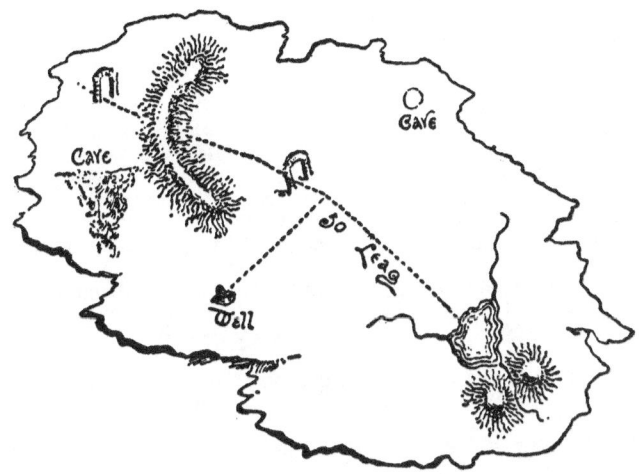

ROUTE TO KING SOLOMON'S TREASURES.

"Why do you want to go to that land?" I asked.

"My father's father came from there," was his reply, and nothing further could we obtain from him as to his reasons for wishing to journey so far.

"If, as you say, you want to go to this great country, can you tell us the way?"

"If my masters, whose deeds are mighty, will trust their poor slave."

"Then describe to us the route we ought to take."

The man was dumfounded, and stuttered and stammered so much, that we became convinced he had no knowledge of the road, but that some motive, perhaps antagonistic to our interests, actuated him.

"Go!" I commanded, when he so clearly displayed his ignorance.

"He has heard of the treasures, and wishes to have a share," was Jack's practical explanation.

After a careful study of the maps, we resolved to leave

the river at Dongola, and then cross the desert toward the mountains marked on our very imperfect map.

At the time we were ready to start, we were short two men, and I engaged two fine-looking Nubians to take their places.

The Nubians were strong, hearty-looking fellows, and betrayed no curiosity, only asking whether we were going into the slave country; they had a wholesome fear that they might be seized and sold into slavery.

They seemed well satisfied with our guarantee of their freedom.

Three days later Jack called me to the poop, on which he was standing, and pointed out one of the finest buffaloes I had ever seen. The head and shoulders towered above the high grass about one hundred and fifty yards away.

We both got our rifles, and I gave the post of honor to Jack, telling him that if he missed, I would fire.

O Brien took aim, and the buffalo apparently dropped dead.

My men were delighted, and asked to be allowed to fetch the animal, or such parts of it as they could carry. Jack gave consent on condition that they brought him the horns and skin.

Off went the men, tearing along through the tall grass as though their very lives depended on reaching the buffalo.

Achmet got hold of the animal's tail, while the others executed a sort of war dance round the body.

Presently up jumped the insulted buffalo, and, charging through the men, he disappeared in the high grass, falling, so Achmet declared, into the deep morass.

As it was getting late, we anchored for the night, and in the morning we were awakened by the groaning of the buffalo in the marsh, not far from where he was supposed to have fallen.

Four of the men, led by Achmet, started off and waded knee-deep in the mud and water of the morass in search.

We lost sight of the men for over an hour, and then beheld four of them carrying the horns and skin of the buffalo, and a good share of its hindquarters, which proved most excellent eating. But where was Achmet? After a great deal of coaxing, I got the men to admit that he was dead.

The buffalo, although wounded, had been very wily to the last, and had tossed Achmet several times before the others could get near enough to dispatch the animal with their knives. They might have saved Achmet's life had they only been a little more courageous.

Although I distrusted the man, yet I felt sorry to hear

of his death, and made the men go back and fetch his body, so that it might have decent burial.

The journey was a very tedious one, and we were getting heartily tired of it as day succeeded day, for our progress was very slow.

With the exception of an occasional shot at some crocodiles, and now and again a buffalo, we had no sport, and I was wishing myself back again at Girjeh or Alexandria, in whichever place Nyassa might be.

Two months had elapsed since we had parted from her, and both Jack and I were constantly thinking of her lovely face and figure.

The noonday sun was shining brightly when at last we reached Dongola, and the easiest part of our journey was over.

We were so pleased to leave the dahabeah that we raced up and down the banks of the river like delighted schoolboys. Our legs were stiff with the continued confinement and cramping position in the boat.

We entered the city of Dongola, and more than ever realized that we were out the pale of that civilization to which we had been accustomed.

Although I had plenty of money, both Turkish and Egyptian, we could not obtain any camels.

To attempt to cross the Libyan desert on foot appeared to us the height of madness; but what was to be done?

The natives told us that Kordofan was the nearest place where we could obtain these ships of the desert, and that meant another twenty days' rowing down the river, and would give us so much further distance across the desert to strike King Solomon's road.

We pleaded and coaxed the people to procure camels for us, but to all our prayers they turned a deaf ear.

One old man, whose age must have been quite patriarchal, had a camel, which he said he loved, but would not sell. If we would engage him he would go with us, and his camel could bear our pack.

It was the best thing which offered, and so we accepted the services of the man and his beast.

"Monty, come here!" shouted Jack, who was talking to a pretty Libyan girl a little distance away.

"What now, Jack?"

"What do we want camels for? is not the river the best way to reach our destination?"

"What river?"

He drew from his pocket a small copy of the ancient map, and pointed out what appeared to be a river as leading to the place called Mer.

"But where is the river?"

That was the new difficulty, and knowing no better way of finding out, we asked the old man who owned the camel.

"By the Great Prophet, he had never heard of any river near there, except the Nile!"

I explained to him that there must have been a river flowing round the mountains we could see in the distance.

But he was positive we were mistaken, and assured us that no river could be found.

We noticed how he trembled, and ascribed it to the fear that we should not need his camel if we found the river, but our surprise was great when he told us positively he would not go past those mountains, not even if the Great Prophet himself commanded him to do so.

CHAPTER VI.

THE LEGEND OF THE MOUNTAIN.

THAT the old man was really frightened could easily be perceived, and as we were desirous of knowing what hidden dangers might beset us, we asked him his reasons for so determined a refusal to journey to the mountains.

For a long time he was silent, and it was only after a liberal amount of bacheesh had been bestowed that he consented to tell us the legend of the mountain.

"At the time when Astaborn reigned over the whole of Ithiopjawan* there was a wise old woman who lived in a cave on yonder mountain.

"She was old and wrinkled, and could scarcely walk, but by the aid of a stick she managed to wander far enough to get the few berries on which she lived.

"There came a time when her legs would no longer bear her, and she had but a handful of berries upon which to subsist. When they were gone she must die. Well, to her cave came a poor, feeble old man, who dragged himself along wearily and craved food. The old woman looked at her few berries, and thought of her own approaching death; but something prompted her to share the small handful with the stranger, and she bade him eat. He did so; but for every berry he put in his mouth there suddenly appeared two on the stone slab which served as a table, until, by the time his hunger was appeased, the woman had twice as many berries as at first. She knew then it was the great God, or one of his prophets, and she fell at his feet. 'Rise up,' he said; 'and from henceforth be ever young! Never shall old age come to thee, nor food fail,

---

* Supposed to have been about 1,500 years before the Christian era.

till thou allowest the stranger to reach the land of the Biommyes or the Macrobii!"*

"When the woman rose to her feet she was alone; but she found she could stand erect, her hands were no longer thin and wrinkled, but plump and youthful. She needed no stick to aid her steps, but was able to run to a little well of water. In this she looked, and found herself young and handsome. Now she was not content with her cave; she wanted the life of the city; but on her way there she was met by the man who had performed the miracle, and warned her that the day she reached the city she would become again old and infirm.

"Taking heed of the warning, she went back and lived a lonely life until the time when Makeda† reigned over the land, when this woman allowed the strangers to pass to the land beyond. It was the great king who flattered her beauty, and by that means bribed her to acquiesce. The moment the king and his people passed she became old, and cannot die.

"Every one who tries to pass her is stricken dead; for she hopes by that means to either be allowed to die or recover her lost youth. She tells of many who have died, and near her cave she gathers up the skulls of them all as a warning."

The old man told his story with much earnestness and fervor, as though the legend was to him bristling with truth.

So positive was he, and so firm in his determination not to assist us in passing the mountain, that we could not laugh at his absurd story, but were bound to give him credit for believing it as he did his religion.

It now became a question as to what we should do. If we started without camels our loads would be heavy, but to travel a thousand miles to get these beasts of burden seemed to us, in our youthful enthusiasm, the very height of absurdity. Accordingly we sold our dahabeah, and made up what stores we could carry, so that each of us would have about forty pounds' weight on [our backs, including our guns and ammunition.

We took five men with us, two of them being the Nubians we had engaged at Korosko, and one the companion of Achmet, whom we had so mistrusted. Taking the most essential papers from the tin case, we left the box in

---

* In the "Leshana Geez," the ancient language of Ethiopia, the word Macrobii was used to designate a race of men which had the power to live forever.

† The Nubian name for the Queen of Sheba, who visited Solomon at the time of the building of the Temple.

charge of the Egyptian magistrate, warning him that if the case was tampered with his life would be the forfeit.

The mountains appeared to be about fifteen miles or so distant, but we soon found that the sands of the desert were very deceptive, and at the end of our first day's march we seemed no nearer.

Oh, the agonies we experienced on that day's journey! Never shall I forget them, although since I have experienced far worse; but then it was all new to me. I had been a pet of fashion, and had never walked any great distance. The pavements of Pall Mall and Piccadilly were the roads with which I was most conversant, for when on the Continent I always preferred riding to pedestrianism; of course I leave out of the question that climbing of the Matterhorn, for that was more like an acrobatic feat than an act of pedestrianism.

But the journey through that desert was fatiguing; our march was through a wilderness of scorching sand and glowing basalt rocks. The heat was terrific; the thermometer, placed in the shade by the water skins, stood at 110 deg. Fahr.

Fortunately we had taken with us a good supply of water, for during the whole of our eight hours' walking we had not discovered one drop of water, either good or bad.

The next day we continued our march, but we were not nearly so light-hearted as we had been. Still no water to be found, but about the middle of the third day we saw to the right a clump of trees, which plainly told us there must be water near.

Even at the risk of losing our way we made for the trees, for our water supply was nearly exhausted.

When we reached the swamp with the few trees growing there we heard a most peculiar snorting.

What it could arise from neither O'Brien nor I could conjecture; but our man Medjid, a Nubian, who was more tractable than the others, and had been, therefore, selected as our favorite, told us it proceeded from a hippopotamus. No sooner had he said so than all the others shouted:

"Wah Illahi, sahe!"* and took to their heels as fast as they could run. Only Medjid stuck to us.

The shouting roused one of the animals from his slumber, and instantly a monster beast rose head and shoulders above the reeds.

I fired at him, but although the ball must have struck him on the head, he took but little notice of it except to take a dive.

* "By Allah, it is true!"

We found that we were on the banks of a lake about a quarter of a mile long by two hundred yards wide.

Could it be that originally there had been a river flowing from the mountains to the Nile, as our maps showed; but that by some means it had got stopped up, and the water had formed the lake?

MEDJID, THE NUBIAN.

We feared the hippopotami, but Medjid told us all danger was past, for those animals will never attack a man unless goaded to it by injury, and the monster I had shot at was either frightened or offended, for he did not make his appearance any more that day.

The four men, seeing that we were safe and needing water, returned, and began loudly to attest their great courage, for they took to themselves the credit of frightening away the hippopotami.

The next morning, after filling our water-skins, we traversed the bank of the lake, and then took a bee-line for the mountains. Before nightfall we encountered another mishap.

The men asked us where we were going, and O'Brien told them that we were bound for the land beyond the mountains.

Instantly they all refused to go any further. They had heard of the old woman, and were too frightened to proceed. It was no use attempting to force them, for we should have been the sufferers, so we reluctantly let them go; but the rascals actually proposed to take our stores with them. It was only by dint of threats that they were made to unload.

We gave them each three days' rations, and bade them get water from the lake.

Medjid, at the last moment, resolved to accompany us.

In the night we were roused from our fitful sleep by Jack shouting loudly to me. I could not understand what was the matter with him, for I was lying close to his side asleep, while Medjid kept watch.

Jumping up, I saw Jack pointing in the direction of the mountain, which rose like a black mass a few miles away from us.

I looked, but saw nothing which should cause alarm.

"See—look there!" he said, in a lower tone of voice—"lights!"

I thought the heat had affected his brain, but after looking for some time fixedly at the black mountain, I saw several small lights flickering on its side.

"What is the matter with you, Jack?"

"Nothing; but look!"

"Those lights," I said. "What of them?"

"It was not the lights, but——"

"What?"

O'Brien grasped my arm and squeezed it until it seemed numb with the pain.

"Great powers!" he exclaimed; "I saw a man burning. The figure was outlined clearly against the dark background of the rocks. I saw him one mass of fire, and thought I heard him appeal for mercy, but none was shown."

"Jack, my boy, you were dreaming."

"No—before Heaven, I saw it."

"No doubt! 'In your mind's eye, Horatio.'"

"Monty! let me entreat you to cease your jests. I am serious in this matter, and I tell you I saw it."

"Very well, my boy, we will agree that you did see this wonderful sight. What then?"

"It was a white man."

"Come now, while I am willing to admit your wonderful sight, I cannot acknowledge that you could detect the man's color at this distance."

"As you like, but we shall have to beware or we may share the same fate."

"Do you want to go back?"

"No," and Jack clinched his teeth with a determined will.

"If I die, and you survive," he said, presently, "find Nyassa, and tell her how much I loved her."

"I will; do the same for me, old boy."

"Yes, Monty, but let us hope that we both will return alive."

"With all my heart."

I fell to thinking what was the matter with O'Brien. Had he really seen some one being burnt, or was it a freak of his imagination?

That I could not solve, for he was so terribly in earnest that whether imagination or actual fact, I was sure that nothing would ever shake his belief in the sight.

Medjid positively declared that he had not slept, but was equally sure that no such scene had been presented to his vision.

Another day's march across the burning desert, our water supply was nearly exhausted, our bodies were faint and the burning heat blistered our faces.

The thermometer now registered one hundred and sixteen degrees in the shade.

By actual measurement we must have marched sixty miles, and the mountains were still another day's journey from us.

Medjid told us that no men had ever passed those mountains. All had been slain when they reached the ridge of high rocks.

He trusted in our powers of magic and would go with us.

We thanked him for the confidence he expressed, and told him we should shield him from harm, or give our lives in the attempt.

We were now traversing a narrow gully which might at some time have been the bed of a river. Probably the water flowed to the small lake at the time our map was drawn.

If we followed its course we should avoid the mountain, passing round the northern end of the range.

So far all had gone well, but we were beginning to feel the want of water, and as far as the eye could reach not a sign of vegetation appeared.

Only a great hope and Jack's faith in his maps buoyed us up and enabled us to persevere.

CHAPTER VII.

PRISONERS.

WE had now reached the end of the mountain range, of which the presiding genius was an old witch with immortal life and a terrific power at her command.

Medjid trembled, but both Jack and I treated the legend like so many others told in the Oriental countries.

We were very sure that no woman, unless she was more than mortal, could bar our right of way.

Our good revolvers would take care of that, and make short work of her if she attempted violence.

I don't like shedding blood, but I am no hypocrite, so do not mind confessing that I would any day rather kill another than be killed myself, and I furthermore declare—though I shall make many enemies by so doing—that there are very many so called human beings that I would kill with less compunction than I would a pet dog. Bear in mind I am not bloodthirsty nor vicious, but as I have previously stated, I believe in candor. If, therefore, the old witch attempted violence, I should not hesitate to use some of the resources of civilization to rid myself of an enemy and the country of a fiend.

We never expected to meet with any such creature, for we had seen no sign of life except that flickering of lights the night before. Now that we were close to the mountain, and saw no trace of humanity, even Jack began to doubt the evidence of his senses.

"And yet I could have sworn I saw quite a number moving about," he said.

Medjid grew more nervous every moment, and I began to fear we should have to go forward without him.

Presently he threw up his arms and fell down flat on his face, shouting:

"Wah Illahi! Wah Illahi, sahe!"*

We wondered what he meant, but had scarcely time for thought before we were entirely surrounded by as ugly a lot of savages as ever drew the breath of life.

They were entirely nude, not even a string of beads decorated their persons, which were as dirty as they were ugly.

We could not imagine a tribe of natives so barbarous, and yet in such close proximity to the Nubians, who were quite refined in their habits and customs.

Yet here was a demonstrated fact, that within one hundred miles of a semi-civilization savages brutal and coarse could be found.

There must have been a hundred of them, men and women.

Only one thing was gratifying—they were without weapons.

But even that was but poor consolation, for we were only three in number, whilst they could boast of thirty to our one.

Our revolvers could bring down several of them, but of what avail would that be, for before we could reload in all probability we should be killed.

"Better see what they want," said Jack.

* "By Allah! by Allah, 'tis all true!"

"But who can talk to them?" I asked, and then turning to Medjid, who had risen to his feet, I said:
"Ask them what they desire."
The Nubian spoke in his native language, but evidently he was not understood.
He tried another dialect but was equally unsuccessful. The third attempt was in a kind of bastard Ethiopian, containing, as I afterward learned, the idioms of the Leshana Mazhaf or sacred language of the Abyssinians.
Without showing whether he was understood, the savages danced round us, gradually making their circle smaller, until they formed a solid ring of black forms around us.
Then every second man stepped forward and the rings were made complete, only now there was a double barrier between us and liberty. Again every alternate man in the inner ring stepped forward, and the three rings closed up with military precision.
I put my hand on my revolver, but Jack stopped me.
"Better see whether they are hostile or not," he suggested.
"Hostile be hanged!" I retorted, "what does it look like if they are not hostile?"
"That is true, but——." The speech was cut short by a savage putting one of his dirty hands over the speaker's mouth, the other hand was quickly in the middle of his back and Jack fell heavily to the ground.
Before I could draw my revolver I was served in a like manner, and Medjid was too frightened to offer any resistance. The savages then carried us in a mighty uncomfortable fashion to the mountain side. They commenced to climb the rocks, and I began to think my body would be quartered, for a savage had hold of each arm and leg, and as each of the four wretches had to select the easiest place to ascend, they often pulled different ways.
If I could have made them understand I would have offered to walk, but the more I shouted the greater violence they used. When our captors had got up the side of the hill some hundred feet or so I was fast losing my senses with the pain I endured.
I closed my eyes for a moment to shut out the strong glare of the sun, but a sudden darkness seeming to fall on me. I opened them, and found we were entering a cave, or rather underground passage-way.
I was carried along for a short distance when a cave was reached into which a little ray of sunlight entered.
Before I was able to realize what the wretches were about I was thrown down violently on the floor. The fall knocked me senseless, but when I recovered my faculties

I found that O'Brien and Medjid were rubbing their eyes, awakening to consciousness at the same time.

"This is a pretty pickle to be in," said Jack, as soon as he saw me.

"A pickle!" I answered. "I am afraid they won't wait to pickle us, but may eat us raw."

"The curse of Cromwell on them!" muttered Jack. I noticed whenever O'Brien was at all excited he adopted the Irish form of cursing, which was as effective as anything else.

Medjid asked what I thought they would do with us, but of course I was as much in the dark as to our fate as he was.

Who were these people? What were their habits? Medjid had never even heard of them, and did not know but that the old witch was the only resident of the hills.

"They must be the Troglodytes," said Jack.

"It is evident they live in caverns, whether they are the people mentioned on your map or not."

"Whatever or whoever they are, I hope they will bring us some water, for I am nearly parched."

That wish was one which found a responsive thrill in each breast, for we had drank the last drop of water several hours before our capture.

All that day we lay stunned and bruised in the cave, the ray of sunlight vanished, and we knew that night had fallen with its heavy mantle on the earth. All was as still as the grave. Not a sound had fallen on our ears since we had been confined in the dungeon.

Our own voices seemed to echo and re-echo along the caverns until we grew almost afraid of the sound.

We had some food in our haversacks, and we tried to eat. Medjid was the only one who could swallow.

I opened my mouth and took a bite of the food, but I was unable to chew. What was the matter? I knew I had lost the sense of taste through thirst, but I could not chew the food. I put my fingers in my mouth, and found the palate and tongue as hard and dry as a piece of dried leather. My tongue was swelling rapidly. I spoke to Jack, and told him; he, too, had a like experience.

The power of speech was leaving us.

"Good-bye, old fellow," came to me as a whisper in the well-known voice of my friend.

"Good-bye, Jack," I answered, feebly, and then I knew it was impossible to speak more.

I had lost all power of motion as well as of speech, and had I not felt the throbbing of my heart I could easily have imagined I was dead.

The night wore away and morning came, bringing with

it the faint glimmer of light. I opened my eyes and caught sight of O'Brien. His mouth was wide open, and his tongue was black and swollen. He tried to speak, but the effort was too much for him. His eyes caught mine, and we knew that, though both were suffering untold agonies, there was life still in our veins.

I was so wretched, and the burning fever was racking me so much, that could I have raised a revolver to my head I should have died a suicide's death.

The sun rose higher, and the air of the cavern grew more sultry and oppressive.

Still no one came near us, and I believed we were to be left there to die.

I resigned myself to my fate, and really wished for death.

I fell asleep, and in my slumber dreamed that my tongue had been bathed with water. It was a dream of heaven. I felt better when I awoke. The cave was dark as pitch, not a sign of light, and no means of getting any, and yet I saw a figure moving about in the place. As it glided around a strange yet dim light seemed to follow it, or, rather, its clothing was in a manner luminous, and yet not sufficiently so as to enable me to see whether the form was male or female.

One thing seemed to surprise me—the figure evidently was draped. Trying to watch its movements I fell again to sleep, and thought that sweet voices were singing soothing songs.

As I dreamed, my sufferings grew less, and I thought I was with Nyassa. Nay, I heard her voice very distinctly saying, "Be of good cheer; all will yet be well."

I was happy in the thought of her presence, even if it was but in a dream; and when the early sunlight came into the cave I felt stronger and better than I had done during our forty hours' confinement.

A woman entered, bearing in her hands a bowl of some liquid, a few drops of which she poured into our mouths. The effect was good, for it seemed to allay the inflammation and reduce the swelling very quickly. Still we could not swallow. A little later she repeated the operation, and again a third time did this poor savage act the part of the good Samaritan. By the time the third application had taken effect we were able to swallow, and then we had a most refreshing drink of milk brought to us by the woman.

We had regained sufficient strength to reach our haversacks for some food, and mighty good it tasted.

We saw no more of the woman for over thirty hours, and we were fast failing back to our state of helplessness. It occurred to me that the savages intended we should starve to death, but that the woman had taken pity and surreptitiously fed us.

In this I found later I was correct. Creeping in slowly she poured some milk down our throats and silently left us. I blessed that woman. A poor nude savage she was, but even the barbarous manner in which she lived had not destroyed the entire human feeling in her breast.

Each night I felt rather than saw the wonderful luminous presence, and heard the sweet singing which I knew could not come from the poor savage woman. One morning when we had been refreshed with the milk, Jack whispered to me:

"It is all right, old boy. We shall come safely through it."

"How do you know?"

"Every night my mother comes and fans my fevered head and sings to me."

"I have heard her," I said.

"Thank Heaven!" ejaculated O'Brien.

The next day when the sun shone almost perpendicularly through the crevice into our prison-house we heard the rush of feet.

A few moments and the fellows who had captured us were in the cave.

They looked at one another with eyes wide open and surprise stamped on their dirty faces.

To them it seemed as if a miracle had been wrought, for after so many days of torture from thirst and hunger we were still alive.

They knew not what to make of it, but after holding a consultation, we were lifted to their shoulders and carried out of the cave.

I tried to speak to Jack, but the effort was too great. As for Medjid, he made no attempt to speak, wherein he was really wise for he was husbanding his strength.

What was to be our fate? I confess I felt downcast, but as I glanced across at O'Brien, I saw a smile on his face, for he was kept happy by the pleasant reflection that his mother's spirit was ever watching over him.

It was a consoling thought, and whatever basis it may have had in fact, I could bear testimony to the nightly visitation and the soothing influence of a light-robed figure moving about in our dark and noisome cell.

We found ourselves carried up a steep incline, though most of the way the road was dark, running through a subterranean passage-way.

CHAPTER VIII.
THE GENIUS OF THE MOUNTAIN.

I SUPPOSE the distance we traveled was not very great, but the inconvenient mode of conveyance added to our weakness made the distance seem many miles, whereas it was doubtless only a few hundred yards.

The air in the cavernous passage was close but not so bad as one would expect, for at irregular intervals air shafts admitted the purer atmosphere and gave a means of escape to the foul air.

When I was near fainting from exhaustion I found myself suddenly roused by being thrown down, or rather dropped, for all four of my bearers quietly let go of my limbs and I fell on the stone floor.

I opened my eyes and saw that I was in a large square cavern, very lofty, and well lighted. On one side the cave was open and I could see across the country we had traversed.

At first I thought I was all alone, but on looking round I distinguished in the far, dim corners the forms of O'Brien and Medjid.

"O'Brien," I called, as I thought, loudly, but, in reality, my voice was but little better than a whisper, and not loud enough for Jack to hear.

O'Brien caught sight of me, and he told me that he, too, called, but his voice was very indistinct. I tried to stand, but my body was too bruised and weak.

However, by dint of a great amount of struggling, I managed to crawl several yards; O'Brien, seeing my movements, followed my example, and in a few moments we were near enough to converse. As for poor Medjid, he had never moved hand nor foot; not a sigh nor groan escaped him, and I thought that, poor fellow, he must be dead.

"What do you make of this?" Jack asked.

"That is more than I can at present answer," was my cautious reply.

"I don't think they are going to kill us."

"Why?"

"They would have done so before this, and if they had wanted us for eating, they would scarcely have starved us."

"There's some consolation in that."

Scarcely had I uttered the words, than two very ugly-looking females entered, but their presence was welcome, for each carried a bowl of steaming soup.

"Perhaps it's human flesh," whispered Jack.

I grew sick at the thought, but, even if I had known it

to be so, I should have taken the soup just the same, for I was hungry and weak.

While we were partaking of the soup we saw the first trace of life in Medjid. No food had been brought for him. I pointed him out to the woman who had brought me the bowl of warm soup, and she nodded her head and left the cave, returning in a few minutes with another bowl for the Nubian.

The bowl held about a quart of soup, and contained a piece of flesh meat, about half a pound in weight. Medjid raised the bowl to his mouth and never removed it while one drop of the liquid remained; he then took the meat and eat it, as ravenously as a hungry dog.

We all felt better, and when the women left, Medjid crawled over to us, and we were able to converse.

We had but little hopes of ever leaving the caves alive, but there was a solace and consolation in company, and we had an opportunity of resolving that, if we had to die, some of the rascally natives should go before us, if we possessed sufficient strength to handle our revolvers.

All day we were left alone, and our jailers seemed to feel very sure that we should not escape, for they never troubled us with their presence. When the sun went down we were getting very hungry, and the savory smell of more soup was very agreeable to us. This time three women entered and we were each well supplied.

No attempt was made on either side to talk, for we had exhausted every language we knew and could not make ourselves understood.

The night was a dark one, and we lay looking out on the desert beyond.

Presently Jack touched my arm and pointed to the side of the cave which was open to the surrounding country.

I distinctly saw figures moving about in front of the cave, each bearing a small lamp. Their object we could not, by any means, understand.

That these were the lights we had seen when encamped on the desert we did not doubt, but their movements were very mysterious.

Watching them we fell asleep, and the sun was high in the heavens before we awoke next morning. We were rather annoyed at having slept so long, for our attendants had been in with the soup, and, instead of awakening us, had left the bowls by our sides, and the contents had become cold and very greasy; however, it was our own fault and we made the best of it; even in that way it was welcome.

After breakfast we crawled, for we were still too stiff and weak to walk, to the mouth of the cave to see if there was any way of escape, but, to our dismay, we found that the rock seemed to overhang the others, and that any one stepping out from our cave would fall a distance of, perhaps, several hundred feet.

How did the lights get in front of the cave?

Here was another mystery, and I was almost of Jack's opinion, that they were spirit lights and not natural ones.

Thinking it would be bad policy to be found so near the mouth of the mountain-prison, we crawled back to the center; but in going I caught sight of a narrow crevice near the edge of the rock, just wide enough for a man to walk in. No doubt that was another entrance to the cave.

Three days dragged their weary length along, and we were chafing at our monotonous imprisonment, yet did not feel strong enough to attempt an escape.

We had gained sufficient strength to be able to walk, and when our attendants brought the soup that night, we walked to meet them.

As I expected, that would bring things to a climax.

Early next morning about a dozen of the nude savages entered the cave, and began jabbering away in a manner entirely unintelligible to us, but satisfactory to them, for every few seconds they gave a grunt of approval.

When the speeches were over we were ordered, by signs, to follow the leader, a big fellow who looked as strong as ancient Milo of Croton, who carried a live ox through the stradium of Olympia, and then ate its whole carcass in one day.

We had but little option in the matter, for we were pushed forward by the others, and found ourselves going rapidly along an uncomfortably narrow passage, until we reached a cave or rather series of caves, for we could see archways leading into other natural rooms.

Here we were left alone, our eyes dazzled by the light after our journey in the dark. As soon as we had an opportunity to glance round, our eyes witnessed a sight which was horrible in the extreme.

On the opposite side to where we had entered was an archway composed entirely of human skulls, fitted together with cleverness and ingenuity; the walls were lined with bones evidently human, but so neatly and compactly intertwined that it was almost difficult to realize that they had been the legs and arms of men.

Whichever way our eyes turned we saw nothing but bones and skulls. We crouched together, thoroughly alarmed and made nervous by the sight. Was it intended to be a prognostication of our fate? It looked so, for we were left alone to contemplate the scene for several hours.

When night shadows began to gather a woman came in, looking hideous in the extreme, and carrying a lighted torch in her hand. By its glare we were able to see that all through the archway of skulls, every alternate one held a small wick made of some kind of swamp reed. These wicks were lighted and gave the arch the appearance of a thousand blazing eyes.

I could not help shrieking with very fear. The sight was more horrible than any I had ever before witnessed.

When all the ghastly lamps were lighted a hundred nude blacks came pouring into the spacious cave and stood round its walls; we were pushed into the center, to await the next move.

Perfect silence reigned, and then a shuffling noise was heard under the arch of skulls.

We looked in that direction and saw what appeared to to be a wizened monkey, enter.

For a moment the nude figure stood upright and we saw that it was an old woman, but so wizened by age and exposure that every bone was visible through the parchment-like skin, and the face was so like one of the skulls that it was difficult to realize its humanity and life. This figure crouched down on a pile of bones just under the archway, and resting its elbows on its bony knees, placed its chin in the fleshless hands.

Was this the old witch of the mountain? Could it be that she had really lived before the time of Solomon? It was easier to believe that she had lived for centuries than it was to realize that she had ever been young and beautiful. If the legend should be true and this old woman was condemned to live forever, what a torture the eternity of life must be!

She sat staring vacantly at us, and then in a croaking whisper asked the leader of the savage band who we were, at least that is what we supposed the question to be, by the motions the man made in answering it.

The old witch then looked at us and spoke, but as we did not understand it was no use speaking.

She tried another language, but of that we were equally ignorant.

Medjid spoke in Abyssinian, but even that she did not comprehend.

O'Brien could not resist his propensity for fun even there, so saying in English to me that he would have a bit of fun with the old lady, he stepped forward, and I was aghast at his audacity.

Sinking on one knee, in the most courtier-like fashion, he commenced an harangue in a barbarous jargon of Latin and French which caused me to have a pain in my side from suppressed laughter. He went on something in this fashion:

"Thou Queen of the Ages, whose wisdom is only excelled by thy beauty, and who art of long life that the world may enjoy the greatness of thy mind! We have heard of thee, and have been sent from the great land to bring thee more power, and to sit at thy feet to learn some of thy great wisdom!"

THE OLD MOUNTAIN WITCH.

"Come nearer!" said the old hag in tolerably good Latin, but of rather an ancient accent.

O'Brien moved nearer to her, and she put out her bony hand and stroked his head.

A look of great astonishment was visible on the faces of the savages, who had not been able to follow the conversation.

It was the first time they had seen the old witch fondle

anybody. Medjid shuddered at the sight, and I trembled for fear she would want to claw me all over in the same way.

"Thou bringest more power, thou sayest."

"Ay, most gracious queen."

"Show me thy power."

Jack rose to his feet and in an aside said:

"What shall I do?"

In a whisper I advised him to show his revolver.

Taking the hint, he drew his revolver from his belt and quietly withdrew all the cartridges but one.

Then showing it to the witch, he said very grandiloquently:

"This, most gracious Queen of the Ages, is the tube of life and death. By its use I can rid myself of enemies without striking a blow, by a breath my foes are swept from the face of the earth."

The wizened old hag stood erect and presented the appearance of being an animated skeleton.

She put out her hand for the pistol, but Jack pretended not to notice her.

"I have heard," she said, "of the white man's magic tube, but never saw one, neither believe I in thy power."

Jack asserted his strength with the aid of the magic tube, and told her that if she would order a goat or other animal to be brought, he would slay it as he had said.

"Slay that!" the old hag commanded, and she pointed the bony finger straight at me. That was a very pleasant predicament to be in, and I wondered how O'Brien was going to get out of it, but he boldly told her that if he did so his power would be forever gone.

"Then slay it!" and her finger was directed at Medjid.

Again Jack made the same excuse, and the old hag roused herself and declared that his power was a farce, that he was a vain boaster, and unless his words could be proved all three of us should be torn in pieces and our skulls be placed on the arch.

She meant it, of that there was no room for doubt.

Jack offered to kill any animal, but that did not please this witch of the mountain. She explained all that had been said, to the natives, and we could see their fingers working with the very thought that they would be able to tear us in pieces.

"I will give thee one more chance,",she said, and then pointed at one of the ugliest and most ungainly savages. "Slay him!"

Jack looked at me for a moment, and said: "I will do it with pleasure, for that is the fellow who nearly tore my legs from my body."

The savages stepped back, and left the human target standing stolidly and with a look of stoic resignation on his uncouth face.

Jack raised the revolver, and then asked that he should be held blameless if he killed the man.

"Slay him!" was the command, and that instant the man dropped dead with a bullet hole in his heart.

No sooner had he fallen than his comrades hastened to the body, and as many as could get a grip seized hold of each leg, and began pulling with all the force of their barbaric physical power. Presently a sickening sound was heard—the man's legs had been literally torn from his body, and carried away in triumph.

The old hag left us, and we were once again alone. "I hated to do it," said Jack, "but it was the only way we could get our lives saved for a time."

The sight had been a sickening one, but we had to endure it, for prisoners cannot be choosers.

CHAPTER IX.
A DASH FOR LIBERTY.

WE wondered whether the ghastly lamps were to be extinguished, or would they shed their sickening light over the charnel house all night.

Our wonder did not last long, for before midnight the old hag came shuffling in; her body was so bent with years that it appeared as though she was walking on all fours.

"Aha! ha, ha, ha! he, he, he!" she chuckled as her old eyes rested on O'Brien.

"Thou shalt be my son," she said. "Come here, my brave boy."

Jack gave a shudder as she approached him, and then as her voice commanded him to draw near, a perceptible shiver shook his frame.

I was on the point of shooting her, but I failed to see how we could escape, even then. At present she was between us and the savages, and therefore her life was valuable. In my case second thoughts were undoubtedly the best.

"Call me Amlekla," she said, with all the coquetry of a young girl of sixteen.

"How old are you?" asked O'Brien.

"Ha, ha, ha! Old, ha, ha, ha! perhaps I don't know, Nay, thou knowest, for every one has heard of Amlekla."

"Just so, most gracious——"

"Mother," interrupted the witch.

O'Brien could not frame his mouth to utter the word, and so coaxingly continued.

"Nay, but tell me, I pray, how old thou art?"

"When the great, wise king ruled across the great water, and my queen, the beautiful Makeda, became his wife, and her son Menilehek* ruled over the whole of Ithiopjawan, I became old, ha, ha, ha!"

The old witch buried her head in her bony hands and laughed heartily.

"Oh, but I was young and pretty, he, he, he! and the fair king wanted to see the land beyond, but wasn't he pretty, and I let him go, and then I became like this, ha, ha, ha! but no more white men have gone. No, no; I tear them up, and put their skulls up there," and she pointed to the arch.

"Count them, my beauty," she said, as she seized O'Brien by the arm. "Never mind, I can tell you; there are scores and scores of them, hundreds and hundreds, and every one who goes near the mountain or who tries to get to the place beyond, ho, ho, ho! ha, ha ha! his skull goes up there."

We were getting tired of this, so Jack continued his questioning, and learned that the old woman claimed to be about four thousand years old.

We also found that the people were a tribe of the Troglodytes, or men who dwell in caves.

"When may we leave and go tell our people of thy greatness?"

The old spitfire was roused. "Leave!" she screeched, "never!" and then with a winning manner which must have been very bewitching some thousands of years before, the old dame coaxed Jack to stay.

"Stay," she said, "and we will have a feast. The Troglodytes shall come and tear him" (pointing to me) "into pieces alive. Oh, wont it be a sight to gladden our eyes, and thou my son shall pick the grease" (flesh evidently) "off his head and put the skull up there."

The old Amlekla went off into a fit of hysterical laughter, and even O'Brien laughed at the thought of the great treat in store for him.

I confess I was loath to join in the merriment. I had often been pulled to pieces by the fashionable gossips at a five o'clock tea, but that was a very harmless proceeding compared with the literal tearing my body would be subjected to, by these amiable people.

When the laughter had subsided, the old hag further offered that I should be torn to pieces by women. That, I

* The Ethiopians say that the Queen of Sheba was married to King Solomon, and that the son born to them was named Menilehek, and became first King of the United Ethiopian Nation.

admit, was more of an inducement, but it was far from being enjoyable.

In talk such as this the night was spent, and when day dawned the lights in the skulls were extinguished and the old witch Amlekla retired to her private apartments.

We were all heavy with sleep, but neither of us felt inclined to risk slumber.

While O'Brien might be safe, Medjid and I stood a good chance of being torn into quarters, and our skulls preserved as a memento, while I did not doubt for a moment that our bodies would make excellent soup for the Troglodytes.

"What shall we do?" I asked.

"I'm blessed if I know, ask Medjid," was Jack's curt response. Evidently being the favorite of a queen did not agree with him, for he seemed crusty and even cross-tempered.

Medjid was in favor of going along the passages, and if we came across any of the natives, fight our way through them, or die in the attempt.

It was the only sensible thing to do, and as we were now strong enough to make the attempt, we resolved to load our revolvers and start on our journey.

By which passage did we enter? There were several archways exactly alike, and all we could be positive about was that we had not passed under the archway of skulls.

While we were debating, about a dozen women came in and began chattering and jabbering away at us; but as we did not know what they were talking about, we let them jabber along.

When they stopped, they looked at us for a few moments with perplexed faces. Seeing that we returned the gaze with interest, they rushed on us, and before we knew what was happening we were on the ground and our arms held firmly by our side.

Then these strange creatures began to pull and tug at our clothes until they had stripped them off.

I had always prided myself on my strength, but I was like a child in the grasp of a giant, and Jack said that Hercules himself would have been powerless against these women.

The clothes, when stripped from us, were rolled up and taken to the cave through the skull gateway, so I surmised that old Amlekla had taken a fancy to them.

There was one pleasing thing even in the midst of all our anguish. The women had left our haversacks, together with the revolvers, rifles, and ammunition. It was, as I rightly conjectured, because they were too much afraid of the weapons to carry them.

Instinct and the law of self-preservation prompted us to fasten on our pistol and cartridge belts, and sling our rifles over our shoulders.

We held a consultation, and determined that we would send Medjid along one of the passageways, with a view of finding a means of escape, and that, should he succeed, he was to return, and we would force our way out, even if we were minus clothes.

Medjid tried every passage, but after he had penetrated a few yards he returned, declaring that all were well guarded, and that no outlet was visible.

I made a resolve, which was a very fool-hardy one, but as it happened, a fortunate one for us. I wanted my clothes. Not only did I feel uncomfortable in my primitive garb, but I had a continual blush on my face, and that was unpleasant.

Leaving O'Brien and Medjid, I moved as quietly as possible into the passage under the skulls. It required a strong nerve, for everywhere I saw fragments of human remains—here a leg partly decomposed, there a heap of bones, and further on I came across four or five dead bodies, some evidently quite fresh. I was now inclined to the idea that the skulls might be those of the natives as well as whites.

I had not found any cave or room in which the old witch could sleep.

Some distance further I walked, when I saw the passage grow broader, and on a pile of bones covered with a lion skin the old Amlekla was lying fast asleep. Close to her were our clothes.

I caught a glimmer of light at the back of her couch, and surmised it must be an opening on the opposite side of the hill.

Even at the risk of detection I was resolved to find out, and so I crept silently along, and, to my great joy, found my surmise was correct.

Seizing the clothes, I made my way as fast as I could to the cave, where O'Brien and Medjid were beginning to get alarmed at my absence.

How full of joy they both were at getting their clothes, and I do not think a toilet was ever more quickly performed. Time was of value to us, and we put on the clothes in the quickest possible manner, and then with our revolvers in our hands, Medjid carrying a big hunting-knife almost as large as a cimeter, we crept cautiously through the archway and along the sickening passage. When we reached the old Amlekla's cave she roused herself and looked round.

Jack pointed his revolver at her, and said if she made the slightest noise he would kill her on the spot.

Whether the hag believed she had immortal life or it was but the fearlessness of her nature I know not, but she sounded an alarm for help.

Jack struck her a tremendous blow on the head with the butt of his revolver, and then we made a run for freedom. We had not got a dozen yards before the old creature was shouting loudly for help.

"I believe the hag cannot die," said Jack, "for the blow I gave her would have stunned a giant."

We had only about fifty yards to go before we should gain the open.

But, fast as we ran, the natives were quicker, and we were surrounded. The savages seemed to come up out of the ground, to flock from every part, and there seemed but little chance for us.

"Fire in front and dash through the devils!" cried Jack, and I quickly obeyed the order.

We had each two revolvers, so were good for fourteen shots each. The first volley brought down one native dead and a second one wounded in the shoulder. The wretches had now armed themselves with arrows, which they threw at us. And terribly annoying they were, for at each moment we were getting pricked with their sharp points.

Volley after volley we fired, and our way was over the bodies of those who had attempted to bar our progress. I did not want to fire our last shot, for the revolvers might be useful at close quarters later, so I unslung my rifle, and passing Jack, swung it over my head and with the butt end crushed in the skull of a big fellow who was most active with the arrows. It did terrible execution, but when it was a matter of physical power, the natives had the advantage not only of strength but numbers as well.

Our revolvers and rifle-shots were our greatest strength.

We had cleared a way, and were nearing the mouth of the cave, when, right in front of us, looking horrible in her deformity, stood Amlekla. She seemed to be rallying the men, and stood there like a skeleton queen giving orders to a body of fiends.

The natives fought with a desperate valor, and I much feared that we should not escape with our lives.

I fired a shot at Amlekla, but must have missed, for she stood in the same position laughing in my very face.

Had she a charmed life, or was my aim bad?

I know not, but there she stood laughing and grinning most hideously.

"Now, fellows," I said, clubbing my rifle, "let us rush for it."

We dashed forward, and with our rifles cleared a path. Amlekla fell, and was trampled under foot. Down went first one and then another until we reached the mouth of the cave. The natives had evidently had as much as they cared for, as they began to fall back, and we were left alone, tired and bleeding.

We had no time to attend to our wounds, for our freedom was not yet secured.

CHAPTER X.

A PERILOUS BRIDGE.

WHEN we reached the open air, we perceived that we had quite a long descent to make; but there was one sight which pleased us, tired and bruised as we were.

At a distance of only four or five miles was an oasis which promised us water and food, for we could distinctly see some birds flying about.

This was an excellent stimulant, and we were badly in need of one at that time. How to get down the hill was the next difficulty. We found that the cave opened out on a wide plateau, which seemed to overhang the hill beneath. To climb down was an impossibility, and to drop meant certain death.

We walked to the end of the plateau, but crouched behind a rock immediately, for close to us were half a dozen of the natives. They looked along the ledge of rock; but, not seeing us, they turned back into a cave. We then proceeded to the other end, and found absolutely no outlet or way down.

What was best to be done?

After a moment's thought we concluded our most likely chance would be to wait until night, and then either dash through the cave at the end in which we had caught a momentary glimpse of some steps leading down the hill, or drop over the cliff.

We found a hiding-place, and were not sorry to get a re

Scarcely had night entered upon its reign before we saw a number of the natives dragging out of the center cave the bodies of the slain, and then we watched them pile them up into a great heap.

A resinous substance was put in great quantities on the bodies, and the flame of a torch applied.

I was about to whisper to Jack a wonder whether the old witch was being burnt, when I saw her dancing gleefully round the blazing bodies, looking more horrible than ever.

We decided that the time for our escape had come, and

A PERILOUS POSITION.

we stole from our hiding-place, cautiously and quietly along the plateau, and reached the steps safely.

No alarm had been given, and so far all was well.

We descended the steps, and found them almost interminable.

A faint shimmering of light told us that we were nearing the open air.

When the last step had been reached we stepped out of the cave, and found that we were standing on a pinnacle of rock which jutted out from the hill, and whose sides were so smooth that no foothold could be obtained to aid our descent. Here was another difficulty, and one which we knew not how to overcome.

It became necessary that we should wait until morning, so that we could see more clearly the way to descend. When the first rays of the sun came over the hill we found that the path down the side of the rocks was easy, if we could but reach another rock which stood over eight feet away from us. How could we reach it? Had we been on solid ground we could easily have crossed the chasm in a jump; but the pinnacle on which we were standing afforded no room for even a step, and the rock we had to reach was also more in the shape of a column. The chasm was a hundred feet deep, and the bottom was composed of multitudes of ragged, jutting crags. To fall was certain death.

We had faced death so much, however, that we were not going to give in until every means of safety had been tried.

A happy thought seemed to strike O'Brien, for he unslung his rifle and asked for mine. He then took our slinging straps, and strongly lashed the barrels together, end to end.

He then asked me to hold him while he pushed the but-end of one rifle to the rock we wished to reach.

It was a frail bridge, but even that was welcome.

To our horror the rifle would not reach by six inches.

"What was to be done now?"

Medjid offered to risk his life for us, in a daring exploit.

"You hold the rifles here," he said, "steadily while I swing myself along them as far as I can with safety. When I reach the end I will leap to the rock, and can then steady the rifles for you."

The offer was a generous one, but extremely dangerous. Could we divine no other plan?

Yes, there was one hope more. The Nubian's hunting-knife was incased in a very strong sheath. This knife and sheath we would lash between the guns, and so lengthen the bridge.

This we accomplished, and so our only chance of liberty and life depended on that frail bridge.

The rifles at either end and a long hunting-knife in the center. If the straps gave way we were lost.

Medjid wanted to be the first to try it, and I admit we were cowardly enough to let him take the post of danger. He grasped the rifle barrel in his hands, and slowly lowered his body over the side of the rock; hand-over-hand he went, the frail bridge bending so in the center that we held our breath in the silence of dread.

Our eyes grew dim with fear, but a moment and the strain on the bridge was withdrawn, and Medjid was safe.

We had drawn lots as to who should be the second one to cross, and the position of honor had fallen to Jack. I trembled for his safety, for he was the heaviest of the three, and was at least a good fifty pounds heavier than Medjid.

He lay down flat on his stomach, and steadying himself with one hand, while the other grasped the rifle barrel, he lowered himself down very cautiously. As his whole weight hung suspended from the peculiar bridge, I was sure the straps would have given way. Slowly he passed his hands along, and then Medjid leaned down, and, pressing his chest on the butt of the rifle to prevent it from slipping, stretched out his hand, and pulled Jack safely to the rock.

I was the only one now to cross, and felt confident that what they had accomplished I could. Still there was no one to steady the rifle at my end, so the risk was as great if not greater than before.

I reached the middle of the bridge, had grasped the knife with my left hand, my right reaching forward for the rifle barrel, when I felt the butt at my rear slip. I seized the barrel with both hands, and only just in time; for the bridge had slipped at the one end, and I heard my rifle fall to the bottom with a doleful sound. I expected to follow it in another minute.

" Keep fast grip!" shouted O'Brien.

I did so, but the barrel was smooth and there was nothing to prevent my hands from slipping off save the little sight at the muzzle. I held on for dear life. For how long? Who can tell? For who is there can devise a method for reckoning time at moments like that? Every heart-throb seemed an eternity. There was I, hanging at the side of a rock to the smooth barrel of a rifle, so near death that the throbbing of a little finger might hurl me on the pointed rocks below.

"Hold tight!" again shouted Jack, and I felt the rifle being gradually raised.

Jack was lying full length on the rock, and had his right hand stretched down as low as possible. Two inches more, and O'Brien could reach me. I was growing sick and faint; my brain was in a whirl. Instantly I imagined I saw the clear, dark eyes of Nyassa looking into mine, and I gripped the rifle firmer. Another inch, and I was safe; but I was a heavy weight for Medjid to lift in that peculiar fashion. I had faith, and that saved me. My eyes were growing dim. I could feel the tips of O'Brien's fingers, then the grasp of his hand on my arm; another moment I was on the rock safe!

The bravery of Medjid and the cool courage of O'Brien had saved my life, and no words of mine can ever testify half warm enough the gratitude I feel for this splendid achievement.

We were not yet out of reach of our enemies, and gathering up courage we commenced the descent, and reached the valley without further mishap.

CHAPTER XI.
FROM THE DESERT TO THE JUNGLE.

WE reached the valley, and, fearful of being pursued, hurried forward across the desert. In our haste at leaving the unfriendly Troglodytes we had left behind the most important part of our equipment for a journey across the desert—our water-bottles. What we were to do we had not the slightest idea, for it would be impossible to travel for days, as we might be compelled to do, without water. Better have left anything else, but there was no help for it. If we turned back we should face certain death; if we went forward death was almost as near.

We had escaped with our lives, but the Troglodytes' revenge would be sweet when they found three men parched, bruised and wounded trying to cross the desert without water.

The oasis we had seen was about six miles from the foot of the hill, and we tried to reach there without resting, but our sufferings were great.

We were tortured with thirst. The glow of the sun from above, its thousandfold reflection from the glowing sand, made our faces smart and our throats burn and our heads ache.

The sight of an oasis so near at hand was very sweet to us and we grew sick with longing. My throat filled with phlegm and my eyes were suffused with water, and I felt that I could weep like a child.

We reached the oasis, and after taking a good drink of the water we stripped and bathed. There is nothing so refreshing on the African desert as a bath. The skin needs water, and drinks it through the million pores as readily as the throat. After we had enjoyed ourselves most thoroughly we sat down to consider ways and means, more especially how to provide the commissariat.

We needed food, for we had only about two or three pounds each of dried flesh and a few biscuits; but we had some cocoa leaves, and we found them very useful when fatigued. Water we could get plenty of while we remained near the oasis, but who could tell how long it would be before we again met with such a liberal supply?

At that moment a bird, half-goose, and yet shaped in the body more like an eagle, flew over our heads and fell dead at our feet, being brought down by a bullet sent after it by O'Brien.

I had never seen any bird like it before, but Medjid said they were very common on the White Nile, but rarely seen so far inland.

Its head was so pretty that I felt I would like to have preserved it to take back to England. The body of the bird was black and white, but its head and neck was a very bright crimson, a horny yrotuberance on the top of its head being red and yellow. It had another peculiarity in the shape of a heavy spur upon the wing an inch long, which was used as a weapon for striking, and was very powerful. Medjid told us that he has known hunters killed by a stab from the spur wing of this species of goose. It made most excellent eating and we heartily enjoyed our meal.

We examined our map to see if we were on the right road, and then I imagined that we had misunderstood the route. If we had gone the road which was marked "bad," we should have given the mountains of the old witch a wide range, passing much to the south, and we thought now that the word "bad," referred to the path across the river to the country of the Blemmyes.

Jack, however, insisted on the original interpretation, and said that if we had gone the lower road we should have had to strike our present path and perhaps encounter the Blemmyes, or go forward and find some more Troglodytes.

What we wanted to do was to reach Mer, and then the country beyond, but if we could not devise means for carrying water, our journey and our lives would be at an end before we reached anywhere near Mer.

Medjid had been exploring and now returned with the welcome news that the oasis was apparently a mile long, and that there was plenty of evidence of the spoor of large game. But that presented another difficulty to our minds. It is surprising what a deal we have to unlearn. We had been led to believe that the whole country from the Nile to Mer was a desert.

Elephants and lions whose spoor Medjid declared he had found, would not live in the desert, hence there must be jungle beyond. If we could secure a lion, or any large animal, all we need do would be to take its stomach, wash and dry it, and we should have a most excellent water bottle.

A WHITE NILE GOOSE.

Leaving Medjid to take care of our haversacks and such things as we thought too cumbersome to carry unless compelled, Jack and I started with our rifles in hand along the banks of the water or swamp.

We had not proceeded far before a magnificent pair of horns was seen above the tall reeds.

"Go slow, Monty," whispered Jack, "and when you get within range secure the horns."

We crawled along cautiously, fearing to disturb the noble beast, when it suddenly raised its head and looked round, evidently confused.

It was too far off to be certain of a good shot, so I waited.

Instead of taking fright and running away, it made toward us.

This surprised me, but made me determined to show how good a shot I really was.

The antelope bounded along, crackling the reeds under its feet as it advanced, and seizing a favorable moment I fired, and I had the pleasure of seeing it jump in the air, and then fall over dead.

To my astonishment the crackling continued, and I had scarcely time to swing out of the way before an enormous leopard dashed right past me, and fell with savage fury on the antelope. It was now easy to see that the graceful animal had not been frightened of us, but that it feared its powerful enemy, the leopard.

Jack claims the credit for the second death, but as both of us fired at the same time and two bullet holes were plainly visible in the skin of the leopard, I think I may claim an equal share of the honor.

Be that as it may, we kept that leopard skin, and many a night have I slept rolled up in its warm embrace.

Medjid made short work of the leopard's interior, cutting out its stomach and cleaning it as well as a professional.

A few days' exposure to the sun, with several washings, had the effect of tanning the skin and turning the stomach into an excellent water bottle. We did the same with the antelope, so we were now equipped with two skins for carrying the most precious liquid on earth.

The antelope was splendid eating, and the horns were the finest I had ever seen.

We hid them and marked the spot on our map, so that when we returned we might try and convey them back to England.

We continued our march, camping again before we left the marsh and water, and entered, as we had surmised, a thick jungle.

When we had started from England we had read stories of African travel and exploration, and imagined we could find our way by compass and trail to any part ever trodden by man; but how different was the fact. Had it not been for Medjid we should never have lived to tell our adventures. Often we should have walked right into the warm embrace of a lion, or fallen into the traps set by the hyena for its prey.

Before we had left Dongola a week we had admitted our helplessness to ourselves, but not to each other; but now we made no secret of it, and O'Brien promised Medjid great rewards if he continued with us to the end.

I had taken a fancy to him, and, as he possessed greater

intelligence than is to be met with ordinarily in Nubians, I often walked by his side and conversed with him.

He could tell us many of the legends of the country, and threw light on some of the things which were dark and incomprehensible to us.

After we had left the Troglodytes, we told Medjid of our intention to reach the treasure-chamber of King Solomon.

"Ah, Baas!" he said, sorrowfully, "then we shall not return again."

"Why, what makes you think that?"

"My father's father acted as guide to a party which thought they knew where the treasures were hid, but not one returned alive. My father heard that some of the party had become slaves to some strange people which lived near the treasures."

"How did the party pass the old Amlekla?" asked O'Brien.

"They went not near the mountains, but went by a dahabeah to Khartum."

"Then, Jack, that is the road marked on our map."

"Perhaps so, Monty, but tell me, Medjid, were they never heard from?"

"Not for many years, and then my father, who was a trader, was selling some ivories, and he heard of a white man who was a slave to some hideous-looking creatures."

"The Blemmyes, perhaps!"

"Most likely," I answered.

We had suffered severely on the desert, but there our sufferings were slight compared with the agonies endured in that jungle. It seemed impenetrable, so dense was the undergrowth, and at every step we were fearful of encountering jungle snakes, or falling into the lair of a lion. Yet it was our only way, and it was of little use being fainthearted, so we persevered, and though making slow progress, continued heading for Mer.

There was no sign of any river, and our map was very inaccurately drawn as regarded distances, but Jack's faith in its correctness was implicit, and he would have as soon thought of doubting his own existence as the evidences he had in his possession of the treasure.

I began to fully realize that we had made a mistake in undertaking so perilous a journey without plenty of men.

I was in favor of going back by way of Khartum, but Jack was obstinate.

"What did we want men for?" he asked.

"In case of attack, or if we find the treasures how shall we remove them?"

This had never presented itself to his mind, for he stood still for some time as though in doubt what to do.

"What shall be done?" he asked.

"Jack, my boy, I left it all to you, and you are captain."

"Then let us go on."

Through the jungle we went, our faces at times torn with thorns, and our feet slipping into the deep pitfalls and holes. It was a hard and difficult march.

When our spirits were at the lowest ebb, a noise of the crackling of the reeds and bushes attracted our attention.

"Elephants," said Medjid.

The noise was getting nearer, and seemed to be right in our track.

Medjid, who was an old elephant hunter, suggested that we should move to the left, and wait the approach of the ponderous animals, and not fire unless we were sure of our aim. The noise ceased, and Medjid declared that we must be near water, for that was the only thing which would stop the elephants in their journey.

We followed the Nubian's instructions implicitly, and soon we were on a little green knoll, in full sight of the herd of between fifteen and twenty very fine beasts. They were a few score yards below us, and were flapping their immense ears with pleasure at the sight of water, for close to them was a pretty little lake, clear and pellucid.

We crept on all fours down the side of the knoll into the jungle at its foot, and cautiously pursued our way until we were within thirty yards of the animals.

"Now, fire!" said Medjid.

"Boom! boom!" went our two rifles, and down went a fine bull elephant, pierced fatally by the bullet Jack had sent home with such unerring aim.

Mine had been wounded, and fell to its knees, and seemed unable to rise. I was for going up to it, but Medjid pulled me back, and fortunately for me that he did so, for at that instant the elephant rose, and was tearing along straight past me. I gave him another dose in the ribs, and the beast staggered, but looked at me apparently astonished.

"Can you send one in his eye?" Medjid exclaimed, quickly; "if not, we shall have a hard fight."

I did not wait for him to finish his speech before I took careful aim, the brute seeming transfixed with astonishment, and boom! went the gun, and the bull dropped in real earnest.

Jack came up at the time, and gave another shot, which went crashing into the elephant's brain, and we had bagged two elephants. The remainder of the herd had scampered away in every direction.

Several of the herd had gone the route we wished to take, so we determined to follow their trail and secure more big tusks if we possibly could.

Our task was easy, for the elephants had left a trail almost as broad as a good carriage-way, beating down the thick brush as if it had only been so much grass.

For three hours we followed them, the broiling sun pouring down with relentless fury on our heads, and then we caught sight of several fine specimens of the kingly leviathans of the forest and jungle.

As we neared them, one old fellow, the patriarch of the herd, a monster bull, standing as tall as the far-famed Jumbo, turned round and faced us, covering the retreat of the others.

It was a grand and affecting sight, for the animal knew his danger. Medjid explaining to us that the peculiar noise he made was the elephant's death winny. He had offered his life to protect the others. We were pitiless, and while we appreciated his devotion and sacrifice, agreed to accept it and take his life.

I had given Medjid an extra Winchester we carried, so begged him to use it, firing at the same time we did.

All three report rang out simultaneously, the crack of the Winchester keeping time to the heavier boom of our express rifles.

The bull dropped to its knees and then rolled over dead.

It had given its life for its companions, and for a few minutes had barred our way.

The hunter spirit was strong in us, and I really believe that even if the ivory of the tusks had been ot no value, we should have continued slaughtering for the pleasure of the sport.

How cruel is man after all! We blame the untutored savage for his brutal instincts and pleasures, and torture a fox and shoot innocent birds merely for the pleasure of so-called sport.

The line which divides civilization from barbarity is but a small and narrow one.

CHAPTER XII.

"O, FOR A DROP OF WATER."

THAT night we had a hearty supper of elephant heart, which was the daintiest and most appetizing dish I had ever eaten.

We camped beside the pool of water where we had seen

the elephants, having had to return there on account of our surplus stores.

There was a silence which was impressive, and as the rays of

> " The crescent moon, the star of love
> Which glorjes of evening . . ."

shone down on the small lake, we felt a refreshing peace fall on our minds.

We slept. Not even taking the precaution of having a watch kept.

In my sleep I dreamt, and my spirit wandered to Nyassa. Why was it that she was so constantly with me in my sleeping and waking moments?

So absorbing was the influence which she possessed over my mind, that many a time I imagined she was with me, and guiding my every movement.

She was my guardian angel, and with thoughts of her the dangers of our journey were of but little moment, and if at last I could press her to my heart and call her my own, Heaven itself would have but little more to offer.

In dreams like this, most of the nights passed away into the oblivion of the ages, and there is no knowing how long I should have remained sleeping, had not a most ominous roar thoroughly roused us all three.

"A lion!" exclaimed Medjid.

And almost before we could rub our eyes open and seize our rifles, we were faced by the king of beasts.

The great eyes glared at us, the monarch's head erect, its long flowing mane hanging over its head and shoulders in silky waves, and altogether presenting a picture of proud and haughty grandeur.

His looks plainly asked why we had dared to intrude and trespass on his territory.

There is a subtle magnetism in a lion's eye which is not equaled in any other animal.

Medjid whispered, rapidly:

"Don't fire until you see it ready to spring, and then don't miss."

The lion was only a few yards from us, and I thought the Nubian foolish for not firing at once.

The animal looked at us, and growled.

We stood unmoved, but with our rifles ready to fire at any instant. We watched every movement of the beast, and could see that it was astonished at our cool presumption in staying there to be killed.

"Keep steady," said Medjid, "and watch its eye."

A moment later we saw it crouch.

"Now, prepare," the Nubian whispered, excitedly.

It was only an instant, but it seemed an hour, before the crouching animal made a spring toward us.

"Boom, boom, boom," went our three guns, and the next moment I found myself on the ground, and hot breath fanning my face.

The violent fall had so numbed my senses that I had no idea of danger, and could not conceive that my life depended on my friends' aim and courage.

Something was pressing heavily on my chest, and I feared my ribs would be crushed, I felt a warm liquid pouring over my face, and it was overpowering me.

"Help!" I tried to cry out, but my voice was gone.

My sense of hearing seemed to have left me, and yet I heard, or thought I did, a rifle shot, but at that instant the weight on my chest increased and I gasped for breath.

Nyassa's lovely face appeared in a vision to me and I knew that her spirit and thoughts were ever with me. With her eyes looking into mine I became senseless or, as I then thought, dead.

When I awoke, later, I felt bruised and weak and could not account for the strange feeling which oppressed my senses.

O'Brien was leaning over me and bathing my temples with water.

"What is the matter with me?" I asked, when I was sufficiently awake to be able to speak.

"You have had a narrow squeeze," was Jack's reply, and when I had thoroughly regained my senses he told me that when we fired at the lion only one bullet struck the beast and that not in a vital part, the animal knocked me to the ground and rested his heavy fore-quarters on my chest. The lion was weak with loss of blood and panting with the excitement, or I should not have written this story of my adventures. Jack found, to his great annoyance, that his spare rifle was not loaded, and Medjid's Winchester was in the same condition. Their carelessness nearly cost me my life. The delay in firing was caused by the time required to load the rifles.

Fortunately, the lion was so weak that it took plenty of time to consider my fate. Before it had made up its mind, a bullet had gone thorough its heart and the heavy carcass was rolled off my chest. Then my friends feared that I was dead, for I lay there motionless, and several minutes elapsed before they could detect any heart-throbs or breathing. By constant rubbing and the application of water I was restored to consciousness.

The lion was a monster, and I have often wondered why its weight did not crush in my ribs.

I was so weak and bruised that we had to encamp for

over a week, our stores were getting exhausted and our last biscuit had been eaten. It was repugnant to our delicate taste to live on flesh alone, but there seemed no help for it. Bread could not be obtained, and even the edible roots, so plentiful in other parts, were not to be found there. When I was strong enough to march we started, and found we had a long desert to cross after leaving the jungle. While I was resting, I had superintended the drying of a quantity of antelope meat and other kinds of flesh, so that we started well supplied with flesh-meat and water, for Medjid carried two skins of water, and Jack and I had also one each; so we had altogether about three gallons of the life-saving fluid.

We left the jungle almost with regret, and went on our way across the desert. The sand was moist for some distance, and karoo shrubs grew in abundance.

We soon found a new enemy which had not before entered into our calculations—this was the fly.

Never before had I experienced such an incessant annoyance as these flies caused. They were at times so thick that I thought we must be again enduring a veritable plague of flies such as bothered the Egyptians of old. These flies were too numerous to count or even to have their number estimated; they covered our clothes and stung our faces and necks until we were nearly maddened with pain.

When the hottest part of the day came we made holes in the sand and lay in them pulling the karoo bushes over us to try and ward off our two great enemies—the sun's rays and flies.

When the evening came, we started again on our journey and for several days endured the same tortures. The heat was intense, our thermometer registering the last day we tried it, one hundred and twenty degrees in the shade, made by our haversacks.

To add to our discomfort we had now drained the last drop of water, and our bodies were so parched that a gallon would have scarcely quenched our thirst, while we had had less than a quarter of a pint each.

Oh, the pitiless fever of thirst! There is nothing so terrible, no anguish so great, no suffering so intense as that caused by the want of water. All that day we walked on, our legs getting weary and our bodies faint. I would have given all I possessed, would have signed a release to all my property in England for a gallon of water.

"If we don't strike water before morning, Baas, we shall be dead men," said Medjid, as we commenced our night's journey.

As I walked along silently I meditated on the absurdity

of our journey. We were enduring all these sufferings, risking our lives and perhaps losing them in the end for what? No benefit to science, nothing which would be of value to the world—no, but all for gold, for wealth, gathered by others and to be appropriated by ourselves. This had not actuated me, but I wanted adventure and sport, and truly I was getting as much as my heart could desire.

I made no complaint. I was even anxious and desirous to go on with our search; but there was one thing which seemed to act like a magnet and drew my heart away from the adventures—Nyassa. I had never felt love before, had laughed at it, scoffed at its power and sneered at those who had made sacrifices for the one they loved. Now I was bound in the fetters, and there was nothing I would not have done, no sacrifice I would not have made for her who was my heart's treasure, my soul's idol. Alas! she was not mine, might never be clasped in my arms; her head might never rest on my shoulder, nay, my eyes, perhaps, would never again gaze into the liquid depths of her glorious orbs, but it was sweet to hope, and a consolation to feel that—

> "Not blind to fate, I see, where'er I rove,
> Unnumbered perils—but one only love."

And then the hope that one day she would be mine nerved me for the dangers of our trip, for—

> "Well my toils shall that fond breast repay.
> Though fortune frown and falser friends betray,
> How dear the dream in darkest hours of ill,
> Should all be changed, to find her faithful still."

I was roused from my meditation, which had caused me to forget my sufferings, by Medjid's voice calling me. I had walked on, leaving Jack and the Nubian far behind. I turned and saw Medjid stooping down. What was the matter? I hurried back to find O'Brien lying on the hot sand, his eyes glazed and mouth wide open.

As I approached he recognized me and put out his hand:

"Good-bye, old fellow," he gasped; "I'm going! tell Nyassa."

I could not believe he was dying, yet it looked very like it. I sought advice from Medjid.

"He will die if no water is near."

I took my water skin and tried to squeeze out a few drops. Alas! I had tried that for myself before. Those carried by Medjid were tried and two or three drops fell on O'Brien's parched tongue.

What could be done? My own mouth was parched and dry. I felt in my haversack and, to my great joy, found in a small flask a half teaspoonful of brandy. It seemed like madness to give it, but even that fiery liquid was better than nothing.

"Leave me, Medjid," I commanded, "and see if water is near."

The man staggered away exhausted and in a high fever, but returned shaking his head. He tried another direction, and I watched him until he was almost out of sight. I thought he fell, but presently I saw him come running toward us.

"Baas, water! water!"

He was able to speak plainer, and I knew he had found a drink.

Between us we carried O'Brien across the sand until we came to a little pool of water. There did not seem to be a gallon in the pool, but I took as much as I could bale out with my hands and threw it on Jack's face.

The skin was so hot and parched that the water seemed to sizzle and boil as if it had been thrown on a hot stove. Another half pint of water cooled his face, and Jack opened his eyes.

He was not dead. That was such a delight to me that I fairly danced with joy.

After giving Jack a drink, or, to be more accurate, pouring some water down his throat, Medjid and I lay down at full length on the sand and lapped up the water, utterly regardless of consequences. To our great joy we found that the water was not stagnant, but a bubbling spring.

It was several hours before we were quite certain that O'Brien would recover, and even then we feared that the weakness would overpower him.

We were in hopes that some animals or birds would come to the water and provide us with fresh food.

We had not long to wait, for a couple of fine specimens of ellands came within rifle-shot, and instead of getting a drink they met their death.

Three months before the sight of blood would have sickened me, but now all three partook of a good deep draught of the warm blood of the beautiful animals.

It is strange how one can overcome a natural repugnance for and even enjoy things which at one time would have been nauseous. But though strange, it is true, and we all felt better for our drink, and would have killed another elland for the sake of its blood if we had got the opportunity.

CHAPTER XIII.

THE BLEMMYES.

FEELING considerably refreshed and having our water bottles filled, we started again on our journey, and for several days met with no adventures worth recording.

At the end of the fifth day we met a deep gully or river bed, perfectly dry, but which ran at right angles to the trail we were making.

"Out with your map, Jack," I said, cheerily, for I had a remembrance of seeing an indication of such a road or river.

We sat down on the sand and looked at our small map.

Yes, there was the mark. It was the one which led from the word "bad" to the Blemmyes of whom we were cautioned to beware.

So the route we were taking had been traversed before, and if the map was really the road to the Treasures of King Solomon we were right.

I called Jack's attention to one of the pieces of writing which told us to be on our guard when we crossed something, what, we could not say, for the writing had become illegible. It may be this old river bed was referred to, and the idea seemed to have occurred to O'Brien as well, for he at once assented and admitted its feasibility.

We rested for a few hours and then resumed our journey on the other side of the gully.

Next morning we saw in the far distance what appeared to be the two mountains near Mer.

The sun did not seem so hot as it had done previously, or we were getting more acclimated, for we took a shorter rest during the day than we had been accustomed to do since we left Amlekla and her barbaric home.

When the evening approached we took a good look round on the wide expanse of sand, and as far as the eye could reach nothing in the shape of life was visible. Neither could we perceive any sign of water or vegetation except the karoo bushes, which seemed to grow without moisture.

We had nearly a pint of water each for the next day, so we determined on a good sleep.

To guard against surprises, we took it in turn to watch. I had enjoyed a good sleep and was almost inclined to rebel, when Jack called me to take my place as lookout.

It was the most detestable part of my work. I never could keep awake if alone, and I would at any time have preferred tackling a lion or meeting an enraged elephant single handed, to keeping watch for nearly three hours while the others slept.

But it was only right that I should take my turn with the others, so I had soon the satisfaction of standing alone, my comrades sleeping, on that vast desert.

I looked round, but no trace of life appeared. Feeling confident, I sat down and meditated, then—I feel ashamed to write it, but truth is truth—I thought I could keep a lookout as well lying down. Of course I never intended going to sleep, but there is an old proverb which says the road to a certain warm region is paved with equally good intentions. To be brief, I succumbed to my drowsiness and fell asleep.

How long I slept I have not the faintest idea, but I was roused by a vigorous kick in my ribs.

I was mad, and inclined to be nasty, for even if I had slept there was no need to administer a rebuke of that kind, and with very unamiable feelings I jumped to my feet to confront, as I thought, my comrade Jack.

Instead of his happy face I saw that which made me stagger back, and as I did so my heel caught against Jack's head, and I fell prostrate over him. Muttering an anathema, most probably in Irish, Jack jumped up and was so startled that he threw himself to the ground in very fear.

The commotion woke Medjeh, and he screamed aloud for Allah to aid him.

What was it which so alarmed us?

A creature in the shape of a man stood erect, proud of his seven feet of body, and looked at us. We returned the stare when we could summon up courage. But to describe the creature, that is another thing.

I have said that his height was about seven feet; his body was nude, with the exception of a leopard skin which was slung from his left shoulder, crossed his breast, and was fastened into a belt on his right side; other covering he had none.

His head was entirely hairless, and shone like a huge black billiard-ball. His face was hideous. The forehead had a huge scar across it extending from temple to temple, one eye was exceedingly small and sightless, while the other was equally abnormal, being of immense size. The nose was originally broad, but had been split straight through the center, giving the appearance of two nasal organs. The creature's mouth was very large, seeming to extend from ear to ear; the thick lips had been further extended by pieces of stone sharpened and pushed through the flesh.

There was nothing human about the face, and yet it would be a libel on the beasts of the field or the prowlers of the jungle to say it was like any animal.

"Who are you?" asked Medjid, in the Nubian language.

The creature only grunted in reply, but raised above his head the spear he carried, and within three minutes we were surrounded by twenty or thirty creatures equally hideous.*

I don't know whether it was cowardice or only prudence which prevented us shooting at these creatures, but I have often thought since we were very foolish in not asserting our power.

However it was, we allowed ourselves to be taken prisoners and marched across the desert for several miles, until we came to the village occupied by the Blemmyes.

The houses, if so they could be called, were merely holes dug in the sand, to a depth of three feet, round the edges were reeds, stuck in the sand to form a barrier against drifting and support the roof, which was also made of reeds.

The Blemmyes were not numerous, but we soon learned that they were men of business. Their principal occupation was that of slave catching and selling.

A party of Blemmyes would start out to the villages many days' march away, and would profess to be friendly with the people. When they had established amicable relations with the chief and the villagers they would watch their opportunity, and, while all were sleeping, would fire the grass huts in every direction. Panic-stricken, the unfortunate victims would rush from their burning dwellings, and the men would be speared to death, while the women and children, bewildered in the danger and confusion, would be kidnapped.

The women and children would then be fastened together, the former secured by a forked pole called a sheba, the neck of the prisoner fitting into the fork, held tight by a cross-piece lashed behind, while the wrists, brought together in advance of the body, were tied to the pole. The children would then be fastened by their necks with a rope attached to the women, and thus form a living chain, in which order they would be marched to the nearest market for slaves.

The captured women and children can be redeemed by the payment of a ransom within a month after capture. The Blemmyes sell the slaves to traders for various articles, especially spears and spirits, for this tribe would sell a dozen women for a gallon of rum or brandy.

In every expedition the Blemmyes reserve for themselves

---

* Manetho, who wrote a history of Ethiopia, by command of Ptolemy II., about 200 B. C., refers to this peculiar race of people, and in the British Museum there are several ancient stones, on whose surface the faces, such as described, are to be found. Barth, in 1853, also saw several of the Blemmyes a little further north.

the handsomest girls, and keep them for wives until they grow tired of their company; they are then marched off to the slave market with other captives, and exchange masters, oftentimes to the great advantage of the women.

When a woman is taken to be the wife of a chief she is tattooed upon the stomach, sides, and back so closely that it has the appearance of a broad belt of fish-scales, especially when they are rubbed with red ocher, which is the prevailing fashion. The women are generally free from hair, their heads being shaved. Their dress is a neat little lappet, about six inches long, of beads or of small iron rings, worked like a coat of mail, and a tail of fine shreds of leather or twine pendent behind. Both the lappet and tail are fastened on a belt which is worn round the loins.

It is not to be supposed I learned all this while marching across the desert with our captors; the information was given me later by Icona, the newest wife of the chief. Icona was a native of the Soudan and had been captured by the Blemmyes and reserved for the chief.

She told me she was longing for the time to come when she would be sold, and she expected it would be soon, inasmuch as she had borne no children to the chief, although with him for two years.

When we reached the Blemmye village, we were pushed rather unceremoniously into one of the holes, called a house, and left there to ponder over the strange vicissitudes of fortune.

Medjid took it badly, for he was certain he would be sold into slavery. O'Brien and myself escaping such a fate because we were white.

We found we were closely watched, and as we did not know what languages were understood by our captors, we were afraid to talk too much. We were rather surprised that they had left us possession of our firearms and all our ammunition.

This was explained the next day however, but was of but little advantage to us.

Every effort we made for quiet conversation was stopped by the entrance of the sentry, who would stand close to us.

We would have conversed in English, but Medjid would not have understood, and it was essential that he should form one of the council. I cursed myself for neglecting my duty on the watch, for had I seen the approach of the hideous Blemmyes, we should not have been surprised and so easily captured. O'Brien generously excused me, saying he most likely should have slept, had he been in my place, but that did not ease my conscience the slightest. Whatever disaster came to us, I was responsible for it, and

78   KING SOLOMON'S TREASURES.

the more I thought of our position the greater became my bitterness of feeling.

CHAPTER XIV.
A TREATY.

WE were not disturbed all that day, and this, while it was to a certain extent gratifying, was at the same time unpleasant, inasmuch as it compelled us to draw upon our own stores of food and water for our subsistence. It would have been pleasanter to have been living on the enemy while we were in their power.

ICONA, THE BLEMMYE CHIEF'S WIFE.

As night came on we thought it advisable to keep careful watch, and this time I did not give way to my propensity for sleep, but was faithful and vigilant.

In the morning we had an opportunity for looking round and examining our prison-house, which was very similar to the general run of houses as described in my last chapter.

OUR PRISON HOUSE.

We determined to wait as long as possible before we breakfasted, hoping that we should be remembered and food provided. The sun had risen some two or three hours when we saw a woman of very pleasing features approach. She carried a pipe, which evidently solaced her in her home life with its unpleasant lord and master. In her other hand she had a large bowl, in which was contained some black bread and some strips of dried meat.

We explained that while grateful for the food, we were very thirsty and would like a drink. The woman hurried away and soon returned with a "billy" full of a hot liquid, which from its fragrant aroma, as well as its delicious flavor, we found to be coffee. It was the first we had tasted since we left our dahabeah at Dongola, and was the most delightful beverage, we thought, had ever passed our lips. We were surprised that these savages, so uncouth in appearance and dirty in their habits, should enjoy coffee, but I conjectured it was a habit learnt at some of the slave markets. The woman talked in the Abyssinian language, and as we understood it, we found a way to loosen her tongue and find out what she knew about us.

She told us her name was Icona, and that she was the favorite wife of the chief. She had been seized when fourteen years old to be sold into slavery; but, when the chief saw her, he took such a fancy to her face and figure that he kept her for his wife. That was two years ago. I imagined she must have been at least twenty-five years old, but girls age very rapidly in these countries.

"Which was the chief?" I asked.

Icona told me the chief was away, but would return that day, and then it would be decided what was to be done with us.

I don't know why it was, but I took quite a fancy to Icona, and felt that she would assist us if she possibly could.

It was risky, but I determined to ask her advice.

"Hush!" and then in a whisper she told us that if she was heard advising us her life would be taken, as these orders were always given by the chief before any journey was undertaken.

Later in the day Icona made an excuse to return to our prison-house, and managed to get the sentries away. She advised us to hide in the sand any weapons we might have, and offer no resistance, whatever the orders might be.

"What will the chief do with us?" asked Jack.

"Most likely sell you as slaves," was the reply, as though that was a blessing and a favor rather than otherwise.

O'Brien came out with an expletive which was hardly suitable for feminine ears; but, as it was in English, most likely Icona did not understand its meaning.

"If he does not sell you," she said, "he may keep you here to build huts for his people."

"How many men are there here now?"

"About eighty, but there will be a hundred when the chief returns."

It seemed hopeless to oppose eighty armed men, but unless so we did we had but a poor chance of obtaining our freedom.

After Icona had left us, we held a hurried consultation and resolved that at night when the majority were asleep, we would force our way through the sentries, even if we had to kill them, and make for the open desert.

It seemed a feasible plan, for we were certainly equal to the two sentries, and if we had to use our revolvers we could be some distance away before the men would be aroused and on our trail. The afternoon wore away and we had not been allowed to go out of the hut since the short time in the early morning.

We were very despondent and felt less sanguine of success as the time for our attempt at escape drew near.

A great noise and hubbub roused us from our fit of blues. We heard drums beating and horns blowing, while continued shouting and clashing of spears told of some extraordinary event.

Our first thought was that a neighboring tribe had made war upon the Blemmyes, but the noise was one of joy rather than a warlike one.

Our curiosity was appeased by the appearance of Icona, who put her head in through the doorway and said: "The chief has come, hide your weapons;" with that she hurried away, evidently fearing to be seen in converse with us.

I did not like the idea of hiding our arms and ammunition, but Medjid thought it wise, for he was of opinion we should have them taken away from us if the chief got sight of them.

We took the advice, and it was only the work of a few minutes to bury our four rifles and revolvers together with the ammunition. The sand was soft and our work therefore was light.

We had hardly completed our labor, when the giant who had taken us prisoners the day before, entered and motioned us to follow him.

We obeyed, and stood outside in the free air, feeling pleased at even a few moments' liberty. The oftener we saw these hideous Blemmyes the more repulsive they appeared.

We followed the man past various huts and kraals, into a stockade made of bamboo canes stuck firmly into the ground, and inclosing a large square in which were several huts, occupied, so we were told, by the chief and his favorite wives. They were no better than the one we had just quitted—in fact, looked even more frail in their construction.

One was if anything a little larger than the others, and this, we rightly conjectured, belonged to the chief.

As we stopped before it the chief, even more hideous than our captor, stepped out and looked fiercely at us.

Icona came out of a hut near by, and stood by her husband.

It was a black representation of beauty and the beast. She was even good looking, while he, with his protruding lips, split nose—from each part of which a huge iron ring was hanging, the badge of chieftainship—and scarred face, presented an appearance the very reverse of pleasing.

Icona acted as interpreter, as the chief did not understand any language with which we were familiar.

"Who are you?" he asked.

"We are from the great country whose flag will protect its sons, wherever they may be," Jack answered, proudly; but the next minute he regretted what he had said, for he saw it was possible England was in bad odor with the Blemmyes, through the attempt to put down the slave trade.

Icona seemed to admire the answer, for she looked equally proud as she translated it to the chief.

"Sons of dogs!" yelled the chief, "you shall go where your flag will not protect you!"

"Great chief," I interposed, "hear me. We are only crossing the desert, that we may know the greatness of the people and see the riches of the land." How much more I should have said I know not, for Medjid pulled my arm and whispered:

"You are on the wrong tack; tell him you will give him ivories."

"Tell him yourself," I said.

Medjid took the hint and stepped forward, made a most graceful Oriental salaam, and commenced:

"Most great and mighty chief, thy slaves were hunting the elephant and can tell thee where the big tusks are, that thou mightest receive them as a present from thy poor slaves. They were heavy, or thy servants would have laid them at thy feet."

"Thou liest," shouted the chief.

"Nay, but let thine own people go with thy poor slave, and if they are not as stated, then do with me as thou seemest fit."

"That's good! I'll tell thee thou shalt go and show my people where thou hast hidden the ivory, and if thou liest thy carcass shall feed the hyenas, and these sons of dogs," pointing to us, "shall be food for the jackals."

"And if it be as I have said!" asked Medjid.

"Then thou and these dogs shall depart in peace."

"Let it be so."

The chief stepped back into his hut, and we were pushed violently along until we reached our prison, into which we fell headlong, for we had forgotten the descent of a couple of feet to the bottom of the hut.

Our sentries were increased to six that night, and early next morning Medjid started off with eight hideous Blemmyes to find the hidden tusks. If he failed to find them our chance of escape was small.

If he succeeded, then we were sure that the sight of so much ivory would be pleasing to the chief.

O'Brien asked how long it would take Medjid to reach the oasis, and we computed that it would be at least three or four days before he could return with the treasure. Till then we should remain at the mercy of the chief, but we had no doubt we should be honorably treated, especially as we had a friend at court in the person of Icona, who spent over an hour with us after Medjid had left, and told us much about the habits of the Blemmyes, which proved very interesting, but did not impress us very favorably as to their honor or character.

CHAPTER XV.
THE CHIEF'S TREACHERY.

MEDJID had been gone on his journey about three hours when Icona came as a messenger to tell us that we were to proceed to the chief's kraal. She was either a good actress and concealed her knowledge, or she was entirely ignorant as to the chief's intentions, for she told us we were bidden to a feast.

When we arrived at the kraal we found that to a certain extent this was true, for a feast was certainly prepared and we were invited to partake of it.

We had no objection, and Icona waited on us. This was a great honor, for only the most favored guests were waited on by the chief's wife.

The chief asked us many questions about England, its laws and queen.

These we answered without giving any offense. He then wanted to know if all the people were free in England.

When we answered that they were, he expressed his pity for a nation like that.

"Who does all the work? Who hoes the ground and puts in the seeds? Who builds the houses? not freemen?"

When we told him that all work was performed by free men and that the workers were paid for the labor performed, he was more than ever sure that it must be a bad country to live in.

He was getting on dangerous ground for us, and we had difficulty in framing our answers so as not to give offense.

When he inquired by what right England wanted to stop the slave trade, I was thrown off my guard and answered that England had as much right to interfere as some tribes had to go to another tribe and steal the people and sell them.

This enraged him, and had not Icona interposed and soothed him, I believe he would have slain us on the spot.

We were sent back to our prison, but scarcely had we reached there than we were ordered back again.

When we entered the kraal we saw a number of the Blemmyes assembled, who quickly formed a circle round us, and at a word from the chief began to strip our clothes from our bodies.

We were powerless to resist and soon stood perfectly nude before the hideous wretches.

While we stood there, wondering what was the next scene in the drama, which might turn out to be a comedy or a tragedy, we saw, to our dismay, some women, not as shapely and good-looking as Icona, enter our presence, carrying a large pail full of some liquid.

This liquid Icona told us, when we got back to our prison, was a brown dye made from the fruit "garra," growing on the soont tree.*

This dye was poured over us, every part of our body being well covered with it. Places where the dye did not penetrate were filled by the women dipping their hands into the liquid and then rubbing the white parts. We were so thoroughly colored that no one would have thought we had ever been white.

When this operation was completed we were marched back to our residence, and as we looked at each other neither could restrain a laugh, though the situation was far from pleasing.

"The old fellow has kept our clothes," said O'Brien.

"Yes, confound him! I wonder whether this dye will wash off?"

"I am afraid not."

There was not much consolation to be derived from our position; but we determined, if treachery was attempted, further than the practical joke of stealing our clothes and dyeing our bodies, we would fight hard against it.

The evening had come, and we were getting used to being without clothes. The flies were the greatest torment, but now that they had the whole surface of our bodies to probe, they were not half so bad to endure as when their united energies were directed to our faces.

"Monty, old boy, if we ever live to get back what a sensation will be caused by the society papers announcing the return of that distinguished African explorer, Arthur Montmorency, Esq., followed by the statement that the aforesaid distinguished gentleman is of a bright chocolate color."

"Have your laugh, Jack. I wish I could laugh like you."

* Acacia Arabica.

"It will all come right, Monty; only promise me one thing."

"What is that?"

"Whenever you see a circus bill and read that a 'chocolate-colored wild man has been imported at great expense, etc.,' don't go to the circus, for you may be sure it is your old comrade, Jack, and I might not like a rival in the boxes."

And with this quaint conceit Jack laughed as heartily as though he really enjoyed the turn things had taken.

The night grew very dark, and we were arranging to sleep in turns when we heard Icona's voice.

"Hush!" she said.

We drew near to where the opening was, and she whispered, "Keep up your courage. I will get your clothes."

That was all, but it was some little comfort for us.

Icona had apparently a desire to serve us, and it would be well to follow her advice as near as possible.

That night we slept soundly, but fearing treachery, the time was divided so that only one slept at a time.

When day broke Icona was quickly on hand with a palatable breakfast, and she contrived to whisper that at night she would give us the clothes, but we must not put them on until we were ready to start, and of course we would have to wait for Medjid.

The day was monotonous, and time hung heavy on our hands

When darkness returned Icona was faithful to her word, and returned all our clothes, telling us to hide them at once or she would be killed, and we should share the same fate.

It was the morning of the fifth day before Medjid, with the party of Blemmyes, was seen returning.

The approach was signaled by the beating of drums, the blowing of horns and other noisy demonstrations.

The old chief could not restrain his curiosity, but came outside the stockade to see the treasures.

Medjid had given the rascals not only ten fine tusks, but the antelope's horns as well.

Medjid looked round in evident expectation of our welcome; but though his eyes rested on us several times, he failed to recognize our chocolate colored bodies. It was only when we addressed him in Nubian that he could bring his mind to believe that we were really the ones whose service he had entered.

"Wah Illahi! bad, bad!" he exclaimed.

"Why bad?" asked Jack.

"Baas will be sold as well as Medjid," was his reply, and the horrible thought came to me that the chief had purposely dyed our skins so that he might dispose of us as slaves, our color not betraying our nationality.

If such treachery was attempted some of the Blemmyes should bite the dust. In this resolve both Jack and Medjid were fully agreed.

"When can thy servants depart, according to thy word, oh, most mighty chief?" asked Medjid.

When the chief heard the question he professed not to understand it, and asked its meaning.

"Did not the great chief promise that we should go our ways to our own countries if we gave him the ivories?" cried Medjid, getting alarmed.

"No," was the cool answer of the monster, "I was wroth because these dogs did praise my enemy, and to appease my wrath they offered me the ivory, which I accepted and spared their lives."

"Great Heaven!" I thought, "we have lost the tusks and our liberty as well."

The guards or warriors pushed us away until we reached the hut. Medjid, however, was not allowed to enter, but was taken to the king's kraal where he was stripped of his clothing, and then sent back to us naked.

We told him of Icona, and he was of the opinion that our only chance of escape was to appear to accept the inevitable, and act as if we were resigned to our fate.

This would throw them off their guard, for they had no knowledge we possessed weapons of any kind, and then we might, through the relaxation of discipline, find an opportunity to escape.

CHAPTER XVI.
SLAVERY.

It was not many hours before we became accustomed to our primitive costume, and, strange to say, that the chocolate tint of our skin seemed to deaden that feeling of bashfulness which we had heretofore felt.

The sun had not risen an hour next morning before several Blemmyes entered our hut, and without so much as an apology fastened a rope round our bodies, pinioning our arms close to our sides. We formed a string of three, I was first, Medjid in the center, and O'Brien bringing up the rear. Then a hideous-looking fellow caught hold of my bare shoulder and dragged me out of the hut; of course the others had to follow.

We were marched in this fashion to the chief's kraal, where the rope attached to O'Brien was made fast to a large pile of bamboos firmly tied together. The Blemmye who was acting as leader had a piece of raw cowhide in his hand, with which he dealt me a vigorous blow on the back. I felt the blood follow the whip and trickle down my body, but the indignity was worse than the blow. By this method we were made to understand that it was our captors' pleasure we should be beasts of burden. Our arms were so tightly pinioned that we were compelled to obey, but I said in an undertone to Medjid that I thought it would be the last time.

All that day we were kept hard at work hauling every manner of thing for a new kraal which the chief was about to build for himself. Not a drop of water or bit of food did we get from sunrise to sunset; the only stimulation we received was the constant lashing with the whip whenever our footsteps lagged.

Darkness came at last, though it seemed weeks since we had started work that morning. Our overseer had partaken in our full view of two good substantial repasts, but to all our entreaties for food or water he was deaf. When night came Icona brought Medjid's clothes, and we were not long before we were all dressed.

The pain and smarting from the wounds on our backs, which seemed festering with the poisonous dye and the heat of the sun, made Jack screech out.

I was, perhaps, more stoical, and exclaimed, with set teeth:

"Some of King Solomon's treasures, my boy."

O'Brien recovered his equanimity and laughed.

We watched an opportunity, and about midnight we resumed our clothing and cautiously crawled out of the hut.

Our sentries had fallen asleep, everything, we thought, favored us.

Icona had not informed us that on the outside of the village sentries were stationed every night, and that we should have to be very cautious in passing them.

We walked on, a revolver in each hand, Medjid having his hunting knife unsheathed, ready to use at any moment, for we intended using that in preference to the revolvers on account of its silent action.

We crept on in the darkness, meeting with no obstacle until we had reached the outskirts of the village, when Medjid stumbled against something which was full in his way.

Before he had time to recover from his temporary surprise the sentry uttered a wild whoop, which was at once answered by fifty voices from all parts of the village.

It was the very last time that the sentry ever gave an alarm, for Medjid's knife went clear through him, and was imbedded so tightly in the flesh that the Nubian had to put his foot on the Blemmye's chest to give a leverage by which he could withdraw the knife.

We started running as rapidly as we could, but we felt very weak and exhausted, and our haversacks appeared extra heavy.

Turning my head, I beheld a sight which was so picturesque that I was compelled to admire it.

About a hundred Blemmyes were running about in every direction, carrying a swinging torch, which, however, gave forth a very feeble light. These torches were held close to the ground, and presented a very pretty appearance as they seemed to skip over the desert.

One fellow held his torch up over his head for a moment, and I recognized the features of the man whose cowhide had left such unpleasant reminders on my back. I noted him well, and when the advance guard set up a hideous whoop, showing we had been seen, we stood still and faced our enslavers.

On they came like a pack of wolves.

"Crack! crack! crack! crack!" went the four revolvers, and I am really proud to say it, four of the rascals fell headlong on the sand.

Again the revolvers rang out, and two more fell beneath the deadly missives.

I showed Medjid how to use one of the revolvers, and took his Winchester, which he did not really understand.

I raised it to my shoulder, and as rapidly as I could pull the trigger sent twenty-five bullets into the midst of that savage crowd.

The overseer had not yet fallen, although I felt sure I had singled him out early in the fight as a mark for a shot.

He was now only an arm's length away from me, and had raised his spear, intending to pin me through as I stood.

I was too quick for him, for either by accident or design the last bullet in my Winchester left the barrel within a foot of the fellow's face, and he fell dead with a countenance so disfigured that even a Blemmye could not recognize him.

I have been in many fights since, but never have I seen such bravery and stolid courage shown as I did that night, for although so many fell, and we were uninjured, they never thought of retreat, but pressed forward and overpowered us by mere weight of numbers.

I felt there was but little chance for us, but at that moment Icona came on the scene, and in the chief's name claimed us as her slaves, a present from the chief.

We were seized by the arms and dragged along until the

chief's kraal was reached, when we were thrown headlong into Icona's hut.

We were her slaves, and she had a right to do as she pleased with us.

The first thing which suited her gracious pleasure was to give us some coffee and food. This we stood greatly in need of, and we were pleased at the change in ownership.

For five days we were unable to leave the hut, our arms and legs being tied very firmly together, but we were well cared for, and the scars on our backs carefully washed and dressed, for Icona had compelled us to strip off our clothes as soon as we became rested after our refreshments.

During our close and unpleasant confinement Icona talked to us very seriously, told us that if we had trusted to her she would have found a way to escape for us, but we were too impatient, and must needs go just when our captors expected we should.

She told us if we would but do as she wished, our escape should be so managed that it would be certain and she too held harmless.

We must purchase our freedom, however, and Icona laughingly told us that we might find the terms very high.

It was a comfort to know that we were owned by some one who could appreciate liberty sufficient to offer us a promise of escape if we only accepted the conditions.

At the end of the five days our arms and legs were very stiff with the strain upon them by reason of the knots and cordage, but it was a great relief to feel once more that we were able to move about.

We saw no signs of our clothing, and we were afraid our weapons and haversacks had been confiscated.

The days passed on, our duties being very trivial, except when the chief was round, then Icona had to make us work apparently very hard.

We made no further attempt at escape, and to all appearance had become resigned to our lot.

We were well fed and waited on by our owner, and when our work was done she told us all she knew about the Blemmyes and other tribes.

She also related wonderful stories about the witch Amlekla.

We dare not ask her about the treasures of Mer and the country beyond, but one day we listened with rapt attention to a story she told of a tribe of men who lived over the mountains and who lived forever, on purpose to guard the treasures which had been placed there by the gods.

We thought of our maps and the Macrobii* who were fain to inhabit the region beyond mer, and wondered whether after all the story of the escritoire was true.

"The Macrobii," said Icona "were fine-looking people, but they killed all who went into their land. They even once killed a chief of the Blemmyes."

This she thought the very acme of daring, but I inwardly thought I should like to have the chance of killing the present chief.

Icona saw but little of her husband, perhaps he was seeking another wife, he only possessed fifteen, and some of them were to be sold next time he went to the slave market, but whatever the reason he never came to the hut which we had to share with her, and she but rarely entered his.

We occupied Icona's hut for nearly two months until we began to fear that she never intended us to escape, especially as she professed a strange passion for Medjid, and indeed for all three of us.

O'Brien chafed under the restraint, and Medjid began to loathe the very sight of Icona. I stood it the best of the three, but then, I was out of favor with the dusky but not bad-looking chieftainess because I professed not to understand her love speeches, and she got tired of paying attentions to me, and concentrated the force of her batteries on O'Brien and the Nubian.

CHAPTER XVII.
FREE ONCE MORE.

Icona had been away from her hut for three days, something very unusual for her, but she had been with the chief, and had so pleased him that we were forgotten. I searched everywhere for our clothes and weapons, but in vain.

We found plenty of food and coffee, so we did not suffer from hunger and thirst.

Being in the chief's stockade, we had a certain amount of liberty, for we could go where we pleased and do as we liked inside the stockade, but the moment we offered to go out, we faced the sharp point of a Blemmye spear.

Wondering why Icona had so neglected us, we began to devise means for escape, and might have attempted something rash had not Icona reached the hut at dark that night.

"He is asleep," she said, as she pointed to the chief's hut, "and will not awake for many hours, I gave him——" and she took some leaves from the inside of her belt, which

* Men who live forever.

I had often seen, but never understood their use until now. They were a strong narcotic, and she had dropped some into the hot coffee and drugged her husband.

"Hark!" she said, in a whisper. "Come near, for I have much to say. You must get away in the morning. I will arrange it."

She then, in a very verbose but hurried manner, said that she had so pleased the chief that he was not going to sell her for a time. He, however, told her we must be sold. That he was going to Wara, at which point he would meet some traders, who would buy his ivory, his cast-off wives, and give a good price for us. As an inducement, he promised Icona he would bring her back a lot of beads, iron rings, and a new lappet as the price he would get for the three of us.

He would start after noon the next day.

"If," said Icona, "you wait until then, you will have no chance; so you must go in the morning."

"Why not now?"

She uttered the Abyssinian word equivalent to the English favorite feminine reason—"because," and then laughed.

When she had left us, we shook each other by the hand in silence and waited.

The time seemed interminable before she returned, but when she did re-enter the hut, we learned that she had given hot, drugged coffee to the sentries, and that soon they would be all asleep.

Our clothes were then given us, and, to our joy, our revolvers, hunting knives, and rifles, together with the haversacks and water-skins.

We had reason to bless the very name of the savage woman afterward, for we discovered the haversacks well filled with a variety of food, and the skins expanded with good water.

We left, quietly and with silent steps, the chief's kraal, Icona leading the way.

The sentries were all slumbering at their posts, and we were safe out on the desert.

Icona told us that she had concocted a clever story. She was going to tell the chief that she had ordered us to make the coffee for the chief, and that we must have stolen some of the leaves and dropped them into it. After the chief had drank all he wanted, she took some to the sentries, as was her custom, and on her return drank the remainder herself.

Thus all were drugged by the same "billy" of coffee. Icona said she would be fast asleep within an hour, from the effects of the drug, which she would take as soon as she got back. With that we parted with the savage, who had befriended us and saved our lives more than once

What became of her I have never heard, for the plot was so successful that we never after saw any of that tribe of the Blemmyes.

As Medjid had conducted a party of Blemmyes to the lake for the ivory, we thought it safer to take an opposite direction, and especially as we desired to reach Mer with as little delay as possible.

All that night, or rather the few remaining hours, we marched as rapidly as we could over the sand, and when daylight burst upon the desert we made deep holes with our hands and the butt ends of the rifles, and lay down in them, fearful of being seen by the Blemmyes, who would be sure to miss us, and search in every direction to recover so much valuable property.

Darkness was the signal for our continued journey, and again by daylight we took the precaution of hiding in the sand-holes.

This we continued for five days, steering our course by the compass and our maps.

Our food and water supply was beginning to get smaller, and the sight of an oasis was pleasant to our eyes.

In the oasis was a delightful little lake, and an abundance of edible plants were growing on its banks.

We could not resist the temptation to take a bath, although O'Brien facetiously remarked that our skins were of the right color warranted not to show the dirt.

We swam about in the water for some time, and when I stood upright on the bank, being the first to leave the water, Jack nearly choked with laughter and water combined, for as he opened his mouth to laugh the water rushed in faster than was pleasant.

I could not imagine what had caused the explosion until I looked down at myself and found I was as spotted as a leopard. The dye had washed off in places and left the skin a yellowish white.

"Monty, old boy, you will be a successful rival to the chocolate-colored wild man, for a spotted man will be the greatest attraction."

"Don't talk so much at random, Jack; look at yourself."

The effect was the same, and we both presented the appearance of spotted specimens of humanity.

What seemed most remarkable was that the more we rubbed the deeper appeared the color of the spots. I washed my face, but could not remove the dye.

As we were going to stay near the lake until we had secured more food, we were bent on taking frequent baths in the hope of removing the absurd appearances from our skin.

Medjid came to us the next afternoon and directed our attention to some shallow water covered with a peculiar slimy substance.

"Wash there, Baas," he said.

It looked far from tempting, especially as the clear lake was so near; but Jack dipped his hands into the thick water and found that wherever the slimy matter touched the dye came off his flesh.

That was sufficient. We were both rolling over and over in the nasty thick stuff, and even rubbing our faces with it. When we came out we took a dip into the clear water of the lake and felt refreshed, but our thankfulness was great when we perceived how white our skin had become.

Another bath in the shallow slime would restore us to the proud dignity of white men. We obtained all the food we wanted without much difficulty, the birds and animals seeking the water quite as readily as man.

The oasis was so pleasant that we felt loath to leave it; but our journey had already lasted longer than we had intended, and I was beginning to desire a return to civilized life.

Jack had been very downcast for a long time, and if his spirits got to a low ebb he was not a pleasant companion.

Had there been a chance of falling in with honest traders, who would have joined us in a return to Khartum, I believe Jack would have voted in favor of abandoning the search.

"I am weary, Monty," he exclaimed as we sat together one night looking into the clear water and watching the moonbeams sparkle.

"So am I, Jack, but what is the use? We set out to find the treasures."

"Hang the treasures."

"Agreed; but first let us find them. I am in favor of going the whole length of our intended journey before we talk about giving up."

"Bravely spoken; but we shall never return."

"What then? Better men than you or I have had their bones bleached on the African deserts."

"But think of the death!"

"Do you care for death?"

"I never did until recently, but now—— Oh, Monty, I want to live."

"So do I, my boy, and intend doing so. I am not fainthearted, for I believe we shall succeed. Let me tell you, Jack, that I have lost all fear of death."

"You have?"

"Yes, for I have become a fatalist. I now believe that every man has a work to do, and that work will be done no matter how he may try to shirk it."

"Perhaps so; but how can that take away the fear of death?"

"My dear old fellow, reason it out. A man dies when his work is done, not before. Now, if I die to-night, that is a proof of what I am contending for, and if I live for fifty years longer, it only proves that my work will not be complete until then."

"Then you mean to say——"

"Just this: there is a time appointed for men to die, and they will not die one minute before that time, and cannot prolong their life a second beyond."

"I don't agree with you entirely, for some men meet with accidents."

"Well, what of that?"

"Does not that prove the falsity of your theory?"

"Not at all."

"What about the suicide?"

"The same thing, exactly. If a man dies by his own hand, it is because eternal law has so ordered it; if he gets killed in an accident, or by the hand of another, it is the fulfillment of the same law. I have grown into this belief out here on the African desert. Tell me why we were not killed by Amlekla, or how we escaped her murderously-inclined Troglodytes? Explain why, when we killed so many Blemmyes, our lives were spared, and through no effort of our own?"

"I cannot explain," answered Jack, seriously, "it is to me incomprehensible."

"I carry my ideas further than that," I continued, "for I believe in the perfection of the universe through love. There never was a man, reasoning, thinking man, born, but somewhere the completion of a perfect man—woman—is also born."

"I scarcely follow you."

"Go back to Holy Writ and read—'Male and female created he them.' If the Great Architect of the universe so ordered in the beginning, he has continued to the present and will do so to the end. For every man or woman born there is the destined mate, and the union results in greater perfection of human kind."

"But if such is the case, why are there so many unhappy marriages?" asked Jack.

"Because marriage is a commercial contract in many cases; in others, man chooses a woman because she is pretty, dresses tastefully, can play or sing with exquisite taste, or is possessed of wealth. A woman selects a man pretty much in the same way. The higher qualities of the soul, the grandeur of love which rises above face, figure, or accomplishments and looks only at the inner beauty, is lost sight of, and bodies are united but souls are unmated."

"By Jove! Monty, I never thought it was in you!" exclaimed Jack, almost bewildered by the vehemence of my long speech.

"It was in and had to come out, you see," I answered, and then changed the conversation to some other topic.

It was but seldom that we conversed so seriously, but something in the atmosphere seemed to act magnetically on our minds, and cause us both to think and talk seriously. It did me good, and Jack said he felt the better for it, so the time was occupied with pleasure and profit to us both. Medjid had been crawling round the oasis trying to get a shot at some swamp ducks, so that we could have roast duck once more before we left the pleasant lake.

CHAPTER XVIII.
THE TWIN MOUNTAINS.

"MONTY, old boy! Monty!" cried Jack early the following morning as he roused me from a heavy sleep.

I turned over, rubbed my eyes, and then was settling myself again to slumber, when my companion once more called me. Thinking there was something wrong, I jumped up, and my nasal organ was regaled with a most delicious smell of roast duck.

This savory dish, with some edible plants we had found, and a plentiful supply of water, made a breakfast fit for a king, though why a king should have a better meal than a hard-working peasant I have never been able to understand.

When we had finished our repast and taken a dip into the lake we were ready to continue our journey.

Medjid walked first, whilst I and Jack followed closely after.

When we had gone a short distance Jack suddenly exclaimed: "It is all true. I have seen it."

"What have you seen?" I asked.

"The treasure," he replied with a sincerity and seriousness of manner which impressed me greatly.

"Explain, my boy?"

"I will. Last night I had no sooner fallen asleep than I saw the figure of my mother standing near me. She did not speak, but beckoned me to follow her. I thought I did so, yet there was this peculiarity, that while I was going forward, close to the spirit of my mother, I distinctly knew that my body was lying beside the lake and near you. We traveled very rapidly, so that only a few moments elapsed before we had passed between the mountains and stood near a monster stone monument, on which was carved the face which we found on one of the papers in the escritoire."

"It is interesting, Jack, but let me point out that so far your dream was but the reflex of what was in your own mind."

"I know it, but listen. At the back of the monument was a peculiarly-shaped piece of rockwork looking almost like those primitive brick bird-traps we used to make when we were boys together. A couple of large stone slabs measuring, I thought in my dream, six feet long by nearly three broad, rested on two stones of enormous size and thickness. My mother went to the one end and pressed on the stone slab, when it caused the other end to tilt like a sway-pole, and I was told to enter."

"Describe that again, Jack, so that when we arrive there we may see what reliance can be placed in your dreams."

"I will do better than that," he answered; "I will sketch it for you," and taking a pencil, he drew the following.

JACK'S SKETCH.

After Jack had made the sketch, he continued the story of his dream.

"I entered the cave under the stone," he said, "and my mother, by some means, got in advance of me, although I left her holding up the slab for me, and she walked down some steps until we reached a spacious chamber which was so full of dazzling brilliancy that I was blinded for some minutes.

I saw all kinds of precious stones and they sparkled so that I was bewildered.

"This is only one of the storehouses," said my mother. "There are ten more, each of which will be yours if you persevere."

"I was overjoyed as you may readily imagine, and knew not how to thank my spirit guide enough, when I turned, and to my regret, found myself lying on the banks of the lake, and Medjid roasting a very prime duck."

Although I was impressed with the dream, I could not resist laughing at the curious climax, and jestingly said:

"Which said roast duck was worth more to us hungry men than all King Solomon's treasures."

Jack O'Brien drew himself up to his full height, reminding me of an Irishman I had once seen in a prison dock charged with high treason, as he stood upright facing the judge, and when asked his name, he replied, "Six foot three of Irish treason, my lord." O'Brien looked just as dignified as he stood on that desert, the sun casting an immense shadow behind him. For a moment he looked at me and then exclaimed in almost tragic tones:

"So you believe the roast duck and doubt my dream!"

It was ludicrous and I could not resist smiling as I answered:

"You see, Jack, I tasted the duck, but you only saw the treasures."

"But they were there."

"That I don't doubt, neither am I prepared to question your dream; for I am ready to acknowledge, to some

"'Unlocked the world of spirits lies;'

while to others it is equally true that

"'Their sense is shut, their heart is dead,'

to all influences from the world beyond the grave."

I had thought much of this subject since the time when the luminous form had fanned us in the caves of Amlekla, and I was beginning to believe in what the world generally designates an apparition."

Admit this much and we shall find there are conditions of mind and body necessary to enable the spirit of the living to converse with or see the soul of the dead, and that while one may see, another standing by will not. The verdict of the senses negative to one, is affirmative to the other, and even if the thing imagined has no real existence, the imagination of it is not the less a reality. Since I had brought my mind to that degree of belief in the truth of apparitions, I have had abundant opportunities of pursuing the investigation, and I now believe that there can be no doubt to the earnest seeker, that we are capable of seeing, and that with the most distinct clearness of every detail, objects which have no immediate external counterpart, and hearing sounds, as well as tasting flavors and inhaling odors, which have no external cause. I was led to reason this out by the thought that after looking at any object in a bright light, we continue, long after we have ceased to contemplate it, to see it depicted in various colors upon a dark ground or under the eyelid of a closed eye.

This fact led to others until I arrived at the belief stated.

O'Brien was a little mollified at my expressed belief in the reality of his dream, but for a long time he remained silent.

"What do you make of it all?" he asked, breaking the silence with a suddenness which made one start.

"All what?"

"My dream," he answered, shortly.

"I scarcely know yet," I replied, cautiously, "for I am not sure how far the brain can act independently during sleep; but this I will acknowledge—if the drawing you have given me proves correct, I will sink my individual opinion, and bow before the great dreamer of dreams."

"Still jesting, Monty; you are incorrigible."

"No, O'Brien, not jesting, but serious; for if you are right in this particular, I shall say that indeed thou art guided by the unseen and mysterious."

"You will find it so, then; be assured of that."

"I think you are right. Something within me tells me so."

Medjid stopped short and waited for us to get up to him, and then he pointed out the two mountains right ahead of us.

"See, Baas!" he said; "is not that smoke coming from that hill on the right?"

"It has that look, Medjid."

And as we looked we thought that one of the hills was volcanic.

We stood with eyes fixed on the hills, gazing with rapture.

Never before had I beheld anything so sublimely grand. The alps in all their glory, with their snow-clad peaks and miles of ice, their lovely valleys and spreading forests, faded into insignificance before the solemn grandeur of those twin peaks.

Like gigantic pyramids they stood, their base being nearly circular and rising gradually till the apex must have reached an altitude of eight or ten thousand feet.

But it was not their height that so much impressed us as the varied colors of their rugged sides. As the sun shone on them they gave one the appearance of being composed of glass studded with multitudinous gems of every shade, color, and shape.

Now the rays danced in wild glee on some immense ruby, then they glinted over the surface of an emerald an acre in size; now the prismatic rays of the diamond seemed to shine forth across the desert. Those mountains looked in that early sunlight like a cluster of gems arranged with the precision and taste of a skillful jeweler.

High up their sides a veil of filmy mellowness seemed to be rising. As we approached nearer we found the smoke-like appearance to be the dew arising from the surface.

"No, not smoke, not dew, Baas!" exclaimed Medjid, breaking forth almost into a fervor of poetic imagery, "but the spirits of the mountains bidding us welcome."

We could not withdraw our gaze from these pillars of a gigantic gateway, and a devotional feeling seemed to take possession of O'Brien, for he stood looking intently at the hills, and then exclaimed:

"Great Father of the universe! how puny is man and the works of his hand compared with the vastness of Thy creative skill."

"Amen!" I responded, fervently, and I, too, felt that the place was almost holy ground. It is ever thus. The sublime and unexpected in nature makes even the skeptic pause in his skepticism and bend the knee in adoration of the unknown God.

The hills were many miles distant, and we had, perhaps, innumerable dangers to overcome before we entered that sacred gateway and passed to the land of treasures beyond.

A joyous feeling took possession of us, and our feet seemed to bound with airy lightness over the hot, burning sand.

It was worth all our sufferings if we gained nothing beyond the glimpse of that grandeur, fresh from the hands of the Great Architect of the universe.

CHAPTER XIX.
THROUGH THE CLIFF.

THE march across the desert was not half so irksome or terrible now that we had the mountains in full view.

So far our map, though so crudely drawn, had proved to be correct. Still there was the doubt that the treasures might not be in Mer or even the region beyond.

Whoever drew the map may have been deceived. We

never found any good reason why the original draughtsman had not secured the treasures for himself, perhaps that difficulty would be solved hereafter.

I taxed my brain to consider all that had been said of Solomon and his immense wealth, and that night while it was my watch I thought over it all, and could scarcely realize that one man could have possessed so much wealth.

If the accounts were accurate, his income must have been about one hundred and forty million pounds sterling every year, and as he reigned forty years his savings must have been prodigious.*

As we were told that this wealth was gathered into treasure cities, and that Solomon reigned over Ethiopia, which included a very large portion of Northern and Central Africa, I was ready to agree that O'Brien had on his side a plausible argument in favor of his search.

I sat and watched the shadows deepen on the wonderful hills, and saw them gradually grow darker until they appeared more like a denser black than the surrounding atmosphere, but without shape or form.

My watch, which had been first, ended, and I was glad to get a rest. Jack was to relieve me, and when I roused him, he leaped to his feet with alacrity, exclaiming:

"All right, old boy, a few more nights will soon pass and we shall be wealthy."

"Don't be two sanguine, Jack. 'There's many a slip'— you know the old proverb."

"I do, but we have a dead certainty this time."

I was soon asleep, and when the day dawned I was as lighthearted and sanguine as O'Brien himself.

We reached, after several days' weary tramp, the great hills, but found that our map was wrong.

As we understood it, a river had once run from Mer, passing between the mountains and emptied itself into the Nile, near Dongola.

We had seen no trace of any river, and now we found we must either go round the hills or climb over a ridge which connected "the twins" as Jack facetiously named these solitary peaks.

This connecting link was apparently of the same material as the hills, and might be the result of volcanic eruption.

The cliff, for so it would be more correct to call it, was half a mile long and rose to between one hundred and fifty and two hundred feet high. When we were able to examine it closely we found that both it and the surface of the high

---

* Reynolds, the careful Biblical commentator, reckons Solomon's income to have been £142,242,034 9s. 7d. per year, or £2,735,423 9s. 7d. per week, and his daily income would be £390,774 16s. 4d. Multiply the pounds by five and we get the equivalent in dollars.

hills was really glass. It presented an appearance of being at some time a surface flow of obsidian, which became cooled in its fall. The peculiar brilliancy of the hills we now saw came from, the prismatic columns and shapes on the mountain side. These configurations were of black obsidian, mottled with bright, brownish red and various shades of brown and green. The brilliant luster of the rock and the strong contrast of color with the black background were very striking.

It was worth all our trouble, suffering and annoyance even if we gained nothing but a view of these remarkable rocks.

"By Jove, Monty, wouldn't the Londoners rave if we could take this cliff back with us and put it in the Crystal Palace grounds."

"And rightly, too, for England has nothing like it," was my reply.

We were so rapt in admiration, that we determined to spend the remainder of the day in examining the hills, and wait till the morrow before we continued our journey.

The combination of colors were the more striking on the hill which we had at first thought to be a volcano.

Down its sides pieces of glass or transparent lava had fallen, and in the process of cooling been broken into small angular pieces, which were again cemented by a later flow, producing many strange designs and beautiful *breccia*.

Through the black and red glass we found dull, bluish-gray patches and bands of pink scattered at irregular distances, all adding to the beauty of this wonderful and conspicuous extinct volcano.

"Monty, come here!"

I looked round, but could not find any trace of O'Brien. Medjid had left us, to try and trace a water well which we had reason to believe must be near.

"Monty!"

"Where are you, O'Brien?" I exclaimed, looking in every direction, but failing to find my comrade.

I had nearly given up the quest, when I almost shared the same fate as Jack. I found him in a great hole, close to the center of the cliff. He had been looking closely at the peculiar rocks, when he felt the sand give way, and before he could save himself he was in a pit seven feet deep.

I lay down at full length, and he caught my hand. But the sand afforded a poor foothold; and at every attempt to rise he found himself getting back to his old position, only breaking away the sides of the pit.

"You must wait there till Medjid returns," was all the consolation I could offer him.

O'Brien made use of his time in clearing away the sand

from the wall of the cliff, and was rewarded by finding a cave, which apparently went a long distance under the rocks.

When, later, Medjid returned from his unsuccessful search for water, we were able to lift O'Brien out of his pit; and then we fell to speculating on the significance of the cave.

All our theories were wild and visionary, and we had, after all, to trust to Jack's propensity for dreaming, to find a solution.

We were eating a breakfast—the last we should have, unless we found more food—when Jack broke the silence by saying:

"I know all about the cave."

"How?"

"I dreamed all about it."

We had got so accustomed to O'Brien's dreams, and had found them so accurate in the main, that we took the statement as soberly as if he had asserted as a fact that the cave was marked on the map of Africa and described in the history.

"Yes, Monty, the map was right," he continued, finding we made no comment on his dream. "Many years ago there used to be the river marked on the map, and its course was *under* this cliff. The river was dried up, and the sand gradually drifted and filled up the channel, as it did the entrance to the cave."

"You think, then, that we could get to the other side through the tunnel?"

"I am not sure about that, for I cannot say how high the sand may have drifted on the other side."

"Baas, wouldn't it be well to search for water and food before going to the other side?" suggested the practical Medjid.

We were both of the same opinion, and we separated, taking different directions in our search.

I was the lucky one, but it was more by accident, for I was walking along, taking but scant notice of my bearings, not thinking to find water so near. I was in deep thought, when a bird suddenly rose up from the sand close to me, startling me with the flapping of its wings.

I knew that where we could find birds water would not be very distant, so I looked round, but could not perceive any. I did see, however, a bird standing some fifty yards from me, and having my Winchester, I fired and killed it. When I went to get the game I was surprised to find myself in several inches of water, and the sand of a very treacherous nature.

O'Brien and Medjid both heard my shot, and were near

enough to see the smoke; they therefore hurried to me, and were quite as surprised as I had been.

It was the first time we had found water without vegetation. We tasted, but found it rather brackish, but even then it was a godsend to us. Explorers cannot afford to be nice or dainty in their tastes, and the most brackish water is welcome on the desert. After securing a few birds we filled our water-bottles and started back to the obsidian cliff.

I was in favor of climbing over it, but Jack was firm in his desire to excavate the sand away from the cave.

Medjid agreed with O'Brien, so they two started to work at the bottom of the pit, while I, with my hands and a Blemmye hoe which I had appropriated, made some rude steps in the sand to aid the ascent.

Two hours passed, and as I was ordered to stay on the top, I obeyed the command and waited for news.

It was not long coming, for Medjid's head was seen emerging from the cave, and his not unpleasant voice called me:

"Baas! Come."

He mounted the steps, and we gathered up our possessions and entered the cave. It may have been a freak of nature, but the walls were so smooth, and the archway so perfect, that never did man make a better tunnel. My wonderment had increased greatly by the time we reached Jack, who was working like Hercules in clearing a passageway through the sand. I saw a faint glimmer of light beyond, so was certain we should reach the promised land without climbing the hills.

All three of us set to work with a good will, and before the day had passed we made such good progress that a few hours would finish our task.

Even O'Brien could not toil night and day, so we rested, and made no attempt to continue our work until we saw the sunlight making the far exit from the cave bright and luminous.

As we neared the end we became so excited that we made but slow progress. Our nerves were highly strung, and the blood in our veins was like boiling lava. Never did children feel greater excitement than we did that last half hour.

Medjid was useless; his emotion was so great that he sat down and cried. He, like Jack, had become sanguine that as soon as we had reached the other side of the cliff we should be in possession of the treasures. I was delighted at the thought; but, perhaps, because I deserved the name of "doubting Thomas," which Jack bestowed on me, or that I was cooler and more calculating in my disposition, I did not manifest my delight and pleasure so demonstratively as did the others.

I reasoned about the subject, and the result of my reasoning was that the treasures were securely hid, and many a hardship would have to be endured and obstacle overcome before we really entered King Solomon's treasure chambers. As the sequel proved, I was correct in my reasoning.

Nevertheless, we worked right heartily, and it was easier than climbing the almost polished glass cliff.

The sand grew less in depth, and now we could crawl out if we so desired, but we continued to make the path deeper for a few moments—then O'Brien could stand it no longer. He was soon on all fours, scrambling over the sand, and five minutes later we heard his voice raised in a song of triumph.

CHAPTER XX.
THE SHADOW OF DOUBT.

WE were through the cliff, and as we looked up at its almost perpendicular wall, we perceived how impossible it would have been to have climbed over it. The country beyond seemed partly desert and the remainder jungle.

When I left Alexandria, I possessed a first class fieldglass, but I fancy I must have left it in the dahabeah at Girjeh, for I had not seen it among our stores when we unloaded at Dongola. It would have been valuable to us on the route, and many times our regret at its loss found utterance in words.

We were wishing for it, when we emerged from the glass tunnel.

We strained our eyes and tried to find some trace of the place marked Mer. As far as the eye could penetrate, nothing but sand and jungle.

The excitement in the cave had been great, but the reaction was terrible. O'Brien walked away from us, and from my heart I pitied him.

When he returned I perceived that his eyes were red. His emotion had been too great.

"Let me look at your map," I said.

With slow and deliberate movement he drew it from his pocket, and handed it to me without a word.

If the map was drawn according to any clearly defined scale we ought to see some trace of Mer. Although how we were going to find it, seeing the river bed was filled in with the drifting sand, was more than I could understand.

In reality we had nothing to guide us but O'Brien's

dreams, and the positive conviction he had that if we were going wrong his spirit guide would make it plain to us.

Never before had two men started out on such an enterprise so badly equipped. It was a regular Munchausen expedition. As I sat looking, first at the map, and then at the wide expanse of level country, I could not help giving utterance to my thoughts.

"We are a couple of fools, Jack," I said.

"In what way, I ask?" he retorted haughtily.

"Think over it all and you will say the same thing. We started out on a dangerous expedition, without camels or men——"

"Of course! If we had a lot of men with us they would perhaps have murdered us for the sake of the treasures."

"Probably so; but we may get killed by the natives as it is."

"No, we shall not."

"I am glad you are so positive, but think again. We have no sextant for finding the latitude and longitude, we trusted to our chronometers; but when they both stopped they ceased to be of value."

"We couldn't carry everything."

"That is true, therefore we ought to have had a camel for our stores. Then we are without food."

"We have not starved yet, have we?" Jack said, almost savagely.

I saw he was getting cross, so I thought I had grumbled sufficiently, and changed the style of conversation.

"See here, my boy, we are in for this affair, and I am not going to back out because of difficulties, are you?"

"Not likely, who said I was?"

"Don't get crusty, old fellow, I meant not to find fault, I had been thinking, and we are pals in this expedition."

"Forgive me, Monty! I am disappointed."

"I am not."

"Not disappointed?"

"No."

"You mean you never expected to find the treasure?"

"I mean that we came for sport—which we have had—and treasure, which we will find."

"You have faith yet?"

"As much as ever, but there are difficulties."

"Of course, but what are they?"

"Come here by me, and I will explain."

Jack had been standing some distance from me, Medjid had gone prospecting for water and food.

O'Brien sat down on the sand, and I opened the map.

"Listen to me," I said, "and follow my ideas; they may be worth something. This map is not drawn to scale."

"Who said it was? it's true, though!"

"Don't fly off so at a tangent, Jack, I never doubted its truth, but what I want you to realize is this: the distance on this map is greater between the mountains and Mer than between the Nile and the mountain, where we encountered Amlekla."

"What of that?"

"It took us a great many days to reach Amlekla's mountains—I know no other name for them—is it not probable we may have a longer distance to go before we see traces of Mer?"

"That seems probable. By Jove, Monty, I should have killed myself with despair if it had not been for you."

"No, Jack, you would not, for that is not be your fate."

"Yes, I believe I should, I was so disappointed."

"I have more to say: have you thought how we shall know Mer when we arrive at it?"

"No! That is—of course;" Jack was confused. "I shall know it by the monument."

"That is the very answer I expected you to give, now don't get offended when I suggest that as the river has been filled in with the drifting sand, the monument may be buried. If it is, how shall we find it? If it is only partially buried, what tools have we for excavations?"

A shadow passed over O'Brien's face as he saw the difficulties growing greater.

"The other map," I said, "may help us. The only distance given is on that, and we find that Mer is fifty leagues from some arch. That arch may be standing, and if it is we can measure back from it to Mer."

"I am in a fog, Monty, and that is a fact. I must dream about it; oh, if my mother would but come. What's that?"

"What?" I asked, surprised at the sudden exclamation.

"I thought something touched me on the shoulder."

"I did not, I never moved. Perhaps it was your spirit guide, you talk so much about."

"Don't jest on that subject, Monty. To me it is as sacred as my religion."

"All right, Jack, old fellow, we owe our present adventures to that same influence."

After a pause O'Brien pointed to the map, and called my attention to the word Troglodytes, near Mer, or between the mountains and the mysterious treasure cave.

"I think it likely we shall see some more tribes of natives before long, and it may be shall discover some wonderful specimens of the monkey tribe."

"What gives you that idea?"

To satisfy Jack I took from my pocket a few leaves of a small Bible. I had not taken a Bible with me, but as I desired to think about Solomon I had torn out the leaves relating to the great king's treasures and wealth.

Here is what the Bible says: "And the navy also of Hiram, that brought gold from Ophir, brought in from Ophir great plenty of almug trees, and precious stones. . . . And the king had a navy with the navy of Hiram: once in every three years came the navy of Tharshish, bringing gold and silver, ivory, and apes and peacocks."

"Now, Jack," I continued after I had read the passages, "if we are near the great treasure caves of Solomon we are most likely in the land which produced not only the gold and silver and the almug trees but the apes and peacocks as well."

"You think, then, that this is Ophir?"

"Quite likely, and therefore I believe that Solomon would store great treasures here, because it was not his custom to risk all in one place."

"I am glad, Monty, we have had this talk, for I was getting very low-spirited."

Our conversation was interrupted by the return of Medjid, carrying with him some birds and a bottle of water.

He had found an oasis about a mile to the south, and after we had eaten some of the food, we journeyed across to the oasis, as we needed a rest and a good bath.

Medjid alarmed us by saying that when he reached the oasis he found traces of naked footprints on the sand, but although he had kept a good lookout, had not perceived any human being.

While we were not averse to meeting the natives, we did not like their sudden disappearance, for not an hour had elapsed, Medjid said, before the sand had obliterated all traces of the marks. That being the case, the tribe must be near at hand.

Our map spoke of Troglodytes, and as they were dwellers in caves, it might be that they had made caverns for themselves in the twin mountains, and were therefore near to us.

We had scarcely finished taking our bath before we saw a cloud of sand rising up between the mountain and the oasis.

It was easy to conjecture that the sand was being thrown up by a number of men in the act of running.

Our supposition was correct, for in an instant we were face to face with a number of blacks, rather more refined in their appearance than those we had seen since we left Dongola.

One of the blacks, tall and majestic in appearance,

* 1 Kings x. 11, 22.

stepped forward, and placing his spear across his breast, asked:

"Who art thou that crossest the mountains to the land of our people?"

Medjid understood the language better than we did, so we let him be our spokesman.

"Thy servants crossed not the mountains but came through them."

"Thou declarest that which the Sun would fain not look upon."

This was a polite way of saying we had deviated from the truth.

"Nay, not so," answered Medjid; "but of a truth it is as thy servant sayeth."

"Then it matters not, for no one from the lands beyond can live when they visit this country."

"Say not so, most mighty chief, for thy servants are men of great power, whose wisdom shall aid thee against thy enemies."

"The king hath said it," was the answer.

"Lead us to the king," said O'Brien.

"Your bodies shall be thrown to the jackals and your heads shall be carried to the king."

Jack looked at me and then in English asked what trick we could show the chief which would prove our power.

I could not conjecture, for I was afraid whatever was suggested, would further exasperate the warrior, who, while desiring our death, was polite and courteous.

"Let the great chief point out to thy servants the enemy he wishes to see prostrate at his feet, and thy servants will show their power," said Jack, impressively.

"Thou sayest well, the king shall see thee."

When the chief had consented to the saving of our lives, we were surrounded and a bandage made of jungle grass was tightly bound around our eyes.

"I don't like this," I said in English.

"By Jove, they shall smart for it," was Jack's response.

We were then seized by the arms and marched off by our captors.

I have no idea which way we went, but it seemed as though we traveled miles. The chief and his warriors singing a chant of triumph, the words of which were in a language entirely different to the one we had been using in conversation.

It was quite pleasing in its musical cadence, and, although we understood that it might be our funeral anthem, we could not help enjoying it.

When our journey had continued for half an hour, we

felt the atmosphere growing denser, and the close, suffocating sensation told us we were entering some caves.

We were led up some steps, and a sudden cessation of the singing and the march led us to believe we were at our journey's end.

The bandages were removed from our eyes, and we saw a most wondrous sight.

Our captors left us alone, and that gave us an opportunity of fully investigating our prison chamber, or the royal palace, we knew not by which name it should be designated.

CHAPTER XXI.
THE SACRED APE.

THE room we were in was a cave of immense size, but well lighted by many lamps placed round its walls.

The cave was nearly square, but each corner had the appearance of being an entrance, or doorway. The roof was arched and very lofty, and was supported not only by the walls but also by columns of black glass, like the lava we had seen on the twin mountains. The walls were of the same material, and the many lamps shone brightly on the surface, the lights being reflected back in almost every conceivable color.

On one side the flooring was slightly raised, and was of some polished substance. In the center of the raised dais was a seat or table, I could not say which it was intended for, as it was very high for a seat, and possessed no back.

Being alone, we examined the place very carefully, and Jack was almost beside himself with joy as he found that the table was made of bars of silver supported by the finest elephant tusks we had ever seen.

The wealth contained in that table, or seat, alone would repay us for all we had expended, and make us wealthy men if we could but convey it to England. I really believe Jack was coveting it as his eyes rested on such barbaric splendor.

I had never seen such a magnificent room in my life. Its crystal walls plentifully besprinkled with rubies, emeralds, and sapphires—or glass which had that similitude—a throne, for it was worthy of the name, made of solid silver and polished ivory work—a king's ransom—a flooring of polished glass—who ever saw such a sight before or since.

And yet though our dreams of grandeur had been based upon the royal palaces of Europe, here in the desert of Sahara we found a room far surpassing anything which our imaginative minds could conceive.

Jack walked round the walls, looking carefully over the surface in the hopes that he might find some inscription or carvings which might give us an idea of the origin of the place."

"Monty, come here."

I went over to the other side and found O'Brien puzzling over an inscription which he had found.

"What is it?"

"Read that," was his answer, as he pointed at the slab.

In bold and deep-cut letters we found traces of several lines of writing, but so obliterated by age that we were unable to decipher more than one word, which was so often repeated that it formed, evidently, the subject-matter of the inscription. That word was in larger characters than the rest, and was written like this: *

KEIΠEN

I thought I was well up in the language of the Orientals, and was given the credit of being somewhat of an Egyptologist, but I could not unravel the meaning of the word.

No other inscription could we find, and the place was beginning to weary us with its vastness and weird appearance. Medjid had remained stationary in the center of the room, and had occupied his time in various devotional movements, which, doubtless, accompanied his mental prayers.

When we had almost begun to despair of either seeing or hearing from any one, the room suddenly seemed animate with life, and several score warriors entered.

At one corner appeared a number of men, each carrying a torch in one hand and a spear in the other. At the opposite corner an equal number appeared on the scene armed with a spear and an immense shield. A similar spectacle occurred at the third entrance.

As the warriors filed in they took their places silently, moving almost like automatons, so exact and precise was every action.

As they stood, forming three sides of a hollow square, the torch-bearers being distributed so that an equal number was ranged on each side, we waited with breathless interest and fixed our attention on the opposite corner.

---

* The same word occurs on a fragment of pavement taken from the ruins of the Temple of Fortune in ancient Præneste, in Italy, and is generally admitted to refer to a peculiar kind of monkey held to be sacred.—EDITOR.

A very pretty sight was presented to our astonished gaze.

First there entered ten girls, their ages ranging from ten to sixteen years, their skins as black as midnight; but relieved by a broad strip of leopard skin, which they wore sash fashion across the chest.

These girls stood on the right side of the raised dais; no sooner were they stationed in their places than they were followed by ten more girls, a little older in years, having no sash or leopard skin, but about twenty rows of beads hanging round their necks and several rings fastened round the ankles from which bangles or pendants were hanging; as these girls marched into the room the bangles and beads struck against each other, making a pleasing jingling accompaniment to the tramp of their bare feet.

These girls stood on the left of the dais, and were immediately followed by ten additional girls of uniform height and appearance. Their dress consisted of a lappet of leopard skin pendant from a broad belt of the same skin round the waist; they had on a head-dress of a peculiar kind of skin, above which was fixed a tiny torch.

Each girl had resting on her left arm a small musical instrument shaped almost like a zither.

When they were opposite to the center of the dais, they with perfect accord dipped on their right knee facing the throne, as I now began to consider the silver and ivory table to be.

When they had taken their allotted places three girls entered; their bodies were almost entirely covered with plumes of ostrich feathers, and each girl held to a rope of leopard-skin, which was attached to the body of an enormous ape.

This ape, a most wonderful-looking animal, jumped with a bound on the throne or table, and uttered the word "Koola."*

This was the signal for the entrance of the chief whose acquaintance we had previously made, and who was accompanied by a very fine-looking warrior, who towered head and shoulders above all the rest, and who wore on his head a plume of very large and fine ostrich feathers.

This man I rightly conjectured to be the king, but we were all puzzled at the appearance of the monkey occupying the post of honor.

The ape sat on the silver table and waited patiently for the proceedings to commence.

* Du Chaillu tells of a tribe of monkeys found in Africa, nearly related to the species called the Nschigombouvie, which utters the word "koola" when desiring the company of its fellows. There was a very fine specimen in the English Zoological Gardens in 1883.

No judge ever looked more calm or unruffled when on the judicial bench than did the presiding genius of the cave.

PORTRAIT OF THE SACRED APE.

When all were in their places the king raised his hand as a signal, and instantly every native male and female sank to their knees and bowed their heads until their foreheads nearly touched the floor.

It was a quaint sight—we, three in number, standing erect, while all the rest were deep in obeisance before the monkey.

The animal could now be seen plainer by us, and we noticed that it possessed many features different to apes we had before seen. There was a certain resemblance to the chimpanzee and gorilla, but in general appearance it was different.

It had an immense belly; its skull was globular, and its ears very capacious. On the face was a look of great intelligence and cunning.

If our fate was to be decided by the ape we were afraid death would be our portion, but as we stood erect staring at it, while all the others were kneeling. we determined to sell our lives dearly, and if we were in any danger I resolved that the ape should be the first victim. I did not like the look of the creature.

"Koola!" it said, after a long and protracted prostration.

At once every one rose to their feet and stood erect.

"Koola va Koubie," again came from the monkey.

We exchanged looks of surprise at hearing one of the strange animals conversing so that it could be understood.

"Kambi chi mavode," and then with its right arm pointed to us.

We were unable to understand the words uttered, and could only get their general meaning from the results. While we expected the pointing meant death, we were surprised to find the chief commissioned by the king to escort us to the raised dais, and placed in front of the throne of the ape.

I ventured to remark to the chief that I had never before heard a monkey speak, and he replied in a low tone that it was only the Sacred Ape that did so.

The old story recurred to me that the monkeys could talk, but refused to do so for fear they might be compelled to work.

When we had taken our places we were ordered to sit down. Our backs now rested against the ivory which supported the great table or throne.

The king raised his hand, which seemed to be the signal for every change. Instantly the girls bearing the zithers began to twang the strings, and all the girls commenced a strange gyration of the body. Their feet never moved, but with that exception every part of their frames was in motion.

Every joint, from the ankles up to the neck, was in endless vibration. The dance or gymnastic performance is really a difficult thing to describe, for it commenced by a slow shivering, followed by a more violent shaking, increasing in its force and power until every muscle quivered and every joint seemed loosened. When the movements became so rapid that to look at the dancers was bewildering, every girl raised her right foot a little and the strange gyration continued; the right leg was slowly elevated during the movements until it was almost at a right angle with the body.

Then the whole performance changed, and the feet began to move in a shuffling manner. Every kind of dance seemed to be introduced, and at one moment we fancied our strange entertainers were dancing the lanciers, the change was made instantly to a waltz, then to the galop, and so on through every conceivable step and terpsichorean movement.

The girls, with the head-dress of lamps, moved in and out of the throng, adding to the beauty of the scene.

It was bewildering and yet entrancing, and continued for a long time.

"Didst thou ever see aught like it?" asked the king in very fair Abyssinian.

"Never," I answered; and then I became a questioner and asked, "What is its meaning?"

"It is the adoration of the Sacred Ape," was his reply.

"Is the ape your God?" asked O'Brien.

"No; but the ape is the presiding genius. Any enemy we have can only triumph by first killing him; and as he is always in the caves, no enemy can come near."

I thought that he was resting on a very frail foundation, for with one shot from our revolvers the ape, whether sacred or otherwise, would be but dead, inanimate flesh.

"Thou art favored! Thy lives are spared!" he continued, after a pause.

I thanked him, and asked when we could retire, but was immediately checked by the king declaring we must remain until the Sacred Ape—whose name, by the way, I learned, was Koolokamba—gave permission.

One of the dancers was seen to throw up her arms frantically and cry out loudly for a goat.

"A goat, a goat!" was taken up by all the dancers, who instantly ceased their gyrations.

One of the warriors left and soon after returned with a grayish colored goat of the masculine gender.

The king examined it and found a tuft of dark hairs on its back, that saved its life. Another was brought in which was all white.

All the time the girl was shouting frantically:

"A goat! a goat!"

Jack was standing near the chief and asked him the meaning of the goat episode.

He explained that while the girls are dancing their bodies are taken possession of by genii, who inhabit the caves.

Sometimes one of the genii gets tired, and then a bogie or evil spirit gets possession of the body, and unless expelled would kill the girl.

The only way to expel or exorcise this evil spirit was by the slaughter of a white goat.

The goat was standing an innocent spectator of the strange proceedings.

When all was ready, a man habited in a goat-skin, slung from his neck by means of a band or collar, seized the goat by the horns and held its head high, stretching the neck to the utmost; the girl who was possessed of the evil one was then dragged forward and forced to lie down with her head under the animal's neck, and her mouth wide open.

The priest or butcher immediately stuck a knife into the goat's throat, and the hot blood spurted out into the girl's mouth.

It was a horrible sight, but possessed a strange, weird fascination.

As the man drew away the knife the girl raised her head until her mouth was over the wound, and then she drank as much of the blood as possible.

It took two men to hold the poor goat steady while its life blood was entering the mouth of the possessed girl.

As the animal became faint with loss of blood, the girl was pulled away and laid on one side to rest.

This ended the ceremony, and the girls re-formed their lines and marched out of the room, the warriors followed, then the ape, accompanied by its three attendants in the ostrich feather costume.

The king, chief, and ourselves were the only ones remaining.

"Come," said the king, and we followed him through the passageway into another room, of smaller dimensions than the one we had quitted.

CHAPTER XXII.
WE BECOME TROGLODYTE CHIEFS.

MEDJID seemed to move about in a trance; never did he betray the slightest concern or interest in the proceedings of which we had been witnesses. A strange expression was on his face, and I felt alarmed. If sickness prostrated him, we should be the greatest sufferers; and if he succumbed and died, our expedition, Quixotic as it was, even with his aid, might as well be given up. So valuable was he to us that O'Brien had suggested giving him a third of all we recovered from the treasure caves, and I was even inclined to be more generous.

O'Brien whispered to me, as we left the large cave:

"What is the matter with Medjid?"

"That is a mystery; I hope he is not sick," was the only reply I could give. I stepped forward and tapped his shoulder.

"Medjid, what ails you?"

"Nothing, Baas."

"But there is something. Tell me; I am your friend."

"I know it—but not now."

Whether the latter part of his answer referred to my friendship or the time to tell me his trouble, I had no means of ascertaining, for we had entered the smaller cave. In this we were left alone for a time; but within a few minutes the chief returned, and looking at Medjid, said:

"Swear by Allah and his prophet that thou revealest not our habitations."

"I swear!" answered the Nubian, making a very low salaam.

The same form of oath, with but a slight alteration, caused by the addition of the words, "Swear by the Allah thou believest in," at the end of the sentence, was administered to us; and after we had taken it, the chief, who told us his name was Benizid, said we were in the mountains of the Troglodytes and the worshipers of the Sacred Ape, and that our lives had been spared by King Gabzenati's command; but if we attempted to escape, we should be killed without any hesitation.*

We answered that while we were willing to be the guests of the most noble nation of Troglodytes, and would never locate their habitation so that others could discover it, we must be free to leave when we so chose.

Benizid grew wrath and declared that he would, were he king, destroy us on the spot, that we were the first strangers ever allowed to live on that side of the great mountains, and that no one in the world ever left there alive.

There may have been some truth in this, for, with the exception of the map, we had no knowledge of these strange people, and we had been told by the Nubians and the residents of all the villages we had passed, that no one lived beyond the hills guarded by Amlekla.

If all explorers had been killed this ignorance could be easily accounted for, and our own safety was, therefore, all the more mysterious.

Benizid made no further remark, and in his anger left us, but returned almost immediately, looking very sulky and cross.

"Come," he said, gruffly, and with heavy hearts we followed. We feared that we were marching to our doom.

Through innumerable passages we walked, until we reached a series of rooms or caves, very similar to the

---

* Herodotus, in his book of "Melpomene," chap. 183, after having enumerated the peoples of Libya, speaks of the Garamentes who hunted the Troglodytes. Strabo, in his description of Africa, also names the Troglodytes; and Pliny cites them as neighbors of the Garamentes and the Angiles.—EDITOR.

council chamber we had first entered, except that they were much smaller.

The rooms were square, the entrance being at the corners; the walls were of the same material, black and varied colored glass, or lava, highly polished. Many lamps gave forth a dim but pleasing light, and round the sides were many skins thrown down, which indicated that they were intended for seats.

We were getting hungry and thirsty, and felt that there was rather too much ceremony.

Jack laughed heartily at the oath we had taken.

"It would puzzle a lawyer," he said, "to find the way into these caves, and I am afraid we shall never get out alive."

Yet the thought was amusing to him.

The chief returned and motioned us to be seated.

Thinking it as well to be prudent we all occupied one skin, so that in case of attack we should not be divided.

Gabzenati (meaning the blue-eyed king) entered and seated himself at the end of the room opposite to us.

To our delight, his entrance was only the prelude to that of a number of girls who brought great quantities of fruits of various kinds, and a delicious drink which seemed to possess the flavor of grapes, but was of a light straw color and quite thick.

After we had eaten of the fruit, the girls took away the empty vessels, and returned with a kind of griddle cake, which was excellent eating, though tasting too much of wood-smoke.

We felt refreshed, and when the repast was finished, the king rose, made a salaam, and clapped his hands.

This was the signal for the entrance of a strangely hideous-looking creature. The head and upper part of the body was decidedly human, but from the waist down it partook more of the monkey than anything else.

To catch a glimpse of the long legs and hand-shaped feet, without seeing the upper part of the body, there would have been no hesitation in describing the creature as a gorilla, but had the lower extremities been covered, the upper part would have stamped the object as human. On the upper part of this female monstrosity, no hair was growing; but on the lower, a thick, long, and shaggy growth was manifest.

Judging from the face, the age must have been very great.

The chief was standing close to us, and whispered for our benefit:

"The Witch Mother."

"Great mother, whose wisdom hast ruled this nation for

so many years, tell me, I pray thee, are these the sons of the moon thou expected?"

This speech from the king increased our wonder, as it did also that of Benizid, who looked far from pleased.

In a harsh croak scarcely like a human voice the witch answered in the one word, "Verily."

"Is it thy will that they should be slain and offered as a sacrifice to the most great Koolokamba?" asked the king.

"Slay them not."

The old witch leaned forward, and croaked out in a miserable voice:

"In the night watches the genii of the air did come to me and say that the sons of the moon were coming to this land, and that they were to be welcome."

"Thanks, mother," said Jack, and then to me in English he added, "You see it is all right; the old woman was told we were coming."

"Then what shall be done with them?" asked Gabzenati.

"Make them chiefs of thy nation, and let them hunt out the enemies of thy land."

"Good!" assented the king.

The old woman—half woman, half monkey—hobbled out, and left us alone with our new monarch.

"Benizid said that thou wouldst fight mine enemies. Hast thou courage?"

I was never of a very egotistic or boasting temperament, so I left O'Brien to answer.

Here let me digress long enough to say that Jack—he was never by any means called John, even by the college professors—O'Brien was a typical Irishman in many respects. He had the gift of gab, and must have kissed the Blarney Stone, which

> " Whoever kisses
> Never misses
> To become eloquent,"

for he had the power to argue, and the facility to get out of scrapes which to others would have been almost an impossibility.

O'Brien thought but for a moment, and then making a most profound salaam, said:

"Most mighty king, thy servants never knew fear, neither lives there an enemy whose power is too great for them to overthrow."

"Good."

"Let thy servants but rest, and they will send thine enemies to feed the jackals."

"Be chiefs of my kingdom, and sons of Koolokamba."

I made a grimace at the last sentence so ludicrous that O'Brien nearly exploded with laughter.

I had been called the son of a sea-cook, the son of the moon; but to be called the child of a most hideous ape was an honor I did not covet.

Benizid left the room, and when he returned he was escorted by the dancing maidens.

Three rings were formed, in the center of which one of us was ordered to stand.

This was the ceremony of initiation. The girls danced around us, but that was not objectionable.

What I complained of most was the perpetual assaults to which were subjected.

The girls pulled my ears, then my nose; they caught hold of my arms and dragged in opposite directions until I feared my shoulder joints would give way. When weary with that, they seized my legs and I fell on my back with a force which I thought was fatal to my spine. One more enterprising than the rest made a dancing platform of my chest, and to the great delight of Gabzenati and Benizid, danced a jig thereon. Another imagined my head formed an excellent seat.

This torture lasted for several minutes and then I was allowed to get up. Jack had participated in the fun and made some of the girlish tormentors howl with pain, for while they were pulling his arms he kicked their shins, and when on his back and unable to use either arms or legs he inserted his teeth into the plump leg of one of his torturers, and the girl winced with agony.

Another surprise awaited us. The girl showed her bleeding leg to the king and he was delighted, and at once made O'Brien the principal chief. Medjid submitted without a murmur, and when he rose to his feet, looking dirty and his costume torn and disarranged, he wore the same placid countenance which had characterized him all the time he had been in the caves.

Having undergone this torture attendant upon initiation into the chieftainship of the Troglodytes we awaited developments, hoping that in fighting the enemies of our tribe, if not before, we should get an opportunity to escape, and continue our explorations.

CHAPTER XXIII.
THE LEGEND TOLD BY THE KING.

THE next day a calamity overtook us. We were separated. O'Brien and Medjid were compelled to go with Benizid to another part of the domain ruled over by Gabzenati, while I was kept at the royal court as a kind of aide-de-camp to his majesty.

Before we separated, we devised a series of signals in case of danger—our revolver reports would echo and re-echo through those caves, and be an excellent mode of communication. With the disadvantage of being divided in case of treachery, there was the other side to be considered. Separated we might learn more of this strange people, and perhaps get some knowledge of the treasure caves.

Gabzenati had taken a fancy to me, and as he was not half a bad fellow, we soon got very intimate.

Were I to copy my journal *in extenso*, I should only weary the reader, therefore I will condense what I discovered into as brief a limit as possible.

I really believe we were the first white men that ever penetrated that part of the Desert of Sahara for centuries.

Gabzenati treated me as an equal, and I lived quite sumptuously, seeing very little of the Witch Mother, who gave me the nightmare whenever I saw her ugly body, or Koolokamba, the sacred ape.

Our food was always brought to us by young girls. In fact, as I found out, all the work is done by the women; the young ones are the wives of the king; the old ones gather in the fruit, lay snares for the antelopes which abound, so they told me, a few miles away, plow up the little patch of land on which grow all the corn and fruit they cultivate—in fact, do all that there is to do. The men have nothing arduous to do, except fight. The laws or customs relating to women are very curious.

Every girl, as soon as she arrives at the age of fourteen, has to become the king's wife. When the monarch gets tired of them, they can become the wives of the chiefs, and after that, of the warriors. So that every woman, if she lives long enough, gets, in name, if nothing more, three husbands—first, the king; second, the chief; and lastly, one of the people. Often this is a mere form, for Gabzenati said he had been married to hundreds of wives he had never seen.

The form was gone through at the end of every three moons, the chief coming with a list of all the girls aged fourteen, and the king proclaims them his wives.

At the end of that ceremony, all who had been married to the king the preceding time were handed over to the chiefs, who did the same as regards their wives.

With this difference: the king and chiefs could retain any they pleased, so that it was possible for a woman to live her whole life with the one husband; the form of transfer had to be gone through, but the wife was not delivered.*

One of the titles of Gabzenati was "husband of a thousand wives." And he facetiously told me that as I had taken his fancy, I should soon have as many as he possessed.

I thanked him for the compliment, but told him that much of my magic power would leave me if I married.

I questioned him about his enemies, and he informed me that his greatest enemy was some evil genii who inhabited a portion of the mountain. They destroyed his fruit and killed his young goats, of which he was proud.

"Tell me all about them," I said, "or I cannot undertake to get rid of them."

With very sober countenance he told me that these genii took various forms and shapes.

"Once," said he. "I was on the mountain side when I saw a little child playing with a kid. Down came one of the genii and carried away the child; but worse than that, it came back and killed the kid."

I was of opinion that these genii were some kind of ferocious birds whose habits were not understood.

When I asked what means had been taken to kill them, he shuddered, and whispered, "That they could not be killed."

I laughed, and told him that my tube, which I carried, would kill them at any time, merely by making a noise.

He doubted me, and when I asked him to show me the place where they lived he became very nervous, and said he would have to consult the Witch Mother.

Gabzenati had a title, "Keeper of the Great Road to the Treasures," and I several times asked him its meaning.

Whenever I did so he would hesitate, walk about, and then commence to talk of something else.

I grew indifferent to it, and as much as asserted that I did not believe any one of his titles.

"Show me your thousand wifes," I said, tauntingly. "Thou canst not!"

"Some I have not seen," was his reply.

"Of course not, and therefore they do not exist. Where is thy great palace, whose walls are like the sun and stars?"

"That I can show thee, but the Witch Mother will not let me."

"I know that, for thou hast not got it, neither is there any road to the treasures."

This taunting he did not like, and so he told me this legend:

* Mela, the historian, mentions similar marriage customs prevalent in some of the tribes of Libya and the northern part of Africa.

"When the earth was young, and the country was divided into the land of cinnamon, myrrh, and elephant-eaters, fish-eaters, tortoise-eaters, and devourers of serpents, there were four great nations which had dominion over the whole land—these were the Troglodytes, the Pygmies, the Blemmyes, and Macrobii. A great king came to visit the queen who had the rule over all, because the Sacred Ape had so selected her, and the great king passed the mountains and dwell in the land of the Macrobii. He made the great road and the treasure-caves, and often great warriors came with camels and horses, and brought gold, and silver, and ivory, all sorts of sparkling stones, and pretty things, and put them in the treasure caves, so that the great king could get them when he desired. When Balkis died——"

"Who died?" I asked.

"Balkis, the queen, whose full name was Makeda Balkis. When she died her son ruled over all, and the genii of the hills, and the great god, Ataroff,* ordered the river to dry up, and the sand to cover the land, so that no one could find the treasure-caves.

"To the Troglodytes they gave the power to kill any strangers who came, and they have done it."

Gabzenati told this legend because, as I was a chieftain, I was eligible as a candidate to succeed him when he died, and I ought to know all about the duties of the king.

I told him of Amlekla, and he shuddered and said that many had tried to kill her, but could not; when I said I had met some Blemmyes he grew furious.

"Those sons of dogs who call themselves Blemmyes are impostors, they slit their noses and scar their faces, while the true Blemmye was born so. Kill them all, and thou shalt be king—that is, after me," he added, after a pause.

I thanked him for the honor, and then my mind reverted to the name of the great queen "Balkis." Where had I heard it? There was a strange, familiar sound with it. Oh, if O'Brien was here, he could tell me at once, for his memory for names was perfection. Balkis! I pondered over it until night came, and then I fell asleep, still thinking of that name. The air was close and sultry, and one of the king's handmaidens fanned me until slumber took my brain and body captive.

Then I "dreamed a dream," one like those which I had thought peculiar to O'Brien.

In my dream I was transported to a land where grew the stately palm; beautiful walks amid beds of flowers and trees laden with fruit seemed to wind in every direction.

* Did Gabzenati refer to Ashtoreth, the false god, after whom Solomon went?—ED.

In the center of the garden a beautiful fountain of pure water greeted the eyes of the weary traveler. I was powerless to stop. Something seemed to ever draw me magnetically forward. A cloudy figure, without shape or outline of form, was ever before me.

I reached a monument and there found an entrance into a dark and gloomy passage. At the end of which I saw a vision of splendor which far surpassed any imaginings I had ever had.

Ranged round the chamber into which I was ushered I saw bars of silver, more in number than the mind could even estimate. Their dazzling whiteness shone as the moon's rays on the grateful earth.

I felt an inclination to stop but was drawn forward still further, until I reached a room composed of diamonds all cut and polished; resplendent in their beauty. I was about to fill my pockets with them, when I thought their brightness vanished, and the chamber was dark. I looked round for a way by which to return, but on every hand nothing but a solid dark wall met my touch. I was confused and sad.

All my dream had been but an imagination, and instead of wealth I had found a prison, where, cut off from food and air, I must die.

In the agony of my soul I cried aloud for help, when I thought I felt a warm hand touch my shoulder. I looked up and saw a face.

It was that of Nyassa.

I wanted to clasp her form in my arms, but it eluded me. I followed, and as it glided further from the arms outstretched, I hurried after it.

Once more the face was turned to me. It was the superbly lovely face of Nyassa. She had saved me; for no sooner had I emerged from the passage and found myself in the garden, than the figure and face disappeared, and I saw it no more.

I awoke, to find myself on the couch of skins in Gabzenati's chamber, and the dark girl still fanning me.

I had made one discovery: Nyassa's name was Balkis. Could it be that Nyassa was descended from the race of royalty established by Makeda Balkis, the Queen of Sheba, who became one of King Solomon's seven hundred wives, and whose son Menihelek founded the dynasty which ruled over Ethiopia for so many centuries?

Nyassa was the daughter of a kingly house, and her ancestors had reigned for centuries. No wonder she was so beautiful, if she was a descendant of that queen whose fair form and lovely face captivated the wise and wealthy king!

I wanted O'Brien, for he might be able to interpret my dream. As it was, I failed to read it, and the only conclusion I could come to was, that the search for Solomon's treasures would lead to a dungeon.

What if it did? If my dream was true and I was rescued by Nyassa, if in the future I could fold her in my arms as my own, what terrors were there in dungeon-vaults, or even torture? I could bear all for her sake. And an eternity of torture would I endure but to call her my own for a brief space! The more I thought of Nyassa the more madly did I love her. My constant prayer was that we might meet again, nevermore to part!

CHAPTER XXIV.
"HAIL! KING THAT IS TO BE."

I WEARIED of my close confinement and loneliness. No news had been conveyed to me of O'Brien or Medjid, so I could only hope that the old saying was true, and no news prove to be good news.

Even Gabzenati had not spent much time with me for several days. I had tried to find a way out, and to accomplish such an object had made friends with some of the girls, complimented them on their beauty, admired their form and figure, and even offered bribes to accomplish my object.

But not one would show me the way out of the caves.

All said, and the excuse came very readily, that I must either ask the king or the old women, for they were too young to be allowed out of the caves.

Unfortunately I never saw any old women, so my chance of obtaining knowledge was but a frail one.

Each passage I traversed appeared to end in a dead wall, the caves leading off the corridors were so much alike that to have experimented with each of them would have taken a very long time.

Food was brought to me regularly, and I had every facility for bathing.

As for company, I had four of the king's wives allotted to me. I believe the monarch had transferred them to me as my share of the thousand wives, but I never troubled myself to inquire whether I was a benedict or not.

There was one girl who seemed to know more than the others, and was specially devoted to me.

She would often come when I was alone and tell me as much as she knew.

The outside world she had never seen, but it had been told her that the way out was through the caves occupied by Koolokamba, and the Witch Mother.

I could never get Shagaffa—for that was the name of the young girl—to converse much about the Witch Mother.

Whenever the old hag was mentioned the girls would shrink away and shudder as though something dreadful would happen even at the very mention of her.

Shagaffa told me that the Witch Mother had lived for many years and that the king had heard his grandfather speak of her as being then an old woman.

As for Koolokamba, he was an object of adoration and worship; so infatuated were these girls with their pagan devotions that they envied the three attendants on the ape.

Horrible as it may be to contemplate, it was a fact that the three ostrich feather covered girls never left the ape night or day, but shared its room and joined the horrible thing in its food.*

But as Koolokamba was sacred, it became an object of ambition to become one of the attendants, and Shagaffa asked me, when I became tired of her, would I ask the king to transfer her to the ape. I expressed my astonishment at the request, but she held it as a part of her religion, that they who assisted to entertain the Sacred Ape, would receive the greatest happiness on earth, and when they died they would become genii and enjoy great power. Gabzenati entered the room and asked me if I would like to go to the place where his great enemy could be found.

It need not be wondered at that I was eager for the chance, neither could I be blamed for feeling jubilant.

I had got my two rifles loaded and my revolvers were each good for seven shots, and with four weapons of so deadly a nature, I felt prepared to meet quite a formidable enemy.

The king had frequently asked me about the guns, but I had evaded a reply. I could see that he was entirely ignorant of their use.

We started on our journey, and proceeded through the king's private cave, and then into that occupied by the Witch Mother, who looked more horrible than ever, especially as she shook her long finger at the king and croaked out:

"Beware! I have warned thee!"

Gabzenati laughed, but went on through a long passage and into another cave, which I found was the residence of the ape.

The girls were with him, and looked unspeakably happy.

---

* Travelers have found, in Equatorial Africa, several instances of the Nschigombouvie Ape living with the natives and recognized as part of the family.

Another passage was traversed and some steps ascended before we found ourselves in the open air.

I looked round and opened my mouth to inhale some of the life-giving atmosphere.

We were very nearly on the summit of one of the twin mountains.

The sight was an entrancing one, and never before had so much natural beauty been spread out before me. The mountain side was even more charming and brilliant when viewed from its summit than it had appeared from the desert.

I pointed to the other hill and asked the king if it also was inhabited.

For a time he hesitated, and then told me that a portion of it was the dwelling-place of some of his people, but that it was very unsafe, as often the gods would send out from its top fire and smoke and kill all who had rebelled against the Witch Mother or the Sacred Ape.

Gabzenati pointed out in the distance the sacred monument of Ammon.

The name brought back to me the story of Solomon's idolatry, for had not the great king gone after "Astoreth, the goddess of the Zidonians, Chemosh, the god of the Moabites, and Mileom, the god of the children of Ammon?"

The monument stood on what used to be an island formed by two rivers, long since dried up. I let the king talk all he wanted, for this was a confirmation of our map, and when we were able to effect our escape, what joy it would be for me to show O'Brien the exact place where the island of Mer was really located.

"Behold, mighty chief and great king," I said, "and tell me what is that?"

Gabzenati looked in the direction and trembled violently as soon as his eyes rested on a strange-looking creature at about five hundred yards away. I am not easily frightened, but a tremor did pass over me as I saw this object. At the distance it looked like an immense bat, with the head of a monkey. Its wings must have been several feet across, and even more than a quarter of a mile away it looked a dangerous enemy.

"It is the devil," was the meaning of Gabzenati's remark.

When I could get him to talk about it, I learned that the creature we saw was one of the enemies so feared by the Troglodytes.

"Shall I kill it?" I asked.

"Man that is born of woman could never do it," was the reply.

"But I think I can."

KING SOLOMON'S TREASURES. 127

"Thou canst not get near enough."

"I can kill it from here, by merely making a big noise."

I had spoken in an ordinary tone, but the air was so rarefied that every word seemed like a shout.

The creature flapped its huge wings and laughed so long and heartily that I confess I thought for the moment that it was some demon of the air, and beyond the power of my rifle to destroy.

The laugh resembled that of the hyena, and sounded harsh and discordant.

"It hears thy boast, my chief, let us return."

"Nay, I will slay it."

Again the laugh sounded out on the air.

"Is it possible," I said, "that the monster knows of what we are talking?"

"Yes. If we were near enough for me to throw my spear, you would soon see whether it understood. Even now, see——"

Gabzenati raised his spear as in the act of throwing.

The bird or beast or devil, rose to its full height, flapped its wings and laughed defiantly, setting again in its old manner conscious that no spear could reach it.

"Come away," said Gabzenati, seizing my arm, "or we shall be killed."

I laughed, and unslung my Winchester which was sighted up to a thousand yards.

The king watched my every movement, and trembled violently as I took aim.

The strange creature rose, and showed its defiance again, but a puff of smoke and a report startled the king, and I pointed to the dead body of the bird, or fiend, as it fell from crag to crag down the side of the hill.

"Now I know, of a truth, that thou art the son of the moon," exclaimed the king, as he dragged me by the arm and pulled me into the passage.

He lost no time in reaching his own apartments, never once stopping to salute the Ape or the Witch Mother.

"Go!" he commanded. "I would be alone."

I left his presence, and got back to my own cave, wondering at the change that had come over the king.

Shagaffa was waiting for me. She had some delicacies of food prepared on which she prided herself.

She was a dear, good, faithful girl, though her color was very black, and her ambition so outrageous.

I did full justice to the food, I had got to like Shagaffa's cooking, and she danced about with joy as I commended her.

She was possessed of a fair share of feminine curiosity, and, therefore, when I had finished my dinner and she was eating, for Shagaffa would never attempt to touch food until my inner man was satisfied, she asked where I had been.

I told her all my adventures, and when I repeated the story of the slaying of the strange creature, she looked at me with eyes staring, and then fell on her face and seized hold of my feet.

"None but a god could have done it," she cried again and again.

I lifted her to her feet and laughed at her for her simplicity. I told her all the men where I came from were as powerful. This she would not admit, for it could not be so, she said, or there would be no enemies of my people allowed to live.

I saw no more of Gabzenati until midnight, when I was roused from my sleep to be told that I was to be the next king of the Troglodytes, the Witch Mother and the Sacred Ape had so declared their wish.

I thought the king was sorrowful, but he answered not when I asked concerning his gloom.

When he had retired, Shagaffa came to me, and in her way congratulated me.

I asked if she had noticed the king's sorrow, and she replied that the king was young and did not wish for death.

I failed to comprehend her meaning until by dint of further questioning, she told me that whenever the Witch Mother and ape announced a successor, the reigning monarch always died within a month.

Although Shagaffa would not admit it, I shrewdly suspected that the one king was quietly killed to make way for the new *regime*.

"Shagaffa," I said, "do you know what a secret is?"

"Yes, my lord."

"What is it?" I asked.

"What you tell me, which torture could not find again in my body.

It was a quaint answer, but I could easily see that the girl knew what a secret really meant.

"Could you keep a secret?"

"Yes, my lord."

"And never tell it?"

"The Witch Mother would have to cut me into little bits before I would mention it?"

"Then listen, Shagaffa, I shall not be king."

"Not king?"

"Hush! we may be heard. I shall escape from here as soon as I can, and Gabzenati will remain king."

"My lord, may I ask thee a favor?"

"What is it?"

"Let thy Shagaffa go with thee."

"Nay, thou wouldst never endure the dangers, but thou canst help me."

"How?"

"Thou canst find out the road, and may hear where my friends are."

"That will I, but let thy Shagaffa go with thee."

"We will see."

With that poor consolation the girl had to be content. She was devoted and good, it was possible she might be useful as a servant, but I did not want her, for I am sure I could never fall into the custom of the country and allow a woman to do all the work. Shagaffa was very active all the next day, and moved about with a lightness of heart which was new to her.

CHAPTER XXV.

ADIEU TO KINGSHIP!

WHEN the day had passed, though day and night were the same in the caves of the Troglodytes, there was a commotion discernible among the dwellers.

The lamps were lighted and extra torches prepared.

I had been kept in solitary confinement all day, inasmuch as no one came near me. My attendants, even, had taken a holiday, all except Shagaffa, who was never far away, but was as silent as a mute.

I found that she had sent the three attendants, or wives, away, for she saw I treated all with the same indifference, and representing to them that I had chosen her for my favorite, and that I desired their absence for a few days, she thought I should surrender to her winning ways and tender devotion. It was a feminine strategy which would have been a credit to a society lady.

Shagaffa learned that a great council of the tribe was to take place in the chamber into which I had been ushered on the first day of our captivity.

Her information was correct, and I soon received orders to accompany the king.

Gabzenati looked very sorrowful as he walked beside me.

"Thou wilt be king many years," I said.

"Nay, it is written."

"What is?"

"Knowest thou not that a king always dies when his successor is appointed?"

"I know it, but——"

"Well, thou art my successor."

"If I died, what then?"

"The Troglodytes would lose their kingdom, for thou art mighty."

I saw it was no use talking to him, so let him be miserable in his own way, thinking I would get a chance within a few hours of leaving him in full possession of his kingly power.

We reached the council chamber, and to my great joy saw O'Brien and Medjid as happy and hearty as ever. Even Medjid was looking more cheerful. I joked O'Brien on appearing so happy.

"Why, Monty," he said, "I am as jolly as a sand-boy, and who would't be? I'm a chief! Just think of that! Jack O'Brien chief of the great and noble Troglodytes, etc., etc.," and Jack laughed at the thought. "And, beside, I have ten wives; how many have you?"

"Not any."

"Fie! fie! what a fib."

"It is true, Jack; but surely you have not espoused the ten."

"Monty, my boy, I am a philosopher. I accept the conditions of society as I find them, and I am not hypocritical enough to say I don't like the girls when I am fond of their society."

"Yes; but you are not going to stay here."

"Thank you; that is good news. I thought I should be compelled to stay for a long time. I have never seen outside."

"But I have."

"How did you manage it?"

"Ah, that is the question; but stay, I must not talk too much, the king is returning, and it would be beneath my dignity to be talking to an ordinary chief."

Jack stared at me as though he thought I had taken leave of my senses.

"What do you mean?"

"If you are a chief, I am soon to be your king."

O'Brien laughed heartily, and old Benizid, who understood the last sentence, joined in the merriment. The warriors had all taken their places, and the girls had trooped in with their bangles and beads. The Sacred Ape was seated on the throne of silver and ivory, his three attendants looking as cheerful as any girls I had seen among the Troglodytes. When Gabzenati made a low salaam to the ape, who answered at once with his usual word:

"Koolo."

Then the king stood up and faced the warriors, and said:

"I am Gabzenati, thy king."

"Thou art," responded Benizid.

"Answer me most truthfully, oh, most great and noble Troglodytes, whose power is from the commencement of the world, and to whom has been given the great master of all, Koolokamba, and the treasures of the great caves. Answer me. Have I kept the great road?"

"Thou hast."

"Has the stranger lived that crossed the mountains?"

"No! no!"

"Have I led our warriors in war and triumphed over the enemies?"

"Thou hast."

"Now listen, brave warriors! There is one enemy which has taken our children and eaten them or cast them down the rocks, which has destroyed our kids and broken our vines. Say, have I killed it?"

"No, Great Gabzenati," answered Benizid; "for man born of woman could not do it."

"Now hark, ye warriors! I swore I would fulfil the conditions of my kingship. I would marry the marriageable maidens, I would give them afterwards to the chiefs, I would fight and conquer thy enemies, but although I have done all I could, the one enemy I could not kill."

"Because," said another chief, "the enemy is a bogie (evil spirit), and our spears would not avail us."

"Brave warriors and mighty chiefs! I, Gabzenati, declare unto ye that your great enemy is dead, that the demon of the air, the bogie of the mountain, the evil genii will never torment ye more. Its body lies at the foot of the mountain, and your befriender who slew this great demon, did it by the powerful magic of a noise when it was three stone throws' away, and he should be king."

"He should!" answered Benizid.

"Gabzenati took me by the hand, placed me in front of the ape and said:

"Behold your king, for he it was who slew with a breath and a great noise, the demon of the mountain. Therefore be it known, that all dwellers in the caverns of the Troglodytes do meet here when the sun has gone its round and swear allegiance to your new king. It is the will of Koolokamba and the Witch Mother."

The warriors looked at each other, and then raised their spears as a signal of submission to the will expressed by the king and then the frolic and dance commenced.

O'Brien came over and stood by m , his face full of wonderment and surprise.

Never was greater curiosity shown by a man than that he evinced as he questioned me concerning the great event which led to my proclamation as king.

When the dance was over and the procession re-formed,

I kept O'Brien and Medjid with me, and took them to my own cave.

After a bountiful repast, which Shagaffa had provided, we conversed on our experiences since we had been parted.

O'Brien and Medjid had been chiefs under Benizid, and had not been allowed any freedom.

They had each received ten wives, and in the midst of so much domestic happiness they spent their time waiting an opportunity for a reunion and escape.

"Well, Jack, are you going to stay with your ten wives or go with me?"

"Can you ask?"

"But think of their wretchedness and loneliness," I suggested.

"Loneliness be hanged! Show me a chance to escape and I will not be here another day, no, not even an hour."

"What says Medjid?" I asked.

"Baas, I am with you."

"Then I will keep my eyes open, and the very first chance we will make a dash for liberty."

"We must keep together," said O'Brien.

"Yes, and don't sleep too heartily, for I may start at any time. Jack—I've some more news. I know the way to Mer."

"You do?"

"Yes, and what do you think? You have not forgotten Nyassa?"

"Forgotten Nyassa! Ask me if I have forgotten that the sun shines and gives heat and light; ask me if I remember that I am a man breathing the breath of life—ask me anything but that, for never till the sun and stars, the moon and this earth shall be consumed, not until ten thousand times a million years have passed shall I forget her, who will never be mine, but is my heart's treasure though others may win her," Jack exclaimed in answer to my simple question.

"What about your ten wives—soon to be grass widows?" I asked.

A shade of disgust passed over his face as I spoke and he made no reply.

Seeing his silence I continued:

"What if I told you that Nyassa was descended from the Queen of Sheba, who visited Solomon?"

"Nothing!" answered Jack. "If you told me she was descended from Venus, it would not surprise me, for she is beauty and wisdom, grace and perfection all united in one body."

Shagaffa, acting under my instructions, had filled my

haversack with good food, providing plenty of biltong, and some excellent cakes which she had baked. O'Brien and Medjid also got a good supply, and our water bottles were filled.

Two hours later we were stealing stealthily along a passage which had been described by Shagaffa; and after a journey which occupied over an hour we emerged from the cave.

We were at the end of the hill, whereas we had thought our entrance was in the center.

The clear air was overpowering after breathing the close atmosphere of the caverns for so long.

We sat down to rest, determined to risk even capture for the sake of our poor feet already so weary with the hard walking in the caves.

We sat silent for half an hour when we unmistakably heard the sound of footsteps.

There seemed to be more than one.

"Listen, Jack!" I said, softly. "We are pursued."

"We will give game," was the answer.

The footsteps ceased, and we were wondering whether it was a trap for us, or that finding no trail the warriors had returned, when a hand was placed softly on my head.

The light of the early morning was yet dim and too misty to distinguish the outline of the person who had thus appropriated me.

I put my hand on my revolver, and asked, "Who art thou?"

"Knowest thou not Shagaffa?"

"What art thou doing here?" I asked, almost angrily.

"Be not wroth with thy Shagaffa, she brought thee food."

"But thou wilt be followed."

"Not so! For thy servant did order that none should follow the king that is to be, who had gone to the grove of the great temple to pray."

I had not given Shagaffa credit for so much strategy. The grove of the great temple was in an opposite direction to the route we had taken, though the start was the same.

When the light grew stronger we found that Shagaffa had brought as much food as we had all previously possessed, and as she felt no fatigue from the burden, we were selfish enough to let her go with us.

Although the ruin of the monument of Ammon was plainly visible from the top of the hill, we could not distinguish it from the level of the desert.

However, as I knew the direction, we started full of hope, and with plenty of food to last for three weeks if we so desired.

I was afraid we should be seen by the Troglodytes, but Shagaffa reassured us by saying that the habits of the tribe would prevent them reaching that side of the hill until several hours later, when we should be far away and out of the range of their vision.

Shagaffa proved to be of great value to us, and what at first seemed an incumbrance, was in reality a blessing.

The days passed without adventure, the nights followed each other in the same monotonous way. Our lives for nine days were peaceful and calm. The only living things on that desert within many miles' radius, we were cheerful because animated by hope; we had something to live for, our lives would not be lived in vain if we did but discover these vast treasure fields.

On the night of the tenth day we were in sight of some ruins, and we felt that Mer was reached, but we were so entirely exhausted that even if all the treasures of Solomon and the Queen of Sheba were within reach of our hands, we should not stretch out our hands or exert ourselves to take possession of the wealth.

I had never felt so weary before; it was something unnatural and abnormal, and I should have fancied myself stricken with some disease had it not been that O'Brien and Medjid experienced the same feelings. I looked round for Shagaffa, and found her fast asleep. So we camped for the night.

CHAPTER XXVI.
AMMON CHNOUPHIS.

THE sun was shining with noonday splendor before we reached Mer. It was easy, as we approached, to see the routes which had been taken by the rivers in times long gone by.

Mer was a pleasant oasis, and several palm trees, though of very stunted growth, still stood there.

We found a very pleasant lake, small in size, but having a very strange peculiarity. On its banks were a number of large stones, on which were engraved characters similar to what I had seen on the Ogham Stone, and some were of as recent character as the Moabite Stone.

One inscription we were able to translate, and it told us the name of the lake, and mentioned its peculiarity. We understood it to mean that we were at the Lake of the Sun, and that its water was coldest at noonday and warmest at midnight *

* Cambyses found a well having the same peculiarity in the oasis of Siwah, in the Libyan desert, over which the Emperor Justinian built a Christian church.

We eat some of our biltong and drank some of the water of the lake, which was of icy coldness, before we continued our explorations.

Our hearts beat rapidly and our faces flushed as we stood upon this wonderful land.

By that lake, perhaps, Solomon had penned some of those love songs which still hold a place in the sacred writings of the Christians. There may have sat that lovely Queen of Sheba, who traveled so many miles to learn from Solomon's own lips the words of wisdom for which he was so famed, and under the spreading branches of the palm Solomon and the queen may have walked and talked of love when the great king visited the land of Sheba.

We saw the ruins of the statue of Ammon Chnouphis, the type and symbol of the Divine Originative Principle.

Although the magnificent piece of work had become injured by lapse of time and the drifting of the sand through so many generations, yet sufficient remained to show that the figure originally was represented sitting on a throne, holding the symbols of life and power, and wearing a crown with a peculiar ornament of feathers, and a band falling behind and hanging down to his feet.

On the gigantic throne were hieroglyphics signifying the Ethiopian name of the deity Amun.*

Scattered round were blocks of stone carved with various characters and hieroglyphics, all of which would prove highly interesting if we could but spare time for translating.

We felt elated at our discovery, feeling confident that no white man had trod that hallowed ground for centuries; but Jack's face was clouded, for he had dreamed of a different monument, and the face we had seen in our drawings found in the old escritoire was entirely at variance with what we had found.

"Cheer up, Jack," I said, "for we have some long distance to go yet before we have exhausted our two maps."

"That is so, but I was positive the entrance was here."

When the day waned I felt restless and could not sleep. Shagaffa was in the land of dreams; Medjid gave evidence of heavy slumber, his snores waking the echoes round; and O'Brien, with a calm, sweet smile on his manly face, seemed enjoying the refreshing virtues of sleep. I alone could not settle myself to slumber, so I left the party, and strolled about among the ruins.

I came across a smaller statue, which seemed perfect in

---

* In Ethiopian and Egyptian mythology Amun signifies the hidden, unrevealed deity. After the 18th dynasty we have a character given to the deity by adding RA, the name of the Sun God, to Amun.

its proportions, and had a face resembling one which seemed to me very familiar.

I gazed at it with rapt emotion, and dreamed—— But was it a dream? I will not say. Jack assured me that it was a reality, and no phantom of the brain.

I record it as it occurred to me, and leave each reader to place upon it his own interpretation.

I was so absorbed in the contemplation of the statue that I scarcely noticed anything but the piece of stone upon which the moon's rays were falling.

I thought I heard a sigh, and looking up, saw a man standing with arms crossed over his breast, looking straight at me. I experienced great amazement at the sight, for the man was not like the Troglodytes, but more like an Egyptian, or it may be a Hebrew.

His form was draped in massive folds of clear white linen, which, instead of detracting from, added to the statuesque appearance of the figure, making it look like a bronze statue habited in shining silver.

The figure was majestic in its calm serenity, yet there was a lithe, supple grace about it which was pleasing to the artistic eye.

Knowing I was in a land where every man's hand would be against me, I put my hand to my belt for my revolver. The draped figure gave me such a glance of contempt that I withdrew my hand, feeling my littleness, and I lowered my eyes, feeling abashed at the tranquil scorn so manifest on the face of my *vis-a-vis*.

I was mortified to think of my action, for had the man been an enemy he had received every opportunity, for I had not noticed him, perhaps, for long after he had been there.

Raising his right arm, the stranger looked at me and asked:

"What doest thou here?"

What answer could I make to this question?

Before I could frame a reply, he continued:

"Thou seekest to fathom the secrets of the past, and to snatch treasures from the hand of death."

"And why should the knowledge of the past be hid from the present?" I asked.

"Think and thou wilt get thy answer. Let the dead bury its dead. Each generation should live for and in itself."

"But knowledge is eternal. It can never die, but once obtained must live through the ages."

"Then thou dost contradict thyself, for thou stated thy search was for the knowledge which was lost. Knowledge, as thou sayest, is eternal, but does that follow that mortals should possess it?"

KING SOLOMON'S TREASURES. 137

"If not mortals, who then?"

"The knowledge and wisdom of the past belong to the immortals."

Who was this, that on the desert could converse and argue on such a subject? My wonder increased, as he continued:

"Dost thou believe that the dust which lies here could become living men and women again?"

"No, for after so long a slumber, after the body has been dissolved into the water and gases of which it is composed, how is it possible it should retain its life and power?"

"Thou talkest well, but like all the Moderns, thinkest the body is the man. I tell thee that those who once peopled this island and worshiped before yonder statue had the power to lay down their bodies and watch them decay, and out of the dust form a new clothing and beautified body."

"Impossible."

"Sayest thou so, and yet thou canst take a grain of corn from the tomb to-day, a grain which was cut by the Ithiopjawan before the Pharaohs ruled Egypt, and throw it in the furrow, thou canst know of its decay, but from that decay the new and more useful corn will grow. So it is with force, which is immortal, and being immortal is also all-powerful."

"Then," I said, "thou wouldst reason that there is no death?"

"What meanest thou by death? If it signifies destruction it exists not. The first germ exists to-day as it did when it was evolved from the Great First Cause. Never has anything been destroyed, but if thou meanest does thy body die and be resurrected in the corn or the trees, or impregnate the air with its gases, then there is a death, but that is not the man. Every man who has ever lived, lives still, and because thou canst not find the body of our great Queen Makeda thou declarest she is dead."

I confess I was surprised and amazed to hear this stranger speak of the once powerful Queen of Sheba; why was I ever to hear of her?

"Is she not dead?" I asked, noticing his continued silence.

"Listen. What said the great Ammon, on this very spot?" The quaint figure stooped and picked up a piece of stone covered with hieroglyphics, and after looking a moment, read:

"'I, Ammon, originated all things. Mine is the world from whence all things emanated, and to which all things return. There is no death, no destruction. I have willed it, and that which is the man shall inhabit the world until the final day.'"

"Is that the meaning of the hieroglyphics?" I asked.

"It is the decree of Ammon," was his answer, and then again facing me he said: "Thou seekest the treasure-caves; by what right wouldst thou rob the living?"

"I have no desire to rob the living," I answered.

"But thou wouldst take the treasures placed here by Makeda."

"How knowest thou my object and my thought?" I asked, feeling perplexed.

"It is given for me to know. Beware how thou disturbest the treasures placed in the tomb."

"And what if it be true? Have I not the right to search for these caves wherein lies hid the wealth of the past ages?"

Instead of answering, he asked me a question.

"Had not the hiders a right to conceal their own?"

"Admitted, but we have also the right to distribute this vast wealth for the world's benefit."

A sardonic smile passed over the man's features as I uttered the last sentence.

"That is the cry everywhere. Wealth! wealth! wealth! Not for ourselves, oh, no, but for others. We seek it to benefit the world; we hunt for it that others may have the advantage. Our generosity is proverbial. But from the time of the first man, wealth has been sought for under the same pretext and excuse, but when obtained the good intentions have been forgotten and the most generous man has become the meanest miser, while the miser has become generous though he made no promises of a liberal hand."

"It pleases thy philosophy to be sarcastic," I said.

"Have I not reason for it? What crime is there, what villainy, name me an outrage which has not been committed for the sake of gold. It has been the bane of the world; religion has been prostituted, justice perverted and men corrupted, for gold; for it, women have sold their honor, and parents sacrificed their children. To obtain it, wars have deluged the valleys with blood and innocent men have fed the jackals and vultures that others might have gold. Even what you have been pleased to call civilization has been founded on the greed for gold. The white man sends his missionaries, but he also sends his traders who steal the land and the wealth from the poor natives. Nay, what better are ye than robbers? Ye come here to seek for treasures to which ye have no right, and if they who have been in possession of them for ages should oppose ye, ye would drain their hearts' blood. Ay, I know, it is gold! gold! gold! Find it, but beware!"

I had stood spellbound during this long speech; its truth I was compelled in a great measure to admit, and I felt unable to answer.

If I had been ready of speech, it would have been of but little use, for when I raised my eyes, I was alone.

I searched round for the strange philosopher, but not a sign of living creature could be seen.

O'Brien and Medjid were sleeping soundly, and Shagaffa was also in a calm and gentle sleep.

I felt alarmed and wanted company. My head felt as if it would burst, and a strange nervousness took possession of me.

I roused O'Brien, and when he sat up and looked at me and saw my bewilderment, I regretted my hastiness. I told him my dream or vision, for the absence of any footprints, and the entire disappearance of the strange being, proved to me that I was suffering from mental hallucination, or that I had seen a vision.

Jack was positive I had been in conversation with the supernatural and regretted he had not been with me.

CHAPTER XXVII.
THE TEMPLE OF THE RHINOCEROS.

My interview with my nocturnal visitant had left a depressing effect on my mind which I could not shake off, however much I tried.

O'Brien was jubilant, for to him it had proved the correctness of his views from the first.

The treasures of Solomon were really hidden near by, and it would be our own fault if we did not obtain them, and on our return to England we should be extremely wealthy.

Medjid had relapsed into this state of taciturnity which had characterized him so much recently.

When I questioned him, he evaded all answer for a time, and then told me that he should never return alive.

He believed in the prophecy of an old witch who had told him that he would never die until he had seen a nation ruled by a monkey.

"Baas, I have seen it," he said, and his voice was low and sorrowful.

"That is true, Medjid, but the wise woman did not say thou shouldst die as soon as thou hadst seen this strange sight. It may be many years before death comes."

O'Brien laughed at Medjid, and by his jests and teasings showed that as the Nubian had not died before he had seen the monkey ruled nation, he must necessarily die after. Shagaffa was the most obedient and willing girl I had ever seen, and I wished many times she would transfer her affection to Medjid, who was really fond of her. If she would do so, and settle in Nubia, where she would be free from all risk of slavery, I thought they would make a happy couple. Unfortunately, she considered herself my wife, though I had in no way given her cause to consider herself such. I could, of course, give her to the Nubian, who would be glad to receive her; but it would do violence to her feelings, and, though she would accept her fate with resignation, I did not like to force her to a union perhaps repugnant to her.

We searched amid the ruins for a long time before we discovered any entrance to the caves.

O'Brien led the way, and we followed, thinking it best not to divide our party. When we got some little distance away from the ruins we found some tall, thick grass, through which walking was very difficult. Jack turned round to speak to me, and in the midst of a sentence he disappeared.

"Monty, help!"

We hurried forward, and found that he had fallen down a steep bank or precipice. Being far from desirous of sharing the same fate, we skirted the pit until we found a far easier and more pleasant way to enter.

Fortunately Jack was only shaken; no bones were broken, and he laughed heartily at his mishap, more especially as he saw before him the entrance to a cave.

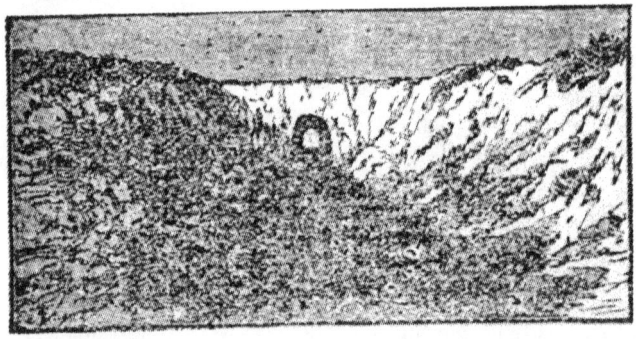

The entrance was arched, and bore evidence of being the work of man.

Leading up to it, though now overgrown with shrubs and brush, could be seen the formation of a well-made road.

"Eureka!" I cried, as soon as I saw it, and found that

O'Brien was not injured. Although we had discovered the caves, our hearts pulsated rapidly, the emotion caused by our success almost overpowering us.

Who should enter first? Should we all proceed together? What action should we pursue? These and many more questions presented themselves to our mind as we looked at that dark archway. After considerable argument and discussion, we agreed that, as all had an equal interest in the treasures, we would proceed together, marking well our route, so that, in case of obstruction, we could return easily to our starting-point.

After partaking of some food, we held our breath through excitement, and plunged into the darkness.

The cave, or, more accurately speaking, the tunnel, was cut out of the solid rock, and presented an appearance of great engineering skill in its execution.

The roadway was as smooth and even as if it were composed of polished marble.

For about a hundred yards we had to trust to our instinct to guide us, for the road was dark; but a faint scintillation of light in the distance encouraged us to proceed.

Our voices echoed through the tunnel so weirdly that we became too startled at the sound to speak.

After we had proceeded nearly a hundred yards, the way became lighter and the air purer. We found airshafts had been cut, but the tops were so carefully concealed that the man who discovered them would require to be a most diligent seeker.

Another minute passed, and we reached an immense cavern, the most wonderful ever beheld by man.

It was as lofty as the dome of St. Peters at Rome, a fact which convinced me that we had been going down hill all the time we had been underground. I had stood in the glorious Pantheon at Rome, devised by Agrippa as a pagan temple, and had noticed the beautiful effect produced by the solid windowless walls, the only light coming through the opening in the roof. I was reminded of this as we stood in the immense cave, for the effect was the same. A large air-shaft in the center of the domed roof admitted light and air, and gave the place the appearance of a gigantic temple.

The roof was supported by several rows of columns cut out of the solid stone, and polished until their surface shone like bright metal. On some, inscriptions were carved, and the history of a by-gone civilization told•in hieroglyphics.

The place had a deserted appearance, and it was probable that we were the first to enter within its walls for hundreds of years.

Rude attempts at carving on separate blocks of stone lay scattered about, and images of monkeys, peacocks, and other animals stood leaning against the walls.

No sign of any treasures could be found, and so impatient were we in our desire for the wealth, that the beauties of the place were wasted on us.

Yet, its very vastness was awe-inspiring. Never had I beheld cathedral with so vast an area. No other building, unless the Coliseum at Rome, could I recall which in any degree approached it in size.

Medjid rambled about, quite as interested as we were.

"Baas! the devil!" he shouted, presently. We hurried to where he stood transfixed with fright, and beheld a huge monster glaring at us with fiery fury in its eye.

We started back, equally frightened with Medjid, and expected to hear the tramp of its great feet, but it moved not.

Its stillness gave us courage to approach nearer—at least O'Brien and I got our rifles in position and stepped forward to see what horrible monster barred our way.

As we got nearer the eyes grew brighter, and I was ready to affirm that they followed me whichever way I turned. We were within twenty feet of the monster before we saw that it was merely an excellent sculptured representation of the head of the Black Rhinoceros.

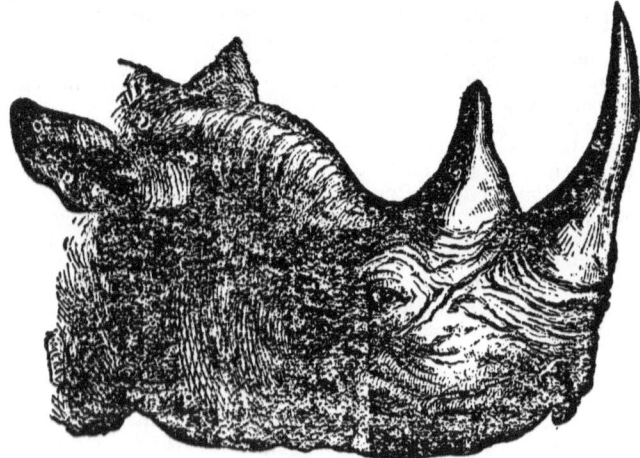

SCULPTURED HEAD OF RHINOCEROS.

I had been told by Gabzenati that there used to be a tribe of Troglodytes which worshiped the rhinoceros, but that for many generations the animals and men had been alike extinct.*

The head we saw in front of us had two horns, and was of the kind which was noted for its vicious nature.

On close examination we found the head to have been made of a kind of black porphyry, the eyes being colored glass, and the horns ivory. On a slab beneath it was an inscription which evidently intimated that the brute was an object of worship.

Never was exhibited to the eyes of man so perfect a specimen of the sculptor's art, and I could not help recalling the old story of the painter who blended his colors so well that when a bunch of cherries was portrayed on his canvass the birds came and pecked at them.

Had I not known the difficulty of killing a rhinoceros I certainly should have fired at the stone head. We had all been deceived by its appearance.

The exit from the great Temple of the Rhinoceros was at the rear of the gigantic head, and as we passed round the piece of statuary our nerves were so unstrung that, I really believe, we all shuddered and half expected to see the eyes turn round to watch our retreating forms.

We were again in a dark and narrow passage, guided only in our march by the speck of light in the distance, which grew larger every step we made. Shagaffa impeded my progress somewhat by insisting on clinging to my arm. She constituted a great difficulty, for I knew it would mean her death if she went back to the Troglodytes; and while she was with us, there were times when her feminine fears were a direct obstruction.

O'Brien seemed so elated that, as he himself expressed it, he thought he was walking on air most of the time.

At the end of the passage we found ourselves in the open air, on the oasis and in sight of the ruins of Ammon's temple. We could not refrain from laughing.

The situation was ludicrous; we had gone through two long tunnels and had visited the Cave of the Sacred Rhinoceros, but no treasures had we found.

Evidently Mer was only the commencement of the great road, and that the caves in which the great wealth of Solomon and Sheba's queen was hid, would be on the road between Mer and the mountains we had seen marked on our second map.

For nearly three weeks we rambled about amid the ruins of the ancient island, but our search was fruitless.

We filled our water bottles and again started on that dreary march which our map declared to be fifty leagues in length.

* See "Schonberg's Equatorial Africa."

tives. She told him we were on a pilgrimage to sacrifice
to our gods; that we were hunting the enemies of the great
and beautiful Troglodytes, and various other things as she
afterward told us, to all of which the old chief had but
one answer. We must first accept his hospitality. Shagaffa said we were possessed of magic power, and that with
a great noise we could kill his enemies.

THE THIEVING CHIEF.

No sooner had she given utterance to this idea than the
chief raised a terrific whoop, and a great crowd of fellows
as villainous and dirty as himself, rose up from the long
grass and outnumbered us a hundred to one.
 This was more than we had bargained for, and we knew
not what to do, until Shagalfa told us we had to kill a man
who had broken the laws of his tribe. We naturally objected, but she pointed out that he would die a most cruel
death if we did not kill him, and that therefore it would
really be a mercy to get rid of him with the great noise.
It was a most unpleasant predicament to be placed in, but
we had got somewhat hardened.
 The criminal was brought close to us and we were or-

"You'll cry before morning," said Jack, and then he, too, started off in an uncontrollable fit of merriment.

In the midst of the outburst a long, bare arm was suddenly pushed between Shagaffa and myself and the bird was seized.

We were all on our feet in an instant, and stood facing a peculiar looking savage, who was evidently delighted at having stolen our supper.

We had traveled so many miles without seeing any natives that we were taken completely by surprise and knew not what to do.

The savage who confronted us was evidently a chief. His appearance, however, was very far from pleasant.

A peculiarity was his head-dress, which I afterward discovered was characteristic of this tribe of dwellers in Sahara.

The hair was woven into a thick felt, which covered the shoulders and extended as low upon the back as the shoulder blade. The members of the tribe, like some fashionable beauties of a few years since, were not at all particular as to whose hair they wore, but were happy to receive contributions from any source. When any death occurred the hair of the deceased was immediately cut off and shared among his friends, to be added to their stock of felt. When in full dress—the men being nude—this mass of hair or felt was thickly plastered with a blue clay so as to form an even surface. It was then elaborately worked with the point of a thorn, so as to resemble the cuttings of a file; white chalk or pipe clay is used to make patterns on the surface, while an ornament made of either an antelope's or giraffe's sinew is stuck in the extremity and turned up for about a foot in length, and the tip ornamented with a tuft of fur, the tip of a lion's or leopard's tail being mostly prized.

The chief, who had stolen our supper, had cowry shells on his head in addition when in full dress.

When the chief saw that we were prepared to defend ourselves, he made use of a little strategy, and handed back the bird, which Medjid seized with such a scornful air that I wonder the savage did not run her through with a spear.

The fellow began to chatter away very rapidly in a language foreign to me.

The Nubian shook his head, for he did not understand a word—fortunately, Shagaffa was able to act as interpreter.

"He desires us to go to his village," she said. "Where is it?"

"A day's march to the setting sun."

"If we refuse?" Shagaffa instead of asking this question began to discuss with the chief the various alterna-

dered to kill him with the big noise. The chief laughed at the thought, for of course he considered it only an empty boast.

Jack volunteered to do the shooting, and he insisted that the man should be allowed to run away as rapidly as he could.

The chief at first refused, but Shagaffa said we would certainly kill the man, or if not, our own liberty should be forfeit.

The poor fellow, who had never faced anything but a spear, was in high glee at the thought of escape.

I trembled at the thought that perhaps Jack might miss. If he did our lives would not be worth much.

The man ran rapidly until he had got some four hundred yards away when "crack" went the Winchester, and the man was seen to spring up into the air and fall back dead.

The chief and the whole tribe now fell on their faces and acknowledged our power.

If we had difficulty in evading the honor of being their guests before, we found it was increased now, for we were quickly elevated to the shoulders of the nude savages and carried in triumph supperless to the village, which we reached just as the sun began to show its glorious rays of light—more glorious in that tropical land than anywhere else.

Shagaffa said that we should be well treated, but I had my doubts, for I did not like the way I had lost my savory-smelling supper, and I never felt happy when compelled to associate with such thieving scoundrels.

To resist was, however, useless; so we had to put the best face on the matter, and accept the hospitality of the chicken-stealing African chief.

CHAPTER XXIX.
OUR WELCOME AT M'KAMBA.

OUR unexpected arrival at the village of the M'Kambas was the signal for great rejoicing. The entire population turned out and welcomed us as if we had been their greatest friends returned after a long absence.

The nogaras were sounded and horns blown with a vigor which showed that the lung power was certainly of the highest order.

When the populace saw our party riding on the shoulders of four brawny M'Kambas they added a war-whoop to their horrid music, for they were sure we were great people or we should not be carried in triumph.

The old chief said something to one of his most trusted followers, who immediately started on a run to a large stockade we could see in the distance. A few minutes later and forty or fifty curious looking objects came waddling out of the courtyard.

They were very short and very fat, and I found they were the chief's wives.

Like the King of the Troglodytes, the Chief of the M'Kambas married all the girls when they arrived at thirteen years of age, but no girl was eligible to remain the wife of so distinguished a man unless she was about as broad as she was long.

Mothers would take their infant daughters and stunt their growth by means of large stones placed at the head and feet while sleeping, and would fatten the bodies with milk. Oh! what happiness it was to us to see some cows, and to learn that we were to have all the milk we wanted.

The female children grew very fat and short under this treatment. When they arrived at the age of ten they were put on the sour milk diet. Every day they were compelled to drink a gallon of curded milk, the swallowing of which was frequently enforced by the whip; the result of this milk diet was extreme obesity. In hot climates milk will curdle in two or three hours if placed in a vessel which had previously contained sour milk. The natives then take it and beat it until it assumes the appearance of cream; they season it with plenty of salt, and we found it most palatable and easy of digestion.

The fat wives of the chief waddled to us, for we were all stationed at about a hundred yards from the entrance to the village, awaiting the full programme of ceremonies.

When the obese beauties reached us they presented a most ludicrous spectacle as they danced round the chief, their husband.

After performing numerous gyrations, they fell on their faces and uttered some few words, the purport of which we failed to understand, and then they rolled over and over, first to one side and then to the other, until Jack fairly exploded at the comical sight.

I was tired of my exalted position and struggled to get off my bearer's shoulder, but the more I kicked and wriggled the tighter he held my legs.

The chief, seeing my anxiety to reach the ground, told me, through the medium of Shagaffa's interpretation, that it was not considered right that such distinguished people should be allowed to stand until the sports were over.

I expect that to Shagaffa the position was a novel one, for the Troglodytes did not believe in showing any indulgence to women, but as Shagaffa had told the chief she was my wife, she too

party. As I looked at her, I could see the calm satisfaction on her black but handsome face.

Medjid, who knew so much of the treachery of the native tribes, had a firm belief we were all to be killed and that the pretended hospitality was but a trap.

However, we must appear to submit and keep our eyes open for a chance to escape. When the obese beauties—pardon the application of the word to such monstrosities—had rolled over a good many times, they managed to rise to their feet, looking very dusty and dirty, and waddled back to the stockade. The nogaras beat and the trumpets brayed, and we were carried into the village, and almost thrown—so violent were the means used to unseat us—into the chief's stockade.

We sat close together and waited for events to transpire. Presently the chief entered, and that was the signal for the commencement of our feast.

A number of tall, slim girls—slaves, as I afterward learned, and captured from other tribes—entered, each bringing a large bowl, filled with the curded milk. It was refreshing and pleasant, and we all four drank heartily. The course was followed by a dish of boiled plantains, tasting almost like potatoes, and succeeded by some kind of boiled meat. I could not help wondering why, when such great plenty was to be found at the village, the chief should lower himself to steal our poor bird.

Before I had partaken of the hospitality of the M'Kambas a week, I had found that the old chief was a regular kleptomaniac, that nothing was safe from his thieving hands.

As we had been on the march all night, we were very much pleased to hear the order that all the warriors and ourselves were to sleep all the remainder of the day.

The heat was suffocating, and I feared that sleep was impossible, but I threw myself down on my blanket in the room allotted us, and tried to compose myself to slumber. I had scarcely closed my eyes before I felt a gentle breeze fanning my face. I opened my eyes and beheld two of the fat girls waving plantain leaves over my head. I was grateful, but could not restrain a smile, as I saw these immense creatures, round whose waist my arms would not reach, standing, puffing with the heat and exertion, and yet continuously fanning, in the hope of soothing me to sleep. I caught sight in the far corner of the large hut of the wavy movement made by the fans, and conjectured that we were each favored in the same way. I had fallen asleep and was losing myself in the realm of dreams, when a strange feeling of suffocation almost overpowered me. I opened my eyes and wondered that I had any breath left.

My fat attendants had grown weary with standing, so had squatted down on the floor close to me, and leaning one hand on my chest, used the other to hold the fan.

I tried to shake myself free, but I found there was a solidity in the mass of flesh which was unusual.

When I found I could not get them to take a hint, I gave one girl a vigorous push, and she rolled over like a ball. The other thought it was a hint likely to be disagreeable so she removed her arm from my chest and continued fanning. Again I slumbered, but not to rest, for I was uncomfortable. I tossed about wearily, and then a horrid nightmare seized me and I thought I must be buried beneath the ruins of some old temple. How long I had remained buried I know not, but I had ceased to cry for help and had resigned myself to death, when I dreamt the stones were being removed and I was free. My eyes opened and I saw Shagaffa bending over me.

For a few moments I did not realize the situation, but Shagaffa petted me, smoothed my brow and called me the such endearing names that I wondered what had so strangely affected her.

When she found I was fully awake, she told me that she could not sleep—no one had offered to fan her—and as she was so restless, she thought she would pass round the room and see if we were all comfortable. She found Medjid musical with his snores; O'Brien was sleeping with a sweet smile on his face, two fat girls waving their fans gently over him, and then she came to me. To her horror she could not find me at first, for the girls had fallen asleep, and as it was far from pleasant sleeping in a sitting posture, they had used my body for a couch, and stretched themselves across me. Shagaffa had to exert her utmost strength to move the ponderous weights, but she at last succeeded. This accounted for my dream or nightmare. I thanked Shagaffa and had to smile when she asked me most seriously if any bones were broken.

The chief heard the complaint which Shagaffa thought it her duty to make, and he apologized by saying that the two girls he had allotted to me were his favorite wives, because they were the fattest, and he supposed the exertion of fanning was too much for them.

We woke to partake of another meal, and then, at the chief's suggestion, we went again to sleep; but although he was very profuse in his offers of some of his wives to fan me or keep me company, I declined. I was not alone, however, for Shagaffa absolutely refused to leave my side. She feared that the "mountains of flesh," as she called the chief's favorites, would come again and crush me.

Toward morning O'Brien came to me and shook me by the arm.

"Monty," he said, softly, "are you awake?"

"Yes, Jack; what is it?"

"Hush! Don't speak above a whisper; let me lie down beside you. I want to tell you something."

"All right, Jack! what is it?" I whispered.

"Gu-r-r-t! Gawoh! gurrah! gwock!"

Jack was snoring, and of all the villainous noises I had ever heard that was the worst. It rumbled along in low, muttering tones, like the distant echoes of a thunderstorm, then exploded like a cannon. It was blood-curdling and horrible, and I gave the snorer a terrific dig in the ribs.

"All serene, Monty," he whispered, and then out came the horrible nasal, guttural thunder.

"Snort! guffaw! gwock!"

This continued so long that I thought Jack had got a sunstroke, and had temporarily lost his reason.

"For Heaven's sake, hush!" I said, "or I shall leave you."

"Don't! listen, but appear to be asleep. I had my head close to the door, and while those fat things—I can't call them girls—were fanning me I heard some voices outside. I thought all had gone to rest, and did not think we were prisoners needing a sentry, so I listened. At first I could not understand a word, and I opened my eyes, that moment the talking stopped." Jack gave utterance to another terrific snore, and after a pause resumed his narrative. "Every time I appeared to be awake the talking was discontinued, so I feigned sleep, but kept my eye open. I saw the girls giving signals at the open door. In a few minutes, when I was supposed to be fast asleep, I felt a hand steal softly to my pistol-belt and an attempt was made to take my revolvers and rifles.

"I opened one eye sufficiently wide to see a villainous-looking fellow as the owner of the hand. I put out my arm and seized the fat girl by the waist and pulled her down, she fell on the fellow's arm and nearly broke it. I professed to be caressing her in my sleep, and held her in such a position, that before my pistols could be taken her ponderous weight would have to be moved.

"She, thinking I was really caressing her, aided me, and drew closer, until I could scarcely breathe.

"I had made a conquest. Well, I stayed some time with my arm round the buxom girl, and kept my ears very well open. I could only understand a few words, but I formed an idea we were to be killed and eaten."

Jack snored again, and I was horrified at his story. Was such treachery intended?

I whispered to Jack to continue his story, which he did after a long pause

"I had two attendants, and as I fondled one the other grew jealous, so I reached out my other arm and pulled her down as well. There was I between two mountains of flesh. I had no need now to use any endearments, for each vied with the other in their wonderfully winning ways, and while the one on the left got so close that I could scarcely breathe, the right side girl pressed closer to me, and I was nearly crushed. I was petted and fondled in all sorts of ways until both fell asleep, and I came across here."

I thought over all O'Brien had said, and I became uneasy. I felt for my revolvers and rifles, and found they were all right. No attempt had been made to steal them, and I conjectured that most likely the native had been more desirous of plundering Jack than killing and eating him.

After an interval had elapsed, and O'Brien had really fallen asleep, I roused Shagaffa, and whispered to her Jack's fear.

After listening to my story, she got up without a word and crossed the long room to where Medjid was sleeping. She shook him, and when he opened his eyes she asked if he had slept soundly.

"No," he replied.

"Tell me what you have heard."

Medjid looked confused for a minute, and then stated he had only been shamming sleep, for he feared treachery, and that he had heard a good deal of talking, but could not understand what it had been about.

When Shagaffa returned and told us what Medjid had heard, we began to fear that treachery was intended. We were, however, for the time, entirely at the mercy of these people, and our safety depended more upon cunning than skill. We must profess to be unaware of their evil intentions and watch our opportunity to escape.

The remaining hours of the night were spent in conversation, and as we had slept most of the previous day, our wakefulness occasioned no surprise.

CHAPTER XXX.
M'KAMBA SPORTS AND CANNIBAL FEASTS.

WHEN the chief entered our hut the next morning his face was one radiant smile. He hoped we had slept well, and expressed a wish we should complain if all was not just as we should desire it.

I thanked him through Shagaffa, and asked him how long we were to enjoy his hospitality.

"Till thy son's sons shall be old enough to follow the chase," was his answer.

Shagaffa smiled as she translated it to us.

"Tell him," I said, "that I have no sons."

That was the prelude to a long conversation, of which the gist only can I find time and space to give. The chief was a philosopher and argued from a strange standpoint for a savage.

He told me—of course I can only give Shagaffa's interpretation—that it was time that I had some sons and daughters. That he had for a long time wanted some white people as guests, so that they could marry some of his wives and bear him lighter children.

He wanted to improve the race of the M'Kambas, and thought the admixture of a little white blood would do much to effect that.

He had, therefore, ordered a grand day of sports to be held, at which, when all were gathered, he would proclaim that fifty girls were to be brought to him as wives, and that he would give me ten, another ten would be O'Brien's share, and he would reserve thirty for himself. That Shagaffa was to be principal wife, and was to carry the whip, and was to have dominion over O'Brien's wives as well as mine.

The old polygamist went further, and said he would order that for every child our wives should bear within two years, he would give us ten slaves.

Shagaffa translated this to me, and I shuddered at the horrible thought. She was delighted, and hoped I would accept the conditions, and settle down, a much married man.

O'Brien laughed and thought his lot was not such a bad one; for only a few weeks before he had been the husband of ten wives, and now he was to get ten more.

"What shall we do?" I asked.

"Appear to accept gratefully. Lull the old fellow into a belief that we are pleased at the thought, and then hop the first opportunity."

This was Jack's reasoning, and I felt that though repugnant to me, it was perhaps the only chance we had.

The day was far advanced before the sports commenced. To us they were hideous and repulsive, and many of them sickening. There was the usual dancing and gymnastic movements, but the most horrible sight was when a number of slave-girls armed with long knives made of sharply pointed hard-wood, stepped forward and commenced a dance or series of dances.

As the girls neared each other they made use of the knives, and in a very few minutes nearly every girl was mutilated, the blood flowing from a score of sharp knife-thrust wounds.

The dance continued, and the dancers got worked into a frenzy of madness. Smarting from the wounds, blinded by blood, and urged on by the beating of the nogaras (drum), they closed in on one another, and while they kept a sort of rhythm with their feet, they struck each other with savage fury.

Three girls were mutilated beyond recognition. One had been stabbed so many times in the stomach that it was a wonder she lived to finish the dance.

One by one the girls fell faint and exhausted, until at last only one was left standing. She was a strong, powerful girl, wounded in a dozen different places, but still lithe and active. She held up the knife from which the blood dripped, and the chief proclaimed her the champion dancer. The warriors lifted her on their shoulders and carried her round, all cheering wildly at her triumph.

When I expressed my horror at the sight, the chief said such sports made the girls hardy, and that the champion could not be the mother of cowardly children.

The field was cleared, and the wounded girls carried to the huts, where the wise women dressed their wounds and tended to their wants. Two were dead, killed in the dance.

When it was noised abroad that there were two deaths, a number of men and women left the field of sports, but shortly after returned for a funeral dance.

The dancers presented a most fantastic picture, and really looked quite picturesque. Their helmets were adorned with long feathers, and a perfect wealth of ostrich plumes must have been worn. From their shoulders were suspended monkey skins, the principal dancers having the skin of the sacred white monkey, the others being content with the black.

Seven nogaras tuned to different notes were beaten until the ears were deadened by the noise. The music was added to, by the jingling of bells carefully concealed under the leather and skins tied round each dancer's waist. The warriors rushed about intermingling with the dancers, and occasionally pricking some with their sharp spears.

The women, generally old ones, joined in the dance, standing outside the ring; with every step they set up a most diabolical yell, blood-curdling in the extreme.

The young girls appeared on the scene later, and added to the melody by the jingling of beads and armlets

The *premiere danseuse* was a woman who was far past

THE M'KAMBA FUNERAL DANCE.

the first bloom of youth, and must have weighed over three hundred pounds, but she danced with a vigor which put many of the young ones to shame, and seemed quite unconscious of her strange appearance.

This strange dancer continued for nearly an hour, and then the most sickening sight of all occurred.

The dead dancing girls were brought in front of the funeral dancers, and after a number of formalities had been gone through, their bodies were cut up and thrown into an immense pot, a fire was kindled and over it the pot was placed.

The heads of the dead girls were placed on spears stuck in the ground, and presented a most ghastly appearance. I was so horrified that I motioned to O'Brien and Medjid to come away, and much to the chief's annoyance, we left before the funeral dancers were rewarded for their exertions by a piece of the boiled flesh and a bowl of the soup made from the bodies of, perhaps, their own relatives.

When this cannibal feast was over, the chief proclaimed his intentions in regard to O'Brien and myself, but Shagaffa told me there was considerable muttering, as we were not liked by the people, and they especially objected to any of their daughters being the mothers of a white man's children. Unlike the chief, they thought it would cause the race to deteriorate. The genuine African, in his rude, natural state, considers his blackness a proof of superiority; the lighter the color the more inferior the race.

I told Shagaffa that we should only appear to acquiesce in the arrangement, and should, at the very first opportunity, make our escape.

When evening came on the chief entered our hut, accompanied by twenty-two young girls, who were in the process of being fattened for the king. These he liberally divided, giving ten each to O'Brien and myself, and two to Medjid.

He also presented a whip made of a strip of cowhide to Shagaffa, and told her what her duty would be.

The girls were to obey us in every particular and were to be true and loyal to us. In case of disobedience, sulky looks or conduct, or if we wished to be amused by the sight, Shagaffa was to ply the whip vigorously. This was the universal custom and so accustomed had the race become to such treatment that the females really expected to receive a whipping quite often, and before I left the land of the M'Kambas I heard more than one of the dwellers in my hut complain that I neglected her because I had not ordered a dose of the cowhide.

I remembered some of the old proverbs which asserted that women required beating.

The English used to say:

> "A spaniel, a woman, and a walnut tree,
> The more they are beaten the better they be."

And even the gallant Italians have been wont to declare that:

> "Women and asses require rough hands."

But I had never expected to find women who wept because they were not beaten, and who really imagined they were unloved and neglected because the whip had not cut into their shoulders.

The hut in which our now large families resided differed from the others inhabited by the natives, inasmuch as only one family occupied a hut, whereas O'Brien, myself, and Medjid, with our twenty-three wives, occupied one large hut.

Outside, and entirely surrounding it, was a high stockade or fence, over which it would be impossible to climb. The entrance was by means of a small and narrow opening, which we found to our dismay was always well guarded. Another misfortune we suffered. The road away from the village which we wished to take, was directly past most of the houses.

We were prisoners carefully guarded. For several days we waited without making any attempt to escape. We had been strictly forbidden to leave the hut. Shagaffa was the only one allowed outside the stockade, and whatever we needed in the way of food she asked for, and the chief at once sent it to our hut. So we were well cared for. We took the precaution not to eat any flesh meat or partake of any soup, fearing that some portion of a human being might have added to its richness. The milk was good, and on that and plantains we depended almost entirely for our food, reserving our own supply for future use. The days lengthened into weeks, and we feared we should never see King Solomon's treasures unless we made some speedy movement to regain our liberty.

We had discussed various ways, but they had all been deemed unsatisfactory, and we might have been discussing till the present hour had not our inventive skill and ingenuity of brain been quickened into action by some news brought by Shagaffa one evening.

CHAPTER XXXI.
A BLAZING JUNGLE.

SHAGAFFA had been to the chief's stockade to get a supply of food, and had received more plantains than usual, and was resting with her load, being tired.

The night was getting dark, and as she sat down in the long grass, just under the shadow of one of the huts, she was unobserved.

Just when she was about to continue her journey she heard some men talking about us. That caused her to stay where she was and listen.

"Why should they take our daughters?" asked one of the M'Kambas.

"Are they kings?" questioned the other.

"The chief has taken a fancy to them, and if he wants them we will get another chief."

"If my girl has a white man's child I will kill her," said another.

The conversation got very warm and animated, and at last Shagaffa heard them plan to surprise us soon after midnight, and take all four of us, O'Brien, myself, Medjid and Shagaffa, kill us, and make us into soup.

The time was fixed, and all the details of the plan agreed upon.

We were now forewarned, but were we ready to meet these diabolical wretches?

Shagaffa was the least alarmed of the party; she had such confidence in our magic that she believed we could easily overcome all our enemies.

An idea occurred to me which I communicated to the others, and seemed to be a feasible plan of campaign.

Fortunately I had shown Shagaffa the secret of a lucifer match, of which I had several boxes left. That evening when the night sentries had taken their positions at the entrance to our stockade, I started Shagaffa to the chiefs kraal for food. She passed the sentries unquestioned, and, having learned the location of the huts occupied by the sentries, she passed quickly along by each, and deftly lighted a piece of slow fuze I had given her for each place.

In addition to those places, she also applied the fuze to the house in which the conspiracy had been hatched, and at a dozen other places all far removed from our stockade. She then returned with quick steps bringing in the plantains and other food from the kraal.

In half an hour we knew that the blaze would ascend from twenty different points and that would be our chance to escape.

Shagaffa had kept our haversacks filled with food, fresh every day, so that we were always ready when a favorable moment arrived.

We now buckled them on, slung our rifles, and saw that all our weapons were loaded.

Our wives watched our movements but could not understand their significance.

At last we heard a commotion, and looking out, we saw the reflection on the sky of a fire.

Shagaffa was sent out to see what was the occasion of the hubbub—I taking care to give her the order in a loud tone of voice.

She reached the gate and found the sentries, and nearly all the inhabitants, running to the scene of the fires.

As they ran in one direction, suddenly a shout would be raised of a fire elsewhere. In the hope of saving the last fired, the crowd would turn that way, only to be confronted with the cry of fire from another part of the village.

That was our opportunity. Bidding Shagaffa run as fast as she was able, we started as though going to the most recent fire, and then, at a favorable moment, doubled, and made for the open jungle. In the excitement no notice was taken of us, and we were at the very least three miles away before we rested.

The grass was tall, and unfortunately our running had broken down a broad trail so it would be easy to follow us. Medjid, who had remarkably sharp eyes, kept them fixed on the burning village, and he saw unmistakable signs that we were being pursued.

A crowd was getting darker and darker, showing that they were leaving the fires instead of going to them. He called our attention to this, and as we looked we saw, not a mile away, the proof of a large crowd of warriors following us.

If we ran we should be overtaken, for we were already well-nigh exhausted; if we remained where we were our death would be certain, for although we could count on fifty-four shots at long range from our two Winchesters and double-barreled rifles, that would only make the remainder more savage. And at close quarters we had four revolvers, each loaded with seven cartridges, in all, therefore, we had eighty-two shots between us and death.

We debated our plan of action and determined to run as far as we could, make a stand and die game, when Shagaffa settled the question for us, and completely changed our plan.

While we had been debating and talking about the possibilities and probabilities of our chances of escape, she had been more active. She had found that the wind was blowing toward the village and therefore from us. With ready, feminine foresight she noted this and utilized it; just as we were about to start on our run, we saw her setting fire to the long grass, and running along lighting it in a dozen different places. We took the hint, and armed with matches we lighted the grass at intervals for more than a quarter of a mile.

In ten minutes, just when the black fiends were within rifle range, a sheet of flame shot up into the air and swept like a whirlwind over the jungle and toward the village.

The natives sent up such a terrific whoop and howl that we shuddered at the sound.

The fire made rapid headway, and the M'Kambas ran with all the speed of their fleet feet, but from the shrieks of agony which went up, I sadly fear some were not swift enough, and fell victims to the blaze which Shagaffa had originated.

We were saved! What mattered it how many were lost? Our lives were of more value than a hundred Africans.

So we thought in our egotism. Yet, is not the life of the same value to a savage, as it is to the civilized? We admit the truth underlying the brotherhood of nations, but hesitate not to sacrifice hundreds of lives, it may be, to save our own. It is true that "Man's inhumanity to man, makes countless thousands mourn."

Our only thought was our own safety, and that we effectually secured at the cost of, perhaps, a score of lives, a burned village, and the destruction of a great amount of property belonging to the poor natives.

The sky was red for many miles with the reflection from the burning grass, and as we watched its progress we saw —I must admit with horror—that the entire village, whose hospitality we had accepted for some time, was wrapt in flames, and in a few minutes entirely destroyed. The women and little children would doubtless be great sufferers, but we were justified in what we did, for, as we reasoned to ourselves, if we had not done so, we should have been stewing in their great pots by that time, and our bodies would have assisted in fattening some of the girls, and strengthening the warriors. It was best as it was.

We walked about seven miles further, and reached the place where we had been surprised by the M'Kambas shortly before.

When we camped for rest we took special care of Shagaffa, for it was her forethought which had in two instances saved our lives, and the warm words of thanks which all three uttered in her ear, made her so excited that she vowed she would never be able to sleep. However, we were all weary with our long night's tramp and excitement, and we had no difficulty in sleeping.

When we were rested and had partaken of food we resumed our journey, and, guided more by instinct than anything else, we set our face toward the point we expected to find the great treasures, and marched across the jungle.

At times we found most beautiful lakes and wells of water.

Sometimes we came across the most exquisitely lovely birds, and to my great delight saw evidences of cultivation in the far past.

What was now but a deserted waste, untrod by white men, unknown to geographers because unexplained, had been at some time a rich, fertile country, and I have no doubt densely populated.

At every step we saw marks of man's handiwork, but far different from anything which could be produced by the natives we had seen in our travels so far. Pieces of stone on which were carved hieroglyphics and inscriptions were met with at intervals, and occasionally we came across a fragment of sculptured stone.

Our progress was slow, for we examined all we met with, and though they spoke to us in an unknown and long-forgotten language, they possessed a significance and gave a pleasure which rewarded us for all our arduous marching, and the terrible trials and sufferings we had undergone.

I was pleased to find that oftentimes Shagaffa would fall behind and converse with Medjid, for I had not given up the match-making idea I had formed at first. I did not know that Medjid would accept her, after she had been the wife of Gabzenati, who kindly handed her over to me, and, therefore, would, if she went to the Nubian, have her third husband.

She was a dear, good girl, and I was desirous of aiding her in life, and she saw that if we ever reached the Nile, and I returned to England, that she could not go with me.

Sometimes I would look round and notice her in conversation with the Nubian, and then she would instantly leave him and come to my side.

One day she volunteered the statement that Medjid was a nice man.

I replied that he was, and would have a nice home for his wife.

"Has he a wife?" she asked.

"No, I believe not; but when he gets back he will want one."

That was all she said; but, to me, it was enough to prove that her heart was going out to the man whose color was only a few shades lighter than her own.

"How far have we traveled since we left Mer?" asked Jack, one morning.

"It seems that by direct line we must have come the fifty leagues," I replied.

"What if we are hoaxed, after all?"

"Jack O'Brien, how dare you stand there and hazard such a conjecture?" I said, as I looked steadily at him.

"You are right. If we fail in this, my hope is gone. My belief in the truth of spirit guidance is lost, and I shall be a mental wreck."

O'Brien had been very quiet and silent for several days, and although he professed to feel a great interest in the scattered vestiges of civilization, I could see he was fast losing hope. I had left England, not for treasure but pleasure, not for wealth but excitement; and those who read this narrative will agree that, for a society man, a west-end club lounger, I had done pretty well in the way of excitement, pleasure and adventure. We had left the oasis and was on land half desert and half jungle.

CHAPTER XXXII.
THE TRIUMPHAL ARCH.

ANOTHER day's weary march and we lay down to rest, watching the sun sink below the horizon. As we fixed our gaze on the beautiful crimson sunset, I saw a sight which made me forget all my weariness.

I leaped up and roused O'Brien, who had already fallen asleep.

"Quick Jack, or you will be too late."

He jumped up, seized his rifle and then looked at me as if he thought I had become insane.

"Look, Jack, what do you see?" and I pointed in the direction of the setting sun.

"Great powers! it is the arch," was his exclamation.

"I think you are right."

Jack was for putting off our rest and proceeding at once to the arch; but when I argued with him and showed that it was several miles away, and that if we reached it we should be worn out and exhausted, he assented to my plan of having a short night's rest, and rising with the sun to pursue our march.

When morning came we were ready for our journey, and although we could not now distinguish the arch, we felt a hope and confidence which compensated us for our early rising, and lent speed to our feet.

It was late at night before we reached the ruins, and we had to defer our inspection until the following morning. Jack was so elated that he sang several songs in his rich barytone voice, and even Medjid forgot his predestined death, and sang some of the songs of the Nile which had often comforted him in his boyhood days. As for me I had never tried to sing without an accompaniment, and as no piano was to be found in the interior of Sahara's great desert, I was unable to sing.

The night had been dark when we arrived at the arch, which had been so rudely and crudely drawn on our map, and therefore we were unable to see what it was like.

But when the first rays of the sun reached us, and lighted up the entire country, we were so puzzled and perplexed, that for awhile we could not realize we were in a desert, far from civilized life.

As we looked at the arch, we saw that it was in every way remarkable.

It rose on a slight elevation, without connection with any other work.

RUINS OF KING SOLOMON'S TRIUMPHAL ARCH.

It was sixteen feet clear, and was composed of two pilasters of stone, cut to the square; above the pilasters were cornices, and from them the arch rose, but ruined at its crown.

It inspired our mind with the idea of its solitary grandeur. There was something in it very different to the gateway of a fortress or temple.

O'Brien thought it was the ruins of a palace, but I formed an idea and I could not get rid of it, that it could be compared only with the Arch of Titus in grand old Rome.

The more we looked at it the more convinced was I that it was erected to commemorate some triumph.

Some great sovereign had wished to eternalize his glory by a triumphal arch.

When was it built? Six hundred years before the commencement of our era we find the Arch of Sakkar mentioned; and in the great pyramid of Ghizeh there is a grand entrance formed on the same principle as the one on which we were looking.

In the ruins of Egypt there are arches in the tombs which date back to the year 1500 before our era, so the arch was no new or modern idea in architecture. Here right in the midst of the great desert were traces of a civilization which proved that at some time in the far past a great and powerful people lived. Poor races, untutored savages, do not raise monuments or erect arches of triumph. The people who created this wonderful piece of architecture must have been conversant with the arts and sciences and their auxiliaries such as geometry, mechanics, drawing, and the strength and power of resistance of various substances. Else how could the arch have been built or the stones been quarried and wrought? How could they have traced this with such great perfection and beauty? How give it the strength to enable it to defy the course of those centuries which must have passed over it and beaten it with their destroying wings?

We were delighted beyond expression, and a prayer of thankfulness went up to the Most High, to the great Architect of the universe for allowing us to reach in safety this convincing proof of the truth of our map.

So interested were we in studying the arch that we had not thought of looking beyond.

When we did so, we thought that we must indeed be in the land of dreams, for a new country opened up before us.

In a direct line from the arch could be traced a road clear and well defined.

For centuries it had been neglected, and the long grass had in places grown through the cracks in the stones, but it was plain enough for us to know that it was one of those masterpieces of engineering skill which can be found in various parts of the world.

O'Brien brought out his map and found that there were two points of interest marked in a line with the arch going from north to south. One was a well at the south, the other a cave.

Here arose a discussion. Should we visit the cave or continue our journey along the great road?

Shagaffa reminded me that it might be as well to get some more water if the well was near, and as no other well was marked on the map, we took the hint and started in the direction of the well of water.

We noticed that a line from the arch seemed to divide the desert and jungle from a fertile land.

On one side of the line nothing but a dense shrub and bush was growing intermingled with tall grass; on the other side, we could see palms and other trees.

The well, according to our map, ought to be a long distance from us, but we had experienced the fact that our geographer had not been very accurate as to his scale of distances.

When we had walked for over an hour O'Brien called a halt.

"What do we want to go to this well for?" he asked.

"Water," I replied curtly.

"Of course, but what I wanted to know was, whether it is not probable we shall find all the water we want, seeing the land is evidently so fertile."

"Thou reasonest like a philosopher," I answered, "but tell me, is it not likely our geographer had some good reason for making the well on the map?"

"It seems so."

"Let us get there, then. Fill our bottles with water, and if we have no use for the glorious fluid, we can easily throw it away."

Medjid walked some little distance by my side silently, and then asked abruptly:

"Do you believe I shall die soon?"

"No; you are the least likely one of the party. But why do you ask?"

"You remember, Baas, what I told you of the wise woman's words?"

"Of course, and attach no meaning to them."

"You don't?"

"No."

"Then what good are wise women?"

"Ah, Medjid, that is a question too deep for me to answer. But what made you think of it just now?"

"I am afraid, Baas, you will not like what I am going to say."

"Say on, I shall not be offended."

He hesitated for a long time, and then, gaining courage from my silence, said:

"When you get to Nubia, will you stay there?"

"No, Medjid. I shall go to the great country from whence I came."

"What will you do with Shagaffa?"

"Medjid! Medjid! that is a problem. Who can say what one will do with a woman at any time?"

"I know, Baas; but will you send her back to those pagans in the caves?"

"No."

"Will you take her with you?"

"I don't know."

"Baas, will you—will—will you sell her?"

If Medjid had asked me if I would chop her up and make her into soup, like the people with whom we so recently resided, I could not have been more surprised.

"Sell her!" I exclaimed. "By Heaven, no!"

Medjid walked away very sorrowful, and I noticed that though he appeared to shun Shagaffa, she sought his company, and, I have no doubt, comforted him in his doleful state of mind. I was on the right way to solve that great difficulty, for Medjid wanted Shagaffa, and she liked him.

But what if she refused to leave me? I could use my authority, and give her to Medjid. She was a Troglodyte, and if we had remained there, she would long since have expected to pass to the possession of a chief, and perhaps, by this time, to the arms of one of the warriors. So she would make no objection; besides, the Nubian could make her happy, which, of course, she could never be if she returned to England with me.

We reached the well near the end of the second day. It had proved a long deviation from our route, but evidently there must be some good reason for it being marked.

It was the first artificial well we had seen since we left the banks of the Nile. The sides were made of stone, and were cemented together very compactly.

It must be an excellent spring, for it had the appearance of being full, and the sun's heat had not dried it up.

We took a good drink, and never was nectar more delicious. Such water I had never before tasted. Of icy coldness, and a clearness rivaling the purest crystal. Every drop, as it passed down the throat, seemed a thirst-quencher *par excellence.*

We sat on the side of the well and drank from its cool waters many times.

I would have liked a bath, but a well was treacherous, and I dare not risk it, but we did the next best thing.

We took some flat stones and hollowed out a space in the clayey soil, large enough to hold a few gallons of water.

We all set to work with a right good will to fill our improvised bath-tub, and then off went our shirts, and we had an excellent wash.

We camped there that night, and when O'Brien and I awoke we found that Medjid and Shagaffa had occupied their time, instead of sleeping, in excavating a bigger space and making a bath-tub large enough for us to get in. They were in the act of filling it when we awoke.

While I was disposed to blame them for losing their rest, I could not but thank them for their devotion and kind thoughtfulness. We all lent a hand in pouring in the water, and then we enjoyed the luxury of a good bath.

I was selected for the first operation, and was followed by Jack.

As soon as I got out of the water, Shagaffa and Medjid took the water-bottles and poured some icy-cold water all over me. I then ran about until my skin was in a delightful glow.

Shagaffa and Medjid enjoyed their bath quite as much as we did, and we had no regret at having deviated from our route to visit this delightful well.

We thought it advisable to return the same way as we had gone, fearing that there might be treacherous places if we crossed to the road by any other route.

No adventures of any moment were met with, and we reached the arch in safety.

CHAPTER XXXIII.
THE CRYSTAL STATUE.

AFTER we had passed under the arch we were in a new land.

And after a day's journey along the wonderful road which had been such a splendid specimen of engineering skill in the centuries which had passed, we realized that we must be in the land from whence the lovely Queen of Sheba went to visit Solomon.

We read that she took to the great king "spices and gold in abundance, and precious stones; neither was there any such spice as the Queen of Sheba gave King Solomon."[*] And later, that the ships of Solomon went and brought back gold and silver, spices and ivory, and apes and peacocks.

I remembered, also, that Solomon built a number of "store cities, and chariot cities, and cities of horsemen."[†]

The air was fragrant with the perfume of spices, and we found large numbers of lignum vitæ trees growing; another

[*] 2 Chronicles ix. 1, 9.
[†] 2 Chronicles viii. 6.

proof that this was the land referred to in the book of Nathan the prophet and Abijah the Shilonite.*

Although the road was now a good one, the walking was far from pleasant, owing to the intense heat, which was retained by its paved surface.

We made but slow progress, but the scenery was so delightful and the air so balmy that we were in no particular hurry.

We had seen on our maps, and heard from the Troglodytes, of the Macrobii, or long-lived men, but had not encountered any of them. We had no particular desire to do so, but still we were curious.

These men, if they really possessed the power of living forever, would prove dangerous enemies, for, while they might kill us, we should be powerless against them. We saw no signs of any mountain range, so conjectured we had many miles to travel.

On our third day's march along the great road we had proof of the great talent possessed by its builders, for we were crossing a valley which had actually been filled in the width of the road, while at a depth of perhaps a hundred feet we could see arched culverts for water ways.

How did Solomon, or Makeda Balkis, or whoever built the road, transport all the stone necessary for that purpose? and from whence did it come?

Answer how did the Egyptians transport those immense obelisks eight hundred miles across the sand, and place them before the temple of the Sun at Meliopolis? Tell me how the pyramids were built, or who fashioned and perfected the Round Towers of Ireland, with their thousands of years of age, and then we may find how King Solomon's road was built.

It was a mystery to us then, and it is so to me still, as I think over it and its great wonders.

Standing by the side of the road, on a slightly lower plane, we came across a statue cut in some kind of hard stone resembling crystal. It was semi-transparent, and as the sun shone on it, it gave back the scintillations of light as brilliantly as a diamond. The face was only slightly damaged by the lapse of time, and the features were most gloriously beautiful.

"Come here, Jack!"

"What is it?" he asked, as he came from the other side of the road, and had not as yet caught sight of the statue.

* The almug trees, mentioned in the Books of Kings and Chronicles, are believed by nearly all commentators to be the lignum vitæ. Theophrastus says that the lignum vitæ, or lignum thya, grows near the Temple of Jupitor Ammon, in Africa, and resembles the Cypress in its boughs, leaves, stalks, and fruit, and that it was often called almuggin or almug tree.—EDITOR.

"Look at that," and I pointed at the beautiful work of art.

"By St. Patrick!" he exclaimed.

"Who is it?" I asked.

"Can't you see. It is Nyassa herself."

I had been struck with the great resemblance, but had not hinted a suspicion of my feeling to O'Brien. I was now confirmed in my opinion.

Whose statue was this?

That we determined to find out if we possibly could.

Leaving Medjid and Shagaffa to find a good camping ground, O'Brien and I scrambled down to the base of the pedestal on which the statue stood.

The base was made of a fine stone, like granite, but from its intense hardness when we tried to chip it, I fancy it was something even harder than that stone.

We searched on every side to find, if we could, some inscription by which the statue could be identified.

As we stood looking up at the figure we noticed that the drapery was almost Grecian in its design, and hung in flowing folds from the shoulders.

A very curious effect was observable as we gazed at it from the rear. The drapery seemed of a different stone to the figure.

In other words, we could discern through the drapery the delicately-molded limbs, and beautifully-proportioned body. So realistic was it that Jack insisted that the body was flesh-colored and of an opaque stone, while the drapery was glass or crystal.

Had any living being stood on the pedestal, with glass drapery over the form, it could not have been more real than was that exquisite work of the sculptor's hand.

I climbed to the top of the pedestal and examined the stone carefully, but could not declare of what nature it was.

To me it was so life-like and natural that I felt if I put my arms round it, I should press the flowing gown close to a warm, living form.

The more I examined it the more was I mystified as to its construction.

That it was no mere illusion I was satisfied.

I saw the elegant and perfectly-proportioned ankle; the knee was just as it came from Nature's grand workshop, a dimple was plainly visible; the figure was so exact to Nature that I felt almost constrained to fall on my knees and pour out my heart-throbbings to it.

I was near the face. It was that of Nyassa spiritualized and transparent.

If I could transport it to England, Jack could have all

the treasures of Solomon, for that one thing alone was worth more to me than all else.

I looked at the face and wondered why when the sculptor could imitate nature so fully and truthfully he could not give it life.

> "How under his forming hands a creature grew
> So lovely fair,
> That what seem'd fair in all the world seem'd now
> Mean, or in her summ'd up, in her contained,
> And in her looks, which from that time infused
> Sweetness into my heart unfelt before,
> And into all things, from her air, inspired
> The spirit of love and amorous delight."

I wished that life could be infused into the marble or alabaster and that the lovely being would be my own.

"Come here, Monty." Jack had called me several times but I was like one in a dream and heeded not his call, until, almost vexed, he demanded what stupid thing I was doing.

I got down to the ground and found him puzzling over some words which he had found on the pedestal.

For an hour we looked at, examined, and traced with our fingers the peculiar letters and hieroglyphics, until we were able to understand some of them, sufficient to know that one of the words was that by which the Ethiopians called the lovely Sheba.

It was as we had suspected. This lovely figure was that of the renowned queen.

But why had she such a striking resemblance to Nyassa! Was it a mere coincidence, or was the charming girl whose friendship we had gained really and truly descended from Makeda, or as her name was originally spelled Maqueda.

The more we puzzled over the matter the greater became the mystery.

Medjid was getting uneasy at our long absence and he began to search for us.

He caught sight of the statue just as the setting sun's rays struck the lower part of the figure.

"Wah Ilahi!" he exclaimed and fell on his face.

He thought he had seen a ghost or specter, and when we told him that it was but a piece of marble, he grew quite excited.

"But, Baas," he said. "I saw through it."

"Not through the statue, but only her clothing."

"That's so; but what is it?"

I explained as well as I could the perfection of the statu-

* Milton.

ary, and Medjid appeared confused and unable to understand the subject.

O'Brien professed to treat the matter lightly, but when I proposed to continue our journey, he declared that he was anxious to stay there another day, as something of importance might be found.

The fact was, he, too, was in love with Makeda's presentment.

"Monty, could we get it to England?" he asked, but had not said to what he referred.

"No. I am afraid it is impossible," was my reply.

"I would rather have it than all the diamonds and precious stones in the world!" he exclaimed, with enthusiasm.

"So would I."

"But you will win her, and I—— Bah! I am a fool. But really, Monty, I love Nyassa more than words can possibly describe."

"Poor fellow! for I, too, am as far gone."

The conversation ended, and we proceeded in different directions to examine the pieces of stone and other things in the vicinity of the statue.

Jack found a large, uncut diamond, one of the largest I had ever seen, and worth a fortune in itself.

The next day, our hearts buoyant and happy, we continued our journey along the magnificent road. What a pity that such a road should now be unused and valueless.

The next few days our path was through a most delightful country. The stately palms and the bushy lignum vitæ trees harbored birds of many-colored plumage. The magnificent and proud peacock was seen to perfection.

Although wild, it had a lordly air about it and its feathers were even finer than of those we had seen in the parks of England.

We reached a point of great interest on our fifth day from the statue.

Many ruins showed that some great city had once stood there. While we were exploring the ruins of houses and temples, we were suddenly surrounded by some fine-looking men who had a superior look to the M'Kambas or other dwellers of Sahara we had encountered. Instead of seeming hostile they had such a benevolent appearance that we were all taken by surprise.

One of their number, who appeared to be the chief—a man standing over six feet high and with long, woolly hair perfectly white—stepped up to us and rapidly asked the question:

"Who are you?" This he repeated in half a dozen different languages; I answered him in Abyssinian, and when he learned we were searchers after truth, and desired not to injure any of the people, he gave us a welcome to the city of the dead, for such he called the ruins among which his tribe dwelt.

I introduced, with due formality, my friend, Jack O'Brien, our guide, Medjid, and Shagaffa.

We were heartily welcomed.

When I asked the name of the tribe, the old gentleman—for such he was in manners and decorum—answered:

"We are the remnants of the Macrobii."

"And do you live forever?" asked O'Brien.

"No, but if we so desired we might do so," was the answer.

"Then why do you ever die?" Jack asked, with surprise on his face to think any one could be found who voluntarily ended his life, when there was no disturbing cause to account for it.

"That would take too long to tell. Let us eat first, and thou shalt know all that I can tell thee."

The old man led us among the ruins, until we came to what had doubtless been a cellar in the old city.

Into this we followed our guide, and found that there was quite an air of refinement about the place.

There was something different to what we had found in other tribes. An indefinable something which made us respect our host.

When we had taken our seat on some stones, our guide and host left us, promising a speedy return.

In half an hour he came to us, bringing some cool water and most luscious fruit; after partaking of which, he suggested we should look round the city.

CHAPTER XXXIV.
THE MACROBII.

THE walls of the building in which we had been seated were massive, and formed of great blocks of stone, similar to that which formed the pedestal of the crystal statue.

The ancient city, as far as we were able to judge, was not a large one, but had been built with great care and of immense strength.

It had evidently been surrounded by walls, for we distinctly saw traces of such means of defense, standing in several places twenty feet high and nearly as many feet broad.

The avenues or streets were broad, and paved with great blocks of stone, between which grass and reeds tried to force their way. At intervals there was a dense mass of scrub and brush, growing doubtless on the site of some ancient garden.

What a sight that was, in the great desert! A city capable of entertaining thousands of inhabitants, built not of the grass which formed the residences of all the tribes we had seen west of the Nile, but of huge blocks of granite. Another evidence of a greater civilization than that possessed by the Africans of the present day.

Our guide explained to us all that he could, but it fell short of what was actually the truth concerning this great city.

Rising before us were columns, beautifully proportioned and reminding me of those of El Karnae; they formed the entrance to the great temple.

Passing between the columns we found ourselves in an immense edifice, clearly outlined, and larger than any building I had ever seen.

I counted two hundred columns in the large hall, which was but the anteroom to the temple itself, and as I gazed on their majestic splendor I wondered what the roof must have been like.

Our host, divining my thoughts, pointed to a pile of broken stone, and we found it to have formed a portion of that ceiling.

Every fragment was richly painted or decorated with sculpture as fine as Mechlin lace.

In the temple proper, the ruins of which are but small compared to the outer hall, we saw fragments of statues which had doubtless been the ancient deities, worshiped in the bygone time.

Standing erect, amid the havoc of ruins, was a statue of Ammon Chnouphis, looking sublimely grand amid all the decay and desolation which surrounded it.

In a sort of bas relief was carved an allegorical picture, typifying the divine judgment.

Between two of the lesser deities of the time the symbols of wisdom were presiding at the decisive ceremonial of divine justice. The recording angel is writing the record of the soul's trial. Before him the God of Silence is seated on the upper crook of a divining rod. His finger is placed on his lips. Finally on the throne, before the doors of the nether world, is seated the great lord and master, the mighty and majestic Ammon, ready to deliver the final sentence, on which are depending the future migrations of the soul till the period of its purification and the length and nature of the new probationary life on which it has entered.

We left the temple and entered another building which was so gorgeously decorated, that we judged it must have been the dwelling of a great and privileged person—most likely the monarch of the city and country.

The old Macrobii stopped before a high wall, painted most beautifully, for even after the lapse of centuries the color of many cases was bright and clear. "Here dwelt the great queen Makeda," he said as he waved his hand round to signify the boundaries of the building.

The place possessed an increased interest to us, now that we knew for whom it had been designed and built. We examined every wall, we picked up the fallen pieces of stone, and peered into every crevice.

I pushed my arm into a large space which had formed, no doubt, a closet, but which was now half choked up with the debris.

I pulled out pieces of stone and several curios. Again I dived my hand into its inner recesses and withdrew it quickly, and, as I was unobserved, I slipped what I had found into my pocket.

I felt almost ashamed; was it not stealing? I had appropriated something which had belonged to another; surely the heirs of that person had a right to the treasure, or if no heirs were living, would not the country be the rightful owner?

We entered another mansion, the pavement tesselated, the walls rich with carvings and painted frescoes, and the ceiling, judging from small pieces which we could identify, must have been the very profusion of richness.

"Here lived Menihelek," said our guide.

"And who was the worthy?" asked O'Brien.

The old man looked almost indignant to think that O'Brien was so ignorant that he did not know who Menihelek was.

After a pause, he said:

"In the days when Makeda ruled over the land, there arose a great king in the East whose words were as the words of a god, and whose greatness was as the greatness of Ammon. His riches were vaster than the riches of all in the world beside. To him Makeda went taking with her gold and silver and spices, and she found him good to look upon, and when she returned, he came with her, and built the great road and this city. And Makeda had a son, its father was the great king and its mother the most beautiful woman that ever lived, and they called the child's name Menihelek, and he ruled over all Ithiopjawan."*

* The Bible makes no reference to Solomon ever having visited Ethiopia, although the Abyssinians have a tradition that he resided on the Island of Meroe with the Queen of Sheba, and that there a son was born to them, whose name was Menihelek. Other writers locate the "City of the Great King" further west, on what is now known as the great desert

The old Macrobii told the story as well as any professional guide, and we thanked him for the information he had given us.

"Come," he said. "It is time for our repast."

We returned to the portion of the old ruins which the chief occupied, and again we had most delicious fruit, and a drink made of spices, which was refreshing and slightly stimulating.

"Will you tell us," I asked, "why you are called Macrobii, and something about your people?"

"It gives me pleasure, though I have but seen one white man before."

"And that was here?" I felt alarmed.

"No." I breathed more freely.

"No, he continued. "I went across the desert when a boy, and saw a white man who killed all he could."

"Alas! your experience has not been a pleasant one."

"You asked after our people; we are but few in number, and shall soon be all gone. Yes, we are Macrobii, but do not care to live."

"Why?"

"What is there to live for? If we could see our children and children's children grow up it would be wise, but, alas! no women come to us."

"But have you no women?"

"Yes, but they are old. For many years no female children have been born to us, and our people are now all old."

I tried to get a history of this strange tribe, but it took a long time to get the few meager details. It would only be tedious to the reader if I gave all the conversation; I therefore quote from my journal the substance as I noted it down at the time.

The Microbii, the old man said, were the direct descendants of a people who came with the great king on his visit to Makeda. They were white and possessed great wisdom, and had learnt how to take the leaves of the coca. the thya, and a root which grew in plenty, and make a syrup therefrom which retarded the decay of the body, and prevented death. These men preferred to stay in this city after the great king returned, and they took to themselves wives of the daughters of the people.

They taught their children philosophy, and showed them how to compound the elixir. Some of the original Macrobii lived until their age was a thousand years, and then they

---

of Sahara. We read in the Bible of three other books on the life of Solomon, which are lost, though the Abyssinians claim to possess the Book of Nathan.—Ed.

grew weary of life and were gathered to their fathers in the tomb.

Their descendants soon learned to value death as most value life. And when they were weary they prayed for death to come, and they slept the sleep of peace.

"It is now a hundred years since a girl child was born to us," continued the old man, "and we will not marry with the Troglodytes, or the Blemmyes, or even the M'Kambas."

"Has no white man visited you?" I asked.

"Yes, but it was before my time. I have heard my father say that a white man came here, when he was a boy, and was searching for the treasures hid by the great king."

I looked significantly at Jack, and I saw his face change color with emotion.

"And did he find them?"

"Yes."

Jack fairly trembled. What if this white man had found them and removed the portable ones? then our journey would have been in vain.

"You say he found the treasures. Did he take them away?"

"No. He said there were too many, and their weight too great, so he would return with a lot of men and with camels and horses from Egypt, and take them."

"But he never returned?" asked Jack, his voice husky with emotion.

"No."

"But would you have allowed them to be removed?"

"Why not? We don't need them, and others may. They belonged to Makeda and the great Sulieman, but their race have long since died out, and none but ourselves remain."

"Wouldst thou show us these treasures?"

"Why not?"

"We might steal them."

The old man stood upright, looked me straight in the eye and then said: "If thou wantst the treasures take them. My father would believe—but I do not—that some one would come and show that they were of the line of Makeda, and then the treasures would belong to them."

The Macrobii was honest, and so I thought I would be equally so with him. "We came to find the treasures," I said, "and to seek knowledge."

"How knowest thou of them?",

O'Brien drew out his copy of the two maps which he had found in the escritoire, and showed them to the Macrobii.

"The same," said the old man.

"Same what?"

"The same as the white man made for my father."

Here was a strange corroboration of our whole story. The white man had made plans in duplicate, and had given one set to the father of the Macrobii.

"How long is it since the white man was here?"

"How long! I shall have seen one hundred and three score winters when the next shall pass, and my father had dwelt on earth five score summers when I was born, and only twelve had passed over him when the white man came."

Accepting the old man's story that he was one hundred and sixty years old and that his father was one hundred when his wife bore him a son, that would give two hundred and sixty years, less twelve, or bring the year to about the date mentioned on some of the documents we had found.

"Where are the other members of your tribe?" I asked.

"Ours is not a tribe," he replied with hauteur. "We are a people."

Then he quickly changed back to his pleasant manner of speaking, and told us that the other members of the family of the Macrobii were attending to their own affairs, making palm wine, or finding the roots to use with the coca and the thya, or gathering the fruit for food.

He further told us that the Macrobii never eat animal food, but lived on fruit and roots, and that they had no weapons because they never had anything to kill. Here was a people practically at peace with all the world—amiable, generous and hospitable. Using no weapons, and not even taking life for food. True, they were very few in number, but what an example they set to the tribes of Central Africa. We were fortunate in meeting with these people, for had not the old man, even if he was a hundred and sixty years old, offered to be our guide to the treasure caves?

We were elated with our success, and when night came slept soundly. Shagaffa did not like the Macrobii, for she had an idea that no one could live without flesh-meat for food.

CHAPTER XXXV.
THE SACRED SCARABÆUS.

WHEN I was alone I drew from my pocket the article I had found in the ruins of Makeda's house. I had felt so guilty when I pocketed it that I was ashamed of myself. I found it was a necklet of immense value. It consisted of over fifty scarabæus, each of which fairly bristled with diamonds and rubies. The necklet must be worth a fortune in itself.

What should I do with it?

It had been my intention of retaining it until we returned, and then placing it in the hands of Nyassa. But I felt that I had no right to do so, for had not Jack an equal right to share in the treasure?

"Jack, old fellow, come here."

I was standing out amid the ruins of the city, and had amused myself by watching the sun's rays dance and sparkle on the gems composing the necklace.

When Jack came up to me I placed it in his hands without a word.

"By St. Patrick!" he exclaimed. "Here is a fortune indeed. Where did you get it?"

I told him, and then suggested he should keep it as a portion of the treasures, of which this was the most important so far, although the rough diamond he had already in his pocket was worth a thousand pounds sterling.

He declined to take it, and then in an undertone, as though unconsciously uttering his thoughts, he said:

"I know what I should like to do with it!"

"I have an idea as well, perhaps it is the same as yours. Write yours down, and I will do the same."

Jack laughed at the boyish trick but tore a leaf out of his pocket-book, wrote a line, folded up the paper and handed it to me. I followed his example and handed my idea to O'Brien.

"Open, and read," he said.

I opened his paper and found written thereon:

"Place it on the lovely neck of Nyassa Balkis."

"Read mine, Jack."

He did so, and our ideas were the same, only mine was expressed in fewer and more abrupt words, for I had written only—

"Give it to Nyassa!"

"Jack, old fellow, we will give it as our joint present, shall we?"

"No, no, it is yours."

"Don't talk such rubbish, there is no *meum et tuum* in this matter. What is yours is mine and *vice versa*."

"All right, do as you please. I am glad Nyassa will get it."

"If we live she shall," was my response.

I had never really known what the holy Scarabæus of the Egyptians really was until Nyassa had pointed out to me at Girzeh some immense beetles at work in vast numbers, walking off with every species of dung, by forming it into balls as large as small apples, and rolling them away with their hind legs, while they walked backward by means of their fore legs. Sometimes a ball of dung would roll into a deep rut, and then another beetle would come to the assistance of the owner of the ball and quarrel for its possession when their joint labors would raise it to the level.

This beetle was the Sacred Scarabæus, and even its worship was typical of the country and its peculiarity. This beetle appears shortly after the commencement of the wet season, its labor continuing until the cessation of the rains, at which time it disappears.

The ancient Egyptians worshiped it as the harbinger of the high Nile.

The existence of lower Egypt depending upon the annual inundation, the rise of the river was observed with general anxiety. The beetle appears at the commencement of the rise in the river level, and from its great size and extraordinary activity in clearing the earth from all kinds of ordure, its presence is remarkable.

Hence the ancients evidently imagined some connection between the beetle and the river, and considered it sacred as the harbinger of the inundation.

How appropriate it would be, then, to give the necklace of the Sacred Beetle to Nyassa, who was the first to show us the genuine living insect in its work of purifying the earth.

Medjid had found in his early search a very fine piece of onyx, which he thought we would like to add to our treasures; but I told him to keep it until he returned, when we would buy it from him at a fair price.

"Baas, may I give it to Shagaffa?"

"Of course you may, you silly fellow—it is your own."

"But will you buy it from her when you leave?"

"Yes. Why?"

Medjid made no reply, and I began to believe I should have to put matters straight between him and Shagaffa.

A little later in the day I was alone with the dusky girl, and I seized the opportunity to talk with her.

"Shagaffa," I said, assuming an air of great seriousness, 'I thought you would be faithful and true to me."

She made no answer, but held down her head.

"Why don't you answer?"

"I am thine!" she said, at last.

"I know that, and I believe you are a good girl and will never leave me while I desire you to stay. Is that so?"

"It is."

"Now tell me truly, Shagaffa, do not the women of the Troglodytes ever feel they would like some man for a husband, but find themselves given to another?"

"Yes."

"What do they do then?"

"Don't ask me," she replied. "Some die, others endure, but some——" and she turned away as though the subject was obnoxious to her.

"Shagaffa, you were given me as a wife, but you love another."

No answer. So I continued:

"Why not tell me all about it?"

"You are too good, Baas——" it was the first time she had ever called me by that title. "I thought once, silly girl that I was, that I would never leave you, that I would show how different I was to the Troglodytes, by keeping to you for life; but, Baas, I found out that the sun could never mate with the darkness, that light could never exist with the black night, and that though I worshiped you as my god, you would never love me as I wanted to be loved."

"Who told you about love?"

"The same who made my heart to beat; who made me like to hear sweet music. The same that showed me the difference between dark and light. Oh! all know what love is."

"You love Medjid?"

Her eyes flashed as I spoke, and then the tears rolled down her cheeks. I saw that the whole love of her heart had gone out to the Nubian.

"Medjid!" I shouted.

Shagaffa tried to run away, but I took her wrist and held her fast.

When Medjid came up to us he looked at us in astonishment.

"Medjid, I have found a treasure which I value very highly, and which I consider worth great riches. Now, I have thought of your faithfulness, and have determined to present the treasure to you."

"But, Baas——"

"Wait a moment. When I have told you what the treasure is, you can then refuse it, and I would rather you do so if you think it unsuited to you." The good fellow opened his eyes scarcely comprehending what I was saying, so I put an end to his doubt by adding: "Here it is. I call it Shagaffa. Take her, and may Heaven bless you."

"Do you mean it?"

"I do! Don't you want her?"

"Oh, Baas, I am so happy. I love Shagaffa more than my life."

"And you, Shagaffa?"

She hung her head, and in low, faint tones said, "I love Medjid and am happy."

"Go then and be happy. And if we all reach Dongola again, safely, I will give Shagaffa such a wedding-present as will make her heart glad. But as for you, Medjid, if you ever ill-treat her or say an unkind word, and I hear of it, I will kill you like a dog."

Shagaffa smiled through her tears and said:

"But my Medjid could never be unkind."

So I lost my wife—in name—and Shagaffa found a third husband.

It was only another episode in African life.

After spending several days with the Macrobii, and learning to admire their simple and childlike ways, we left the ruins of the great city, and guided by the Patriarch of the Macrobii, wended our way along the great road.

Our guide knew the best camping-places, could point out the wells of coolest water, and show where game could be procured.

For himself he would gather a handful of fruit, and that would suffice for his meal.

The road seemed more wonderful the further we traversed it. Its surface, even though unused for perhaps two thousand years, was even and clean, and must have been the very perfection of road-making when it was first opened for the chariots and horsemen of the powerful Queen of Sheba and the more powerful Solomon.

For four days we continued our journey, finding occasional relics of great value which we secreted until we should return.

When we had ended our fourth day our guide suggested that we rest the next, for after that we might have to walk in difficult places and have but scant rest.

We therefore took his advice and slept and rested all we could during the whole of the next day.

When the sun rose on the morning of the third day, our guide prostrated himself and adored the wonderful orb, and so glorious was it, as seen shedding its golden rays on the wide expanse of country that we could scarcely refrain from following so excellent an example and adoring the great life-giving power—the emblem of the Supreme being.

CHAPTER XXXVI.

THE HALL OF IVORY.

"The groves were God's first temples. Ere man learn'd
To hew the shaft, and lay the architrave,
And spread the roof above them, ere he framed
The lofty vault, to gather and roll back
The sound of anthems, in the darkling wood,
Amidst the cool and silence, he knelt down
And offered to the Mightiest solemn thanks
And supplication . . ."

"These words of Bryant's came across my mind as expressive of my own feelings when by noontime we had climbed down the side of the road and stood in one of the most lovely groves I had ever seen. The palm, stately and grand, the thya tree and trees of every kind known to the tropics grew there in luxuriance.

The air was redolent with sweet perfume wafted by the zephyr breeze from innumerable spice trees. The birds sang sweetly, and the stately and haughty peacock moved about in all its native grace and beauty.

We stood for awhile admiring the solitude of the grove, and then followed our guide until we forced our way through thick brush to a huge ruin, apparently a portion of the side of a pyramid.

Instantly we recognized it as the one we had found the drawing of, and the same that Jack had seen in his dream. The ruin before us was erected of huge stones; but they were not dressed to the square, and the mortar was only employed to give a superficial polish.

The Macrobii told us that this was the ancient grove of Milcom, the god of the Ammonites, who numbered his worshipers in every part of the country.

The gigantic face on the stone was supposed to be that of Milcom, who was the giver of the rain and dew, the glory and substance of the sky.

The Macrobii told us that the people who worshiped here in days long gone by, looked upon the face as an oracle, and they consulted it, and received answers to their supplications.

The ruin is fast crumbling to decay, but sufficient of it was seen to show how vast had been its proportions when first erected.

The face which remained entire, we measured, and found to be seven feet eight inches in height by seven in breadth.

"Now, Monty, what think you?" Jack exclaimed, triumphantly, "you see my dreams are all true."

"Not so fast, Jack. You had a drawing of this which

you found in the escritoire, so the dream may have been but the reflex of your own brain vision."

"Stuff and nonsense, but what about the entrance to the cave?"

"That will be a test, I admit."

When we had signified our readiness to continue our journey, our guide led us round the ruined pyramid or temple to a large open space in the grove, the center of which was occupied with gigantic stones so much resembling those which Jack had seen in his dream that I shuddered. A cold chill passed over me, and I could scarcely speak.

As for O'Brien, he fairly danced with joy.

I took the drawing from my pocket, and it was so exact that I could almost imagine it to have been an actual sketch taken on the spot, instead of a drawing from memory of a place seen in a dream.

The Macrobii paused when he got to this entrance, and asked if we were still desirous of finding the treasures.

Such was our object, and we would face any dangers or endure any hardships.

He then went to the slab, just as Jack had seen in his dream, and tilted up the end, bidding us walk in as he held it. We did so, and a moment later he was with us, leading the way along a dark passage.

"This is the entrance nearest the city," said the old guide. "The entrance for the chariots is on the mountain side near the end of the great road."

"But how far are the mountains?" I asked.

"Do you mean to the summit?"

"Yes."

"About five days' journey from here."

"Then how is it we did not see the mountain range?"

The old man looked pleased at the question, and then told us that we were in the mountains, that we had been climbing the mountain all the way from the Triumphal Arch; that the road was so gradual in its ascent that no one could believe they were going up the mountain side, yet such was the case. We walked along as rapidly as we could, following in a direct line our guide, whose form could be seen but dimly.

We were amazed at the purity of the atmosphere, but this was accounted for by so many air-shafts having been sunk, through which, as the foul atmosphere escaped, the light streamed in.

After walking several miles, as it seemed to us, we reached a large cave almost similar in its form and construction to the cave of the Black Rhinoceros we had seen at Mer. At one end were three figures seated in state.

They were the gods of the Ethiopians at the time of Makeda. One god represented wisdom and knowledge, another had a lyre by its side and was typical of the fine arts; while the third was a nude female figure, perfect and lovely, the marble being tinted to a natural flesh color. The face almost Grecian, long hair caught up by a scarabæus and then falling gracefully like a wave down the back. This was the goddess of love, and typified *la grande passion*, better than any statue, ancient or modern, I had ever seen. It was chaste as marble, and yet warm in its tints as the glorified body of a perfect woman.

In all the majesty of nature, in all the evidences of creative skill, there is nothing more beautiful, more perfect or sublime, nothing more nearly approaching Divinity itself than the female form when untortured by fashion and its suicidal contrivances.

The ancients often deified the female form, and the poets in all ages have made their angels women.

On the side immediately opposite the three deities was a colossal statue, so mutilated that it was impossible to say for whom it had been intended.

The upper part of the head was destroyed, all that was left of the lower was a portion of the chin, showing a very long beard, which fell over flowing garments to the waist.

Our guide said it was the great king, meaning Solomon, and that it had been placed there by Menihelek, the son of Solomon and Makeda.

In another portion of the building was a bas-relief representing the fight for the supremacy among the animals.

Seated in the center, on a high throne, was the ape, who held aloft a crown which he had won. Near by, but occupying inferior positions, was the lion and the rhinoceros, the peacock and a small eagle.

The ape had won the supremacy, and, next to man, had dominion over the beasts of the field and the fowls of the air.

We passed out of this monster cave into a passage, or hall, filled with fantastic-shaped stalagmites and stalactites, some of which represented, very fairly, natural objects, while others conveyed to the mind such weird designs as looked almost supernatural.

In the next large cave we entered, we lighted the lamps which the Macrobii had provided for us and then we saw a most wonderful effect.

As we looked up at the vaulted roof we beheld an excellent representation of the moon and stars shining in the blue firmament. As we gazed in wonderment, we saw the millions of little points sparkling and twinkling as realistic as though they were the stars themselves. Jack insisted that every one of the points or stars was a diamond, and that they had been by some means affixed in the roof as a safe method of storing.

If the idea was a correct one, there was no doubt about the safety of the gems, for the dome of the roof must have been nearly three hundred feet high.

So far we had only seen a succession of passages and large caves, and began to desire a sight of some of the vast treasures.

"The great king," said the Macrobii, "intended closing up the entrance on the mountain and making the secret way by which we have come the only way to his treasures. Therefore he filled those nearest the mountain and left these empty."

Whether this was told us as an encouragement I don't know, but I began to weary of our march. I had no taste for being so long underground, and when I learned that we should be several days without seeing the sun, I asked why we had not climbed the mountain and entered that way.

"The road is difficult," was the reply.

We had been in the cave for three days before we saw anything in the shape of treasures. Statues innumerable, all of vast dimensions and absorbing interest. Pieces of statuary which had not been seen by white man for hundreds, perhaps thousands of years; but these were not what we were searching for. Medjid and Shagaffa had not a word of complaint. They were so happy in their love that they were as ready to spend their honeymoon under ground as anywhere else.

To those who say that real honest love can only be found in those of light skin, I would say that "if there is an elysium on earth" these colored people, the Nubian and the Troglodyte had found it.

On the morning of the fourth day since entering the subterranean halls, we entered a large cave, which must have been at least five hundred feet long by as many broad, and with a height of half as many feet.

Here we found ivory in such abundance that I could not imagine so much had ever been obtained since the killing of the first elephant.

Round the walls, tusks were piled solidly to the height of four or five feet. Jack, who was always fond of figures, began to reckon and compute the number.

He counted the number to a yard, and then estimated the length of the piles, but he soon got bewildered for he had already reached into thousands of millions, and he laughed as he threw down his pencil.

"I give it up," said he, "but if we had a thousandth part of this, couldn't we rule the ivory market."

"Jack, has it ever occurred to you how we are going to get these things home. You can only carry one tusk, and perhaps the bar of gold will be so heavy that you could not carry even one away."

"My dear fellow, I never thought of that when we started, but it has puzzled me lots of times since."

"We may get enough to pay our expenses and perhaps a few relics for our friends besides, but that will be all."

Besides the great piles of tusks, I saw something which filled me with wonder. As I moved with my foot the dust of centuries, which had gathered on the floor, I found that the whole cave or room had been paved with polished ivory.

In the center was a table large enough to dine a hundred people; its legs and supports were made of tusks elaborately carved, and its top was polished ivory inlaid with rubies, emeralds and sapphires. Several small statues stood round the table, each made of ivory, some almost covered with gold.

"I have it," said Jack.

"I see you have," I laughed, for Jack had rested his hand on one of the statues.

"I don't mean this statue," he answered.

"What then?"

"How to get the treasures home."

"Well, how is it?"

"When we get back we will tell what we have seen, and form a limited company to fetch the treasures."

"Good idea, but not for us. We should pe paid for our secret in capital stock, for if we asked cash, no one would believe our story. The expedition would start, and the whole of the subscribed stock would be swallowed up by the time old Amlekla was reached, the company would fail, the stock would realize about one per cent., and a new company would step in—in which we should have no share —and bring back the treasures. That is the usual thing, my boy. If you are bent on this thing, I will wait until the failure, and then I'll purchase stock in the new company."

"Botheration take you, Monty! You are never serious!"

"It is because I am so serious that I speak as I do. In too many instances these stock companies are only so many traps for catching dupes, and in other cases the original inventor, discoverer or idealist, gets shunted after his secret is known, and others make wealth while he starves."

"I am afraid you are right."

To change the drift of the conversation I suggested that

we dust the chairs and table and, for once in our lives, eat from a table worth many thousands of pounds.

The resolution was carried and, amid the glitter of rubies and emeralds, and on a surface of polished ivory we drank the health of King Solomon (in water) and toasted the lovely Queen Makeda.

CHAPTER XXXVII.
FACING DEATH.

WHEN our repast was finished I suggested we should leave this wonderful palace of ivory and continue our journey.

I asked our old guide how long it was since he had gone through these caves.

He answered that he had not been there since he was a small child, and then his father took him through to teach him a lesson.

"To teach you a lesson?" I repeated.

"Yes, to show the folly of hoarding up what can never be used. My father always said that we were not to be anxious about the future, but to let each day find food for itself."

Philosophy was the last thing I expected to hear in that wild region; and yet where could there be a better place for wisdom than in the wise king's treasure-house?

We entered another hall, which was so dark that we had to again light our lamps.

"I don't know what to make of this," said the Macrobii, "for all the passages should be lighted."

We stumbled on for some distance, and heard a strange rumbling noise.

The next instant I was seized round the waist from behind, and dragged off my feet.

What did it mean?

Medjid was shouting for us to come back, and I was struggling in the arms of some one I could not see.

"Who is it? What do you want?" shouted O'Brien.

"Come back, if you value your life!" answered Medjid.

"Come, dear Baas," came in the gentle voice of Shagaffa, and I then knew she was responsible for my ungainly mode of exit.

We got back into the Ivory Palace as quickly as possible, and then I found that the rumbling noise we heard was caused by the falling in of one of the walls of the ivory cave, and the Macrobii at the same time declared our passage was blocked.

A huge bowlder had fallen only a few feet in f of him, and more were being loosened.

How strange, that on the very day we had got into the treasure caves there should be that upheaval of the rocks and the effectual stopping up of the way to the diamond and gold caves!

There was a fatality about it which seemed to strike us all with fear.

Medjid actually trembled. Shagaffa clung to him with fright, while O'Brien declared that he was sure his hair had turned white.

As for myself—suffice it to say, I thought my end had come, and that, after all the speculations of the future, I was to be buried alive under the walls of King Solomon's treasure caves!

It was unsafe to stay even in the vast room devoted to the ivory storage, for one side had already slipped, and we could see far up above us the glimmering of stars, though it was noonday.

We must retrace our steps and depart without the treasure.

The Macrobii started rather gloomily, but almost before we left the large room, he came back wild with excitement.

Even our retreat was cut off. The passage had fallen in, and it was impossible to climb over the scattered rocks.

The rumbling continued, and we knew we were in the throes of an earthquake.

What could be done?

There seemed no way of escape.

Our lives would be sacrificed in the struggle for wealth which we had not earned or even gathered together. Our names would be dropped from the very mention of our friends, and in a few short years we should be entirely forgotten.

Such is the eternity of a man's name.

It was horrible that five human beings should be buried alive in the midst of so much wealth.

Was there no escape?

"There is but one chance," said the Macrobii.

"One chance!" that was joy even to our troubled minds.

One chance for life. How eagerly we bent forward to hear the old man describe our only hope.

He pointed above to the stars. "There is an opening," he said, "or we should not see them. We must climb up the side here."

If that was our only chance we might as well lie down and die at once.

It was an impossibility.

Still the love of life is strong in all, and when the old man said he should try it, and O'Brien declared there was nothing out of the range of possibility, we gained courage and determined to try our one chance.

If we failed we should only die, and better die fighting for life than to give up all hope like cowards.

Before we started O'Brien had tried to get some of the rubies from the table, but they resisted all his efforts.

Our difficult climb commenced.

Shagalfa came to me and said she was sure we should all die, and then put up her face and said:

"Kiss me just once, Baas."

I pressed a kiss on her lips, and then our perilous attempt to escape began.

The Macrobii started and made good headway. I followed, then Shagalfa, O'Brien and Medjid.

For two hours we continued to toil upward. It seemed like as many weeks. Every step was fraught with danger, at each movement we felt the rocks and earth giving way under our feet.

The wall up which we had to climb was almost perpendicular, and therefore all the more difficult to obtain a foothold.

After three hours' battling with the shifting earth, we found ourselves safe and uninjured, but very tired, on a huge rock, large enough for us to stand or, sit upon for a short rest.

We looked up. The stars had disappeared, and we saw the azure vault of heaven above us. This gave us hope and new courage, for we knew we had not more than a hundred yards more to climb.

Again we started, and toiled on for an hour, never resting, but using one hand to make new footholds even while we grasped the side of the bank with the other.

Another hour passed, and the top looked as far off as ever. There was no rest for us; we must go on, and on, or drop to the bottom, mangled corpses.

Our hands were losing the sense of touch, and our feet began to tremble as we touched new footholds.

If we got no rest, we must even now, within a few yards of safety, give up and die.

My brain began to swim; I had lost all care for life. I would just as soon die as live. Such was my feeling.

Mechanically, I suppose, I must have continued stepping up higher and still higher. I had lost all consciousness; I knew not whether my companions were alive or dead, neither did I care. All feeling had left me.

"Courage!" I heard, like a soft whisper, but I had no sense of either hope or fear left. The next minute I felt my arm seized, and a wrench which almost tore it from my shoulder gave me a twinge of intense pain.

I felt some water on my face and opened my eyes. I was lying on the green grass on the mountain side, safe and alive. I looked round and saw O'Brien, Medjid and Shagaffa.

For a moment I missed the Macrobii, but I caught sight of him bringing one of our water bottles, and then dashing the water in our faces.

He had got to the summit first and had then pulled each of us to the top. What a narrow escape we had! Even now the beads of perspiration stand on my face at the thought.

We rested all the remainder of that day and all night, and then declared we were ready to return.

"But the treasures?" said the Macrobii.

"They are lost to us and the world," said Jack.

"No, not so; we can go to the other entrance, for most likely that will be open."

Strange as it may appear, yet it is the truth, the hope of gaining the treasures made us resolve to go on and again risk our lives for gold.

CHAPTER XXXVIII.
WEALTH GALORE!

WE felt none the worse the next day for our perilous fight for life, excepting a stiffness only natural.

But when we breathed the pure air, and felt its invigorating influence, we laughed at fear and declared we were ready once again to test the truth of our maps, and find the other treasure caves of old King Solomon.

It took us all that day until late at night to reach the road, and then fortunately we found a most picturesque little lake of ice-cold water. We drank our fill, we replenished our bottles, and then enjoyed a plunge into the water.

It was the most refreshing bath I had ever taken, and I felt to have lost all my stiffness and fatigue in that water. The higher we climbed the road, the less vegetation we found forcing its way through the stones, and therefore we had a better opportunity of examining the bed of the road.

We had three days' march before we reached the summit of the hill.

Looking back, we saw how beautifully the road had been graded, and were surprised at the gentle ascent to so high a point.

On the other side of the hill, at a distance of about a mile, we saw another arch similar to the one at the commencement of the road.

This proved the correctness of our maps, and showed what a careful observer the draftsman had been.

We descended the hill, and saw stretched before us a plateau, strangely excavated, and looking more like a fortification than anything I could think of at the time.

THE MOUNTAIN CAVE ENTRANCE.

In the center of the plateau was a large circle cut out of the solid rock and formed by a lower roadway. In the perpendicular walls of the circle were several entrances beautifully arched.

Each entrance was large enough for a chariot to pass through.

Under the roadway was another arched entrance, which the Macrobii told us was for the horses, as there were remains of large stables in the rocks near by the entrance.

Everything was cut and designed with the same precision as the road itself.

Even if we found no treasures we were well repaid for our journey. The scenery was delightful and picturesque.

On one side stretched a wide expanse of desert as far as the eye could reach, on the other the lovely oasis over which we had passed.

In the distance we could see dimly the twin mountains of the Troglodytes standing out in their bare and rugged grandeur. And as I pointed them out to Shagaffa she shuddered with fear, and wondered whether as we returned we should escape the terrible creatures.

Our guide was very thoughtful, and said he would not allow us to risk our lives until he had first found the entrance and saw whether all was right.

For several hours we waited his return, and we began to think that some evil had come to him and that perhaps he had met with accident or death, when we saw his white, wooly head emerge from the entrance gate.

"Ah! Baas," he said. "The earth trembles have filled up most of the caves—but one is open. Come!"

The Macrobii suggested we should leave Shagaffa on the outside, but she declared that she would rather share the danger.

Once again we started, and went all safely through the gateway. We began to laugh at the dangers.

Our laugh came too soon. No sooner had we got past the first entrance than we saw our guide began to climb a pile of rocks.

We followed, wondering how we could possibly get down again, even if we safely reached the top.

After a troublesome scramble up broken pieces of stone, we saw a hole about the size of a man's body through which we had to crawl.

When we did so the sight was very bewildering.

Standing on a small platform, about ten feet square, we looked down at the abyss beneath.

"Down there," said the Macrobii guide.

"But how?" I asked.

"This way, Baas!" he said.

I watched the old man lower himself over the rock, and then his head disappeared; he had dropped about eight feet.

"Be careful! for the rock is small," he shouted.

I began to feel that it would be better to draw back, but was ashamed of my fears.

"Are you going?" asked O'Brien, almost angrily.

I scrambled to the edge, my heart palpitating violently, and then, when I was hanging by my hands, I confess I would have gone back if I could have drawn myself up, but that I felt to be impossible. Holding my breath, I loosed my hands and fell with a sickening thud on the rock beneath, and should certainly have fallen had not our guide caught me.

"Steady!" he said, "and watch me."

The same maneuver was gone through again, and another fall of about the same distance.

No less than four such drops had to be taken before we reached the bottom. Shagaffa was the bravest of all, for she made each fall steadily and fearlessly.

If it was so difficult to get down, what must it be to ascend?

I began to fear we should never succeed in getting out of our prison cave; but, with wealth on every side of us, perish in its midst.

When we were at last at the bottom, the Macrobii led

the way through a long, dark passage, broad enough for a chariot to pass along.

The rocks had been placed there, so we were told, with a view of effectually closing up the cave at that side, for formerly there was a chariot-way right through the caves.

Nearly a hundred yards had to be traversed before we reached the place where the treasures were stored.

This cave was a large one, and filled with cases made of the lignum vitæ wood, all heavily barred and sealed.

I cut one of the seals from the first box and put it in my haversack.

When I submitted it to an authority in numismatics, he offered me a thousand pounds for it, for he declared it was a veritable seal of Solomon.

I keep it as an heirloom, and value it more than all my other treasures.

For nearly two hours we hammered away with stones at the lock, and our labor was well rewarded.

The box-lid sprung open, and we found the entire chest filled with diamonds of all sizes, ranging from small ones of about five carats to others as large as small hen's eggs.

What a treasure! What wealth!

But how could we carry them?

To remove so vast a quantity was an impossibility.

We agreed to put all our food and stores into two haversacks and fill one with the diamonds.

In addition to this we filled our pockets and Shagaffa said that now she had learned the value of clothes; she had often wondered of what use they were.

When we got all we could carry, we started back.

The stones were heavy, and we wondered how we were going to get up the rocks with such an immense load.

The Macrobii, however, showed us a way by which we could crawl out, but which it would have been impossible to use in the descent, as we should have had to go the entire distance head first.

It was tedious but far better than having to climb up the perpendicular rocks.

We reached the open air safely and sat down to rest.

"How in the name of St. Patrick did they get those big rocks there?" asked O'Brien.

Neither of us could answer that problem. The rocks must have weighed a hundred tons each, yet they were quarried and drawn to the top of the hill and placed in position in the cave entrance.

We camped there that night, and on the following morning started on our homeward journey.

In due time we reached the great city, and spent a week resting at the house of our guide.

I wondered how we could repay him for his trouble, but whatever we suggested his answer was the same.

"No, Baas!" he said. "I am an old man and the exercise has done me good."

When we were on the point of leaving I gave him my watch, which had pleased his fancy so much.

I explained to him its action and movements, and he danced like a young child, so pleased was he with his present.

I hated to part with it, but it was the only thing which he had felt any interest in, and we felt we must give him something.

He insisted on going with us as far as the arch, and when we had camped another day, he volunteered to show us a safer road than the one which we had taken on our journey to the caves. Our new route lay by way of the well, and there we camped long enough to get a good supply of game and recuperate our wasted energies.

The old man gave us such explicit directions that we felt we should not lose our way.

The time had come for parting with our aged philosopher, who boasted his hundred and sixty years of life.

He shed tears as the hour approached, and turning to us, asked that we send no white men to the caves, but if ever we liked to come, he would welcome us, and if he rested in the tomb every surviving Macrobii would be our friend.

His last words struck us as strange.

"If ever," he said, "you see Makeda—for she still lives; her soul was too good, too great, ever to die—tell her that the treasures are hers, and that the Macrobii who served her and her son have faithfully guarded them."

With these words he left us, and we felt like parting with an old friend.

We watched his form gradually growing less in the dim distance, but never once did he turn his head to look back. Our faces had been a glimpse of a new world to him, and he was exceeding sorrowful at having parted from us.

We stayed another day and night at the well, and then resumed our journey.

The bag of diamonds was heavy, and it took all our strength to carry them. Neither of us could endure the weight for more than half a mile. Shagaffa insisted on taking her share of the burden, but although Medjid was almost cross with her, and offered to carry the bag for double distance, she insisted.

"Shagaffa," I said, "I shall not love you if you carry the bag."

She only laughed, and retorted that I had never loved her.

But she was happy, and perhaps more so for having her own way, for all know—

> "He is a fool, who thinks by force or skill
> To turn the current of a woman's will.
> For if she will, she will, you may depend on't,
> And if she won't, she won't, and there's an end on't."

We traveled on, passing the twin mountains which towered above us many miles to the north, and we were fortunate in not seeing any more of the Troglodytes.

I wondered whether Gabzenati still was king, and Benizid his principal chief.

We have never heard anything about that wonderful people since, so I am unable to satisfy the curious.

CHAPTER XXXIX.
HOMEWARD BOUND.

FOLLOWING the directions implicitly we continued our journey to the oasis where we had seen the Blemmyes.

Our treasures and surplus stores were just as we had left them, and the lion skin, even though we were so heavily weighted, I determined should go with us.

We wasted no time there for fear of another surprise, but struck the road to the south.

When we were on a parallel line with the mountains inhabited by the old witch Amlekla and her strange people, we fell in with some traders going to Khartum.

They had a quantity of camels to spare and we arranged to purchase four of them.

We had considerable haggling over the price for we were afraid to tell of our riches, and our firearms we did not want to part with.

We concluded a bargain, however, at last.

Though, even at the last minute, the chief trader wanted us to give him Shagaffa in addition to the price agreed upon.

We assured him she was a free woman, but he only laughed and said that all were free until they were sold.

O'Brien was shrewder than I was, and was constantly on his guard, watching every movement of the rascally fellows, and in one instance saved our property and perhaps our lives.

A cry was raised that they were short of food, and they demanded that we should open our haversack and produce the food we had secreted away.

This was only a ruse to find out what treasures we were

carrying, and Jack's subtlety and cunning tided over the difficulty and restored all to good humor.

We reached Khartum safely, and chartered a dahabeah for our journey north. Just as we were ready to start we missed Shagaffa. She had been with us only a few minutes previously.

We searched in every direction, but for several hours without any result. Medjid was nearly mad with the thoughts of his loss, and we felt equally bad. A muffled cry smote upon our ears as we were passing a house in a low and almost deserted quarter. Instinctively we knew it proceeded from Shagaffa, and regardless of consequences we burst in the door and searched the house.

On the top floor we saw the devoted girl gagged, and her arms pinioned by her side, while over her was standing the chief trader.

A blow from O'Brien's strong hand knocked the scoundrel to the floor, and Medjid, before we had time to prevent him, had stuck his knife through the villain's heart.

Shagaffa was saved and her abductor dead.

The neighborhood was unsafe for us to tarry in, so we released Shagaffa and made the best haste we could to our dahabeah.

We were only just in time, for the traders' friends had followed us, and, as the boat was pushed into the water, fired at us with their old-fashioned muskets.

We returned the salute, and had the satisfaction of seeing two of the fellows fall to the ground, dead. After a long and tedious sail, relieved by occasional fights with crocodiles and hippopotami, we reached Dongola safely.

Here we went to the house of the old chief who had offered his services as guide, and made an arrangement by which Medjid and Shagaffa should have a good income for the future. We secured our papers from the Turkish magistrate and prepared to leave, when Medjid and Shagaffa asked to be allowed to go to England with us. We could not well refuse, so our party was again united.

When we reached Girzeh we learned that Nyassa Balkis had returned to Alexandria, and most likely was now in England.

It was just twelve months since we had left Girzeh, and what changes must have taken place! We could not help wondering whether our names had been remembered, and whether Nyassa was still unmarried.

Business delayed us at Girzeh for nearly a month, and the time hung heavily on our hands.

With what joy at last we reached Cairo, and how delighted to jump aboard a train bound for Alexandria!

Shagaffa had never seen a dahabeah before, and her astonishment was great, but when we entered the railroad cars, her face was a picture. She clapped her hands and laughed with glee. Then she put her head out of the window, and I was afraid she would get hurt.

One thing was a great trouble and annoyance to her: She could not get accustomed to clothes, and I heard her tell Medjid how pleased she would be to get to England, for then she would throw off her clothes and be once more free.

I could not refrain from laughing at the idea, and when I told her what I had overheard she pouted her lips and pretended to be quite sulky.

"When I come to see you I will wear these horrid things; but at no other time will I do so."

She felt uncomfortable, and could not imagine of what use the clothes were.

By the time we had reached Alexandria she had become a little more reconciled.

We went to the European Hotel, on the Grand Square, and I represented Medjid as a chief who was traveling to see the world. He was therefore treated courteously, and Shagaffa was made quite a pet of by the ladies.

When we had purchased some new clothes, we presented ourselves at the house of Nyassa's guardian and received a very warm welcome.

Nyassa had only gone to England two months before, and the banker was highly delighted at our prospect of going soon, for his daughter was to join Nyassa, and he had been puzzled how to get her there, his old friend, the captain, having joined the majority, and gone to his last account.

By a strange coincidence the banker's daughter was called Nyassa, and was a charming girl of seventeen summers.

A few weeks later we were all on board the good ship De Lesseps, homeward bound.

But how we missed the jolly captain. Medjid and Shagaffa were registered on the ship's books as "Monsieur Medjid Monty and wife."

Medjid insisted that if he must have a second name he would have none but the one by which he had heard me called so often.

The good ship landed us safely at Southampton, and when we reached London we were so bronzed that our friends did not recognize us.

CHAPTER XL.

ONE YEAR LATER.

The sun was shining most gloriously over the banks of the river Thames, as I sat on the verdant lawn which reached from my residence at Richmond to the river.

I was seated in a little rustic chair watching the merry couples as they paddled past in their frail canoe, or sat looking spoony at each other in a row boat.

The cigar I was smoking had been a good one, and I was watching the white ash as it projected a good two inches from my mouth.

I was wondering whether I could manage to smoke to the end without dropping the ash, when a pair of soft white arms were thrown round my neck, and the ash dropped to the ground.

"Did the poor boy lose his ash?"

"Nyassa, my own."

"Yes, love, I am your own, and I bring you news."

"But I thought you were in London."

"So I was, a short time ago, but I hurried home and found two letters awaiting me. Oh, such news!"

"What is it?"

"I won't tell you—yes I will—but give me a kiss first."

I gave her one, and then she said:

"Who do you think will be here for dinner?"

"Nay, dearest——"

"Why Jack and Mrs. O'Brien, and his excellency, Medjid Monty and Lady Monty," and she laughed.

But to go back in my history. I found Nyassa Balkis single but not heart whole, for she told me with a charming naivete that I had taken the largest share of her heart with me over the desert.

Two months later we were married, and Jack O'Brien accepted the inevitable with good grace and acted as my best man.

The first bridesmaid was "Cousin Nyassa," and she made an excellent partner for handsome, dashing Jack.

Medjid and Shagaffa were there, and that wild young lady had not thrown off her clothes yet.

They had been made pets of by society, and Medjid was highly amused to find himself dubbed "his excellency," and Shagaffa "lady."

The diamonds proved worth a million and a half pounds, so as we divided equally into three shares, we had made £500,000 each by our fifteen months trip in search of King Solomon's treasures.

I forgot to say that Nyassa—my Nyassa, as I often called her—wore on her wedding day the handsome scarabæus necklace which I had found mid the ruins of the Queen of Sheba's palace.

We had been married ten months, and Jack O'Brien had just returned from his honeymoon bringing his Nyassa with him to our house, as his first place of call.

"I got Nyassa after all," he said, that evening after dinner.

"So did I," I replied, and then we laughed as happy husbands can afford to do.

We were all happy, and if I could be sure of such glorious results following, I would recommend all my single friends to go and search for King Solomon's treasures. But if Amlekla still lives, and the Blemmyes are as rampant and hideous as ever, and seeing that there are no other Nyassas in the world, I say, be content with what you have and don't seek buried treasure.

Nyassa O'Brien was more charming as a wife than she was as a girl, and Jack is as proud of her as if she were descended from King Solomon in all his glory.

That reminds me, that out of curiosity I searched into the records of the Balkis family and traced back Nyassa's genealogy to Menihelek, who ruled over Ethiopia. If he was the son of Solomon and the Queen of Sheba, then my wife is the direct descendant of the wisest and wealthiest king who ever lived and reigned.

Some day I'm going to try and get the statue of the first queen, the lovely Makeda, brought to England, but if I do it shall stand with its transparent robes in my own park.

Nyassa says if the clothes are as transparent as both Jack and I intimated, the statue had better stay where it is, but Lady Shagaffa Monty declares that the less clothes a woman wears the more lovely her form and figure.

The two ladies don't agree on that topic, but Shagaffa is determined that the young colored Monty shall grow up with her opinion firmly impressed upon her mind, for when you visit the lovely estate owned by Medjid, you will in summer time see a little naked baby being fondled by its mother and almost worshiped by its father. I often tease Nyassa and tell her if ever we have children they shall grow up to abhor clothes, but I get my ears boxed for my pains. And now my story is finished. I lost my *ennui* and gained a wife. I searched for King Solomon's treasures and obtained the great king's descendant for a wife. I am the happiest man in all the British isles, although when Jack is around he qualifies it by adding: "Except Jack O'Brien."

To young men about town I would say, go to Africa rather than give way to *ennui*, and if you gain a good wife you will have greater riches than all the treasures of that king who declared that all was vanity and vexation of spirit. I searched for adventure and found it, but I would not part with a single hour's happiness which I have with my dear Nyassa for all King Solomon's Treasures.

[THE END.]

MUNRO'S LIBRARY.

Vol. 50.　No. 739.　　　July 5, 1887.

Entered at the Post Office, N. Y., as Second Class Matter.
Munro's Library is issued Tri-Weekly.

"BESS."

A COMPANION TO "JESS."

By the Author of "King Solomon's Wives," "King Solomon's Treasures," "He," "It," etc., etc.

[John De Morgan]

Entered according to Act of Congress, in the year 1887, by Norman L. Munro, in the office of the Librarian of Congress, at Washington, D. C.

NEW YORK:
NORMAN L. MUNRO, PUBLISHER,
24 AND 26 VANDEWATER ST.

"BESS."

A COMPANION TO "JESS."

By the Author of "King Solomon's Wives," "King Solomon's Treasures," "He," "It," etc., etc.

CHAPTER I.

HOW THIS BOOK CAME TO BE WRITTEN.

I NEVER thought a few weeks ago that I should be preparing a story of real life for the press, though if it comes to a question of adventures, I have no doubt I could make the hair of my reader's heads stand on end, and cause the nervous to peer into ever cranny and corner the moment the evening's darkness fell on the earth, for I have been a traveler.

Ay, and something more. For I have seen service in India and Africa, and in my younger days I had a brush with the Russians in the great Crimean war.

But let me tell who I am, or else you may be tempted to throw down the book and declare that it is only some inane fiction.

I, Henry Waldo Adair, captain in her Britannic Majesty's Tenth Regiment of Cavalry, after knocking about the world for over a third of a century, returned home a few weeks ago to settle down and prepare for the enemy that finally conquers all.

When I reached London I felt just like a fish out of water. Everything was strange to me. Even the way people conversed was peculiar. I knew more about life in the jungle and society in the barracks than I did about the queen's drawing-rooms, fashionable parties, or balls.

It was true I was out of place. I had only been in England for a month or so at a time ever since I started out as a youngster to win my spurs in the Crimea.

After fighting there, and seeing the fall of Sebastopol, and making the acquaintance of Florence Nightingale in the hospital of Scutari—God bless her—I was invalided home—no; that was not my luck, but to Malta, and there I stayed for six months.

Ensign Adair was promoted to the position of lieutenant for distinguished bravery on the field—bah! that is what the order said, but the secret was that I happened to have a good deal of influence with my colonel, and then my old father was a master of foxhounds and a member of Parliament and a thick and thin supporter of the government, that was what got me my promotion.

Well, I had a taste of Indian life, then I got somehow to China, and afterward to Africa.

Now that brings me to this story.

I had been stationed for some time at Natal, and had taken part in the various disturbances which occurred in the colony.

Later I was in the Zulu war, and in the troubles with the Transvaal.

Now what could I do in London? Society was so different, and the manners and customs were not so free as in the Cape colony.

I was just on my way to the War Office, for I was on half-pay—my father had long since gone the way of all flesh, and my promotion ended when I got a captaincy—and was meditating arranging to take up my residence again in Africa, when I saw a man coming toward me, whose face was like a revelation.

Who was he?

I knitted my brows—a habit I have—and set to work to think.

But thinking is getting to be a slow process with me, and every step we took brought us nearer to each other.

We looked and stared, and then, as neither could recall the other's name, we shook hands.

"I have met you before?" I said.

"Most likely," was the reply.

"India?" I asked.

"No."

"Africa?"

"Likely. I am Captain——"

"John Niel!" I added at once. "Of course you are, and I am Captain Waldo Adair."

"Bless me! This is a pleasure. When did you return?"

I told him. The War Office was forgotten, and we were soon lost in the mysteries and strange reminiscences of the past. We strolled into Morley's Hotel, and over a bottle of wine fought our battles over again.

"Where are you living now?" I asked.

"Down in Rutland, near Oakham."

"Ah!"

"You must come back with me. Now, no excuses. I won't hear any—the train goes from King's Cross in two hours. Say, will you come?"

I never stopped to think. I cared not for what others might say about my speedy acceptance of the invitation. I never paused to consider that my friend might have a wife and a lot of children, but on the instant, said:

"Yes, I will."

"Good!. Why, Bessie will be delighted."

"Bess?" I queried; and then the thought came to me that perhaps Bess, whoever she might be, would not be so well pleased at her house being invaded by a savage from the wilds of Africa."

"Bess!" he replied. "Yes; don't you remember her?"

"Can't say that I do. Oh, you mean Bess Jones, that kept the canteen——"

"No, no, Adair. You knew Silas Croft?"

"What, of Mooifontein? Yes, of course I did."

"Well, his daughter."

"I thought her name was Jess."

Captain Niel sighed, drew the corners of his mustache into his mouth, and then in a whisper, which sounded almost sepulchral, answered:

"She died; but her sister, Bessie, became my wife."

"Oh! And old Silas Croft?"

"He died a year ago, now, and lies buried in the little graveyard near our house. By the way, we call our little place Mooifontein."

"Any children?" I asked, hoping that he would quickly answer in the negative.

"Yes, one, little Jessie; and she is the sweetest, cutest little thing, so like her aunt Jess in many ways, that, do you know, Adair, I sometimes think--but there, I won't bother you——"

"Tell me, Niel, what you were thinking, for I may be interested."

"I was about to say that I sometimes think that Jess Croft's spirit is very near her little namesake, and is molding her as she would wish her to be."

"Very likely it is so, John Niel; for I believe those who have gone before us are very near the ones they loved on earth, and it is comforting to think so."

"Very; but where are your togs, old fellow, for the train won't wait for us, and I wouldn't miss it and disappoint my Bess--no, not to be crowned King of South Africa?"

"I have been staying here," I replied. "You see, it is handy to the War Office."

"Well, square up your bill and come, for you shall not sleep in any hotel again for a long time, or my Bess and little Jess have lost their power to charm."

And that was how I got to John Niel's house, and through going there this book was written.

We arrived at Oakham and found a dog-cart waiting to take us across country to the new Mooifontein, presided over by Captain John Niel and his wife, *nee* Bessie Croft.

After we had left the railroad, Niel was unusually silent.

He was evidently deep in thought, and as I mentioned various fine bits of scenery in the country we were passing through he would merely give a quiet assent.

Once or twice I caught myself wondering whether I had made a mistake in accepting the invitation, and whether Niel was imagining that his wife would look upon me as an intruder.

But the thought left as quickly as it came, for I knew honest John Niel must have changed his nature if he gave an invitation as a mere matter of courtesy.

Still he looked so strange and was so thoughtful, that at last, in my usual blunt manner, I blurted out:

"Confound it, Niel, what is the matter with you?"

He laughed, but it was a forced one; his face crimsoned and showed that he was very much confused.

"I was far away," he said, after a short glance round. "I was in the Transvaal."

I knew not then the meaning of his thoughts, but afterward, as will be seen, I realized that his spirit had soared away and was by the side of a grave far over across the ocean, in which a loved one lay moldering to dust.

Presently the stalwart fellow gave himself a shake and, pointing with his whip to a pretty ivy-covered house in the distance, said:

"That is Mooifontein."

His whole manner changed and one would fancy that he was a young lad just from school, to see how delighted he was to be near home.

As the dog-cart drew up to the door, a handsome, comely woman, with face slightly bronzed, came out and was quickly folded in Niel's arms.

Then a little toddler, about three years of age, came out, and putting up its arms, cried out:

"Tiss ittle Dess."

A hearty kiss was imprinted on the little one's mouth, and then I was remembered.

"Forgive me, old fellow. Bessie, this is Captain Waldo Adair; you remember him, don't you?"

"No!" she answered, as she offered her hand.

"But I remember you, Mrs. Niel. I was at your house one day when Jantje set the dog on me, and you came out, caught the dog, and shook your hand at your Hottentot. Do you remember?"

"I think I do! Oh, yes, it was you who warned father against Frank Muller."

"It was, and now I am here to warn you against that husband of yours, who fills your house with South African rooibaatjes."

Bess laughed heartily, and we were soon on the best of terms.

We partook of a good tea, and then the evening was spent in pleasant stories of the past.

"Mrs. Niel," I said, "why don't you write your reminiscences, they would prove highly interesting."

She only laughed, and looked at her husband, who said:

"She is always writing. I shouldn't wonder if she hasn't already done something of the kind."

"Well, my boy, you ought to do so as well."

"Come now, Adair, you have seen everything. You were in that terrible charge where every participator was a hero:

> "When can their glory fade?
> Oh! the wild charge they made!
> All the world wondered.
> Honor the charge they made!
> Honor the Light Brigade,
> Noble six hundred!"

After saying which in melodramatic style, Niel marched up and down the floor as though he felt the martial zeal within him.

"Plenty of time for that," I replied.

"So say I, about my life," responded Bessie quickly.

The subject dropped for the time, and I spent nearly a month with the hospitable friends of my South African days.

Little Jess was a perfect love, and I can well understand how Niel got his ideas about the spirit of "Aunt Jess" watching over the little one, for often there was a far-away look on the tiny face, and to each question the youngster would reply, "Don't bodder me, I'm tinkin'." I was compelled to tear myself away, for I did not wish to wear out my welcome; besides, I had some business matters to straighten out, and so the hour of my departure drew near. Just as I was stepping into the dogcart to be driven to Oakham by John, Bessie put a package into my hands, and bade me not open it until I reached London.

My curiosity however was excited, and the train had scarcely drawn its long and winding length out of the station before I opened the parcel.

Inside I found two smaller packages and a letter.

Breaking the seal of the letter, I read:

"MY DEAR CAPTAIN ADAIR,—You were kind enough to say you would like to read our story. We have both been guilty of writing down our experiences, and though we have not read each other's memoirs, we trust them to you. If you think them worth publishing, they are at your disposal, though I must warn you that we are entirely at sea about writing for the public gaze. Still, we leave the manuscript with you, and whatever comes of it, we hope the blame will rest on us, the praise, if there be any, we dedicate at once to our little Jess.

"Your sincere friends,
"JOHN AND BESSIE NIEL."

So my good friends, I thought you had been writing. Well, whatever you have penned will be interesting, and I for one shall read it with pleasure.

I opened the packages, and reached London some hours before I thought I ought to have got there, so absorbed was I in the interesting narrative.

I have determined to publish the story pretty much as it was written, having taken very little liberty with the text.

I now drop my pen for a time and leave Bessie to tell her own true adventures, thoughts and feelings.

CHAPTER II.

BESSIE'S INTRODUCTION.

WHEN I determined to keep a journal, I never thought that any one would see it except myself, but since Captain Adair has been with us, I have thought that it was possible my story might be interesting, especially as so much has been written about my dear sister Jess, whose grave is far off among the trees of the Transvaal.

Whenever I think of Jess, and can read her great character so much more clearly, I wonder that she was so brave. She loved John so much, I wonder did he love her? If he did, he never let me know it.

Bless him, he is the bravest and best man that ever lived.

I ought to think so, for did he not bring father and me away from that horrid South Africa, and did he not work hard as a land agent, until by his sheer industry he was able to purchase our dear little home?

And when father died, oh, how he grieved for him.

Then there is little Jess. What a sweet little winsome thing she is, and doesn't John love her. Oh! he could not love her so much if his heart was with any one else.

No, I will not wrong him. If he did love Jess once, his whole love is with me now.

But what am I writing all this for? Captain Adair wanted my life-story, not a treatise on my joyous home. But I am so happy that when I begin to think about the past the present looms up before me, and I am almost ready to dance a reel, I am so happy.

John has never seen my journal, and the sly fellow has actually kept one as well, so our story ought to be complete; but I wouldn't have my journal published, no, not for all the queen's crown and jewels, and all the wealth which she possesses.

So what have I done?

I have rewritten all that I thought would be interesting, and so have kept the journal as a sacred thing. John may see some parts of it some day—it is the only secret I ever had from him, but there are portions too sacred for even his loved eyes—too sacred, no, I do not mean that—but I have written on its pages my thoughts and feelings and—but then I was in love with him, and was afraid I should lose his love, or perhaps that he would never love me, so I wrote just as I felt at the time, and that wouldn't be nice for him to read, now would it?

And when I first saw John, I shall never forget it; I thought he was cold, that no love could ever enter his breast, and I wrote in my journal some lines Sister Jess once showed me.

> " There are hearts of so ashen a mold,
> So senseless, so sluggish, and cold,
> That, though love to their pulses should hold
>   His torch all aglow,
>   They never would know
> That the flame had been near them
>   Unless they were told."

Then I thought that perhaps men like John Niel really loved more than those who fell in love so quickly that they often burned their fingers, for Jess used to sing another verse which I shall never forget. It ran:

> "There are others so quick to ignite
> At a touch of love's magical light,
> That they 'catch' at the very first sight
> Of a pair of bright eyes,
> And, enkindled by sighs,
> They burn and consume in the space of a night."

And it is better to know and love one of the cold ones than the hasty lovers who love so quickly, for fear their love might consume in the night.

There was quite a great deal in my journal like this, and now that I know my husband so thoroughly, I, of course, would not like him to see all I have written. Now would you, if you were in my place?

So I rewrote my diary or journal, and when I had done so, I wrote this chapter, so the preface was written after the book, and the first chapter when the last was concluded.

I have reversed the order of procedure, and have given what ought to have been a postscript as an introductory chapter.

I must say something more, however, and that is that I don't know much about writing stories. I can only tell just what took place, and it may be that no one will care to read about Bess.

I was eight years old when I reached my uncle's house in the Transvaal, but, young as I was, I had an adventure which I never told even to Jess, though she was to me both mother and sister.

I had not been at uncle's place more than six months or so, when some Boers came to sell a number of ostriches.

"Is this Om Croft's diggin's?" asked a Boer boy about fifteen or sixteen years old.

I looked round to see who it was that the young Boer addressed, and finding I was alone, I concluded the question was intended for me, so I answered:

"It is, and what do you want?"

"Well, you're spunky, I like you," was his rejoinder.

"What do you want?" I asked again.

"Got some ostriches."

"Eh, what?" I exclaimed, not understanding quite what the boy had said.

"Come an' see."

I went with him, and saw some ten or twelve young birds, prettier far than any which uncle possessed.

"Where did you get them?" I asked.

"One of them belongs to me. See that one with the ring round its neck."

I remember I admired it so much that the boy proposed I should mount its back and have a ride.

I was terribly afraid, but after a little urging I got up on the bird's back, but not before I was assured that all I had to do was to hold tight by the neck.

The beautiful creature swayed its graceful neck to and fro for a moment, wondering what new experience it was to undergo, and then I felt its wings rising, and like a whirlwind it swept across the veldt.

I grasped it round the neck and held on for dear life; but on the creature went until I felt sure it was trying to fly with me on its back.

Uncle had been attracted by my screams, and ran in the direction the bird was going.

Of course the more he shouted the greater speed was shown by the ostrich, and I had the greatest difficulty to keep from falling off.

After a few minutes I lost my fear, and really enjoyed the ride.

Across the country we went with the speed of the lightning, it seemed.

There was an exhilaration which I had never before experienced.

I never thought then of danger. Did not know where I was being taken, and, what was more to the point, I did not care.

I was happy, and could have clapped my hands with delight, only for the fear of falling off the bird.

We came to the avenue of gum-trees, and my ostrich turned suddenly, as though each tree was an enemy ready to take its life.

On toward my uncle's house it sped; it really appeared as if nothing could tire it.

Away we went, until the bird, suddenly seeing my uncle and the Boers in front, was about to turn and fly in another direction.

"Billy," the owner of the ostrich, thinking I had ridden far enough, walked away from the others, and faced the bird as it flew, rather than ran, in another direction.

He lowered his body in the long grass, and the bird did not see him.

When it was within a few yards from him, Billy suddenly jumped up, sprung forward, and threw his whole weight against the legs of the great bird.

As he twisted his arms round the long, thin legs, the bird fell on its side, and I was shot over its head a few yards in advance, falling in a heap in the tall grass, and presenting such a curious figure that Billy laughed, and declared that for the life of him he could not tell which was my head or my feet.

Fortunately I was unhurt, and Uncle Silas laughed heartily at my adventure.

Jess looked grave and serious, but then she was three years older, and three years make a wonderful difference at the age we had reached.

The ostrich was bought, and for a long time was the finest my uncle had, but at last it grew so vicious that no one dare go near it.

That was the bird that John Niel killed when he arrived at Mooifontein, and which gave him such a hearty but unpleasant reception.

That ride was my first adventure with ostriches, and I have mentioned it in my introduction because Billy became a friend, and will be often mentioned in my story.

Poor old Billy! He loved me in his honest Dutch fashion, and when I saw his dead body, with a bayonet thrust through the breast, I could not help crying. For he was devoted to me, and when—— But I am only anticipating, so I must leave Billy, and let my story tell of his future career.

CHAPTER III.
MY GIRLHOOD DAYS.

I DON'T know how it was, but Jess and I were as different—as old uncle used to say—as chalk and cheese. I was delighted to be out in the fields, roaming over the veldt, or feeding the ostriches, while Jess was always wanting books, and was never so happy as when she could get a newspaper or a book to read. She delighted in music too, and could sing all sorts of weird songs, which I am sure she had never seen or heard before, but just improvised them as she went along.

I was "a terror" to her, and the poor girl constantly told me I should never grow up to be a nice young lady.

Now that was what I had no desire to become. I was annoyed to think I was a girl. It seemed to me at that time that there were too many girls in the world, and I wished I had been born a boy.

But as I was not, why I had to make the best of it, but a regular tomboy I undoubtedly was in those days.

"Let Bess alone," Uncle Silas used to say. "She is young and full of life, and will come out all right in the end."

So I was allowed to grow up pretty wild as regards my amusements.

I had been one day out with Uncle Silas, and was very tired.

He left me sitting on a gum-tree log, to the top of which—about four feet—I had climbed.

The sun was just about setting, and cast a beautiful golden ray of light over the scene.

I was thoroughly enjoying the rest, and was, for a wonder, deep in thought. How long my reverie would have lasted I cannot say, for it was disturbed by the sound of a horse's footsteps.

Presently the horse stopped, and then the softer sound of a human footfall was heard.

The sounds stole upon me gradually, as it were, and I did not pay much attention to them till a man's shadow came like a dark cloud in front of me, and then I looked round.

I saw at about twenty yards, a young man, very handsome, but with a scowl on his face which I did not like.

"Hello! You there?"

I looked round again; such a salution was a strange one, especially when addressed to a girl, but I had forgotten that I was wearing one of Uncle Croft's old jackets and a big Boer hat. Seeing that my back was nearly to the stranger, and he could not see that the lower part of my body was in feminine attire, I knew he had mistaken me for a boy.

"I hear you!" I said. "You needn't shout."

"Indeed!" sneered the stranger.

"I'm not deaf," I said, rather annoyed at the brusque manner of the man.

I now twisted round, and as he saw my petticoats, he raised his hat as an acknowledgment of my sex, and said: "A girl; well, I'm blessed!"—this was in an undertone but loud enough for me to hear.

The new-comer was a fine-looking man, with a long beard which swept his broad chest.

We stared at each other for some time without either speaking a word, and when the stranger said:

"I like you—there is something about your face which pleases me. You are not a native?"

"No! Indeed I am not," I answered indignantly.

"I meant no offense," he said at once.

I never though he did, but I was annoyed at his manner. I knew that the word "Native" was usually applied to the Hottentots and Boers, and therefore it was easy to understand my indignation.

"I am English," I answered.

"Ah! Have you a father living?"

"No," I replied shortly.

"A mother?"

I could not refrain from bursting into tears at the question which reopened the old wound.

"I am sorry if I have offended you, but——"

"You haven't offended me," I gasped out between my sobs; "but I don't know who you are, and you have no right to question me. I shall not answer any of your questions."

"You won't?"

"No."

The new-comer only laughed at me, and as he saw I was about to slip off my perch, he approached and said in Dutch, forgetting himself:

"*Wacht en beeche.*" (Wait a bit.)

Before I really knew what he was about he had lifted me off the tree, and then with a comical twist of his mouth, said:

"See here, my dear! You think it smart to be so

saucy and pert, but whoever you are, I'm glad for your sake I am in good humor, for in some moods I would just touch a young filly like you up with the whip, and make you answer."

"That you couldn't do," I replied, tossing my head independently.

"Indeed! Well, I like your spirit. Tell me where you live."

"Over there," and I pointed over my shoulder.

"So; but at whose house?"

"Uncle Croft's."

"Oh, so you are 'Om Silas Croft's' niece, are you?"

"Yes, meinheer."

The man frowned and then said:

"Well, I am going to see your uncle, and so we shall meet again, and—by the way, what did you tell me your name was?"

I had not told him my name, but I was thrown off my guard, and answered quickly:

"Bessie Croft."

"So. Good-day, Bessie—won't you give me a kiss?"

I hated that man from that moment, and before my story is ended it will be seen I had good cause for my hatred.

At the time I merely turned away and walked in the direction of home.

The man followed, leading a horse as handsome as himself—and I could not close my eyes to his very handsome face—and without a word we reached the door.

Uncle Silas was outside smoking a huge pipe, which was the envy of the Boers for miles round. I passed him without speaking, but as I entered the house I heard my uncle say:

"Ah, Meinheer Muller, so you have returned I see!"

"Yes, Om Croft, and right pleased am I to get home again."

"What are the prospects through the country?" I heard my uncle ask, and then with almost a savage manner, our visitor replied:

"The d——d English are trying to stir up strife, but they won't succeed. We can manage our own affairs here well enough."

"I think so, but the English would rather protect us than destroy our government."

"That's as may be; but I say, uncle, that Bessie of yours is a pretty girl, and a sharp creature too. I'm blessed if I don't wish she belonged to me."

"She is a good girl, and so is her sister."

"Her sister?"

"Yes, but I forgot, you have been away over two years and so have not seen my little English singing birds, who have been with me nearly eighteen months."

"Indeed!"

I heard no more of the conversation, but I took a hearty dislike to Frank Muller, which only grew in intensity as the years passed over.

From that time Frank Muller was a constant visitor at my uncle's house, and I was always wanted whenever he came, for to my disgust and horror he asked about "Willful Bess"—as he was pleased to term me—and then uncle, who was so proud of his English nieces, would send for me, and I would be expected to sing or do something to entertain the handsome half-breed, for Frank Muller was half Boer and half English.

At that time he possessed a very great influence in the affairs of the little South African Republic, and even held an official position in the government.

My uncle was English to the backbone, but as he was a resident in the republic, he was loyal to the government, and was even a member of the Republican Parliament, and was considered one of the fathers of the country.

Therefore he and Frank Muller had always plenty to converse over, and there was a good reason why Muller should visit my uncle so often.

Still I was then too young to know that, and I imagined that his visits were only for the one object—an annoyance to me.

My hatred was shared by the Boer boy, Billy, who found time to see me very often.

Billy could talk good "Englees," as he called it, and therefore we got on well together.

Nearly a year passed from the time I made the acquaintance of Frank Muller, when I was walking down the Blue Gum walk with Billy one evening.

We stopped suddenly, for right close to us we heard voices.

We moved along as quietly as possible, for we imagined some quarrel was taking place, and we might not be wanted as witnesses.

Those were lawless days, and life was not held to be very sacred. Instead of getting further away from the voices as we intended, we were really much nearer.

"Hush, Bessie! Listen!" said Billy, taking hold of my arm and squeezing it so tightly that I was nearly crying out with the pain.

We could distinguish a harsh, gruff voice, and one that was evidently a woman's.

It was impossible to retreat, and so our only chance of safety was to crouch down on the grass and wait until the disputants had gone.

"What do you want here?" I heard the man ask.

"Oh, I love you so much," was the reply of the woman.

"Did I not tell you I would not be followed. And now you have left your home, and tracked me here."

"I was mad."

"Of course you were, I could have told you that, but what did you come to this place for?"

"I thought there might be some one to whom you whispered words of love," she said.

A harsh, coarse laugh preceded the answer of the man.

"What, at Om Croft's? Not a bit of it, there are only two chits of little girls there."

"Why won't you marry me?"

"Are you crazy?"

"Perhaps I am; but you said you loved me, and oh! I did, I do love you so much."

The man muttered something which we did not hear.

"Who is it?" I whispered to Billy.

"I don't know. Hush!" he answered.

"I think it is Meinheer Muller," I murmured, softly.

"Hush! or we shall be discovered."

The voices were hushed for a few moments, and then I heard the man say:

"Swear you will never seek me out again."

"I cannot."

"I will give you money, and when you are married I will find your husband a good job."

"Oh, Heaven! Money, when I have given love. No; I will follow you, will haunt your life, will be at every house you visit, and all shall know of my ruined life through my love for you."

"You will do this, will you?" he said, slowly.

"Before my Maker, I swear it."

"Bah! what care I for a woman's threat? But I swear you shall never utter one word against me."

"Marry me and we will be so——"

The sentence was unfinished, and a strange silence ensued.

A moment later Billy raised his head, and saw a man stooping over a woman engaged in searching her clothes.

This lasted only a minute, and then the man walked away stealthily; he passed so close to where we were concealed that I was sure we should be discovered.

I was curious and wanted to know who the man was, but I dare not hold up my head for fear I might be seen.

A few minutes later we heard the sound of a horse galloping over the veldt, and at the same time I seized Billy by the arm and asked:

"What's that?"

I trembled so that I could scarcely stand.

We heard it again. It was a groan. Was the woman in pain?

I thought, and Billy agreed with me, that she had fainted.

Again the groan broke the stillness of the evening.

It was our duty to see what was the cause of the groaning.

Surely, the man had not left her and she in pain. It was cruel and heartless.

Perhaps he might have gone for assistance. If so, we should be discovered.

Another groan, and then a low, stifled cry:

"Help!"

"Come along, Billy," I said, for I could not endure it longer.

We pushed our way through the long grass, until we reached the place where the woman had fallen.

What a sight met our view!

On the ground lay a white woman, her clothes disarranged, evidently through the search we saw made by the man, but, worst of all, from her bosom was running a stream of blood.
She had been stabbed.
I gave a scream. Who could help it?
Billy was a boy, and had often seen similar things, so he just pushed me away, and, as I thought, contemptuously, as he said:
"What good will screaming do, Bess?"
Of course I knew it was no good, but then I was a girl.
What was to be done?
Billy knew just how to act in such cases, so I followed his directions.
We lifted up her head, and then Billy, while I held her up, tried to stop the blood flowing from the wound.
"Oh!" the poor thing groaned.
"Who did it?" asked Billy.
"He——"
"I know that, but what is his name?"
Whether the woman understood it or not, she made no answer.
"What is your name?" I asked.
"Mary——" The poor dying woman gasped for breath. She tried to finish her name, but could not do so.
"You hold her just like that," said Billy, "while I run to the house."
It was horrible, and so I proposed that he should stay while I went for assistance.
"I can run faster than you," he said; and without waiting for any further objections on my part, he soon showed his heels in the distance, and only a few minutes passed before my uncle and some men were seen coming with Billy to the woman's assistance.
"Why, Bessie, my lass," said Uncle Croft, "what is all this about?"
My nerves were so highly excited by the watching over the dying woman, that, instead of answering, I began to cry.
Uncle lifted the woman's head off my knee, and I heard him ask:

"Who knew her?"

No one responded, and then the voice of my beloved uncle came again:

"It is all over. She is dead."

That started me again, and I felt as though I should die with nervous fright.

To think I had been alone with death, and that, with her head resting on my knee, the woman's spirit had taken flight.

They searched her pocket and clothes, but there was not the slightest trace of any name.

An informal inquest was held, but none of the neighbors seemed to recognize her, and so she was interred in the little graveyard, where afterward my dear sister Jess was buried.

Billy was closely questioned as to who the man was that had been seen with the murdered woman, but beyond the fact that he wore a beard and was dressed in dark clothes, no information could be obtained from my companion.

When, however, they found that Billy persisted in his statement that the murderer was a white man the inquiry ceased, for in those days a white person could scarcely do wrong.

The scene made a lasting impression on me, and I could not nor never have rid myself of the thought that the murderer was Frank Muller.

Once, some years later, when Muller was praising my name, and declared that Bessie was the sweetest name ever possessed by woman, I said carelessly:

"Did you not once say the same of Mary?"

He turned pale and walked across to the window. After a moment's pause he asked in a low voice:

"What do you mean?" and then, before I had time to answer he continued, "No, I never cared much for Mary."

I tried to follow up my advantage by saying:

"That woman who was murdered and buried in our graveyard was called Mary."

"Ah, poor woman," he replied; "so I heard. I wonder who she could have been."

The mystery was never solved, but I still believe that when the secrets of our hearts are laid bare it will be found that Frank Muller, the smooth-tongued Boer, was guilty of shedding the blood of the woman who had loved him beyond his deserts.

But what a storm of indignation I roused in the house when I incautiously mentioned my belief to uncle.

"No, no, Bess, my girl!" he said. "I don't like Muller, and believe he is a dangerous man; but a murderer—why, Bess, you ought to be ashamed of yourself for even thinking such a thing."

Jess was just as strong. Her gentle nature could not conceive such a possibility. To her mind, only the lowest, the most illiterate, and the poorest among white people would ever commit a murder, and as Muller was rich, passably well educated, and with a good standing in the Republic, it was wrong to even think of such a crime in connection with him.

That was how Sister Jess reasoned, and I professed to be convinced, but my opinion has never changed.

I have learned that murder is a crime which is indulged in by the educated at times, and John is of the opinion that there are many murders committed which are never suspected.

The scene of the finding of the murdered woman and her death in my arms is ever before me, and will be, I expect, as long as life lasts.

From that time on my life was an even one, nothing of great importance occurring, and therefore I turn over the pages of my journal until I approach the time when Captain John Niel was expected at Mooifontein.

CHAPTER IV.

VISITORS AT MOOIFONTEIN.

MY sister Jess was of a strange and almost morose temperament.

She was always sad. If she sang, her songs were nearly always gloomy; if she spoke of love, her softest accents were tinged with melancholy; even when any new enjoyment was proposed, which particularly gave her pleasure, she would sigh as she expressed her thanks.

Jess was peculiar in many ways.

Since she had returned from Cape Town, where she

had been at school for two years, her manners were still harder to comprehend.

Yet she was not really unhappy. No; there was a pleasure hidden under all that morose exterior; and if one could ever touch those chords, if a loved one was ever able to cause her nerves to thrill and her bosom to heave with the passionate yearning of love, I believe her whole nature would undergo a change.

One day I teased her about love, and said I was sure she had met with some one at Cape Town who had captured her heart.

She sighed. I pressed my inquisitive talk upon her, and then she sighed again, and said she had sometimes dreamt about love, but they were only dreams, and that love itself was only a fancy on this earth, a glimpse of the spirit which pervaded fairyland.

She sat down at the piano and let her fingers run carelessly over the keys, and then she sang softly:

"I dreamt that I passed thro fairyland,
My love and I on our way,
From this dull earth to a better sphere,
And the fairies bade us stay.

"We lingered awhile in that bright land,
My love and I were so gay,
And almost forgot while tarrying there,
We were only on our way.

"The fairies all sang from morn till night,
So happy and blithesome they,
With purest joy, and no evil thing
E'er shadow'd their cloudless way.

"'Twas too bright to last, for naught so chaste,
Save in heaven is found, I ween,
And this was true, for when I awoke
I saw it was all a dream."

She closed the piano and looked brighter than I had seen her for a long time. There was a new light in her eyes.

"Jess, tell me, dear, was that song your own experience?" I asked.

She laughed, and then almost crossly answered:

"You are young, Bessie, or you would not ask such a question."

Nothing more could I get from Jess at that time.

A few mornings afterward, uncle came into the room, and I saw he was rather excited.

"Jess, my girl, get the spare room ready, can you, for we are to have visitors."

"Visitors?" she asked, without showing much surprise, although we were often a year without seeing a strange face.

I was more demonstrative, so I caught hold of uncle's arm and kissed his hand.

"Are they nice?" I asked.

"What, the kisses do you mean?"

"No, you silly old uncle, you know I mean the visitors."

"Oh!"

"That wasn't an answer to my question."

"Your question, really, Miss Inquisitive, what do you want to know?"

"You are an old bear, that's what you are," said I; and then feeling ashamed of my petulance, I said, "Tell me, Uncle Silas, are they old or young, married or single, black or white?"

"Now that is a pretty string of questions to ask an old bear, but I suppose I must answer them—let me see—one will be old, yes, nearly as old as I am, the other, well I don't know whether he is five or fifty, my correspondent calls him a boy. Married? well, I should say so, for the old one has been married, let me see if I can remember how many times, I know he once told me that he had to go to the burial ground to count the graves when he wished to remember the number."

"Oh, uncle!" said Jess, who was terribly shocked at the light way uncle was treating the subject.

Jess left the room, for she knew the dear old fellow would tease her if she stayed.

"Has he buried all his wives?" I asked, my natural curiosity prompting me.

"No, he has one now about your age, Bessie."

"Oh!" I said, with a shudder, for I didn't like the idea of a very old man marrying a young girl.

As uncle made no further comments, I asked a few minutes later:

"Where are they coming from?"

"Durban!"

"Oh! and when?"

"Well, Bess, you are determined to get all the details, so I may as well answer at once, and tell you all about them:

"The old gentleman is Thomas Hardy, a lawyer, and the boy is his son.

"I knew the old fellow twenty years ago, but have not seen him many times since. He is coming into this neighborhood on business and pleasure combined, and may stay a week or longer. Now, is there anything else you would like to know?"

"No, uncle!"

"What, are you satisfied? Well, I will chalk it up, for I never knew you satisfied before," and Uncle Silas walked out of the room rubbing his hands and laughing.

I followed Jess and told her all I had learned. She betrayed no curiosity, but took all the information as a matter of course, and went on with her work, preparing for the visitors as if it was a constant occurrence in our household. The eventful day at last arrived, and Thomas Hardy and his son arrived.

The "boy," as the old gentleman called his son, was nearly thirty years of age, and was one of the most peculiar specimens of humanity I had ever seen. When he entered and was introduced to us, he had one set expression, which never varied.

"Mr. William," said my uncle, "this is my niece Jessie."

Jess put out her hand, which he took, and with the most comical contortions of his face, said:

"Ah! Miss Jessie. How do!"

Jessie could scarcely restrain herself, for melancholy as she was usually, she had a keen love of the ludicrous.

She came across and took my hand, saying:

"This is my sister Bessie."

To which the Durban swell, as no doubt he considered himself, remarked:

"Ah! Miss Bessie. How do!"

At that moment I felt wicked enough for anything, and seeing the Hottentot, Jantje, by the window, I beckoned him.

As he entered, Mr. William turned his eyes on the

hideous specimen of a native African, and I addressed him.

"Mr. William, this is Jantje."

"Ah! Jantje. How do."

This was too much, for even my uncle had to bury his pocket handkerchief in his mouth to keep from laughter.

If the son was peculiar, what can be said of his father?

He was the most eccentric-looking creature I ever met.

Dressed in an old-fashioned style, which even uncle had long since discarded, his clothes old and threadbare, some of the buttons gone, and a piece of string answering for them, even that peculiarity was nothing to his head.

Perched on the top of his cranium was a wig which was many sizes too small for him. In consequence, the sides, instead of fitting close to his head, stood out like a mushroom, under which could be seen a highly polished scalp.

The old gentleman, seeing our attention was attracted to his wig, put up his hands. When he found how the sides projected, he adroitly turned the wig slightly, exclaiming:

"I beg pardon, ladies, but one's hair does get disarranged by traveling."

He again put his hands to his head and gave the wig another twist, and then another, until he had managed to get the top of the wig, which was fluffy and parted on one side, at the back, and the back, without any parting, was on the top.

I laughed, and then uncle burst forth into one of his hearty guffaws, which seemed to shake the house. Mr. William looked to see what we were amused at, and then caught sight of his father's very comical appearance.

Instead of speaking, he walked up to the unconscious old gentleman, and took the wig between his fingers and lifted it off his father's head, placing it on the table.

Mr. Hardy was indignant, and as he stood shaking his fist at his son, his head as smooth as a billiard ball and quite as shiny, we all laughed heartily.

It was rude but irresistible. Who could refrain under such strange circumstances?

I could not, neither could staid Jess.

The old gentleman took it sensibly, even joining in the laugh against himself.

The two veterans talked of their early life in the colony, and about the various political parties which had at different times ruled the destinies of South Africa.

This discussion absorbed their entire attention, and we were left to entertain William Hardy.

This was the most difficult thing to do, for though we spoke about nearly every subject of which we had any knowledge, he seemed entirely ignorant.

To everything he replied:

"Ah, yes, that's good."

In despair, Jess asked him if he could sing.

"I cannot play," he answered.

"I will play," she said, "if you will sing."

"No, you sing."

"Won't you oblige, Mr. William?" I asked.

"Really, ah! that's good."

Jess left the piano, and again asked him to sing. He made no reply, but sat down at the piano, thummed on the keys for a few moments, and then in a good voice, sang:

> "The wheel of the world goes round and round,
> Those who are uppermost soon may be
> Rolled over the rough and dusty ground,
> While those that were down rise rich and free.
> But while the wheel unceasing rolls
> Over and over and over again,
> Will it sunder our hearts and kindred souls,
> And leave us apart in sorrow and pain?

> "Around and round the wheel goes and goes,
> Now we go up and then we go down;
> To-day we look down from the top on those
> Who to-morrow may be the *elite* of the town.
> But what is the top of the wheel to me,
> Though it lifts me up with the larks to the sky,
> If it takes me where I never can see
> The face the angels might covet on high?"

We were surprised and astonished at the song, for it had been impossible to get any conversation with the strange young fellow, and now he had really enchanted us all with his singing.

We hoped, the ice being broken, we should be able to draw him out of his shell a little, but not a word did he utter until he wished us good-night, when he retired to rest.

CHAPTER V.
A RIDE FOR LIFE.

"Does your son like hunting or shooting?" Uncle Silas asked next morning as we sat at breakfast.

"He is passionately fond of both," answered old Thomas Hardy.

"Then, Jess and Bess, will you accompany William to the north, near Hans Coetzee's place, and you can have some sport."

Nothing would please us better, and that uncle knew.

I asked whether Mr. Hardy would enjoy such sport.

"Ah, good," responded William, which we took to mean that he would like the trip.

Uncle Silas had some good horseflesh in his stables, and so I gave orders that the horses should be saddled.

At the last moment, however, Jess withdrew, declaring that as she had a slight headache, and there was so much to do at home, it would be better for us to go without her.

An hour later saw William Hardy and me scampering over the plain, and for the first time the youth tried to talk.

"What kind of game shall we bag?" he asked.

"Partridges," I responded.

"Ah, good."

"Then if we go far enough we may meet some springbok, and, it may be, a few vilderbeeste."

William's eyes seemed to flash and snap at the prospect of sport.

It is strange how a gun will change some men. Taciturn and morose in the house, without life or animation, give them a gun and they will show their true mettle.

Man is, after all, a fighting animal, and dearly loves a chance to shed blood.

Our good pointer dog had shown that there was game near, and William got ready so that he could show his prowess.

"Where could the birds be?" I looked as the question was asked, but although my eyes had got well used to the warm red grass and could quickly discern game, I was now at fault.

William was riding slowly along until he had nearly reached the dog.

"Whir!"

The sound came so suddenly that our horses felt inclined to run away.

Several braces of birds had risen, and our sportsman eager to show that it was not the first time he had handled a gun, fired.

The birds flew away, as it seemed, laughing at us, for the shot had missed. The other barrel was fired, with the same result.

The birds scattered, and were quickly out of sight in the long grass.

Presently two fine partridges rose.

"Bang!" went the gun and one of them fell to the ground.

Another shot, but it went wide of the mark.

A few minutes and more birds rose, and another was added to the bag. I thought it well to praise our gunner, and I did so in a few words.

"You are laughing, Miss Bessie," he said.

"No, indeed, I am not. Why should I?"

"At my bad shooting."

"I think you have done well."

The words had scarcely left my mouth, when the horse which was ridden by William kicked against a mimosa thorn, which infuriated the animal.

The horse, usually quiet and submissive, was now furious and high spirited. It started to run and I followed as quickly as possible.

Away went Black Dragon, as his horse had been named.

Mimosa bushes were cleared, rocks were leaped as though they were as nothing in its way.

I saw that its rider was losing all control.

My horse was the quickest of the two, if I could but get it to exert itself.

I knew the plain, and our guest did not.

Right before him, only five miles distant, was a huge precipice, which would be certain death to horse and rider, if they went over.

I felt certain Hardy did not know of this danger, for, to all appearance, there was a stretch of many miles before him.

"Stop!" I shouted, but of course it was only wasted breath, for my voice would not carry so far, and even if it was heard, the rider had lost all power over the horse.

"Shoot it," I cried again.

"Oh, why wouldn't he do so?" I was desperate.

A mile more had been traveled and the horse showed no signs of exhaustion.

It was not likely that it would do so, for it had not been out for several days, and was accustomed to vilderbeeste hunting, and therefore to quick and long journeys.

The only thing I feared was the precipice.

If I had only got a gun I would shoot it, for I knew I could do so and not hit the rider.

My horse did not care to go very fast, and Black Dragon was gaining on me rapidly.

I must do something desperate. For I had to overtake and head off the other horse, and had now only three miles in which to do it.

What could I do? My horse was slackening.

I applied the whip, but that it did not care for.

If I had spurs, I would have goaded it into a quicker speed.

What was the matter with it, for Romola, my horse, was usually so high spirited?

"Stop! Turn to the right!" I shouted. It was of no avail.

I took a pin from my dress and stuck it into Romola's shoulder. It was a cruel thing to do, and I hated myself for the act as I saw the tiny drop of blood spurt out.

But I was responsible for our guest's safety.

Black Dragon was making a bee line straight for the precipice.

A few minutes only and he and his rider would be

dashed over, and I should arrive to see their mangled bodies away down in its depths.

It was horrible!

Romola was gaining ground, but not enough.

Again I stuck the pin, this time in its flanks, and now I had roused its anger.

Away it sped like the wind.

I could feel myself cutting the atmosphere as I dashed along. 'Fortunately, I was a good horsewoman. It was an impossibility to throw me. Of that I was firmly convinced.

Romola stumbled. "Great Heaven, help me!" I prayed; and again I buried the pin in the horse's flesh.

Away we went, faster and yet faster.

Black Dragon was only a few lengths ahead.

A stiff breeze had arisen, and of course it beat in our faces, so that every word I uttered was borne away from the one I wished to reach.

"Stop! For Heaven's sake, turn to the right!"

It was no use. My voice was not strong enough to overpower wind and speed.

A terrific clap of thunder startled us at that moment, for it was entirely unexpected.

Its effects were different on the horses, for while Black Dragon increased its speed, Romola felt inclined to stand still.

There was scarcely half a mile between the horse and death.

Again I urged Romola forward, and lashed it until I felt myself to be almost a fiend.

I was within a length of the other horse.

Now I was abreast, but still too far to the windward for my voice to reach the rider.

I had got ahead. What if my horse refused to obey the reins.

I should then be dashed over the rocks to certain death.

I pulled at the rein. I felt the horse's head jerked round, but apparently it cared not.

I tugged and pulled, and at last, within a few yards of the black beetling rocks, I was able to head off Black Dragon.

As I got up to it, I seized the bridle and lashed

Romola; by this means I pulled Hardy's horse round with mine.

A few moments and we were able to stop our steeds, which were both covered with thick foam. We dismounted, and then my guest almost taunted me with stopping him.

He had enjoyed the run, and never knew a horse he could not control.

At first I was angry, but I was almost breathless, and holding Romola by the bridle, I merely said:

"Come!"

Hardy followed me, and I led him back to the edge of the cliff.

When he looked down the three hundred feet of rocks, black and jagged, whose top was hidden by the long red grass of the African plain, he saw the danger which had been averted, and fell on his knees before me.

Taking my hand he kissed it, until I raised my whip and said, with an assumption of anger:

"Get up, you are making a great idiot of yourself."

"You saved my life, Miss Croft."

"Oh, I know that. I wasn't going to see my uncle's guest killed if I could help it."

"I shall never forget your bravery."

"Rubbish! But unless you want to be drowned you will have to come down the rocks to a cave, for that thunder is but the precursor of a good rain storm."

As I said it, some great heavy drops came pattering down on our faces, and we both knew enough of an African storm to be sure that shelter would be far preferable to the drenching we should be certain to get.

After securing the horses, for whom, poor brutes, we were unable to obtain shelter, Hardy followed me down the rocks until we reached a cave, which Jess and I had often made use of in similar emergencies. We were only just in time, for the very instant we entered the cave the rain came down in torrents, and the thunder burst upon us with more powerful effect than was ever made by artillery.

It roared through the valley, and as rock after rock was reached it seemed that the terrific noise was beaten back.

The sound was fearful. Our ears were deafened, and

when the long peal, with its hundreds of echoes and re-echoes, had passed, the silence was even more frightful.

The lightning played upon the rocks, and seemed to find every bit of glistening metal on their surface.

Each flash lighted up the chasm, and every shining bit of surface looked like a glittering diamond. It was a grand and yet a fearful sight, and I could not help thinking that in all the wonders of creation there was nothing which showed the grandeur of nature, and at the same time brought into contrast the littleness of man, so much as a thunder storm.

The skeptic may, in the life and activity of the city, where the ingenuity and skill of man is seen to its fullest capacity, doubt the existence of the Supreme Being, but let him go out into the broad expanse of prairie, let him be many miles away from human habitation, and he will then feel, when the lightning flashes and the thunder roars that there is a mightier ruler of the destinies of the universe than chance, and that while everything is kept in motion and in order by the laws of nature, that far above these laws is the great Lawgiver, who doeth all things well.

I was thinking of these things as I crouched down in the further recesses of the cave, and watched the brilliant flashes of the lightning, and heard the peals of heaven's artillery.

Jess never gave me credit for deep thought, and whenever I spoke of serious things she treated me almost like a child, but I very often had spells of "considering" as Uncle Silas called it, and I had one in that cave, forgetful of the presence of my companion.

CHAPTER VI.

A LOVE PROPOSAL.

My fit of "considering" might have lasted a long time had I not been roused by the sudden breaking out of the silent William Hardy.

From the time we had entered the cave he had been silent, never speaking but once, and that was when a particularly vivid flash lighted up the chasm, and I exclaimed:

"Oh, how lovely!" to which he responded with his usual pet formula:
"Ah! good!"

I gave him such a look that I did not wonder much that he should prefer silence to such indignant glances. I had no patience with him. Was he bashful? If so, I pitied him. Was it affectation? Then I despised rather than pitied.

I have often thought a bashful man was an outrage on humanity, and really bashfulness ought to be treated as a disease.

I met with a young girl who lived at Majuba, and she dearly loved a young farmer, who by his constant visits to Kate's house seemed as if he was smitten.

But he was so bashful that poor Kate knew not what to do. She tried everything but without success.

Kate was nearly heart-broken, but her farmer lover used to go and sit silently in the house evening after evening, never speaking a word. Such a man ought to be shut up in a lunatic asylum. If fate had been pleased to make me a man it should not be said I was shy.

Was William Hardy bashful? That I did not really know.

My reverie in the cave was broken and my thoughts of the grandeur of the storm dispelled by the sudden jerking out of the words:
"Bessie—Miss Bessie."

I turned, for I had almost forgotten the existence of young Hardy.

"Oh, Mr. Hardy. Yes, what is it?" I replied confusedly.

"I think you saved my life," he said.

"Not a doubt of it."

"I am grateful—no; I don't mean that, I——"

"Oh, don't say anything about it. If your life is any good to you I am pleased I saved it; anyhow, I did not want you to lose it while riding Black Dragon." And then a spice of mischief crossed my mind, and I added, "Besides, the horse is a really valuable one."

"Then it was the horse you wished to save?"

"Of course. I wouldn't lose Black Dragon, not for all the money I possess."

"Oh!" The exclamation was like a groan, and I could scarcely keep from laughing, as I asked:

"Are you in pain?"

"Yes, Miss Bessie, I am."

"Oh, really, I am so sorry. Where is the pain, and can I do anything for you?"

I glanced at William Hardy, and the poor fellow really looked ill. I was alarmed, perhaps the excitement of the exercise had been too much for him.

He placed his hand over his heart and with a sigh said:

"The pain is here."

"Poor fellow, it was the hard riding. When you get home, Jess shall give you a good strong dose of brandy and catnip, and it will set you right."

"No, Miss Bessie, there is only one thing will cure me."

"What is that?" I asked, wonderingly.

"You."

The one word came upon me, causing greater surprise and suddenness than the first thunder clap.

For a moment I did not understand, but immediately the truth flashed across my brain that it was a love proposal, and then all the hilarity in my nature came to the surface and I exploded into such a hearty laugh that fairly outvied the thunder in sound.

My laugh quickly stopped when I saw the woebegone face of my companion, from whom I could not escape unless I wished to get a thorough drenching.

"I beg your pardon, Mr. Hardy," I said, "but you looked so serious that I could not avoid laughing."

"I was serious, Miss Bessie; and when I think that you saved my life, when I know all your worth——"

"That is but little, for I have not a shilling of my own, and Uncle Silas may not leave me anything," I said, trying by the interruption to turn his thoughts in another direction.

"I did not mean that—I don't care if you have not another dress——"

"But I do, and I don't thank you for your strange indifference to my comfort."

"Really, Miss Bessie, how can I make myself plain?"

"Mr. Hardy, don't seek to be plainer than you are, for people admire beauty in these days."

"Bessie Croft."

"That is my name." I was desperate, for I did not want the poor fellow to make a definite proposal to me, for I did not love him, and so I seized every opportunity to ward off the dreaded climax to his speeches.

"My dear Miss Bessie, hear me. I love you, more than you have any idea I could love."

"That would be very easy, Mr. Hardy, for I don't think you could love very much."

"You are cruel, but when I knew that you had saved my life, as I looked down the rocks and saw that but for you I should have been——"

"Food for the aasvogels by this time."

"Yes, indeed, and I thought to myself, my life belongs to Bessie Croft, so I resolved to ask——"

"Has the rain stopped yet, Mr. Hardy? You are nearer the entrance than I am."

"Never mind the rain. I love you, Bessie. Don't be so cruel to me. Won't you——"

"Start for home as soon as the rain moderates, or uncle and Jess will be uneasy, and as for your father——"

"Bother them all, it is not often I feel inclined to talk."

"No; that is true, I know," I said, wickedly.

"Oh, do listen to me——"

"I think I am doing so, and do you know, Mr. Hardy, I think you should cultivate conversation more. It looks so strange for a man to sit without talking, and especially when there are ladies in the sit-kamie" (sitting-room).

"But I must say to you now all I have wanted to say to you. When first I saw you, I said to myself—that is the girl I would like for a wife, and all last evening I looked at you——"

"Yes, I thought you were very rude to stare as you did."

"I could not help it, for, Bessie, I feel lonely. I am rich, and could give you a good home. Will you be my wife?"

It was out. I knew not how to stop it.

We were prisoners in a little cave scarcely ten feet square, and I was at his mercy.

"Bessie, say you will be mine," he continued, seeing that I was silent.

"Mr. Hardy, I am always ready for any amusement. I enjoy a joke as well as any one, but there are some subjects which are too serious for jest."

"Jest, Miss Bessie! I was in earnest. I love you, and wish to have you for my wife."

"If you are really serious, I am sorry, Mr. Hardy, but how could I think you really meant it, when only yesterday morning you did not even know of my existence."

"Yes, I did."

"Did what?"

"Know of your existence. Your uncle has written quite often about you, and I learned to love you even before I came."

"So you were sent here to try and get one of Silas Croft's nieces to take back with you to Durban, were you?"

"No, no. Indeed, no one has ever hinted such a thing."

"I hope not; but in any case you would be disappointed, for of course I could not be your wife."

"Could not?"

"No, Mr. Hardy, you can readily see why."

"Indeed, I cannot."

"Then I must speak plainly. To me marriage is as serious as death. I would rather dash myself over the rocks there, and be forever at rest, than marry a man I did not love. Oh! it would be horrible. And sometimes when I think about it, I almost resolve that I will never marry, for fear I make a mistake."

I had spoken seriously, perhaps more so than the occasion called for, as I had no doubt the love of William Hardy was one of those will-o'-the-wisp affairs which would disappear as rapidly as it came.

He tried to take my hand, but I drew it away, and then, with all the seriousness of which he was capable, he said:

"Miss Bessie, I love you, and you would soon learn to love me."

"That I cannot answer for. If I loved you, Mr.

Hardy, I would say so, but I would never marry without love."

"But you would love me afterward."

"I might or might not. The experiment is too risky for me to try it."

"I shall die if you refuse me. Oh! Bessie, I never loved like I love you. I never felt for any such passionate fervor. I never thought I could ask any one to marry me as I ask you. Oh! do have pity on me. I loved you the very moment I saw you."

"Listen, Mr. Hardy, to what Jess sings:

"'There are hearts so quick to ignite
 At a touch of love's magical light,
 That they "catch" at the very first sight
  Of a pair of bright eyes,
  And, enkindled by sighs,
 They burn and consume in the space of a night.'"

It was unfortunate that I had quoted this verse, for Mr. Hardy at once replied:

"Yes, I know that, Miss Bessie, but let me quote from the same song, which I know:

"'There are hearts of a different strain
 That thrill with an exquisite pain,
  Yet their pulses still beat
  With an equable heat,
 And passion aye strives to consume them in vain.

"'Love glows in such hearts like the wine
 Drank by gods in the beakers divine
 On the mythical mount of the nine,
  And believe, O believe,
  Fairest daughter of Eve,
 Such a love now glows god-like
  In this heart of mine!'"

As he repeated these lines, which I of course never expected he would know, when I quoted a verse of the song, he again tried to seize my hand.

I thought it was time for this nonsense to stop, and so I said, seriously:

"I am honored, Mr. Hardy, by your proposal, but you have my answer. I do not love you, and therefore cannot marry you."

The effect on him was terrible. I saw his whole body

shake with emotion, and the color forsook his face. He thought he loved, and the disappointment was poignant.

I felt sorry for him, and remember I was but a young girl, and he was the first suitor for my hand. I felt I would like to soothe him. His evident distress was more than I could bear.

"I am so sorry," I said.

"Bessie, I love you. My heart's love is yours. Never shall I again say the same to a woman. For I want not life if I cannot have you."

I felt really grieved, and my heart was softening to him. Perhaps I might love him, I thought. Should I give him hope?

I moved nearer to him, and was about to whisper a word which might have given him some peace, for I was relenting, and should have told him to wait until I knew him better; but the madness of his passion overwhelmed him, and before I was aware of it, he had thrown his arms around me and smothered my face with his kisses.

I hated him then, and if I could have killed him I would have done so.

I left the cave—my indignation was so great that I could not speak, and climbed to the top of the cliff. It was still raining, but I mounted Romola and started for home.

I had gone about a mile when I was overtaken by William Hardy, who was so profuse in his apologies, that I could not but accept them. Poor fellow, I felt really sorry for him, but all thought of bidding him hope had gone, and I do not think I could ever have loved him after those kisses burned into my flesh like hot coals.

By the time we had reached the residence of Hans Coetzee, we had become good friends, but were on the same footing as when we started, except that I felt I could never again trust to the honor of William Hardy.

CHAPTER VII.
DREAM FACES.

I HAD never believed in dreams, never thought them worth a second thought, and oftentimes would laugh at and ridicule Jess because she would have it that dreams were oftentimes the forewarners of coming events and troubles.

Since I have reread my journal for the purpose of culling thoughts and fancies, facts and adventures for this story, I have thought much about what Jess used to say about dreams.

I well remember how she once talked with me for several hours, trying to impress on my mind the importance of giving heed to a dream I had just told her.

She said that all human knowledge originated in dreams, and that the spirits of those who had gone from the earth life, and were resident with the happy in the great beyond, oftentimes made use of dreams as bridges, whereby they might span the gulf between our world and theirs.

The idea seemed to me at that time to be highly ridiculous, for I was more given to rompish amusements and practical work than I was to fancy or phantasies.

I was a farmer, and uncle, when he was especially pleased with me, and desired to sound my praises to his friends, would call me "Farmer Bess." I am not going to boast about my "manly" acquirements, because nearly every girl in Africa at the time had to set to and work.

I can tell you there were not many idlers. But you see there was no society. No parties or concerts or balls to go to, so we were up at four in the morning and often in bed by seven at night.

In the morning there was the milking, then the feeding of the horses and chickens, the looking after the eggs, etc. After breakfast Jess would do the housework, and churn the butter, and various other work of the kind; while I would wash and purify the ostrich feathers, or, if one of the birds got loose, mount Romola and hunt the bird.

Now, with all these varied duties, we girls of the South African Republic had not much time to think about dreams.

On the night following the day when I had received an offer of marriage from William Hardy, I was a long time before I could get to sleep, and Jess was particularly cross with me for my uneasiness.

When I did fall into a sound slumber I dreamt.

It was not one of those fleeting visions of the night

which can be accounted for by the condition of one's health.

But every detail was worked out with a care and nicety that admitted of no room for doubt.

Only one thing was misty, and that was a face.

The dream commenced by my passing through again the events of the day, and I was shown how, had I accepted William Hardy's proposal, I should have been miserable for life.

Then the scene changed, and I was mounted on Romola, accompanied by William Hardy and his father.

We reached Hans Coetzee's house and partook of some refreshment which seemed to stupefy us.

How long we remained under the influence of the drug I could not say, but when we awoke we were in a tented wagon and were being driven across the country. Our hands were fastened to our sides and we were prisoners.

I was thrown into a small room, and fell on the floor in a far from graceful position, the others were separated from me.

I had remained there for some time when Hans Coetzee entered, his broad, Dutch face beaming with smiles, and he took out his knife and cut the cords which bound my hands, when this was done, he began to apologize.

"We never intended to bring you here, Miss Bessie," he said. "It was all a mistake, and you will be sent back to your uncle as soon as possible. Let me, however, give you some good advice. Never go riding with people you don't know."

I dreamt that I asked many questions, but old Meinheer Coetzee refused to answer.

I was soon on my way back, and no one seemed surprised that I was alone.

My dream seemed to change and I was this time a prisoner in the hands of the natives, Hottentots and Kafirs, and it appeared to me that my life was in danger, when suddenly there burst in on my sight a face the like of which I had never before seen. It impressed me so much that I knew the owner of that face was to exert a powerful influence over my life.

He had a sword with which he cleared a way for me

through the blacks, and then folding me in his arms, saying, "Bessie, I love you."

My soul went out to his and I felt as I had never done before. While I was in his arms, I felt the grasp grow feeble, and nothing remained but a misty, shadowy face which I felt I should remember as long as life lasted.

I was again free, and though I had faced death, there was a calm feeling of contentment which was new to me. When I awoke, my body was bathed in a cold perspiration, and I told my dreams to Jess.

She made me retell them, and when I had finished, she advised me not to go out with the Hardys again, and to be very careful about my horseback rides.

The dreams affected me strangely, for I felt that they were out of the ordinary run of night visions, but the significance I could not then understand.

In the morning I walked with uncle to the ostrich inclosure, and on the way I asked him, what was the business on which the Hardys had come.

He laughed and then said, "William is fond of sport."

"Yes, uncle, but the old gentleman does not hunt——"

"No. Well, I can trust you, Bess. You see that flag-staff?"

"Of course, uncle."

"Well, what would you say if the Union Jack should float from it."

"So it does, uncle, on the queen's birthday."

"I know that, my dear, but what if the English flag was to be hoisted at Pretoria?"

"I don't understand you, uncle."

"Can you keep a secret, Bess?"

"Yes, uncle, you know I can."

"Then what would you say if England was to rule here as well as in the Cape colony?"

"I should be very sorry."

"Sorry!"

"Yes, very sorry indeed."

"Why, Bess, you are English."

"I know it, uncle, but—of course I don't understand these things—but I think the people who now govern have a better right than England."

"You are not patriotic."

"Yes, Uncle Croft, I am. You must remember I

came here a little girl and I have learned to love the Republic."

"And now you have arrived at the mature age of sixteen, and so——"

"Don't laugh, uncle, but what has all this to do with Mr. Hardy?"

"Why, my dear, he is an English agent, and if he is successful the English flag will float over us."

"I shall be sorry, for I am sure the people do not wish it."

"Of course they don't, they are like children, they never know what is good for them."

I knew it was no use arguing with my uncle about England, for he was a monomaniac on that subject, and believed that no country could govern itself properly unless as a portion of the great British Empire.

Had my dream anything to do with that political trouble just looming on the horizon?

Time would tell, and though I felt uneasy, I was too young and full of spirits to allow myself to be troubled by any fears of revolutions or wars. There was one thing which impressed me more than anything else, and that was the remembrance of the face I had seen in the mist and shadow of the dream.

Who was it? And should I ever meet its possessor, or was it a spirit face which I should not behold until death had claimed me, and my body moldered in the grave. Then my spirit, stripped of its incubus of earthly flesh and ties, might soar aloft to a purer realm where the one dear one might be found, and eternal happiness and bliss be mine.

I was fond of speculating on the future, and though my natal days had been so few, the life of hard work, and the mixing with people older than myself had developed my mind so that I thought as one ten years older. No one ever imagined me to be less than twenty, and some declared I was much older even than that.

I was, I suppose, a queer girl, so at least they all said, for as uncle would sometimes remark, I had a man's head and a girl's body. Well, I am not responsible for that, but through life I have tried to do my duty, and at the same time feel an interest in events of the time.

CHAPTER VIII.
PLOTS AND INTRIGUES.

The Transvaal Republic had rather a curious history. In 1848 the Orange Free State was a prosperous republic, but English greed or statesmanship, according to which standpoint it is viewed from, looked on this little republic and determined to annex it. Many of the Dutch farmers had a great objection to this change of government, and they crossed the river Vaal, into the land of the Betjuana tribes, preferring life with savages to allegiance to England.

They established a republic, which was recognized by England, the European powers, and the United States, and England, Portugal, and Holland guaranteed the independence of the little state.

For several years the republic was prosperous, and its sturdy sons became known as the hardiest, bravest, and most enterprising of all the South African colonists.

In 1876, however, they highly offended the English Government by proposing to make a railroad to Delagoa Bay, in accordance with a treaty between the Transvaal Republic and Portugal.

If this railroad were made, the British colony of Natal would lose considerable revenue from the loss of customs duties on the Boer goods sent through that colony.

The English love of money showed itself, and the colonial government sent its agents through the Transvaal to try and stir up strife between the tribes, and thus afford a pretext for annexation.

That was the condition of affairs when Thomas Hardy and his son were the guests of Silas Croft at Mooifontein.

Two or three days after the dream which had rather disquieted me, I was asked to join a party for a gallop across the country.

I was never loath to accept such an offer, for there was something about a race over the plateau which pleased me more than anything else.

The day was pleasant, and the early approach of spring manifest on every side.

William Hardy had said no more of love since that day

in the cave, and I had begun to believe my hold upon his heart was gone, and to congratulate myself on the fact.

His father was so eccentric that I never could really believe he was an agent of the English Government.

The party was made up of the two Hardys, Uncle Silas, and myself. Jess, as usual, staying at home as housekeeper.

We rode for about two hours and then paused at the residence of Frank Muller for a rest.

My dislike for this man had increased since I had first made his acquaintance, and whenever I saw him smile on me, the face of the murdered Mary seemed to pass before my eyes.

We dismounted, and were heartily welcomed by the half-breed.

As we entered I saw that there were several gathered there, among them being Hans Coetzee, Karl Kruger, and another, whose face I had often seen but with whom I was not acquainted.

He was a handsome, dashing fellow, who looked as if he could fight or make love with equal success.

It might have been imagination, but I felt convinced that my presence was not wanted there.

Various pretexts were made to send me from the room, and then I heard Muller say:

"What made you bring Bess?"

"To avert suspicion, for we were watched."

"Oh! What can we do with her?"

"Take my advice, Muller," I heard my uncle say, "and let her hear all, she will never breathe a word."

"You think that is best?"

"I do."

"And so do I," said another.

"Well, be it so, but we have to take care what we are about."

I had heard every word, and was rather pleased than otherwise at the confidence they placed in me.

After dinner, which by its careful preparation showed that we were all expected, Muller opened the discussion by asking Mr. Thomas Hardy to say what he thought was the best course to pursue.

I had drank a cup of coffee and a strange feeling of

dizziness came over me. I was glad to accept the proposition to lie down in the next room.

My senses were bewildered and I expected every minute to faint.

A few minutes later my uncle said he was annoyed to think his niece was so ill, and suggested that a doctor should be sent for.

I heard Muller whisper that he had fixed me for an hour, for "gals were mighty bad folks to keep a secret."

The whole truth burst upon me at once, I had been drugged, but fortunately the narcotic had not been strong enough, and though I was incapable of exertion, I was conscious of everything that was said.

My uncle was very anxious about me, but he was calmed by the assurance that no harm could possibly come to me.

I heard Hardy declare that the English were determined to annex the republic, and if it could be done by peaceable means so much the better. If, however, the Boers would not consent, then war would be declared, and the Betjuans armed and brought into the field against the whites.

"You must not forget," I heard Hardy remark, "that the Betjuans number six hundred thousand, while you at most can only reckon on forty thousand people."

"Well, what terms do you offer?" asked Muller.

"Terms!"

"Ay! How much shall we get, and what better shall we be?" the voice was again that of Muller.

"Well, really, gentlemen, I cannot say; but I do know that for every member of the government and each voortrekker there will be a good round bag of gold which will make his horse sweat to carry it home."

"I am for annexation," said Muller.

"And so am I," responded my uncle who was a voortrekker.

Two others were also of the same opinion.

"What say you, Kruger?"

"Do you want my sentiments?"

"We do."

"Ay, this is a free meeting and we want each to say as he thinks."

"If that is so," remarked Kruger, with dignity, "I

will speak even at the risk of offending. We have a free
republic and treaties with all the great nations. I am
for letting well enough alone. I was born free, and free
I wish to remain."

"And would you be less free under the English flag?"
I heard my uncle ask.

"It is well to ask that, Om Croft. Let me tell you
that a government from Pretoria is freer and better than
one from London. We have less taxes to pay——"

"Taxes, that is all you think about," said Muller.
"We shall have really less, for all the Betjuans will have
to pay taxes."

"Don't make such a mistake," said Kruger, "the
Betjuans will then refuse to work, and we shall be
slaves."

"You are the only one who seems inclined to grumble.
What says Joubert?"

"I don't like to speak," said that person.

"Why?"

"I might offend."

"No, no. Speak out."

"Then. I tell you that the man who takes English
gold for his vote is a knave, and ought to be hanged to
the first tree."

Then there was a commotion, and from the noise I
made sure there would be a fight. I tried to rouse myself, but the effects of the opiate were holding me in
fetters stronger than my will.

To my dismay I heard Uncle Silas ask the Hardys to
see me home, as he had some business to attend to, and
had a long round to take.

Oh, if I could but have spoken, but though I tried, my
tongue like my limbs was bound, and I was powerless.

To make my agony the greater, my uncle came into the
room and kissed me. His kiss seemed like a farewell,
and was far from pleasant. I thought it was cruel to
leave me like that, especially to leave me in the power of
William Hardy.

I heard the door close, and then for a short time all
was silent.

But after the lapse of a few minutes I heard a whispered conversation going on. What could it be about?
Why was it necessary to speak in whispers?

I opened my eyes, but the room was dark, at least that is what I thought for the time, but in reality it was the effect of the opiate on my brain.

"Is she unconscious?" I heard some one say, and it appeared as if the speaker was close to my couch.

I had a strange sensation at the moment. It seemed that a hot wave passed over my face.

Three times it passed over me, and the third time, I overheard some one say:

"It is enough, you singed her hair."

"Great Heaven!" I thought, "is it possible they have passed a flame over me to see if I was unconscious?"

That thought was my last for some time. I imagined I was dying, and as my senses grew dim and I lost the power of even opening my eyes, I resigned myself, feeling sure that my last hour had come.

I prayed, but it was a feeble attempt. I knew no more. I had become entirely unconscious.

CHAPTER IX.

ABDUCTION.

"Where am I?"

I remember asking this question, but it remained unanswered.

My senses were returning to me, and I thought a cold breeze was fanning my face.

I heard no noise, could it be that I was really dead, and was being borne away from earth?

I felt calm and easy, but at the same time a little of that feminine curiosity which I possessed in common with all my sex would obtrude itself on my mind, and I thought I would like to know where I was going.

"Where are you taking me?" I asked, but there was no answer.

Had I really spoken, or were the words only formed in my mind, and not articulated.

For quite a long space of time I remained unconscious.

I felt a sudden shaking as though my couch had been lifted up and dropped.

"Oh!" I exclaimed, but even that cry was unheeded.

I tried to rouse myself, and thought I heard some one talking.

My ears were strained to catch the sound, but not a word could I distinguish.

I then endeavored to sit up, but that was impossible.

Another hour or so passed, and then I was able to open my eyes, and to my horror I saw I was in a tented wagon, and worse than that, I discovered that my arms and legs were firmly secured so that I could not rise. My dream at once recurred to me, and I thought I was a prisoner.

"Help!"

At last I was heard, and I saw the head of old Hardy pushed through the front curtain of the tent.

His wig, as usual, was turned round, and made him cut a most ridiculous figure.

"Oh, Mr. Hardy," I said, "where am I?"

"In a wagon, my dear," was the suave reply.

"But where am I going?"

"Home."

"I am glad of that, but I am tied down to this bed."

"Yes, my dear, you have been very sick."

"Sick!" I repeated.

"Yes, dear Miss Bessie, and——"

"But why tie me?"

"You have been delirious, and we had to do so, for fear you might hurt yourself."

"Where is Uncle Silas?"

"At home."

"Does he know?"

"Of course he does, and we are taking you to him."

I could not converse, my senses were so confused, and everything was dim and indistinct.

I tried to sleep. Treachery never entered my mind. What object could any one have in taking me prisoner? I did sleep—at least I lost consciousness for some time; when I woke I felt weak and exhausted.

Who was that talking? I listened, and heard what made me very uneasy.

It was the elder Hardy who was speaking.

"It is awfully risky," I heard him say, "but we must go through with it. If she rouses we must give her auother dose. It will never do for her to give an alarm until we are across the Vaal River; then we can do as we please."

"But if she is obstinate?"

"See here, Will. It is necessary that you should marry one of old Silas Croft's nieces, and you chose Bess."

"I know that, father, but——"

"I understand what you would say—you want to know what you can do with a wife who is rebellious."

"I haven't got a wife yet."

"No, but in a few hours you will have; and if she resists—well—another drop of coffee—she likes coffee—will render her so that she will know nothing about the ceremony; and when that is over, well——"

"Well, father?"

"Need you ask? Is it likely a girl is going to rebel against a good-looking husband?"

"I love Bess."

"So much the better; it will be pleasanter for all concerned."

The whole plot seemed to come to me then; and as soon as there was a lull in the conversation I let my mind work out the details.

I could see that I was drawn into a dastardly plot for some reason which I did not then understand, and that the drugging at Frank Muller's was a portion of the plan; though I will do even Muller justice, and say that I do not believe he knew of the abduction, for he had been very attentive to me, and had even said, if ever he married, he would like me for a wife.

I was to be taken across the Vaal River, and there, by strategy or force, married to William Hardy; and the old scoundrel thought that I should then submit easily.

I should be under the English flag, and I had learnt that, under cover of its folds, the most dastardly crimes were committed in South Africa.

What was my uncle doing to allow me to be taken away by his professed friends?

For a time I was so unjust as to imagine that he had been a consenting party; but on clearer thought I knew my dear old uncle would never act in such a manner.

It was a deep-laid plot, but its reason an incomprehensible one.

What would it benefit old Hardy that I should be his son's wife?

It was evident that William was not the organizer, or even a willing participant in the plot.

What was my best plan of action?

Escape was next to impossible, for I was a close prisoner in the tented wagon.

Resistance, or even a show of it, would cause me to be again drugged.

I could not refuse all food and drink, for it might be days before a chance of liberation came.

What was I to do?

Oh, if Jess had been with me to advise.

My dream!

A memory of it flashed across my mind at that moment. I was released by Hans Coetzee, and later by a form which gradually faded into mist.

I felt stronger even through that thought of the dream.

I could not see my way clear yet, but for the present I would appear to believe I was being taken home, and would even accept the love of young Hardy. This would most likely throw them off their guard, and give me, at least, freedom of my body.

Nearly an hour passed, and the uneven nature of the road required that the whole attention of the Hardys should be given to the horses.

In consequence I was not able to hear any more of the conversation, and was left entirely alone.

The road became a little more level, and then the old gentleman paid me a visit.

"Ha, ha!" he laughed, in his eccentric fashion, "so the pretty Bessie is awake. Feeling better, eh?"

"Yes, Mr. Hardy, but how is it we have not yet reached home?"

"The roads are bad."

"I am aware of that; but even so, as we rode over them on horseback, I think we ought to have got further than this."

"Well said, ha, ha, ha. The little Bessie is reasoning, therefore the delirium has left her."

"Mr. Hardy, tell me why we are not going the nearest way home."

"I would have informed you before, but did not want to disturb you."

"Tell me now, please."

"Well, we are not on the road to your uncle's house."

I wondered whether the time had come for me to be made acquainted with their intentions, so I waited for further statements to be made.

"No, Miss Bessie, we are going toward the Vaal."

"What for, Mr. Hardy?" I asked, as calmly as possible.

"Well, you see—— But I had better tell you the truth."

"Oh, yes, do please, for I am so anxious to see uncle and Jess."

"Well, my dear, I—really now, I don't like telling you."

I wondered whether his hesitancy arose from a fear of telling the truth, or from his desire to obtain time that he might think out a story.

I therefore waited for him to continue. When he had whistled a little, said a few words to the horses, he turned, and with that inane grimace on his face that so annoyed me, he said:

"You see, Miss Bessie, I am taking you to Durban."

"To Durban?" I exclaimed.

"Yes, to my home."

"But, my uncle?"

"He will join us there, and Jess—your sister will be there before you."

"Indeed!"

"Yes. You see there is going to be some fighting."

"Fighting?" I repeated.

"Yes."

"What about?"

"The fellows won't give up their government."

"Why should they?"

"Because England could govern better."

"I don't think so, but what has that to do with my leaving Mooifontein as a prisoner?"

"I see I have to tell you all."

"It will be better." I spoke calmly, for I was very desirous of finding out all he had to say, and thus—with the knowledge he did not know I possessed—might circumvent his plans.

"Then I will be honest with you. Ha, ha, ha. When you were taken sick at the house of that good voortrekker, Meinheer Muller, Kruger and Joubert, who are leaders of this wretched little republic, would not listen to my plans, and so the next day there was war declared——"

"Who by?"

"The English, of course. And the rascally Boers are in possession of all the best places, so I promised your uncle I would take you away at once to Durban."

"Indeed! And my sister and uncle will join us?"

"Yes, Miss Bessie," said old Hardy, looking relieved.

"It is false!"

He looked at me; his small, steel-like eyes glowing almost like a ferret's as he repeated:

"False!"

"Yes, Mr. Hardy. You are not taking me away because of any war."

"How do you know that?"

"Because," I answered with a sneer, "you and your son are such great patriots you would have stayed behind to fight."

"I am too old, ha, ha, ha."

"Too old too fight, but not to old to try and bribe the leaders to sell their country."

"You are bitter."

"What are you going to do with me?"

"I have told you the truth."

"But what does your son say?"

"Oh, Miss Bessie, can you ask?"

"Why not; he once professed to love me."

"So he does now, he would give his life for you."

"Oh, Mr. Hardy, that is very great nonsense, for he would not wish his future wife to be compromised."

"I don't understand you."

"You say he loves me, and that one day he hopes I shall be his."

"That is the truth."

"Then how will he like it, when he is told that his wife traveled for miles strapped down to a bed, her only companions being two men."

"Ah! I see, I see. Why not marry William, and that would settle it."

"But where is he?"

"Driving."

"He is a very gallant lover."

"I will send him.'

"No. I will not see him until I am free from these fetters."

"And then?"

"Why, don't you think a girl would prefer conversation with a good-looking young man to an old scarecrow——"

"Like me. Ha, ha, ha, that's good."

My speech had the desired effect, for my hands and feet were freed, and I was able to sit up.

"Now tell me, Mr. Hardy, how long have I been away from uncle?"

"He left yesterday at three o'clock——"

"And it is now——'

"Six o'clock."

"Oh!"

I motioned for the old fellow to leave me, and I felt once again free.

I sat down and celebrated my release from captivity by a good cry.

I had acted a part for so long, and forced down my feelings, so that now the reaction had set in, and the tears would come.

The old fellow had made a miserable mess of his story, but he evidently thought I accepted it as gospel.

As I look back, I often wonder that I had courage to do as I did; but then I had been eight years a resident of the Boer Republic, and with the exception of my sister, had no female companions. I had grown up a regular farmer, and had perhaps as much coolness and a certain kind of bravery as many a man.

I wondered what the result would be.

Of course I intended to escape, but how?

At present I had no idea which way we were going, and I must appear to acquiesce until I not only knew the location, but fell in with some who would aid me if I made an appeal to them.

When I had recovered from my fit of weeping, I

stepped outside the tented portion of the wagon and felt the cool refreshing breezes of the March evening.

The old man was driving, and the young one was walking at the horses' heads.

"Ah!" said Mr. Hardy as he saw me, "so you want a sniff of the fresh air."

"Yes, even prisoners like and are entitled to that."

"Don't say prisoner, Miss Croft, you should say guest."

"Perhaps it would be more polite, but not so true," I retorted.

The camp was pitched by the banks of a small stream, and the two Hardys prepared the evening meal.

I watched every movement, for I was determined I wouldn't be drugged again for want of watching.

I was satisfied that all partook of the same coffee—which was really delicious, and as I did not think it possible to narcotize the bread and meat, I was able to make a good supper.

CHAPTER X.

THE PLOT.

I RETIRED to my bed—the tented part of the wagon had been given up to me entirely—and rested.

Instead of sleeping, however, I was thinking, and fortunately so, for I learned much about my abductors and their plans.

I suppose my heavy breathing had disarmed suspicion, and I was thought to be asleep.

After some hours had passed I strained my ears, trying to understand a whispered conversation.

It was in vain for a long time, but at length I heard William Hardy say:

"I don't like it."

"I should think just the opposite," said his father.

"Oh, father, let us go back, and act with honor."

"Impossible. Marry the girl; she is more than half willing."

"Ah, if I could but think so."

"It is the truth. On the morrow you talk to her and you can win her consent easily."

Can he, I thought; we shall see about that. I can play

a game with you, Master William, which perhaps may astonish you.

"But, father, why do you wish me to marry one of the girls."

"I have a good reason for it."

"Of course you have, but I want to know it as well."

"You shall after the marriage."

"Then see here, father, I shall never know."

"What do you mean?"

"That unless you tell me I will never speak of love to Bess again, and will not marry her."

"What nonsense."

"Call it what you please; I am not a child nor will I be treated as one. Tell me or——"

"Or what?"

"I will expose the whole plot to Bessie."

"Ha, ha, ha! That's good, but what good will that do?"

"I will help her to escape."

"And would she escape, think you?"

"Why shouldn't she?"

"Hark ye, William Hardy, Bessie Croft is no fool, if you are."

"Father! What do you mean?"

"Why, she would rather marry you now, even if you hated her, than escape."

"You are mad."

"No; I am not. Let her escape and I will circulate the report that you and she were together for several days and that you cast her off after——"

"Stay I would strike to the earth any man, even you, my father, if you ever dared to utter a word against Bessie Croft's honor and fair name."

Well done, William. I felt that I would like to thank him for his speech, but I was supposed to be sleeping very soundly, and so must remain quiet.

"Don't get angry, for as you know the very fact that she left Muller's with you in a tented wagon, sending the horses home by a messenger, after her uncle had expressly left orders that she was to return home at once, would destroy her name; and I tell you, William Hardy, it is only as your wife she can go back to Mooifontein."

"Then the decision will rest with her, for I will tell

her everything, and I will go back with her, and your
scheme shall be known to Silas Croft."

"You are a fool."

"Am I? I am your son. Tell me your reasons and I
may act as you desire."

"I suppose I must. Do you know I am a poor man?"

"No."

"Well, I am, and I have hard work to live at all."

"You surprise me, father."

"Very likely, but it is the truth. If those rascally
Boers will only hoist the English flag voluntarily I shall
get ten thousand pounds, but if we have to fight for it
I don't get a penny. Now if you marry Bessie or Jess
Croft, I don't care which, you will be a rich man."

"Is Silas Croft so very rich?"

"No, but the girls are; or to be more correct, one of
them is."

"How is that?"

"The story is rather a long one, but as you won't
trust me, I suppose I will have to tell you; but first let
me make sure that Bess is asleep."

The elder Hardy entered the tent and appeared satisfied that I was in the land of dreams.

However, he was suspicious, so he proposed that they
should leave the wagon and go to where the horses were
corraled.

"No, father, I am not going to stir from this wagon,
there are too many snakes around to suit me."

"Well, I suppose you must have your way. You
know the parentage of the girls, don't you?"

"No."

"Do you remember, about eight years ago, a man
coming into my office at Durban, and asking about the
Transvaal? He was drunk and abusive, and I told you
to fetch in my sjambock, and I would give the chap a
thrashing?"

"Yes."

"Well, that was their father."

"No."

"I say, yes."

"You see, old Silas Croft's father was a clergyman in
England, and he went and got married a second time—
more fool he——"

"Father!"

"I mean he was a fool in his second marriage, for don't think, Will, I am one of those who believe a man should only marry once. I have married—let me see, how many wives——"

"Never mind that, father, go on with your story."

"You see he married a young woman who had money. It wasn't for love he married. Bless you, Will, I've known some young fellows marry, and think they have got perfection, but the wife dies, and they get another, and then they find out what true happiness is. Well, the old parson, Croft, reversed that. His first wife was an angel, and as bad luck would have it, his second was a tartar. She bore him one son, and then killed the old fellow."

"Killed him!"

"Well, yes, nagged him to death. I tell you, my boy, there is many a good man gets into a lunatic asylum, or into the grave through the constant fault-finding or nagging he is subjected to at home."

"I don't think I will risk it," said William, almost dolefully.

"If a young man is rich, I say never marry. But if he can get rich by a marriage, why the trial is worth making."

The old rascal, I thought. So he would only marry to get money. And then I hoped he had a good scolding, shrewish, nagging wife. Was I wrong?

"Never mind preaching, father; tell the story."

"Well, the little boy grew up, and was a wild, harum-scarum, drunken fellow; but he married a nice young lady, at least I hear she was, for I never saw her. He beat her, and ill-used the poor thing in every way, until she saved up her money and ran away from her husband, and started for Natal. Before she had been two days at sea she died, and on her death-bed she called her two children to her, and commissioned them to find their uncle at Mooifontein.

"She was so poor, that the passengers raised enough money by subscription to send the children along to old Silas."

"Yet you say that the girls are rich. Where do they get it from?"

"Don't be impatient. The girls' father married again, but somehow his heart yearned for the children in Africa, or at least that is what he said—the truth being that he wanted to see what his brother Silas was doing, and whether he could get a few hundreds from him. So he came out here and raised a rumpus with Silas.

"On his way out, he stopped at Durban and called to see me, for I was Silas Croft's representative at that point, and, as you know, a good many feathers and a tidy lot of ivory came along."

"Yes, father, and I rather suspect your commission was bigger than Uncle Silas ever dreamt it was."

"Ha, ha, ha! that's good. Well, business is business, you know. Now, I found that Jack Croft was poor, and he was mad to think he couldn't do as he pleased with Silas, so he raised a rumpus.

"He didn't get the girls, as you know, neither did he get any of his brother's money.

"He got such a reception that he swore he would be revenged on his brother. Why, Will, you wouldn't believe how the sjambock did score his back. It was a treat to see it. He got to Newcastle that night, and at the canteen he began to spend what little money he had, and that wasn't much. There was a great crowd of drunken fellows there, and Jack Croft got betting with them. He lost about twenty pounds, but he won a little bit of land, about half an acre. 'By gosh, I'll go and settle on that!' he said, as he handed the deed to me. 'Hardy, old boy,' he said, 'I am a landed proprietor now, and I must make a will. Get a paper, old fellow.' I got paper and drew up a will for him. He left the land to whichever of his nieces was the first to leave the uncle's house, providing that she married without her uncle's knowledge or consent. Now you see the drift, don't you?"

"Well, father, it appears to me that all this bother and even crime is for half an acre of land, worth at most, I suppose, a 'scotchman' (two shillings). What became of Jack Crofts?"

"About two hours after he made the will he got drunk, and a Kafir or Betjuan, I forget which, struck him such a blow with a sjambock across the nose that he burst a blood-vessel and fell dead."

"And the will?"

"That I have; and as I was the executor, of course I am all right."

"But how much is this land worth?"

"What do you think?"

"I have already said—about a scotchman; and I am sick of all this intrigue and crime for a paltry half acre of land."

"Don't be in such a hurry. The land is at Basta Marica——"

"What, the diamond fields?"

"Yes."

"And the land is worth?"

"A hundred thousand pounds."

"Great Jupiter! I'll marry Bess to-morrow, even if I have to force her. But her uncle gave consent?"

"No. I told him you wanted Jess—do you see?"

"And he?"

"Said he would see you hanged first."

"But he was friendly?"

"Very; but he is in my power a little, and under the surface he hates me."

"Oh!"

"So I get my revenge on the uncle for his hatred, and get the money into the family as well."

"Who is protecting the property?"

"That I have managed all right. Muller will protect my interests."

"Muller?"

"Yes; you seem surprised."

"I am, I thought you were cuter."

"What do you mean?"

"Why Muller will be after Jess before we can get Bess and the money."

"No. I have deceived Muller, who thinks that the girls cannot inherit until they are of age."

"Oh!"

"Now, my boy, you see the whole thing."

"Not quite."

"What perplexes you now?"

"What did you desire me to act the bashful for?"

"Ha, ha, ha! That was a good joke. Ha, ha, ha!"

"Don't laugh there like a grinning hyena, but tell me."

"That is a nice way to talk to your father."

"In this business we are partners, not father and son."

"Oh! Ha, ha, ha! Good."

"For mercy sake stop it and answer my question."

"If you must know, I will tell you, the bigger fool you appeared the better opportunity you would have for bagging the prize."

"I see now what you meant, but I did appear a fool."

"Just as great as you were."

"Thank you, but what is that?"

"Lie quiet and listen."

I can assure you I was deeply interested in the conversation, but would like to have found out what would become of the property in case neither Jess nor I left Uncle Silas Croft without his consent.

I was started by the sudden stopping of the interesting conversation, and wondered whether it was possible that help and perhaps freedom was at hand.

Young Hardy pushed his head into my apartment so suddenly that I was afraid he saw my open eyes.

He, however, retired without a word, and I breathed again freely.

CHAPTER XI.

THE BETJUANAS.

"HARK!"

"I heard it again," whispered the old man.

"So did I."

"What can it be?"

"A lion perhaps."

"No, for the horses would have given the alarm before this."

"Go and see, dad, what it is."

"Not likely; go yourself."

"And if I am lost what becomes of the Basta Marica diamonds?"

This conversation was carried on in such a faint whisper, that it was only by raising my head and resting it on my hand that I could catch a word.

For a long time there was silence, and I began to think that my abductors had fallen asleep.

I sat up on the rude bed, and tried to look round, but all was dark. Not a sound was to be heard.

Yes, a sound did break in upon my ear. It was a strange one, and appeared to be directly under the wagon.

It was harsh and grating.

Could it be that something was eating through the wagon?

I had heard of, but never seen, a small animal which would eat its way rapidly through the thickest wood and attack its victim in that way.

I was afraid of it, and my fears had been increased by the knowledge that the Basutus worshiped it as the devil, and the Betjuans looked upon it with superstitious awe.

What should I do? I was half inclined to rouse my jailers, for they at least were human.

The noise continued, and I could stand it no longer, so I crept out of the tent and touched William Hardy.

He gave a jump as though startled. His face was as white as the northern snows, and his hands trembled with fear.

"What is it?" he gasped.

"Don't you hear anything?"

"Yes."

"Well, what is it?"

"Heaven only knows."

I was annoyed at the cowardice of the two men, for the elder had laid his full length on the seat and was too frightened to even raise his head.

"Why don't you get up and look under the wagon?" I said.

"No, I dare not."

"You coward, give me a pistol and I will."

"No, don't go, don't, there's a dear, good girl. I love you so that I cannot endure the thought of harm coming to you."

"You love!" I sneered. "What rubbish is that. You love, and have not the courage to protect and defend the one you say you love."

"But I should be killed."

"Poor fellow, give me the pistol and I will defend you."

I really believe the arrant coward would have let me leave the wagon and brave whatever danger there was, had not a new complexion been put on things just at that moment.

A sudden shock was felt and the body of the wagon fell to the ground. The four wheels had been removed and of course there was nothing to prevent us getting a severe shaking up.

"What the devil is that?" asked the elder Hardy.

We had been without lights, fearful of attracting attention of either animals or natives, but now we felt it advisable to light the lanterns.

As soon as the light illuminated a space round our fallen wagon, we saw we were completely surrounded by hideous-looking Betjuans and Kafirs.

As soon as the lamp light fell on our faces, the wretched looking creatures set up such a hideous yell that I for one wished that I could stop my ears and keep out the discordant noise.

They shouted and danced and yelled until it appeared that pandemonium had been let loose.

"What do you want with peaceful travelers?" asked William, but unfortunately in the English language.

They only yelled the more, and as none of them would utter any word we were at a loss what to do.

"We are English. Please don't hurt us," whined the elder Hardy.

This was not understood; but when the old man took out of his pocket a miniature English flag which he carried, believing it to be some sort of a protection for him, he did that which they readily understood, for they pounced upon the old gentleman, took the flag from him, and each treated it to some indignity.

It was then torn in pieces and thrown away.

We were seized, our arms and legs bound, and in that very uncomfortable position we had to remain until morning.

We were heartily glad when the sun's rays first struggled over the hills and lighted up the surrounding country.

The night before, I alone had been a prisoner; now we all shared the same indignity.

What would be our fate?

I had heard that there were some tribes of Betjuanas that delighted in torturing the whites who were so unfortunate as to fall into their power. Could it be that we were to be the victims of such brutes?

"Oh, woe is me," cried old Hardy.

"Curse it, we have got into a nice pickle," responded the son.

I remained silent, for I was very much alarmed at the turn of events in my young life.

I had only commenced to enjoy life's pleasures, and my heart was heavy at the thought of the death which I might have to face in a few hours at the hands of these savages.

A fate worse than death might be mine, for I had heard stories told how young maidens were stolen and compelled to live with these brutal creatures, who had neither honor nor morality to restrain their brutal passions.

"I wish we were at Pretoria," said the elder Hardy.

"We were fools for ever coming this way."

"The risk was worth it."

They seemed oblivious of my presence and talked in the agony of despair as though I were a participator in their schemes.

"Why didn't you shoot?" I asked at last.

"Shoot, Miss Croft, why, what good would that have done?"

"The more you killed, the less there would be to torture us."

"But they would have been savage."

"You are cowards, both of you," I hissed, between my clinched teeth.

"Cowards!"

"Yes. Men who steal a girl and try to force her into an unwelcome union should be possessed of some courage."

"What do you mean?" asked William.

"Oh, innocence!" I sneered; "let me tell you, guests of my uncle as you were only a few hours ago, that through a vision I know all your schemes, and as there is a God above I shall be victorious, for your plans are all of the Devil."

I had spoken with vigor. I had learnt from the conversation I had overheard that both of the Hardys were superstitious, and I resolved to work somewhat on their fears.

"What schemes do you speak of, my dear?" asked the elder Hardy, and at the same time, in turning his head, he accidentally slipped the wig round a little. One of the savages saw it, and in an instant had snatched it from his head and was holding it up on an assagai.

I could not help laughing, for the old gentleman's head was as smooth as a billiard ball and not a vestige of hair was on its surface.

The Betjuan after twirling the wig round for some time on the point of his assagai, thought he would see how it suited him, so he put it on his dirty, greasy head.

"Oh, my poor wig; what shall I do? I can never wear it again."

"I don't think you will ever want it," I said.

"Why?"

"We shall all be roasted and eaten before many hours have passed."

"Do you think so?"

"I am sure of it. I have heard Uncle Silas say often that the Betjuanas of this district were all cannibals."

"Oh dear, oh dear!" the poor old fellow sighed. "What shall I do?"

"You are getting punished soon for your treachery. By the way, have they found many diamonds at Basta Marica on my property?"

My question was like a dynamite bomb in its effect on both father and son.

"What property, my dear? Ah me, I fear the delirium of fever is returning."

"No, it is not. You know what property I refer to. My uncle was saying only the day you came that Jess and I ought to get a copy of father's will."

"How did your uncle know of it?"

"You had better ask him that. You see, my father was not a good man in many ways, but he loved us, and always intended providing for us; and the purchase of that land at Basta Marica we used to look upon as a mad freak, until we heard Muller and others talk of the diamonds found upon it."

I had spoken at random, for I was inclined to press my advantage as much as possible, and the idea got into my mind that if I could only make them believe that Muller was not true to them, they would, for the sake of revenge, tell me all.

"Believe me, Miss Bessie, I knew nothing of all this, until last evening," said William Hardy, with an earnestness which showed he was speaking the truth.

"I am glad you say so," I answered, "for I should have been sorry to believe you were without honor."

"Thank you, Miss Bessie. You know I love you——"

"Or the diamonds?"

"Have I not told you I knew nothing about this until a few hours ago?"

"Yes; but how can I believe you?"

"Why should you not?"

"Because, William Hardy, you have been playing a part."

"I do not understand."

"Where is all your bashfulness?"

"I—ah, I really——"

"No, don't try to assume it again. Both uncle and I knew you were trying to appear a bigger fool than you really were."

"You are complimentary."

"The citizens of the South African Republic believe in plain speaking."

One of the Betjuanas here came up to us and undid the cords which bound us to our unpleasant resting-places.

As soon as we were free and able to stand up, he gave us a push, and with a grunt motioned for us to go with him.

We were prisoners and had to obey.

It was no use opposing. One little sign of disobedience, and we should feel the poisoned point of one of the assagais unpleasantly pushed into our bodies.

In Indian file we marched—I occupying the middle place.

At a distance of perhaps a quarter of a mile we found the huts of the Betjuans.

CHAPTER XII.

FORTUNE AND RESCUE.

The huts were arranged in a circle, the center of which was occupied by a large dwelling, which we rightly conjectured was the kraal of the chief.

Outside the circle was a stockade or fence made of canes stuck in the ground, and plastered over with a preparation of cow dung and clay.

This substance rendered the fence or wall proof against even a rifle bullet.

The Betjuanas, like the Zulus, were great fighters, and when they were safely within their kraal, it required considerable prowess and skill on the part of an invading enemy to wage successful war with them.

We pushed forward until we were in the presence of the savage chief.

He was in full dress. On his head he had a tall and rimless white hat, which he had confiscated from some prisoner.

Round his neck he wore a necklace of human teeth, for the Betjuanas break the jaws of their victims and use the teeth as ornaments.

On the upper part of his dirty black body was a rude drawing in red chalk. What it was intended to represent I never knew, but the old fellow seemed very proud of it, for he constantly looked down admiringly at his broad and capacious chest. His loins were covered by a kind of skirt or petticoat, which I am free to confess I believe had been made for some white woman, but which he had appropriated. His legs and feet were bare.

All his attendants were nearly nude.

I felt very uncomfortable, for I had never seen so many of the natives together before.

"So!" said the old chief, whose name I soon learned was Marabasta.

The expression may have been English or Betjuanan, we knew not what answer to make.

The chief looked at us very intently, and then saw—as for the first time—the shiny bald head of the elder Hardy.

Marabasta stepped forward and rubbed his hand over the surface of the smooth head and then gave a grunt.

Every attendant did the same.

The Betjuan who had stolen the wig, now brought it forward and as he laid it at the feet of his chief pointed to Hardy.

Marabasta grunted again, and tried to fix the wig on its owner's head.

The funny positions in which he placed it, and the awful grimaces Mr. Hardy made, as the touch of the chief was rougher than pleasant, caused me to laugh so immoderately that it proved contagious, and every one joined in the burst of merry laughter.

This pleased the chief, so he continued the amusement, at times pulling the wig over Hardy's face, and then putting it on one side.

Then a new idea occurred to him, and he put the wig on one side, and with a piece of charred wood made a very fair representation of eyes and mouth on the side of the old man's head.

The large ear looked positively ugly as it was made to do duty for a nose.

When he had finished all his fun, he gave the poor old fellow such a kick that it laid him sprawling on the ground.

William had on a coat of quite a fancy pattern, and this was coveted.

With no gentle touch it was taken from his back, and soon the bare body of the chief was adorned with the check coat.

My turn came next, and I had to suffer the indignity of having my dress skirt taken off, and I soon saw the old chief trying to fasten the waist band round his capacious stomach.

I had at that time rather a slender waist, and the attempts to get the band round forty inches of waist when it was only made for twenty-two was so ludicrous that I forgot my strange appearance, and laughed until the tears ran down my cheeks.

I knew not whether Marabasta was only bent on fun, or whether this all was but a prelude to torture.

While the coat was being stripped from William Hardy's back, I happened to espy a revolver in the pocket, and under the pretense of helping the savage remove the coat, I took the revolver and slipped it in my bosom.

During all this time not a word had been spoken which we could understand.

The savages seemed determined to have all the fun they could with us, and occasionally their love of a joke caused us considerable pain.

One of the Betjuans crouched on all fours at the back of the old and cowardly Hardy, and then another native gave the old man a push, and he fell over the crouching form of the savage amidst the grunts and roars of all.

It was fun which none of us appreciated, but we had to endure it.

After they had done all their slender imagination could suggest to make the two men uncomfortable and miserable, they turned their attention to me.

My spirit was roused, and while I knew resistance was useless, I resolved to sell my honor and life dearly.

One big fellow tried to strip off my clothing, but I smacked his face with such force, that he started back shrieking with pain.

That was the signal for several to seize hold of my clothes, and very soon a goodly portion was in ribbons, but when they tried to take them from me I could stand it no longer, so I drew the revolver from my bosom, and in an instant one of my tormentors was dead at my feet and another wounded in the chest. I had only time for two shots, for I was quickly overpowered, and a blow on the head stunned me.

When I awoke later I found I was nearly stripped, and was in a hut bound tightly to a post in the center.

What had become of my fellow-prisoners I did not know.

I was weak and exhausted. To lie down and die would have been pleasant, but I must endure.

I was so firmly bound that I could not move my arms or legs, not even an inch.

My head was hot and my tongue parched.

It was night, for the darkness was most intense.

The early morning found me very indifferent, for my sufferings had been so great that nothing could add to their intensity.

When I had given up all hope and resigned myself to my fate, I thought I heard some voices speaking in the English language.

If I could but shout, but that was impossible.

I tried, but my tongue seemed so swollen that it filled my mouth.

The voices were plainer, hence I felt that they were getting nearer the hut wherein I was a prisoner.

Presently an intense heat was felt, and I realized that fire had broken out.

Was I to be burned alive? Oh, that would be horrible.

"Help!" The word was formed in my throat but no sound came from my lips.

I heard the sound of guns being fired, and then I saw a face—it was that of a white man—and I again tried to speak.

The man was young, and though his face was disfigured with black from the incessant firing which was now going on, I thought in my girlish imagination that it was the one I had seen in my dreams.

I could not speak, but I felt the approach of the man who wore the dress of an English soldier.

He came near, saw I was bound, and then he cut the thongs and I fell to the ground.

I knew no more until I awoke later and found myself in a wagon, covered with a blanket and a man's coat.

I felt refreshed, but very weak.

It seemed to me that Hans Coetzee was near me, for I could not mistake his broad jolly Dutch face.

I was so weak that I never once roused until, as I heard afterward, twenty hours later I was in my uncle's house at Mooifontein.

I may as well tell the story of my release and conveyance home here, though it was some weeks before I was strong enough to hear it.

War had been declared by England against the South African Republic, and a number of patriotic Boers, led by Joubert, and including Hans Coetzee, attacked the English near the Betjuan village.

The natives fought with equal valor against both Boers and English, and the triangular fight waged furiously for some time until some soldier fired the village.

The English were driven out, and the Boers were about returning to their homes when the few remaining huts were searched, as two Boers were missing. In their explorations they found me lying on the ground, and as Hans Coetzee was one of the party he recognized me, and I was placed in a wagon and driven home.

The elder Hardy had been killed, but the younger one was only slightly wounded. He asked the protection of the English soldiers and joined in their retreat.

Although the English were defeated in the fight, bribery and corruption had conquered at Pretoria, and the first time I was able to look from my chamber window I saw the flag of England floating from the flag-staff on the green in front of our house.

"We are English subjects once again, Bess, my dear," said my uncle, when I was well enough to converse. I only murmured——

"I am sorry for it," and I saw a shade of sorrow pass over my dear old uncle's face, for he was such a lover of his native land, that no faults could ever be committed by her government, and I really believe he thought England was, on earth, a reflection of Heaven's glory. He lived, however, to think differently, and before he died, he confessed that had he his time to live over again, he would be less enthusiastic about England than he had been. Poor old uncle, he was a regular Briton in thought, and act, and feeling.

CHAPTER XIII.
CAPTAIN NIEL'S STORY.
Prelude by Captain Adair.

I HAVE been told to use my discretion in the publication of this story of the career of the young South African girl Bess, and so I have thought this would be a very good place in which to introduce a portion of the story of my friend, Captain John Niel.

He feels bitter because his promotion came so slow, but had he known the inner workings of the military service as well as I did, he would have wondered how it was he ever became captain except by purchase. Those old days were good ones for the rich youngsters. Days never to return. Lieutenants would grow gray in the serv ice if they were poor, while a young ensign, whose military knowledge consisted of a fat bank account and an extra suit of regimentals, would go with a hop, skip and a jump over the gray-headed lieutenant's head, and before one had time to turn round grade after grade was passed and the topmost round reached before the smell of powder had passed between the hairs of the mustache up the nostrils of the soldier.

Those were the good old days—of course for the rich. Then again my friend felt hurt because his expenses were more than his salary. Well, some people are never satisfied. What does a man want more than glory? I have known a soldier fight up to his knees in blood, seize his superior officer, who was lying wounded on the battlefield, and then carry him through the thickest of the fight to a place of safety. Did the fellow grumble? Not at all. Why should he? He lost both legs and one eye; but didn't the queen with her own hand pin a silver medal, which cost nearly two shillings, to his breast, and did not a grateful country allow him a pension of seven pence a day for life?*

A man who becomes a soldier does so because of the glory of the thing.

And yet I want no more active service.

" Let paint who will the scenes of glorious war,
They'll never catch me leaving England more;
The country's call may have a pretty sound
To greenhorns; let the clarions resound
For those who like fields far and hot-fought fights;
But I prefer cool days and quiet nights."

But why recall?

" Objects o'er which none ever can rejoice,
The vision of the dark and gloomy fray,
Where starving soldiers in the trenches lay;
The scarlet corses on that cursed field,
Where crops of Taurid grass now fatly yield?"

But this is not my book. I am only its editor, and, I suppose, ought not to have obtruded my own personality, but I wanted to soften down some of Niel's grumbling, and at the same time let the patient reader know that I have

* This is, unfortunately, true of British military life even at the present day.—ED,

cut out, with my blue pencil, a very great deal which the
captain had written, for what we have to do with prin-
cipally is the connection of the captain with Mooifontein
and one of its lovely inmates, the charming Bess.

So I put my pen aside and let John Niel speak for himself:

The Captain's Journal.

Life is a queer thing, and I have been thinking since I
settled down as a land agent in England and started to
write up a journal or autobiography, call it whichever
you please, that my life has been like the world, all con-
tradictions.

For twenty years I was a warrior, and saw some active
service, and then pulled up on an ostrich farm in South
Africa, but that was a strange fate which took me there.
No sooner did I prefer hunting ostriches to Zulus,
Afghans, or Hindoos, than I had to fight again; and
then found I was a rich man, or, at least, was engaged to
marry a rich woman. Here was a consummation de-
voutly to be wished.

Then, lo! the fortune was like a mirage and vanished.
Now I am a small tenant farmer and land agent, married
to the sweetest, dearest creature on earth. Poor dear!
She little knows that my heart was with another, and that
one her own sister Jess. Honor triumphed over love, and
I married, but oh! how hard it was at times—— But
there, I am not going to fill up a book with my moraliz-
ing; I want to jot down some events in my life, so that
when any one reads it, they may understand the story of
Bess—that's my wife, you know—and see how fate
brought us together, and—yes, I will confess it, I believe
I am beginning to love her with my whole soul.

It is little Jess which has brought about that feeling,
for who can find in the wide world a sweeter, dearer little
angel in human form than little Jessie.

I never look at her peculiar beauty without recalling
to my mind some pretty lines I once read in Jess Croft's
album at Mooifontein. She said she had copied them
from some English paper, but they just described my
little Jessie.

"BESS."

> " Would you know my little love?
> Would you know my little pearl?
> My wee, wee girl?
> She has eyes of softest brown,
> She has hair all curling down
> Round a neck so soft and white,
> With a pinky shade, it quite
> Sets you thinking of a grove—
> Hawthorn grove in richest blossom.
> She has lips so ruby red,
> Dewy red, and oh, so sweet!
> Dewy red, and cool to meet!
> By her forehead's milky spread,
> She has great thoughts in her head.
> She has wonder wise and deep,
> She sits watching the cold stars,
> And the moonlight, like a ghost,
> Steals through the window bars.
> She sits, brooding quietly by night,
> She blushes at a word,
> With a glance her heart is stirred!
> And her love speaks rich and strong
> In the wordless stores of song
> That are gathered from the stars
> And encircled in her eyes;
> In her lash's upward curve,
> In her gently breathed sighs.
> Now you know my little love!
> Now you know my little pearl,
> My darling little Jessie."

Now that just describes my little one, and if my mind sometimes wanders away to a far-off grave in South Africa, the sight of little Jessie brings me back, and I feel she is a connecting link between Jess in heaven, and those who are still on earth.

I was twenty years old when I entered the army.

Wasn't I proud of my first regimentals?

Talk of the Queen of England or any of the royal princes, I was bigger than any of them at the time.

I walked up and down the streets of my native town the day before joining, and as I held my head erect, it was as much as saying—Now, Canford shall live in history. Its name has never been heard spoken except by its own sons; no one has cared about it, and few out of the county could say whether Canford was a borough, a town, or a village, but a chance for fame has come.

I, John Niel, am going to the wars, and when in the future the papers are read, the old man shall say as he

looks over his spectacles. "Ah, John Niel, of Canford, I
must go and visit the birthplace of so noted a man." In
the House of Commons some statesman will arise, and in
moving an extension of the franchise will say that Canford must be included in the new parliamentary boroughs,
because it was the birthplace of the great hero, John
Niel.

That was just how I felt and how my thoughts ran on
that eventful day when I was no longer plain John Niel,
but Ensign John Niel of her Majesty's —th Royal Infantry.

I had the regimentals and my commission, but what
would be the result?

I was so proud that it was near evening before I got
taken down a peg, and then it was by a friend of my dead
father, a good Irishman.

"John," said he, "in Skibbereen, where I come from,
there were once some old women on the village green contending about a very large egg which had been laid by a
hen, the property of one of them. Now, it had been
resolved that the egg should be marked and put under a
setting hen, when, lo! two began wrangling, and all
about whether the chicken to be hatched from the egg
would be of the male or female gender.

"The words got so high that at last some blows were
struck, and then the hair began to fly and the cheeks to
get marked with scratches. All at once one of the bystanders cried out, 'Why don't yez crack the egg and settle the dispute?' The advice was taken and the egg
broken, and so were all their hopes as to the gender of
the chicken. Now, John," he said, "wouldn't it be as well
for you to wait until your egg is hatched before you sound
the praises of the great hero, John Niel, of Canford?"

I felt bitter at this traducer of my military hopes and
enthusiasm, and put down—what I was pleased to call—
his venom to envy and disappointment because I had so
good a chance before me.

I think differently now, for I had fourteen years in the
army, and I don't think I was much of a hero after all.

There was one, however, who believed me to be a shining light in the British army, and that was my aunt—
God rest her soul.

"John," she said to me the morning I was leaving to

join, "John, life in the army is expensive, and your pay will not support you, so I shall allow you sixty pounds a year as long as you are ensign, eighty pounds when you become a lieutenant, and a hundred and twenty when you have been a lieutenant two years."

I thanked the good old lady, and had she lived, I suppose I should still have been in the army.

I am not going to tell of all my experiences of barrack life, or how I spent my time in the camps at Aldershot and elsewhere, that is of no interest, at least in this story. I had always a great desire to go to Africa, and when the Abyssinian war broke out, I was delighted to think my regiment was ordered to the front.

It was to be a grand march through the enemy's country, and medals for everybody when we returned. I found the brilliant prophecies far from fulfilled, for we had some stubborn fighting and some adventures while in the Abyssinian country.

I was sent out on one occasion with a small party to reconnoiter, and felt proud of the position.

In the ravines grew dense thickets of bamboos.

Having no native guide, we had to mark our route by certain signs left on the canes, so that we might with ease find our way back. We reached the village, around which were assembled a number of natives.

We counted only fifty having weapons, and they appeared desirous of peace.

Having made a note of that place, I ordered my men to continue in another direction.

A scout who had been sent by me in a westerly direction, returned and reported that a number of natives were engaged in some strange maneuvers close to us.

They massed first in a solid square, and then would quickly disappear and gather some yards away.

Their movements were suspicious, and we knew we had been seen and were in for a fight.

I threw out an advance guard, five men on either flank, while five brought up the rear, I occupying the centre position.

Before us lay two rocky hills covered with trees, high grass and brushwood, in which I now distinctly saw the dark bodies of the natives.

Hardly had we entered the pass when "whizz" went an arrow over our heads.

This was the signal for the fight.

Fortunately, the enemy was armed only with arrows, while we had our rifles.

For ten minutes the fight continued, with only one result, the wasting of great quantities of arrows on the part of the natives, and the loss of ammunition on our side, for not one was wounded. The rattle of musketry, and the wild appearance of the savages, swarming in every direction and firing at us constantly, was sweet music and a picturesque scene to me.

One of the enemy—probably a kind of chief—distinguished himself in particular by advancing to within fifty or so yards, and standing on a rock, he deliberately aimed five or six arrows at me, but each one went wide of the mark.

I was now determined to show how good a shot I was, so I took a rifle from one of my men and pointed it full at the breast of the chief.

There was a report and a cloud of smoke, but over and above that, I heard the laughter of the chief, for I had missed him.

That was the first time in my career as a soldier that I had singled out one man and fired.

And that shot was a failure.

When I returned and gave in my report, proud that I had fought an engagement with the natives, instead of praise I received a censure, for Sir R. Napier was relying on these very natives to ally themselves with our men and so completely hem in the Abyssinians.

My desire for military glory was the cause of England having to trust to its own soldiers instead of relying on the prowess of native spearmen.

I had one other adventure which I record here, for the purpose of encouraging those who desire the character of military hero.

I was sent out with fifty men to attack an advance guard of the enemy, and received instructions as to the exact position in which they were encamped.

Our information, however, was wrong, for the place was deserted, and we found no signs of the way in which the natives had gone.

I concluded that we should find them in a dense wood to our right, so I gave orders to proceed with caution and rout them out of the forest.

We had not proceeded far before a slight crackling of wood was heard, and we saw in the distance several forms apparently creeping toward us.

I gave orders to fire, and a rattle of musketry awoke the echoes in the forest.

There was no return fire, but I saw several objects moving about, and to all appearance crawling toward us.

Again a volley of bullets resounded on the air, and we heard two or three shrill cries, and saw the enemy retreating.

Our firing had attracted the attention of Lieutenant Silver and thirty men, and they came to our assistance.

We chased the enemy some distance, and then to our annoyance, as well as surprise, we saw them make for the trees and rapidly climb them.

At the same time one of us fell over a dead body.

There was a loud shout of laughter went up from all, for I had charged and routed the enemy, but every member of the foe was monkey.

I felt ready to end my existence then, for how should I feel when the news was telegraphed home, that Lieutenant Niel had vanquished a herd of chimpanzees.

Silver comforted me by saying he should have acted in the same way, and promised that not a word should be said about it; but three days afterward I met Sir R. Napier.

"Lieutenant Niel," he said, "I hear you have distinguished yourself," and then he burst out in an uproarious laugh. I colored a bright crimson.

"Never blush at valiant deeds, my dear sir; never fear, I shall report the affair, and you will get a medal from— from the Zoological Society, ha, ha, ha!"

I hated our general then, but later I entered Magdala by his side, and was mentioned in the dispatches in such a way, that when I returned I got the Abyssinian medal.

CHAPTER XIV.

AGAIN IN AFRICA.

I pass over my career until I was again ordered to duty in Africa.

I was with Sir Garnet Wolseley in the Ashantee war, and many adventures I had there.

I found out what Africa was like, never before had I realized the strange grandeur of an African forest.

In the early morning, when the first rays of the sun strike down and drive back the dark clouds of night, a dense white steam seems to fill every part of the forest; the eye cannot carry the vision to the top of the great gray trees majestically towering to the heavens; the rain drops ceaselessly drip, drip on the thick undergrowth, and a cold, sticky, slimy dampness is felt in the atmosphere.

Near by noon, the hot sun has triumphed, and like a great ball of fire, sends its rays right into the depths of this primeval forest, and has changed the slimy, sticky dampness into an almost unbearable heat.

The hour of noon passes and the powerful, sullen sun blazes upon the silent forest, its rays falling in nets of gold on the great gray stems which raise their gigantic trunks a hundred feet without a single branch, and then fork in massive limbs, every one of which would make a forest tree.

Another hundred feet has to be reached before a dense foliage of dark green leaves, some of which are large enough to shelter a score of men, lies outspread in the full glare of the terrible African sun.

Up there the thermometer would reach to close upon boiling point, but the rays of heat got broken and filtered through so many thicknesses of green, that in the undergrowth the same thermometer would only register at noonday about one hundred degrees in the shade.

The night comes and the rain-drops fall like great showers of bullets on the green leaves, and from them to the dry, parched earth beneath.

I walked through this great Ashantee forest, and I felt a sensation of awe creep over me.

The littleness of man and the magnitude of creation was made manifest.

Sunshine and fog, darkness and light, rain and drought are all the same to this great forest.

Now and again the lightning flashes through it, and shatters one of the leviathans, the fall of which is like the noise of an earthquake.

Under the dense undergrowth innumerable hidden rivers make the journey through it dangerous; huge poisonous fruits hang in tempting clusters on every hand.

They are full of juice, slightly acidulous, and just what is needed by the hot and parched traveler.

Great orchids, the growth of a couple of thousand years, hang over the path; spiral creepers, some several hundred feet in length, twisted like great serpents, cling from tree to tree; terrible snakes go hissing along, and in this great ocean of foliage and wonders, which has defied man's machination from the time when the Great First Cause thundered forth His edict, and nature sprung into existence, man looks small and puny, and seems lost in, as it were, the depths of a mighty ocean.

So vast is this great wealth of vegetation that nothing but monkeys and snakes can live in it, for the animal world sickens and dies.

Through this forest I was sent by the special orders of Sir Garnet Wolseley, to seek for a tribe of natives supposed to be friendly with the English.

For several weeks we wandered about in our fruitless search.

I was stricken with a terrible miasmatic fever, but I would not give in. I was determined to persevere until death claimed me for its own.

I had but fifteen men with me when I started, but at the end of a month I had lost four of them, and had to leave them buried beneath the foliage of the forest.

I would rather face death on the battle-field than in the depths of that terrible eternal stretch of woodland.

On the field of strife the rattle of musketry, the boom of the cannons, the whizzing of bullets, and the clash of steel, all make so much music that the soul seems inspired, and death loses half its terrors; but a soldier must obey.

One morning a clear light was visible in the distance and we hoped the edge of the forest was being reached.

What thankfulness came to our hearts.

I could scarcely crawl along, but still would not give in. I took fifty grains of quinine a day, and I am sure that kept me alive.

I was John Niel, of Canford, and did not intend to die in the depths of that forest.

The trees grew farther apart, the undergrowth was scantier, the poison fruits had disappeared and we saw a stretch of level plain away off in the distance. It was only just in time, for we emerged at the very moment that I lost strength and had to be carried on a litter.

A little distance off was a croom or native village.

The mud walls and thatched roofs showed that it was the place we had been searching for so long. I ordered a rest for a few hours, and then on the following morning we were ready to move forward.

I was too weak to walk.

My men now only numbered six able-bodied, the rest were like myself, prostrate with fever.

We were met half way by a number of natives who feared we were warriors, or, as they called us, "slayers," come to destroy their croom, but when they saw how feeble we were, they returned and brought with them the medicine man.

He looked at me first and then took from a bag some leaves which he at once began to chew; when he had reduced them to a pulp, he spat out the mass into his hand.

He ordered me to close my eyes, and then he put some of the filthy stuff on each eye.

Was it magic?

That I know not, but almost at once the fever seemed to abate and I felt refreshed.

It may be that these savages know more of the laws of nature than we do, or they may have a psychologic power which, in olden times, was called magic or witchcraft.

The application was renewed several times and I was transformed into a new creature.

I told the medicine man that I was desirous of seeing their chief.

He wanted to know whether we went as friends or foes, and from whom we came.

I was proud of my queen and country at that time, and said that I was from the great white queen whose people were all over the earth.

"And does your great white mother want to take our little croom from us?" he asked through an interpreter.

"No; but to give you other crooms," was my reply.

Before I left the country however, I saw I had promised more than I could perform, for the independence of the little nation was destroyed, and merged into that of the more powerful but long antagonistic one of Ashantee.

The next day I was carried into the presence of the chief, or rather queen, for I found this nation was governed by a woman.

Surrounding her was a large bevy of the ugliest woman I had ever seen. Their attire was different from any court dress which I had ever looked upon.

The queen whose name was Swaiguon wore a necklace of beads, and she, as well as her ladies in waiting, were attired in a costume which for economy might be recommended, but had no other advantages, at least, not in my idea of the dress for the "female form divine."

There were no men admitted to the consultation. The queen was fully informed beforehand by the medicine man of the intent of my mission, and as she could speak English there was no need of an interpreter.

She introduced me to her daughters and their babies, and I made my first blunder, for I thought to compliment the august lady by saying she looked young to be a grandmother.

This I found out was an insult, for in the country ruled by Swaiguon a lady would be complimented by being asked about her great-grandchildren.

"Young!" she almost shrieked, "oh, woe is me, I was fourteen before I had a child."

I was told by the medicine man that in the hot climate of the gold coast a woman matured so early, that most were married when they had reached the slender age of nine years, and that at thirty they were considered old women.

After I had made suitable apology, in the shape of a string of beads, for my insult, I was introduced to the "fetish woman," and to each of the lady attendants in turn.

My clothing attracted attention, and the queen sadly wanted me to take it off that she might see how she would look in the regimentals of an English officer. I pleaded various excuses, but they were of no avail until one of the ladies found my medicine chest.

This was a source of great amusement to them, but annoyance to me.

I argued with them. Told them all sorts of evil would happen if they spilled the powders and tinctures, but it was of no avail.

I resolved on an expedient to save my medicines.

Calling the queen to my side, I said that all should have a taste of the wonderful drugs if they would bring the small case to me.

This acted like a charm, and I replaced all the bottles.

A spirit of mischief took possession of me, and I took up a bottle of the strongest spirit of ammonia.

I asked the "fetish woman" to smell it, but the queen pushed her aside, and put her nose to the neck of the bottle. I withdrew the stopper, and Queen Swaignon took a good long sniff.

She put her hand to her head, gasped for breath, and then:

"A—a—a—ishi—ishi—ishi." A good hearty sneeze.

Not one, but many, not a solitary sneeze, but a fusillade.

The hut shook with the sneezes, the women clapped their hands, the thatch of the roof seemed to rise with the heartiness of the applause, and when the queen had recovered her breath, she allowed all her ladies to take a good sniff, with the same effect as it had produced on the queen.

But what a pandemonium!

Imagine thirty fat women all sneezing at one time, but in different keys.

The gamut ranged from deep bass to a high soprano.

Weak as I was I could not restrain my laughter, though every minute I expected that the savage monarch would have her revenge by ordering my execution.

Everything must come to an end, and the sneezing fit had its day. When nature was exhausted or the effects of the ammonia had worn off, the sneezing gradually died away into the softest sounds, but a more discordant noise took its place, for every baby began to show the strength of its lungs, and my hut became more than ever like pandemonium.

This was an uproar which did not excite my risible faculties, and I tried every means to keep the noise from my ears.

The queen, seeing it, ordered all to' leave the place, and I was glad, but expected that now my time had come.

CHAPTER XV.

A QUEEN'S LOVE-MAKING.

I LEARNED that my men were well attended to, and was about to resign myself to a comfortable sleep, when the queen, who had retired with the others, entered the hut which had been set apart for my use.

I was annoyed, for though I was loyal to my queen at home. I did not see why any monarch should interfere with my comfort.

I was about to expostulate when Swaignon uttered in good English the one word:

"Sleep!"

I turned over to obey the command, and almost immediately felt a soothing influence over me combined with a gentle breeze.

I opened my eyes, and to my amazement found I was being fanned.

Now—thought I—ye folks of Canford, what would you think if you knew that your townsman, John Niel, was being fanned to sleep by a real live queen?

It was not long before nature gave way and I was enjoying "Tired nature's sweet restorer, balmy sleep!"

I know not how long I slept, but during my slumber I dreamed of home, and then of scenes of carnage. My dreams were not all pleasant, neither were they all the reverse, but when the mind had wandered off into the realm of slaughter the dream would not end, but, by an imperceptible motion, would glide off into some pleasant episode of my past life or some vision which would be pleasing.

When I did awake I saw the queen still by the side of my improvised bed, her arm gently swaying to and fro and the fan still stirring the gentle breezes which were so full of new life to me.

"How can I thank you?" I asked.

She made no answer for a short time, but looked at me with her clear, large eyes, which made her black face really appear almost beautiful. In fact I pictured to myself what a beautiful woman this semi-nude queen would be if the lower part of her face had been as beautiful as the eyes and forehead.

Don't think I was in love with the dusky grandmother of a squalling babe.

No, but I could not help having more than an ordinary feeling for one who had been so thoughtful.

As she had not answered my question as to the most acceptable thanks I could offer, I put my hand in my pocket and drew therefrom a plain gold ring. I had bought it of a poor soldier who wanted money, a poor fellow whose bones were already bleaching on the field where he had fallen, and who died, as he had told me, without kith or kin. The ring was of no use to me, and I was generous enough to offer it to the queen.

She was delighted. It was the first finger ring she had ever possessed. She leaned over me, and took my nose between her finger and thumb and gave it such a pinch and a shake that I almost forgot she was a woman and was about to strike. Fortunately I remembered I was greatly indebted to her for the sleep I had enjoyed and so I held back my hand.

I suppose the scowl on my face showed that I was not pleased with the attention, for she looked at me, her great eyes filled with tears, and asked:

"How doth the children of the great white mother show their joy?"

I saw it all. The nose pinching was a caress, and the harder she squeezed it the greater was I to understand her love to be.

I am free to confess that, with such evidences of affection, I could do with considerably less, and would prefer ordinary friendship to the warmth of love.

I told Swaignon that friendship was shown among white people by hand-shaking.

I had to give her a practical illustration—not one hand-shake, but many.

She was not satisfied, and said it was our ignorance that caused us to be satisfied with such a cold expression of feeling.

"And does the wife shake the husband's hand?" she asked.

"Oh, shades of poets of love, forgive me!" I exclaimed, inwardly, after I had answered Swaignon in the affirmative.

Imagine a lover's farewell to consist of a hand-shake!

Why, Bessie wants a kiss if I only go out for an hour on the farm; and if I stay in the house she wants my arm round her waist and the pressure of my lips on hers at least twice an hour.

But, then, Bessie is white, she is young and pretty, her lips are like luscious cherries, and her breath like the choicest perfume, while my questioner out in Africa was black, with a waist as large as mine; her breath was perfumed with garlic, and, as I love truth, I could not say she was pretty.

Hence I did not want to kiss her, but I had to do it.

I felt very much as a child does over a dose of very nasty medicine. I delayed it as long as I could, and then took it because I saw no way to avoid it.

This is how it came about.

"What is a kiss?" she asked.

I told her as well as I could, and, to my horror, she asked me to kiss her.

For a moment I was horror-struck, and then summoned up courage to say that husbands kissed their own wives and never thought of kissing the wife of another man.

She readily understood my meaning, for Swaignon immediately answered:

"I have no husband. He is dead."

Now, who could resist a widow?

Did not the immortal Weller warn his son to "beware of vidders."

I was convinced that if I valued my liberty, I must obey to some extent the queen, for I was entirely in her power; so, after a great deal of arguing, I gave her a kiss.

"Some more," she said; but I pleaded that I was tired and so obtained a brief respite.

Whether it was the effect of the kiss or some strange psychologic power I don't know, but when the day had nearly waned, Swaiguon told me she loved me, and had chosen me for her second husband, and the grandfather of two little colored babies.

This was something for Cauford to talk about.

"John Niel, our fellow-townsman, has been married to a queen."

Wouldn't the gossips chatter about it at five o'clock teas, and shouldn't I be the lion of the town?

True, the queen was a black woman, but the color, like beauty, was only skin deep, and the fact that she was hereditary monarch of a nation, would cover a multitude of defects. At least so I had always found.

I made all sorts of excuses, and among others, I told her how the great white mother who had sent me would, perhaps, put me to death for delaying with the answer of Queen Swaiguon; but to this argument she replied that we would go together to the great white mother and give the reply in person.

I then pleaded for delay, until I was strong enough to give her a definite answer.

"Answer," she said, with hauteur, "the subject has no answer to make to the monarch, the subject obeys."

I was astonished to hear such ideas from a savage, but she told me that she had been educated by missionaries, and that she had promised them that all her people should be Christians when she came to the throne.

"And did they embrace Christianity?" I asked.

"They must have done, for each had a share of a missionary."

"What do you mean?"

"They eat them," and she laughed so heartily that her great white ivory teeth looked almost like a fence of pearls round a huge cavern.

The fact that this Christian (?) queen, who had been educated so carefully, should allow the missionaries to be eaten, did not add materially to my comfort, and I wondered whether it would not be better to accede to her request and become her husband until "something better turned up."

"Give me time," I urged, but I found she was inexorable, and I must consent to be the queen's husband or else take the consequences of disobedience of a royal command. "My queen," I again pleaded, "I am weak and sick, let me sleep again, and when I awake——"

"You will be my husband."

She rose from the peculiar squatting position she had maintained since the nose pinching, and left the hut.

I was really exhausted and desired sleep, but the seriousness of my position would not allow me to fall into a very refreshing slumber for some time.

At last exhausted nature had its triumph over a restless mind, and I slept.

I was roused by the infernal noise made by the beating of tom-toms and various other rude instruments.

I guessed what it meant.

It was a wedding march—not as played on an organ whose sounds rolled in delightful harmony through the vaulted aisles of some grand old cathedral, as I had once pictured in my youthful imagination, but played by nude painted savages to celebrate my marriage to Queen Swaiguón.

There was one way by which I might accomplish my mission and perhaps save myself from a repugnant marriage.

When the bride entered my hut she was gayly dressed. She had added considerably to her attire, for she now wore a silk apron, the color a flaming red, and which had evidently been a portion of a wrap or shawl at some time; on her head she wore a gold band in which were stuck several ostrich feathers; she had the ring on her finger, several anklets on her right leg, and quite a goodly number of rings round her left arm.

This was her full bridal array.

"Swaiguon," I said, looking at her as lovingly as I could. "My queen, the great white mother, is making war upon the Ashantee dogs. Will you not let me lead your war lions against the dogs and in aid of the English."

"And wouldst thou leave me on our marriage day?"

"Think, queen, how grand it would be for us to enter Coomassie together and receive the thanks of the great white chief who has been sent by the queen mother."

"And what should I get?"

"Thou wouldst doubtless be queen over Ashantee as well as thy own people, and rings of gold should be on each of thy arms and legs, and round thy waist should be silk and gold."

"Sayest thou so?"

"Even as thou desirest."

"I will leave thee and think."

Once more I was alone, and to my great joy, for evidently my words had taken effect, and it was possible I should reach Sir Garnet Wolseley and render material aid to the English forces.

Once with our own men I should escape the obnoxious marriage with the dusky queen, who in the ways of allurement was a Cleopatra without the latter's charms of face or form.

CHAPTER XVI.

A SAVAGE CONFLICT.

An hour passed and I was still alone.

I was beginning to be anxious about my men for not one had been allowed to be near me since I arrived in the croom.

I was of too much importance to be waited on by ordinary rooibaatjes (redcoats), so none but the queen's body guard could come near me.

Another hour was gone and still no attempt was made to relieve my solitude.

I walked up and down the courtyard of my hut uneasily and wondered why I should be kept like a prisoner.

Then the thoughts came that perhaps my men had been served like the missionaries and eaten.

If so, I swore I would kill the queen for allowing the act of cannabalism.

When I was about worked up to fever heat, the old medicine man entered my hut and motioned me to follow him. I was pleased to do so, and I was taken to a large yard in the center of which was a fire, and suspended over it a caldron.

I looked round at the assembled people and was gratified to find ten of my men present, the eleventh had died the day we arrived at the croom.

Queen Swaiguon was standing near the caldron surrounded by a number of "Kojoors" (magicians) and witches, male and female.

On the ground I saw the entrails of various animals used for prognosticating future events.

The witches formed a circle round the caldron and began to make a most horrible noise as a kind of invocation.

They were dressed weirdly, for on their heads they wore chaplets composed of dried lizards, crocodile teeth, lion's claws, tortoise shells and other strange things.

While round their loins they had a girdle made out of snake skins.

As the witches chanted, they threw articles into the caldron and I could not help recalling the witch scene in "Macbeth," and fancied that if their invocation or chant had been translated it would have read:

> " Eye of newt and toe of frog,
> Wool of bat and tongue of dog;
> Adder's fork and blindworm's sting,
> Lizard's leg and owlet's wing;
> For a charm of powerful trouble,
> Like a hell-broth boil and bubble."

The assembly was for the purpose of testing, by means of the witches, the advantages of an expedition against the Ashantees.

An old and horribly ugly witch took a fowl, and as she proceeded to kill it, asked——

"Shall our queen be the Inkosikaas (female warrior chief) against our enemies, the Ashantees?"

As the bird was dying it protruded its tongue, which was an answer in the affirmative.

Several other questions were propounded and I learned that the result was to be something after this programme—I was to marry the queen at once, and together we were to lead the warriors against the Ashantees; Swaiguon was to have the title of Inkosikaas, and I of Baas, or master warrior.

If we were victorious, we were to be declared king and queen, but if we failed I was to be killed and eaten.

This was a wonderfully pleasant thought for me, for

there was that terrible forest to pass through, and danger lurked on every side.

Not only that, but I had no idea how many Akims could be gathered together, and I knew the Ashantees numbered several thousands, and were able, sturdy fighters.

There was no help for it, and so I did what I could to prepare for the position I was to occupy.

Two days later we were in the depths of the forest, and our forces consisted of about five hundred native warriors.

They were armed with spears and bows.

The arrows were all poisoned.

Our new guides found a nearer way than I had traversed, and we reached the skirt of the forest within a week.

Scarcely had we emerged from the darkness of the woodland than our warriors set up such a prolonged and hideous yell that I was startled.

The cause of it was easily seen, for right before us was a camp of the enemy.

The warriors of Ashantee were a fine-looking lot; they averaged nearly six feet in height, and they had arms as large as an ordinary sized man's leg. Their muscles were as hard as iron, and their sinews like bands of steel.

Swaiguon could scarcely restrain herself, she was so desirous of having the first blow at the traditionary enemy of her people.

I counseled prudence and caution, and as I was the leader my words came with authority.

We approached as near as we dare, and then we sent such a shower of arrows into the camp that completely disconcerted them.

The Ashantees made a desperate charge on our position, and then commenced a scene of savage slaughter.

My forces had only spears for close fighting, while the foe was armed with swords as well as short spears, with very sharp, knife-like blades.

The queen fought as desperately as any of the men, and seemed to bear a charmed life.

She raised her spear as in the act of throwing it at one of the leaders of the foe.

He sprung on one side to avoid it, but with the quickness of a lightning flash she had sent it through the heart of a nearer antagonist.

So firmly was it imbedded in his flesh that she had to put her foot on his naked body to give her additional strength to withdraw the spear.

My sword was useful, and fortunately the small contingent of English soldiers, eleven including myself, was well armed. My men had heavy bayonet swords, and at every blow, the steel could be heard crunching through bones as well as flesh.

For two hours the fight continued and we stumbled over the dead bodies, fighting oftentimes behind a barricade of dead men.

It was sickening, and those who glory in war should witness just one such sight.

Our Inkosikaas, Swaignon, was more like a fiend than a human being.

She was all the time in the thickest of the fight and certainly did as much execution as any two of her people. A pile of dead had been gathered together to one part of the field, and she at once jumped on the mountain of flesh and hurled her defiance at the foe.

Both sides were getting exhausted, and we were having the worst of it. It was only a question of a few minutes before we must surrender, and that meant death to each one of us.

"Did yez hear that captain," said one of my men, a wild Tipperary boy.

"No, what did you hear?"

"They're coming."

"Who?"

"Our friends, hurroo!"

And sure enough it was true.

A detachment under Major Butler approached us, and our impending defeat was turned into a victory. The slaughter was terrible, for we adopted all the barbarity of savage warfare and took no prisoners but killed all who fell into our hands.

The victory was ours; and, as it happened, that engagement was the pivotal one of the war, for not a single serious encounter did the English have until Coomassie was burned.

When we rested after the fight, Butler came to me:

"Niel, my boy, we thought you had been skewered long ago."

"I'm alive, you see."

"Yes, tell us all the adventures."

"I can't now, but—my goodness, where is she?"

"Who?"

"My wife according to Akima customs."

"Your wife!" exclaimed Butler.

"Yes. I'll tell you all later."

Weak and exhausted as I was I searched the field for Swaiguon.

No one had seen her fall, but she was not with the living.

Just as I was abandoning the search, I heard my name called in a very feeble manner.

Looking round I saw the head of Swaiguon, that was all, for a dozen dead bodies had fallen across hers.

I managed to remove them, and then she gave a sigh of relief.

She was wounded in so many places that I at once saw she was beyond human aid.

"Baas John," she said, "I'm dying."

"I fear so," I answered. "But you fought well."

"Did I? It was all for you. Stoop down."

I did so. And then she said:

"I love you. Oh, I did not want to die, for we would have been so happy."

It was best that she should die, for I had found that she really had for me the great love of her whole nature. And when a savage loves—it is no light matter. It is her whole existence. She loves with such intensity and passion that everything else has to make way for it. I have seen African women, when love has entered their souls, murder scores of people, so that they might be near the one object of their extreme love and adoration.

She rested her head on my arm, and looked up into my face imploringly—I stooped down and kissed the lips already wet with the death dew which now covered her face.

Swaiguon was dead, and I would not leave the field of carnage until I had seen her buried beneath the green turf of the ground on which she had proved that mighty deeds of valor could yet be performed by one of the gentle sex.

CHAPTER XVII.
THE FALL OF COOMASSIE.

COOMASSIE was burnt.
Where was the necessity? Alas! who stops to think when engaged in war!

The people of the village were peaceable, and certainly the British had no quarrel with them, but because their king and England's rulers had a dispute, innocent lives must be lost.

I was with the army in front of Coomassie. Even now I shudder at the thought.

Nothing more horrible has ever been perpetrated in all the annals of war. Yes, I forget myself, I was witness of a scene later which was even more brutal.

The men of Coomassie were all out of the village fighting like very demons. They fought to protect their homes, and who is there that would not fight for such an object?

The Ashantees were driven back and Coomassie surrounded.

"Surrender!" shouted the English general.

"Never!" was the defiant reply.

Again the musketry rattled, and the brave fellows fell like stubble before the scythe.

"Surrender!" again shouted the English.

"We will if our lives are spared and our women and children protected," was the valiant answer.

What response did England's general give?

"No quarter."

Once again the British soldiers charged, and hundreds more of the warriors died, their faces to the foe.

Only about five thousand were alive out of the twenty thousand that had faced our forces the day before.

The hot sun shone down on the putrifying bodies, and already the stench was frightful.

The Ashantees made another stand, and it was evident that they would never surrender while a man remained alive.

"John Niel, fire Coomassie!"

That was the order I received. I shuddered as I read it, and thinking that there was some mistake, I rode up to my superior officer.

"Shall I clear a passage for the women and children?" I asked.

Never shall I forget the look which was turned upon me.

"Read the order, sir, and obey!"

I again tried to soften the terms, and so said:

"Sir, the women are in the village."

"What have you to do with that? A soldier's duty is to obey. Do you refuse?"

"No!"

"Then fire the village at once."

What was I to do? If I obeyed the order I should cause hundreds of innocent women and children to be killed.

If I disobeyed another would carry out the order, and I should be disgraced and shot.

I valued not my own life, but to be shot as a mutineer, to have my name branded with dishonor was more than I could endure.

If there was but a chance of letting the people of England know why I disobeyed the command of my superior, I would have endured the punishment, but there was not. Sir Garnet Wolseley was not only in command, but he allowed no dispatches to be sent home to the newspapers until he had edited them.*

I saw there was not a loophole for escape, and I must perforce obey.

I did so very reluctantly, and I think I am more tempted by this circumstance than anything else to write this story of my military life.

With my own hand I set fire to the town or village, and the flames spread rapidly.

The Ashantees turned to fight the flames and save their little ones and their wives.

As they did so the order was given to fire, and the troops sent a volley of bullets into the midst of the brave savages.

* This is a fact, and relates to every campaign in which England's "only" general has had command.

The women ran screaming from the huts, carrying their little ones in their arms.

The bullets whizzed through the air, and then the order was given:

"Fix bayonets! Charge!"

On rushed the intrepid soldiers. Men, women, girls, boys, and even tender infants were spitted on the bayonets, and as they fell the flames wrapped round their bodies, and soon only a few hundred were left to tell the story of the savage fury of the white foe.

Once when I sat down to think of the cruelties of war, and especially the savagery indulged in by the British in Africa, Bess came to me and as she threw her arms round my neck, asked:

"Don't you think, dear, that a day will come when, here in England, the same things will be suffered?"

"No, Bess, dearest," I replied.

"You know what Lord Byron prophesied?"

I had to confess my ignorance, and she recited for me the lines:

> " But when the field is fought, the battle won,
> Though drenched with gore, his woes are but begun;
> His deeper deeds as yet ye know by name,
> The slaughtered peasant and the ravish'd dame;
> The rifled mansion and the foe-reaped field
> I'll suit with souls at home, untaught to yield.
> Say with what eye along the distant down
> Would flying burghers mark the blazing town!
> How view the column of ascending flames,
> Shake his red shadow o'er the startled Thames?
> Nay, frown not. Albion! for the torch was thine
> That lit such pyres from Tagus to the Rhine;
> Now should they burst on thy devoted coast,
> Go, ask thy bosom who deserves them most.
> The law of heaven and earth is life for life,
> And she who raised in vain regrets the strife."*

I was much struck by the force of the prophecy as recited by Bess, and I could not help feeling that there might be a fulfillment some day.

When the war was over I was again complimented, and, what surprised me most, was gazetted a captain.

Surprised me! I should say so, for the English army is the worst in the world for promotion. A man may en-

---

* "The Curse of Minerva," by Lord Byron.

list as a private and if he is as able as Wellington the chances are he will die in the same rank as when he entered. But who can wonder at it, when there are so many royal princes, German cousins, and lazy, idle, worthless sons of dukes and marquises, who want all the honor of high military titles? Of course they must be served first, just the same as in the church. The friend of my lord is made a bishop, even though he has been a failure as a priest, while the worthy curate who really does believe in religion and soothes the suffering, is allowed to starve on forty pounds a year.

> "And while the good bishop in wealth is rolling,
>   His slaving curates scarce get bread to eat;
> As he his soul with choice old wines consoling,
>   Fit follower of the apostles' feet,
> They, as their wretched stipend they are doling,
>   The bishop, in three months, spends more in meat,
> Must recollect, although it seems odd, rather
> That he, in God, is their right reverend father."

Yet such is the state of things in England at the present time.

As to our army, of which I happen to know more, my friend Adair gave me some lines he had written about the great duke who is the commander-in-chief of the British army. And as they show how he occupies his mind, it can easily be seen why the army is so very dissatisfied.

> "The duke's mind is likely burdened now
>   With doubts about the army's straps and buckles,
> And care is seated on his massive brow,
>   Because he fears how military 'suckles'
> Will to his next new button edict bow;
>   Whilst many a line his Guelphic features puckles
> As he decides he will, in any case,
> Curtail the width of sergeant-major's lace."

Well, to leave my reflections. When the war was over, my regiment was ordered south, and for a time we remained in barracks at the Cape.

I once wanted plenty of action, but now I was glad to escape the scenes of bloodshed which appalled me so much.

The quiet of barrack life was perhaps not so very agreeable, but it was better than burning women and children.

CHAPTER XVIII.

VISIONS OF THE NIGHT.

Early in 1877, I was sent with a company of men to the valley of the Vaal River, and while there met with an adventure which had a great influence on my future life.

I may be superstitious, yet I think I am rather too matter-of-fact to believe altogether in dreams and visions.

England was engaged at the time in an attempt to overthrow the Republican government of the Transvaal, and to establish in its place a colonial government under the English flag.

I don't wish to pose as historian, and give all the causes which led up to such a resolve, neither does it matter for the purposes of my story, whether the reasons assigned were honest or not.

Suffice it to say we received in our barracks news that we should most probably see some hard fighting in the South African Republic.

England had sent agents to try and corrupt the government of the little Boer Republic, and so change the flag without the shedding of blood.

It was in March, 1877, when I was placed in command of a body of men, and ordered to camp as near the frontier as I could without attracting suspicious attention.

For some days we lay in camp inactive, and had but little news of what was going on in the republic.

At last the order came, and we were told to cross the line and fight our way to Pretoria.

The night before we started I slept uneasily in my tent.

I was haunted.

No other word will express my feelings.

When my eyes closed and I was losing consciousness, a cold perspiration would cover my body, and I would start up in abject fear.

Of course there was nothing to be seen.

The sentry was walking to and fro before my tent, and reported:

"All's well."

Again I tried to sleep, when it appeared to me that I was suffering from some terrible wound, and was watched over by a female whose face was hidden.

Her hand had a soothing influence over me, and I felt I loved her. Who was she?

That I could not tell, but this I did know, that my whole soul went out in rapturous love to her.

She was not beautiful in figure, her face I did not see.

But I felt that life would be a paradise if shared with her. No other love had ever taken such a hold upon me.

Yet there was a peculiar consciousness that she loved me as much, and that she tried by every exertion of her will to prevent me seeing it, or to even acknowledge it when I pleaded with her for her love.

It was a constant struggle, that I knew, but I felt also that she was not for me.

When I put out my hand to touch her, I only struck empty space; she was not there.

Once I felt her hot breath on my face, and I put out my hands to fold her to my heart. My hands fell to my chest, grasping nothing but the air.

Like a will-o'-the-wisp she eluded me, and yet I would have given my soul for her love.

I awoke, and tears of disappointment ran down my cheeks.

I slept again, and I was married, but not to the one I had loved so much in my dream.

How it came about I did not know. I dreamt again, and this time I saw the field of strife, and as I was about retreating, for I thought that we were beaten by savages, I heard a female's voice calling for help.

I searched everywhere but could not find any one.

"Who are you?" I asked.

"Thy wife," was the reply.

"Where are you?"

"In distress."

But I awoke from my dream feeling thoroughly uncomfortable.

I had never believed much in these airy visions of the night, and I really laughed at my nervousness caused by a dream.

I, a soldier, a leader of others actually trembling and quaking because I had been dreaming.

The bugle sounded the signal for marching, and we were soon on our way into the coveted territory.

For several days we saw no signs of any enemy, but at last, near the hour of midnight, we heard a commotion near us.

Soldiers sleep with one eye open, so we were soon ready, and in less than half an hour were fighting Boers and Betjuans.

These latter were fearful fighters. Their mode of warfare was of the most savage type.

If they wounded a man, they at once proceeded to rip up his stomach and disembowel him.

I had no fancy for such fiends, but soldiers cannot be choosers.

The Boers were manly, straightforward fellows, and fought better than any foe I had ever met.

But what strength! I saw some of them take a sword, and with one cut, slash a man right through his body.

In every case one blow was enough. Every cut with the sword meant death.

We fought as the English soldier knows how to, but it was no use.

We were outnumbered, and retreat was our only chance.

The little village was fired, and I discovered that the fight had been more severe than I had ever conjectured.

Out of three hundred men I had in my command, I could only count eighty. I was blackened with powder, but had not even received a scratch.

How I escaped I cannot say.

As I was passing a burning hut, I thought I heard a female crying for help. I went in, and saw a Betjuan woman very sick, and unable to move.

Never thinking of consequences, I carried her from the burning dwelling, and then visited every hut.

I was being pursued by the foe, and bullets whizzed past my head every second.

I entered a hut, and to the center pole saw a woman bound.

I think she was white, but most likely a Boer.

I cut the cords which tied her to the post, and as I did so, saw some grinning Betjuans at the door trying to cut off my escape.

I could not wait to carry out the woman, nor even to take a good look at her, but gripping my revolver with one hand and my sword with the other, I made a dash at the door.

Two fell beneath my bullets, and several other found my sword-blade so sharp, that they were pleased to fall back and allow me to escape.

As I was leaving my arm was seized by a white man, and my sword was just ready to cut him down, when he shouted:

"For Heaven's sake, don't strike! I'm English."

He looked such a miserable coward, that I hoped, for the credit of my country, that his statement was not true.

"My father was killed," he whined.

"You——" I paused, for I knew not what to call him. "Your father, why, you are too old to have a father living."

"He was living a few hours ago, but they killed him as they will me. Oh, save me, save me, English soldier."

We were hurrying forward, and those who say English soldiers cannot run, should have seen the remnant of my troop, for they ran—and I was not far from them—never stopping until we had crossed the Vaal and were again on British soil.

I was ordered to Durban, and there found that the cowardly Englishman who had joined us in our retreat was named William Hardy, and was a lawyer, notary, and general agent.

His father had been killed in the engagement.

I found that the elder Hardy was an agent of the colonial government, and had been one of the principal "persuaders" of the voortrekkers and the government of the Republic in the annexation to England.

In other words—Thomas Hardy was the tool used to bribe patriots to sell their country, and the son told me that of all he came into connection with, only Kruger, Joubert, and two others refused to accept a bribe.

Napoleon the First used to say that if he put gold lace on his republicans he could make them all imperialists, and on this principle England acted in the Transvaal.

The bribe was sufficient to get the so-called patriots to

sell their country, but bitterly did they regret it before the English flag had floated a year over Pretoria.

CHAPTER XIX.
BESSIE RESUMES HER STORY.

NEVER did any one get more attention than I received at Mooifontein.

Sister Jess seemed almost to worship me, while as for uncle, he thought that a whole lifetime would never be sufficient to atone for his carelessness in leaving me to the tender mercies of the Hardys.

He was, however, like one whose life was a blissful dream. He would go out and look up at the Union Jack as it floated from the flag-post, and stand for hours in admiration of the flag of his youth.

Jess, too, was proud of it. Perhaps it was because she was three years older than I, but I could not feel enthusiasm for the English flag.

I suppose it was a disease at that time, brought on by hearing the continual praises of my native land from my uncle and Jess.

Sometimes, when Uncle Silas would praise England and its sons, I would remind him that Thomas Hardy and his son boasted that they were English. When he would speak of the honor of his native land, I would be particularly sarcastic, and ask if bribing traitors to sell their country was an evidence of honor.

Uncle found that his brother had really purchased or acquired a small piece of land near Marica, and that several valuable diamonds had been found on it.

The diamond craze was at its height and people would pay fabulous sums to secure little tracts of land in the neighborhood.

While we could find the record of the deed, we could get no copy of the will, and uncle, as our guardian and next of kin, commenced an action against William Hardy to secure possession of the land.

Under the existing laws, it was necessary that I should live in Durban six weeks before I could bring the action against a resident of that place.

It was while there that I had a narrow escape from being murdered, and as it had to do with my career in

South Africa, the facts may be of sufficient interest to recount.

Jess had an old school friend living at Durban, and it was arranged that I should spend the six weeks with her.

I had with me some diamonds from the property at Basta Marica, and, what was of more importance, some documents which proved my father's marriage to my mother, and the birth of Jess and me. These papers uncle told me never to show to any one, nor to let the lawyer have them in his possession for even a moment.

He had such a distrust of lawyers, and knowing the colonial courts as he did, his confidence was not very strong even in the administrators of justice.

I had been staying with Marion Delorme for several days, and was beginning to enjoy the change from the country to the city.

The house occupied by the Delormes was one of the oldest in Durban, and fortunately—as it turned out—the floors creaked when any one walked over them.

I had met William Hardy several times, and he had renewed his offers of marriage to me, but of course I was not going to give myself to such a poltroon.

He was not aware that I knew the alleged conditions of my father's will.

One object of our lawsuit was to get the executor, William Hardy, who had succeeded his father, to disclose the contents of the will, so that if the provisions were objectionable we might get it set aside.

On the evening of the tenth day at the Delormes', I felt nervous and fidgety.

There was an undefined and indefinable something which seemed to be the precursor of evil hanging over me.

Have you never felt, reader, that strange sensation, that something is about to happen which will be unpleasant and uncomfortable?

That was just how I felt that evening.

Marion had been particularly bright and happy all day, and we had been for several miles horseback riding.

It may have been the reaction; but whatever it was, I retired early to my room, but was too miserable to sleep. I walked the floor, tried to read, but was so uneasy that

I could not rest. About midnight I felt so nervous that I determined to ask Marion to share my room.

She slept in the next room to mine, and a door opened from one to the other in addition to that which led into the hall.

I opened the door and found her sleeping very soundly, and I disliked to disturb her.

My nervousness increased, so I went to her bedside:
"Marion!"

The fair sleeper turned over, but did not wake.
"Marion, dear Marion!"
"Bess! what is it?" she asked, starting up in alarm.

I told her, and she wished me to lie down beside her; but I had put the papers and diamonds under the pillow in my room. I had no difficulty in persuading her to join me.

I had not undressed, for I was far too nervous.

Marion got into bed quickly, and scarcely a minute elapsed before she was soundly sleeping.

I sat down on a chair beside her, not removing my clothes.

How I longed for the morning's light! I watched the window to catch the first gleam of sunlight.

Marion had been with me perhaps two hours, when I was just falling asleep, exhausted, but started with a sudden fear, for I thought I heard some one trying the door which led from Marion's room to mine.

I listened intently, and at the same time took the papers and diamonds from under the pillow and secreted them in my bosom.

I held my breath, and heard the same sound repeated at the door of my room which opened into the hall.

The handle turned and the door opened slightly.

No one entered, so I thought I would wait for further movements.

I heard the creaking of footsteps along the corridor and down the stairs.

I awoke Marion, and she only laughed at my fears.

"It was my father, who always looks in my room before retiring," she said, and was quickly asleep.

Her reply was a natural one, and I returned to bed—but not to sleep.

I grew nervous, then a strong feeling of courage took

possession of me and I determined to look out and see if any one was moving about.

I went to the hall door and found to my horror that it was locked.

Locked, and from the outside.

I was frightened then, but went to the other door, that, too, was locked.

We were prisoners.

What was the motive for locking us in?

Was it a practical joke of Marion's father?

I returned to the bedside and tried to rouse Marion. She turned over, and partly woke up.

"What is it, Bess?" she asked, almost angrily.

"Oh, Marion, we are locked in."

"What?"

"Locked in! We shall be murdered."

"Don't be such a goose. Papa has only thought it would be a good joke."

"Do you think it was your father?"

"Of course. Who else could it be?"

"Perhaps some one got into the house and wants to rob me."

"You silly baby! Do you imagine everybody knows you, and wants to get your few papers. What good would they be to any one?"

"I don't know."

"Of course you don't. Get into bed, you little stupid."

I determined I would not rouse Marion again, whatever happened.

It was not pleasant to be laughed at, even if my fears were foolish.

I went to the doors and tried to force them, but as they opened inward, it was impossible.

I heard, as I thought, a noise in the yard almost directly under my window.

I crawled up to the window, fearful of walking across the room in case I was being watched.

The moon was at its full, and as I neared the window it seemed that I could not possibly look out without being seen.

I opened the venetian slats of the window and looked through, but of course could not see what was going on beneath.

I listened and fancied I could hear footfalls on the ground.

I grew bolder and opened the window.

I could now see the whole of the garden.

I saw two men talking, one of whom was very like in form to William Hardy.

The other looked round, and I caught a glimpse of a most villainous-looking face.

I was now convinced that Hardy was intending to rob me of my papers, and perhaps by this means deprive Jess and I of our property.

I knew very little of law, or I should have had copies taken of the papers and only had them with me, secreting the originals in a safe place.

My uncle was one of the old style men who believed his money was safer in a stocking between the bed and mattress, than even in the Bank of England.

I was therefore cautioned not to let the papers go out of my possession.

I have many times since wondered why I was the one chosen for such an important trust, for I was considered wild and tomboyish, whereas Jess was staid, sober and sedate.

It may have been because we could not both have been spared, and I was an important witness, as I had listened to the conversation between the two Hardys.

That was the only reason I could give for my presence in Durban instead of my elder sister.

One thing puzzled me. The conspirators must have an accomplice inside the house.

Who could it be?

Marion's father was as true as steel, and her mother was the dearest, sweetest matron that ever lived.

There was but one other, and that was Arthur Delorme, a cousin of Marion's, but who was also a kind of foster-brother, inasmuch as his parents died when he was an infant, and he had been adopted by Marion's father and mother.

He might be the accomplice, for I learned from my friend that she was to have been married to Arthur, but the engagement was broken off on account of his wild habits and his fondness for bad company.

I could not understand why Marion slept so soundly.

But that was soon to be explained.

I formed my plan of action. I was locked in the room, and could not escape by the window.

The thieves, I was sure, would enter by the door leading from the hall, because they would not wish to arouse Marion, whom they imagined was sleeping in her own room.

I resolved that when they entered the room I would leave by the same way and then trust in Heaven for my chances of escape.

I had got into position by the door, partly shielded by some dresses which were hanging on pegs.

Scarcely had I done so than the window was darkened by some object. I looked tremblingly across, and saw a human form, suspended by a rope, gradually lowering itself to my room.

I at once recognized it as Arthur Delorme.

He appeared to be guiding his descent so as to bring his feet upon the center of the window sill; having done so he gazed into the chamber.

The moon shone brightly into the room, and he could see that the bed was occupied.

"All right," he said in a whisper; and then I heard the never-to-be-forgotten tones of William Hardy ask:

" Does she sleep?"

" Yes, the stuff on the pillow has done its work."

Here was the key to the whole thing. The reason Marion slept so in my bed was that some narcotic drug had been placed on the pillow, the fumes of which meant sleep.

"Give her another dose," said Hardy.

I trembled now, for I was certain the identity of the occupant of the bed would be discovered, and I should be lost.

Arthur walked on tiptoe to the bed, and then taking a sponge from his pocket, he poured the contents of a vial on it, and placed it over Marion's nose.

He then tied something round her head.

After feeling under the pillow, apparently without finding what he was in search of, he went to the window.

" They are not there."

" D—n you, they must be."

" They are not, I tell you."

"You are a fool," said Hardy from the garden.
"Come up, and do your own dirty work."
"Open the door then."
Arthur moved across the floor and opened the door. As he did so, his hand was within a few inches of my face.

I anticipated being discovered, and my body was covered with a cold perspiration.

The door was opened, but I dare not go out for fear of meeting Hardy, who was now so desperate that I did not think he would hesitate at even murder.

In a few moments Hardy entered the room, and then I heard him ask:

"Had you any interruption from Marion?"
"No, she sleeps in the next room all right. I gave her pillow a dose as well."
"Good."
"Now, we must secure the papers and the girl. My share will be the papers and Bess, you can have the diamonds."
"Good."

William Hardy went to the bed and wrapped the counterpane round the body of Marion, and lifted the unconscious, drugged girl from the bed and placed her on the floor.

I ought to escape, but felt fascinated and could not move.

"D—n the girl, where are the papers?"

I saw Hardy search the bureau drawers, and then he found a package of papers and a small bag; these he imagined to be what he wanted.

With an expression of joy he moved to the window, and the two scoundrels raised Marion and lowered themselves and her down the rope to the garden.

"D—n you," I heard Arthur say, "you did not lock the door. All will be discovered, and I shall appear to be in it. Go back at once."

"Go yourself."

I heard the unmistakable sound of some one ascending the rope, and I knew I had not a moment to lose. I passed through the door, and moved as rapidly as I could down the stairs.

Arthur, I found, entered the room and locked it on the

inside, so as to give the appearance of no one having entered by that way, and then, as I afterward found out, he had climbed the rope and unfastened it, passing me on the stairs a few minutes later, and out of the house.

I went to Mr. Delorme's room, and was some time before I could rouse him.

When he opened the door, he looked as though I had frightened him, and well he might, for I was as white as a ghost.

"Why, Miss Croft—Bessie—what is the matter?"

"Murder—oh, sir!"

That was all I could say, for the next instant I had fallen on the floor in a faint.

It was not many minutes before I recovered consciousness and then I told my story.

"And you allowed them to take my Marion," exclaimed Mr. Delorme, with a touch of agitation in his voice.

"What could she do? I think she has acted well," said Mrs. Delorme, with motherly warmth of feeling.

"Who was it, did you say?"

"William Hardy."

"And who else?"

I did not want to hurt the old folks by saying that Arthur, their own adopted son, was one of the miscreants, so I answered:

"There was another man whose face I did not know."

"Oh, Bessie, what shall I do if anything happens to my Marion?" exclaimed old Mr. Delorme, and his eyes were filled with tears.

"Where is Arthur? He must be roused, for he will help us in our search," and Marion's mother seemed to pin all her hopes on Arthur, who, as I well knew, was the guilty party.

CHAPTER XX.

ARTHUR DELORME.

"Ay, Arthur, where is he?"

"You forget, father," said Mrs. Delorme, "that it is still night. Arthur will be in bed and asleep."

"If he has come home yet."

"Oh, father, you are very harsh on poor Arthur, he is only like most young men, sowing his wild oats."

Mrs. Delorme could not hear Arthur Delorme blamed, had she not held him to her bosom as an infant, and could it be that he was wild and past redemption? No, whatever others might say, she would not believe it of him.

"Mary," said Mr. Delorme to the maid-of-all-work, who had been roused, "go up to Mr. Arthur's room and tell him to come down."

A few minutes later the young man entered his father's room, and his face was pale, his eyes bloodshot and dim.

"Father, what is it?"

"Bessie here——"

Arthur Delorme had not seen me, for I had unconsciously seated myself behind Mrs. Delorme, and was hidden from view.

"What of her?" asked Arthur, still unconscious of my presence.

"Some one has broken into her room and taken——"

Mr. Delorme was not allowed to finish, for Arthur worked up a frenzy of passion.

"Burglars here! Mary, go for the police! Surely the dogs ought to have given warning. But how did you hear of it?"

All this was said in an excited manner, either caused by nervousness and fear, or actual indignation.

It was well acted.

Mr. Delorme did not know but what I had been seen, and therefore continued:

"The burglars are known, Bessie told us——"

"Bessie—told—you?" he repeated, in a strangely excited manner.

"Yes, Mr! Arthur, I——"

There was no opportunity given for me to finish my sentence, for, as soon as I rose from the chair and let the lamplight fall on my face, Arthur gave a shriek, and, throwing his arms in the air:

"Great God!" he exclaimed, and fell to the ground.

"What does this mean?" asked Marion's mother.

"He will tell you, Mrs. Delorme; but are we not wasting time? Should not some one be sent after William Hardy and Marion?"

This question had the desired effect, for it averted attention from Arthur, and at the same time sent Mr. Delorme in search of his daughter.

Mrs. Delorme was nearly frantic with grief, and Mary and I got her into bed and sent for the physician.

When I was able to leave her, I went into the sitting-room, intending to await the return of Marion's father, and then to leave the house, seeking protection elsewhere.

In the room I found Arthur, his face white and his body trembling.

"Oh, Miss Bessie, how did you get away?"

"Get away?" I asked, in astonishment.

"Yes, how did you escape?"

"Through the door?" I answered, coldly.

Could it be that he had not realized the mistake made? It was hardly possible, but there certainly was a look of genuine surprise on his face.

"Have you told Marion?" he asked, after waiting for me to speak for several seconds.

"Mr. Arthur," I remarked with cold hauteur, "are you jesting about your crime, or acting a part?"

He strode across the room and looked so savage that I almost expected he would strike me, but I never moved.

When his rage had somewhat cooled, he said, his voice tremulous and weak:

"What do you mean, Miss Croft?"

"Just what I said, Mr. Delorme; you have helped to commit a crime, and now you jest over it."

"Jest, no; believe me, I would blot out all knowledge of it if I could, and wish I had been at the bottom of the bay before I ever saw William Hardy. But tell me how did you escape from him?"

"I was never with him—at least in Durban."

"But I helped him lift you through the window and lower you to the ground."

"You are mistaken, and you are either a fool or were too excited to know what you were about."

"Miss Croft, tell me, please, for my brain is going mad, what became of you after you got to the garden."

"Do you mean, Mr. Arthur Delorme, to tell me that you really believed you drugged me, and lowered me by a rope through my window, after robbing me of papers and other things?"

"You know all. Did he tell you? Oh, Heaven, what a scoundrel he is! I will shoot him before the sun goes down."

"Who are you talking of?"

"William Hardy."

"I assure you that I have not spoken to him for several days. When you drugged Marion——"

"Marion!"

"Certainly, she was in my bed. I was not there."

"Great Heaven, is that so?"

"Of course it is. You abducted your own cousin, and even now Mr. Delorme has gone to the authorities to see if she can be rescued from her cowardly abductors."

"What a fool I have been!"

"You have. Now listen and I will tell you all I saw and know."

I then told him that I saw him come from his room by means of a rope, saw him drug Marion by means of a sponge and chloroform, and, in fact, related all the events of the few hours.

The story was so minute and circumstantial that Arthur looked as though he wished the floor would open and let him through into oblivion.

The perspiration stood in great drops over his face, and he had scarcely strength enough to stand.

"It will hang me!" he muttered.

"Mr. Arthur, I did all I could to shield you, for I never mentioned your name; but William Hardy may do so, and then——"

"They will hang me! Oh, what shall I do?"

"I should confess all, if I were in your place."

"To father"—Arthur always called Mr. Delorme father. "No; he would never forgive me. There is but one thing for me to do——" and before I thoroughly understood how, he had drawn a pistol from his pocket and fired.

Fortunately, he was in too great haste, and so the bullet merely grazed his hair, and his life was saved.

Before he had time to fire again I had seized his arm, and we had a struggle. He forgot that he was a man, and struck me on the face, and again on the shoulder; but a girl who has lived on an ostrich farm and fought the feathered monsters has even more strength and science than a city youth who has been fond of the wine cup.

I wrenched the pistol from his hand, placed it in my pocket, and then, when I was master of the situation, I burst into tears.

I was but a woman after all, though I had overcome a strong man.

When I had finished weeping I was alone.

I dried my eyes, and went up to Mrs. Delorme's room.

The poor woman was delirious, and my presence made her worse, for she raved about me and declared that I had killed her daughter.

I loved Marion so much that her words cut me to the heart; but I never thought any physical injury would be done to Marion.

I expected every minute to hear her voice; for when William Hardy found he had abducted the wrong woman, I was quite sure he would manage to find some excuse for his act, and escort the fair Marion back to her father's house none the worse for her strange adventure and abduction.

Marion was of so thoroughly romantic a nature that I felt sure she would really enjoy the notoriety the abduction would give her.

I little knew how thoroughly the wretches had done their work, and how she suffered a fate which was horrible to contemplate.

The facts I only learned by degrees afterward, some of them from Marion herself, but I have gathered them together from various parts of of my journal, and have written the story here in consecutive form.

CHAPTER XXI.

THE ABDUCTORS SUSPRISED.

When Mr. Delorme left the house on the morning of Marion's abduction it was scarcely daylight. The sun was only just struggling through the clouds, and very few people were astir in Durban.

He at once went to the residence of William Hardy, and heard there that the owner had gone into the country, and would not be back for several days.

Marion's father was furious, for he believed the excuse was only part of the plot.

The old housekeeper was positive, and declared she could take her "'davy" that Mr. William had not been there for three days.

Mr. Delorme next went to the house recently occupied by the elder Hardy, and learned from the widow, whom he roused from slumber, that William had called there three days before to say he was going across the Vaal, and would be gone for perhaps two weeks.

In agony Mr. Delorme walked about distracted.

When his presence of mind returned to him, he went to the civil authorities and made a complaint against William Hardy for abduction.

The officer in charge for a long time refused to entertain it. The accused was of such great respectability, and besides was an agent of the government. Was there not some mistake?

Mr. Delorme was confident, and as he told me he almost lost his temper.

"Could it not have been your nephew?" suggested the officer.

For a moment Marion's father was horror-struck, but he remembered that officers of justice were always suspicious, and so, choking his indignation, he replied:

"Arthur fainted when he heard of the abduction of his cousin."

The only satisfaction Mr. Delorme could get was the promise to send out the officers to investigate and trace the young girl.

With that he had to be content, and so in despair he returned home.

The days passed and no word was received of the missing Marion.

Arthur was nearly beside himself with grief, and did his best, short of telling the story of the abduction, to find his cousin.

Had he but had the courage to tell all he knew, much

misery might have been averted, but he had pleaded so hard with me not to betray him, that I had not the heart to refuse his request. I have many times since wished I had not listened to him, but he professed he would be able to find Marion quickly, and if I told all I knew of him, he would be lodged in jail and would then be powerless to effect her release.

The argument seemed plausible, and I was too innocent of the world's ways to see things in their right light.

The days lengthened into weeks, and I had returned to Mooifontein before Marion was found, and then Mr. Delorme sent for me, and I heard her story.

As I have said, I got the whole details only after considerable time, and even then only in fragments.

When Marion was lowered into the garden she was at once taken away by the man who was acting under the orders of William Hardy.

A few hours later she was placed in a darkened room, and into it was ushered her chief abductor. He had not seen her face, nor of course could she see his.

A third party was afterward admitted and a form of marriage was gone through in the dark.

I found somewhat later that the man who performed the ceremony had been told that Miss Bessie Croft was suffering from such weak eyes, and that her health was so very delicate, that the ceremony must take place in the dark.

Some one answered on behalf of the unconscious Marion, and in due course the words were said which declared Bessie Croft to be the wife of William Hardy.

"I congratulate you, Mr. Hardy," said the minister, "and hope your bride may soon recover her health."

The minister left, and then Hardy made preparations for a trip into the Transvaal.

His idea was to go by easy stages to Mooifontein, hoping by the time I got there I should have become reconciled to my fate.

The bride was left alone for two or three hours, and was then, while still unconscious, placed in a covered carriage and driven across country to a small village where the first part of the honey-moon was to be passed.

Hardy had not stopped to examine the papers he had

abstracted from the bureau, so confident was he of the success of his scheme.

The village of Batapi was reached by Marion, who was still unconscious, the dose she had received being a very strong one.

It was dusk before Hardy, flushed and excited, arrived at Batapi, and then he ordered plenty of wine for himself and factotum.

"Ah ha! One Croft," he said. "I have outwitted you even now, and the lawsuit—why, a wife cannot proceed against her husband. Poor Bessie. Won't she fume and cry when she awakes in the morning and finds me by her side?"

More wine was drank, and Hardy was fast reaching a state of inebriety.

He chuckled to himself, well pleased with the success of his strategy.

A sudden idea seemed only just then to have occurred to him.

What was to be done about clothes for the bride?

She had been taken from her bed fifteen hours before, and had nothing on but her night robe and blanket.

Nothing could be procured in the village, and so he must wait until the next morning, when he supposed Bessie would be glad enough to send to Mr. Delorme's for her clothes, and to acknowledge her elopement.

The hour of ten had arrived, and Hardy went, for the first time, to look at his bride, who lay just in the position she had been left so many hours previously. Not a sign of consciousness was there; she might be dead, but for the fluttering of her bosom, which rose and fell in regular cadence as the heart fulfilled its mission.

Hardy entered the room, and then broke forth into such a torrent of profanity that would shock even an old colonist.

With a string of oaths he called his factotum, and pointing to the bed, asked:

"Who is that?"

"Why, Mr. Hardy, her is the girl you married."

"You are a liar!"

"Very likely, sir, but seein' as how I have done as you told me, I ain't to be blamed."

Another torrent of oaths followed, and Hardy asked:

"Who is that girl?"

"Marion Delorme."

"Where did you get her?"

"Now, that is a likely question to ask me. Didn't yer honor give her to me in the Delorme garden?"

"Curse it! Curse that fool Arthur, he has done it all. Never mind, I have the papers; but curse him, perhaps even they are no good."

He left the room and went into the sit-kamie, and took the package of papers from his pocket.

The first he opened was a letter from Uncle Silas to me; the second a short one from Jess, and so on through all the package.

His rage knew no bounds. He swore like a madman, and stamped his feet furiously on the ground.

"We shall both hang for this," he exclaimed.

"You will, sir," answered the factotum, who gloried in the name of Van Blude.

"What do you mean?"

"Why, sir, didn't you write me a note?"

"Curse it! what of that?"

"And didn't it say as how I was to be in a certain garden, and take charge of such parcels or property given to me?"

"What of that?"

"Well, not much, only as how I can prove you give the gal to me, an' told me to bring her here."

"Curse you, give me that letter."

"Not if I know it."

"I'll give you a hundred pounds of good money for it."

"No you don't, nor five hundred neither."

"See here, Van Blude, if we are both arrested, I have influence and you haven't, and if you are believed you will go to quod (prison) for a time, and be as poor as ever."

"Well?"

"Give me that letter and I will give you five hundred pounds and you need never go back to Durban."

"And the gal?"

"Drop her into the Vaal or——"

"What?"

"Keep her for yourself."

The man thought for a time and then agreed to the terms with some slight modification. The girl was to be killed and Van Blude was to get six hundred pounds.

Hardy was well pleased with his escape, for, of course, he had no idea that he had been watched, and never imagined that Arthur or Van Blude would turn queen's evidence against him.

Van Blude was a villain, but Hardy knew too much about his past career, and had therefore a pretty good idea that he would never care to go on a witness stand.

"By Jove," said Hardy, forgetful that he was alone. "By Jove, I have it all down fine. I'll spring the marriage certificate on them, and that will do the trick just as well as if I had the girl. It will put Bess out of court, and hang me, I didn't want her. If she had been mine, well, I guess she would soon have joined the great army of father's wives."

The fellow laughed as though he had given utterance to a good joke.

He spurred his horse, and just as he was entering Durban he overheard the conversation between two farmers.

This was what he heard:

"Will Hardy will have his neck stretched over that affair."

"What do you speak of?" asked the other.

"Why, he broke into Baas Delorme's house, and took a lot of things, and the daughter as well. He has the girl with him now."

"Where is he now?"

"That they don't know, but all the constables have warrants to take him dead or alive."

"Is that so?"

"It is, and there is a hundred pounds offered to any one who will shoot him, and two hundred to any one who will bring him alive."

"Crikey, but I'd rather shoot and make sure."

"So would I."

Hardy had not been recognized, so he stuck spurs in his horse's sides, and put as wide a distance between him and the farmers as possible.

If what they said was true, it wouldn't be safe to venture near Durban for some time.

He would get into the Transvaal, and then there were

plenty who would swear to an *alibi*—if they were paid for it. Besides, it would all blow over for a time, for none had seen him enter Delorme's; and if Arthur turned queen's evidence, the weight would be against himself, and Hardy prided himself he could come out as an accomplice and not principal.

In the meantime he was worried in his mind, and felt the most poignant anguish, not because of his crime, but simply on account of its discovery.

> "To what gulfs
> A single deviation from the track
> Of human duties leads even those who claim
> The homage of mankind as their born due,
> And find it, till they forfeit it themselves."

CHAPTER XXII.

A VILE SCHEME FRUSTRATED.

JIM VAN BLUDE sat musing for some time after his master had left.

His life had once been innocent, but that was so long ago that it was hard to recall it.

But never had he been a reckless criminal until he had fallen into the toils of the Hardys, and since then there was no crime which had a name but he had been guilty of it.

He had given up William Hardy's incriminating letter, and had got three hundred pounds in his pocket, the balance he was to get when he reached Delagoa Bay.

This was a matter of precaution on the part of Hardy, for it would insure the absence of Van Blude.

What was to be the next move?

In the house he was master, for it belonged to him, and whenever Jim wanted to pose as a respectable farmer, he would retire to this place, and do a bit of gardening, or raise some truck for the market.

A wicked, cruel thought came to Jim. Up-stairs was a girl under the influence of a narcotic. She was dainty and sweet; true, in a state of unconsciousness, she had been married to William Hardy; but what mattered that? She was deserted, and Van Blude had received money to kill her.

"I won't kill her," said the desperado; "why, bless

you, it would be a shame. I'm blowed if I don't have her for my wife. Let me see," he continued, "she will remain asleep for a good many hours yet, and we can be far away from here. Yes, that's it, Jim, you are a married man now. Bless you, when she wakes and finds she is really Marion Van Blude, she will be as proud as Old Nick;" and then he gave a hearty guffaw.

Poor Marion! So soft and gentle, so loving and pure, to be the victim of such a criminal. It was awful to contemplate.

Jim was about to retire for the night when an end was put to all his visions by a note, which was placed in his hand by a Kafir mounted on a fleet horse.

The black would not say from whom he received it, neither would he speak a word as to his destination.

Jim thought it strange, but he opened the note, and read:

"Fly! All's blown, and the beak (magistrate) knows all, and the quod gate is open."

"By Jiminy!" thought Jim. "If that is so there is no time to lose. Van Blude, my boy, escape is now of more importance than a young wife. Marion, my dear, we must be like the swells. We must go on a tour for our honey-moon."

Marion was saved for a time. The tented wagon was got ready, and a team of oxen yoked to it, and half an hour later Jim was driving the still unconscious Marion away in the direction of the Portuguese settlement at Delagoa Bay.

The hours of darkness were spent in the journey, and in the morning Jim camped out in the open, and began to rack his brains to find some excuse ready for having a young and lovely female in a state of *dishabille* in his wagon.

He had finished his breakfast and was smoking a pipe, when a new arrival appeared on the scene.

This was an old pal of Van Blude, and known as Lawyer Joe.

The new-comer had been a lawyer in good practice, but he had fallen from his high estate, and then found out the truth of an old saying, which he often quoted, "*Facilis descensus Averno.*"

"Just the man I wanted!" exclaimed Jim, for another idea had struck him during the night.

"In trouble, Jim?"

"Yes an' no. But I want your advice."

"Which I can give. And, as you know, Jim, my law is as good, and perhaps better, than what you pay for."

"I know that, Lawyer Joe."

"Well, state your case."

"Suppose—mind, I say only suppose—that I was to get a nice gal, an' trick her so as she wouldn't know what she was a-doing, and then she went an' married me. Would the marriage be all right?"

"See here, Jim, state your case squarely. You haven't done so. Honor bright, between pals, you know."

"Well, Joe, then here it is. A high-up friend of mine wants to marry a gal right bad, and he goes for to steal her, but by some hocus-pocus he gets the wrong gal. Wall, the gal gets a dose of sleepin' fast, and while like that a parson is brought into a dark room, and, of course, the eyes of the gal are so bad she mustn't see the light, an' he marries the gal to my high-up pal. Now, the answers are all given squar', but by some one else. After it is all over, the fellow finds out he has married the wrong gal. Is she his wife?"

Joe thought for a minute, and then delivered his opinion.

"In some countries she wouldn't be, but in Natal, why, she is as sure the wife of your friend as if she knew all about it, and she can only get free by a divorce."

"That's good. What's the lay now?"

"I am a gentleman of leisure just now."

"So am I, only——"

"Well?"

"I'm going to Delagoa Bay."

"What for?"

Jim told all, and took Lawyer Joe into partnership at once.

They resolved that they would use Marion as a means of extorting money from William Hardy.

Jim Van Blude's matrimonial intentions were short-lived, and he saw how it would pay him better to treat Marion as though she were William Hardy's wife.

"Where is she?" asked Lawyer Joe.

"In there"—and Jim pointed with his thumb to the wagon.

Lawyer Joe went to the wagon and stepped back.

"My gracious! it's Marion Delorme."

"Do you know her?"

"I did. She once smacked my face because I tried to steal a kiss. By jingo! I'll have one now; I'll taste the lusciousness of those lips."

"No, you don't!"

"Stand back!"

"I won't; she is in my care, an', by thunder, I'll put a bullet through the man who hurts that gal."

"Don't flare up like that, Jim; a kiss won't hurt her."

"No matter; she sha'n't be touched by you."

"I was only joking, Jim."

The two became good friends again.

Lawyer Joe knew where he could obtain some clothes about Marion's size, and he left his friend for three hours.

When he returned he had a goodly assortment of girl's clothes.

He was not a bit too soon, for, as he got back, Marion had opened her eyes and was asking where she was.

Jim threw in the clothes, and said:

"Dress yourself, miss, an' I'll answer all I can."

"But these are not my clothes."

"Never mind, if you don't put 'em on you will have to go without."

Now, as Marion had been over twenty-four hours without clothes, she was not long in appropriating those provided for her.

"Where am I?" she asked.

"Can't you see?" asked Jim in reply.

"What am I doing here?"

"Spendin' your honey-moon." And Jim laughed.

Marion could not understand her surroundings at all, and certainly did not like the look of Jim Van Blude, so she thought it best to humor his sense of fun, and so asked:

"Who is my husband?"

"Perhaps it's me, an' perhaps it ain't," was the reply.

"Look here, miss," spoke up Lawyer Joe, "I said miss, I meant Mrs. William Hardy."

"What?"

"I was going to tell you if you don't interrupt."

"Go on, then."

"Well, you were married to William Hardy of Durban, and he has sent you to Delagoa Bay in our charge; he will write you and say what you are to do while there."

"You are telling me lies, sir. I am not married."

"But you are, I was present at the time." And Jim Van Blude laughed at the remembrance.

"And my father?"

"Oh, I know nothing about him. I wasn't there when he got spliced."

"Where am I?" she again asked.

"You are going to Delagoa Bay."

"What for?"

"That I cannot say. I have my orders, an' unless you keep quiet I shall make you."

Marion was possessed of sound sense, so she determined to submit, apparently, and watch an opportunity to escape.

She was very hungry, and relished the coarse food as much as the greatest dainty ever placed by her good mother on the bountiful table at home.

The journey continued by easy stages to Delagoa Bay, and when there Marion was placed in charge of a woman who was faithful to her friends, even if her character was not free from many faults.

For several weeks Marion found no way to escape.

She was imprisoned in a room from which there was no outlet save a constantly locked door; and the window, which was only a few inches square, opened out into a small yard inclosed with a high fence.

She had written several letters to her father, but although Jim had promised to mail them, it is scarcely necessary to say that that they were never placed in the post-office.

She chafed at her confinement, but would never acknowledge herself the wife of William Hardy.

After being a prisoner for several weeks, she thought the house was unusually quiet, and the very silence became oppressive.

She tried the door, it was not locked: she went downstairs and out into the street unmolested.

Her jailer had for once forgotten her caution, and neglected to fasten the doors.

Oh, how sweet was the fresh air after the stifling closeness of that small room.

She walked about the streets, and seemed to have no thought except that she was free.

Turning a corner, she came full tilt against Jim Van Blude.

Didn't he swear? And wasn't his hand heavy as he placed it on Marion's shoulder?

It was only there a moment, for the action was seen by an old hunter who was passing, and he let go all the force of his muscles, and Jim was in a very undignified position in the gutter.

The hunter then bestowed his attention on the girl.

"Why, it's Miss Delorme, as I'm a living sinner!"

"Mr. Quatermain, oh! oh——" and then Marion cried.

The old hunter, Allan Quatermain, lived at Durban, and knew the Delormes well. He had been north hunting, and was going to take a cruise by water from Delagoa Bay to Durban. He had not heard of Marion's flight.

"Take me home; oh! take me away from here," she sobbed.

"Of course I will, my dear; and as for you, you skulking rascal, get off with you, or I'll let you know something of old Allan's knife as well as fist." This was said to Jim, who had scrambled to his feet.

The fellow slunk away, leaving Marion with Allan Quatermain.

She told all the story of her imprisonment as she knew it, and the old hunter thought it the strangest yarn he had ever heard.

He waited no longer than was necessary, and soon Marion was at home with her friends.

Not the happy, smiling, jolly girl that had left there a few weeks before, but a withered, wizened, frail thing without a smile, and with no flesh on her bones.

Her cheeks were sunken, her eyes stared from her head as if they would burst the cords which held them, and she started at the slightest sound.

Her return led to a clearing up of the mystery.

Allan Quartermain was the means of extracting a confession from Jim Van Blude—he paid a good round sum for it—and then Arthur Delorme confessed.

According to law, Marion was William Hardy's wife, and for the sake of her name he was forced to acknowledge her; but she was never allowed to live with him.

She had but small chance, for he was sentenced to a long term of imprisonment. Arthur Delorme turned queen's evidence and escaped the punishment, while Jim was wise enough to keep out of the way.

A few months after Hardy commenced his term in prison, he ended it by taking his own life, and by a strange coincidence, the same night the pure spirit of Marion Delorme took its flight.

The effects of the narcotic and her subsequent imprisonment, together with her mental anguish, killed her. She was really murdered, and in my place. I had learned to love her well, and as I stood by the grave and saw the coffin lowered into the silent ground, my heart was heavy and very sad.

I often think of Marion, who was so gentle and loving; and if I did wrong in allowing her to take my place that terrible night, I am sure her blest spirit has long since forgiven me; and though I shall always have doubts as to whether I acted right, I know that her father and mother have never thought harshly of me, for only a few days ago my John was at the post-office and brought me a letter full of warmth and love from Mrs. Delorme, and also sending a little present for my darling "ittle Dess," who bears two names, I would have you know—for on the church register the little mite figures as Jessie Marion Niel; but she is too small for the name and so we call her Jess, and when we do so, our souls seem to see the smile of approval on the face of that purified saint, the Jessie Croft, my darling sister, whose dust mingles with South African soil.

CHAPTER XXIII.

"CURSE HER! I WILL BEND HER WILL TO MINE."

I HAVE written the whole story of Marion Delorme, so must go back to the time when she disappeared so that my own story may be told.

When the search for Marion proved unavailing, her father and mother mourned her as dead.

I wanted to leave the house, for it appeared to me that my presence must be painful to them; but they had learned to love me like a daughter, and on no account would they part with me.

When our law case was called, we were able to prove quite easily that my father did acquire the small piece of land at Basta Marica, and, of course, it was admitted that the elder Hardy was the executor and trustee under the will; but we wanted the will itself—and had good ground for asking that Uncle Silas should be appointed executor for us instead of a stranger at Durban.

There was a plausibility about our claim that won for us the sympathy of the people; and now that the Transvaal was annexed to England, and that Uncle Croft had been specially applauded for the part he took in the annexation proceedings, we expected to have a very easy victory.

William Hardy did not appear for a long time, and it was only when the court declared a decree of outlawry against him that he stepped into court, looking very different to what he did when he was our guest at Mooifontein.

He fenced for a long time, but at last had to produce the will.

It was a strange one, and originated in the spiteful feeling that my father entertained for his brother. The paper was beer-stained, and smelt of powder, but it was written by my father and duly witnessed.

It set forth that the testator was possessed of half an acre of land at Basta Marica, and then went on, with an evident idea of humor, to say that it was his desire that his brother Silas should never have or exercise any authority over it.

That he wished the land to go to whichever of his

daughters should anger irrevocably her uncle Silas, or whichever should first run away from the uncle's house and marry without his consent.

In case neither did so, then the land was to be divided from the northeast corner to the southwest corner, making two triangles, one piece to be given to each daughter at the time when she arrived at the age of twenty-one.

In case one died, the surviving daughter to have the whole of the land.

Then followed a kind of codicil, which declared that it was the testator's wish that one of the children should have the whole land, and that he would rest better in his grave if he knew that Bessie had quarreled with her uncle or run away.

I suppose it was because I was high-spirited that my name was so specially mentioned.

The judge heard the will read, and then asked if it had ever been proved.

After an answer was given, the old judge frowned and tried to look wise, as he declared:

" That the will was such a strange one that either the lawyer who drew it or the testator must have been insane."

Uncle's counsel spoke up:

"They both were."

" I think so too, brother," responded the judge, pleased that some one coincided with him.

When the story was told of the abduction and the rescue by Hans Coetzee, and then the second attempt at abduction of myself, and continued absence of Marion, who had fallen a victim in my place, we easily won our case.

The will was ordered to stand good, but the name of Uncle Silas was substituted for that of William Hardy.

We went back to Mooifontein in high glee.

The land was very valuable, and the diamonds we got the first year were worth many thousands of pounds, but we could not use the proceeds—the whole was to accumulate until the conditions of the will were fulfilled.

The money realized was placed in the bank at Pretoria, and we were soon known to be wealthy girls.

We had no end of offers to run away, and all sorts of people, Dutch Boers and English military officers all professed to love us, but I often said to Jess that they loved the diamonds better.

The quiet of our life was broken by the appearance of Allan Quatermain, who had been invited by uncle to pay us a long promised visit.

The time was opportune, and the old hunter was extraordinary good company.

Uncle Silas invited Frank Muller, Hans Coetzee, and several others to visit us during the stay of Allan Quatermain; and a rare good time they had.

One day we planned a hunt for vilderbeestes, and our horses were brought out to the front of the house. I was riding Romola, and Frank Muller was riding a coal-black horse.

He would persist in riding by my side.

There was something about him which caused me to detest his very presence.

We had not ridden very far before Mr. Muller managed by some means to get me into a rather spirited conversation, and insensibly we slackened our speed.

Jess was riding by the side of Mr. Quatermain.

"Miss Bessie!" said Mr. Muller, "don't you think that old hunter fellow is very partial to Jessie."

"I do think it likely, Meinheer Muller, for no one could help liking my sister."

"Don't call me meinheer."

"Why?"

"Because I am English now. And as I have told you my mother was English by birth."

"I am sorry."

"Sorry my mother was English!"

"No, Meinheer—I mean Mr. Muller, but sorry you are English."

"Have you any objection to say why?"

"Not the slightest, but I might offend."

"No, Miss Bessie there is nothing you could say which would offend me; please tell me the reason you are sorry."

"If such is your desire."

"It is."

"I am only a girl, Meinheer—I mean Mr. Muller, but I have thoughts sometimes which may be all wrong. You are a native of this country. England has no right

to it at all. The people never gave their consent to the
change."

"You mistake, Miss Bessie," Muller interrupted,
"there was the great 'bymakaar'" (meeting).

"I know about that, Mr. Muller, but I also have been
told, that only those who were known to be favorable to
England were admitted."

"Well, what else would you say? Girls will never understand politics."

"Indeed!"

"Tell me, please, why you are sorry I am in favor of
England."

"Because your first allegiance should be to your native
land, and its enemies should be yours. Now, England
bribed and fought and conquered by such means this
land, and therefore all natives should have irreconcilable
hatred and mistrust of the usurper."

"Why, Miss Bessie, you are a traitor."

"No, but only a patriot."

"But you are English."

"I was born so, but by long residence here, I became
—what do you call it—naturalized, and then became a
South African Republican."

"Oh!"

"Let us change the subject, for as you say, girls should
not talk politics."

At the same time there was nothing I liked better. I
suppose it was because I had not many female companions, and so talked with Uncle Silas and the men about
politics.

I had asked for the subject to be changed, but was
sorry, for the very next minute Frank Muller asked:

"Do you know how rich I am?"

"No."

"Well, I am the richest man in the Transvaal, and as
you are fond of politics, I may tell you that I shall never
rest until I am ruler of all South Africa; I am trying for
it."

"Indeed!" And I laughed, but I saw Mr. Muller was
serious, for the next minute he continued:

"There is one thing, however, which makes me very
poor."

"You said you were the richest man, how, then, can you be poor?"

"If a man had all the wealth of South Africa, and could not get a bit of bread to eat, he would be very poor, wouldn't he?"

"I should say he would be very unfortunate."

"Well, I am just in that way; there is one thing I want, and that I cannot get."

"Indeed!"

"Do you not wish to know what it is?"

"I am not very curious, still, of course, I would like to know."

"Will you help me to get that which would make me very rich?"

"I will if I can, Mr. Muller. What is it?"

"A wife."

I laughed, and touched Romola with the whip, which caused our pace to be a little accelerated.

"Why do you laugh, Miss Bessie?"

"At the thought that a wife would make you richer. Why, Mr. Muller, you have no idea the expense a wife is, there would be dresses and bonnets, not to mention jewelry."

"But what are all these things to the peace of mind and——"

"The curtain lectures."

"Miss Bessie, I'm serious."

"So am I. Just fancy, memheer, you would have to give an account of everywhere you went, of every one to whom you spoke. You would have to be home at a certain time every evening, and not be allowed to go out again, you would not be allowed to smoke, or if you did, you would be grumbled at and called extravagant—oh, you don't know what a woman is yet."

"But I wouldn't marry one of that sort."

"That you couldn't be sure of. I am sorry to say that many women profess all sorts of things until they get married, and then they change."

"You speak strangely."

"Did you not ask me to be serious?"

"Certainly, but no true woman would change as you say."

"If she loved, she would not be such a faultfinder; if

she loved she would not want her husband to be tied like a galley slave; but a great many fancy they love when they really do not."

I had talked like this for I was really dreading that Frank Muller was about to propose to me, he had given such hints before.

"I am in love, Miss Bessie."

"Are you? well, I pity you—but what is it you love? Is it your horse, your farms or your newly adopted government?"

"No, it is an angel."

"Really I never thought you were an idealist."

"Yes, Miss Bessie, I love an angel. True, she is in woman's form, but her mind is perfection, while her features are as beautiful as ever graced a human form. She is young, but has captured my heart; oh, no one can tell how much I love her. Do you know I feel that life without her would be misery. Miss Bessie, what would you advise a man who loves like that to do?"

"Seeing I am not a man, I can scarcely say, but I think the best thing he could do would be to shut himself up in an insane asylum."

"You are cruel."

"You asked me for advice."

"But would it not be well for me to marry?"

"If she loved you, and was content to give herself, angel as she is, to one who can change his country so easily, I should say yes."

"You are sarcastic. Miss Bessie, do you not know, have you not seen that I love, I worship, I adore one who is far above me, but whose very name is——"

"Jantze," I called and at the same time struck Romola and cantered off to where the Hottentot was sitting in the long grass.

As I went I heard Frank Muller mutter:

"Curse her, I will bend her will to mine."

"Will you, I thought, no, Meinheer Frank Muller, I have read you too well, and you are not the one I should care about spending my life with.

CHAPTER XXIV.

"BESSIE, I LOVE YOU."

THE party returned to Mooifontein, and Frank Muller had no other opportunity of finishing his love proposals.

The principal sit-kanie was a very pleasant room, furnished in European style, and carpeted with mats made of spring-bok skins.

In the corner was a piano, and by it a book-case, filled with standard authors.

Jess was fond of reading, and she had gathered together a very good collection. Of course there were Dickens' works; what library would be complete without them? Then there were the strange, weird, and mystical works of Bulwer Lytton. Jess would sit for hours dreaming away over the wonderfully fascinating "Zanoni," and her face would flush with an intense excitement as she tried to read between the lines of the "Strange Story." I liked the books passably well, but they were too deep for me. I did admire "Vanity Fair," and I confess I was fond of "East Lynne," but—there! I am not going to tell you what books I liked or disliked. I have been led to these remarks by the thought of that dear old book-case at the African Mooifontein.

After supper the men smoked. Quatermain and my uncle preferred pipes, while Frank Muller and Joubert, for whom my uncle had taken a great liking, smoked cigars.

I don't think there is anything more fragrant than the perfume from a good cigar, but oh, horrors! the odor from a bad one is worse than words can describe, and the smoker ought to be disinfected and quarantined after each smoke.

I sat down at the piano and played two or three selections, but I confess my thoughts were far away from my music.

Uncle insisted that Jess should sing.

She required much urging, and even when she sat at the piano, she declared she did not know what to give us.

"Sing that piece which you were playing last evening," said my uncle.

Presently her rich, clear voice was heard above the harmony of the piano as she sang.

> "I have dreamed bright dreams of a future life.
> Of a world all bright and fair,
> Where we'd rest in the sunshine of joy and love,
> With never a cloud or care;

> "Of glist'ning rivers, like threads of light,
> Winding through valleys green;
> All around us flowers, pure, dazzling, and bright
> The loveliest ever seen;

> "And shady bowers and spicy groves,
> Where balmiest breezes blow;
> Laden with fragrance, fresh and sweet,
> As floods of incense flow.

> "But this was only a beautiful dream,
> Which fancy painted for me;
> The half of its beauties we'll never know
> Till we pass o'er death's dreamless sea."

Jess had a voice remarkably sweet; it was not cultivated, but was really beautiful. I almost envied the captivating power she possessed.

Up! rang the sweet voice, until we could almost fancy that the singer was really in the land of which she was singing. Right away it seemed to soar, until lost within heaven's gates, and then like the soaring and descent of the lark it came back to earth, and as the last line left the sweet lips of my sister, and the song told of "death's dreamless sea," her face resumed its cold, sad expression, and she was no longer the transfigured Jess, but was my own strangely cold but loving sister again.

She left the piano, and soon left the room. To me she once said that when she sang such a song her soul seemed to burst through the barrier and mount aloft, until it held sweet communion with those loved ones who had gone before.

Allan Quatermain said he had never heard such music before, while Joubert was in ecstasies.

Usually cold and unimpassioned, he seemed to be lighted up with enthusiasm.

"My dear sir," he said, "Miss Croft has a voice which far exceeds anything I have ever heard. I could listen forever to it."

"Are you fond of music, meinheer?" asked Allan Quatermain.

"Fond! Music is my life. No other art so reveals the sublime emotions of the soul, no other art is capable of depicting the glories of nature, the character of the soul, the whirl of passion, or the cry of the suffering. To me music is of God, godlike. It presents everything in a new light, and even makes the soulless into patriots."

"I don't care much for music, unless it is a simple love-song," remarked Muller.

"Love is, of course, all music, but in everything it is grand. Why, if our people had been musical, and had expressed their thoughts in verse, we should have had our free flag still flying instead of——"

"Stay, Joubert, you are verging on treason you know," said my uncle, with a laugh.

I happened to pass at the back of Muller at the time, and I heard him mutter to himself:

"How I hate that man."

"Meinheer Joubert, as you are so fond of music, you surely sing," said my uncle.

"Very little," was the modest reply.

"Sing that little for us then, please."

"No, you had better excuse me."

"No, no, we can't take any excuse."

"But you had better."

"Can't do it, eh, Uncle Silas?" said Quatermain.

"But my song you may call treason."

"Never mind, out with it, we are all friends here, and never think of inflaming the masses."

Joubert sat down to the piano, and after playing a few bars, broke out in a wild, impassioned song of war and vengeance.

One verse is all I remember.

> "We bear our wrong in silence,
>   We store it in our brain;
> They think us dull, they think us dead,
>   But we shall rise again.
> A trumpet through the lands shall ring,
>   A heaving through the mass.
> A trampling through their palaces
>   Until they break like glass.
> And still as rolls our million—march,
>   Its watchword brave shall be—

The coming hope, the future day,
  When wrong to right shall bow,
And hearts shall have the courage, man,
  To make that future *now*."

There was a silence in the room as Joubert rose from the piano.

Jess had been attracted by the music and had returned.

"No wonder, Meinheer Joubert," she said, "that one old writer exclaimed, ' Let me make the people's ballads, I care not who makes their laws.' "

"Thank you for the compliment, Miss Jess. I learned the song when I was in England, and therefore all the credit I am entitled to is for the poor singing."

"That's a dangerous man," said Muller in a low tone to my uncle.

"You think so?"

"Yes, for if he teaches the people such songs I am afraid the English flag would go."

"Come, Muller, it is your turn to sing."

The handsome Boer went to the piano and then got up again. "No," he said, "I cannot play, but I will sing if Miss Bessie will play."

"What is the piece?" I asked with unconcern.

He hummed over a well-known air, with which I was conversant, and I sat down to play, but regretted it.

Mr. Muller had a strong barytone voice, and with eyes fixed upon me, he let the strong, full tones float out in the room:

"See the fair moon looking down from the skies,
  Light of my darkness, I love thee to madness;
Ah, my star destiny shines in thine eyes.
  I was but made to re-echo thy gladness!
    Pleasure I sing thee!
    Passion I wing thee!
All that would gladden thee fain would I bring thee."

When Frank Muller had finished the verse, he leaned over as if telling me about the music, and said:

"Bessie, I love you, will you be my own?"

I made no answer, but rose from the piano and left the room.

I felt it was an unmanly act of which he was guilty.

No gentleman would ever take such advantage of a girl.

I hated him.

Yes, the words are strong, but not one whit stronger than I felt.

I hated him, and in my bitter rage I could have killed him.

He vowed that night, so he told me some time later—that I should be his.

Two enmities were made through that musical evening, for Frank Muller conceived a deadly and bitter enmity to young patriotic Joubert.

CHAPTER XXV.
I PLAY THE EAVESDROPPER.

"QUATERMAIN, I am getting old," said my uncle a few evenings later.

"Why don't you sell out?"

"No; I love the place so well that I could not leave it."

"Then take a partner."

"Easier said than done. Now, if you were to think of settling down on an ostrich farm, why, I would entertain the idea."

"I! Oh, no, thank you, I have lots of work on hand. I reckon I shall die as I have lived, a hunter."

"Do you know, Quatermain, I have had an idea lately that you would marry again——"

"Marry again?"

"Yes; is there anything strange in that?"

"No; but I never thought of such a thing."

"Now, you don't say so. Why, I couldn't help remarking the other day what a splendid couple you and my Jess made."

The old hunter laughed heartily.

"Jess! Why, bless me, I have a son nearly as old as she. What would she do with a wizened, dried-up old fellow like me?"

"Don't call yourself old, or I shall begin to count up the years of my antiquity. Why, Quatermain, the first time I met you I was older than you are now, and that is —why, let me see, it must be nigh on twenty years ago."

"Yes, all of that. But, putting aside reminiscences, I confess I would like Jess to spend my life with."

"She is very different to other girls."

"That is just what I like about her."

"Very few seem to understand her."

"No, I should say not. The two girls are very different. Jess is all for study; she can paint and sketch, she writes poetry, and even books; not that she has ever had any printed, but they are better than some that are. But Bessie is my favorite. Farmer Bess is the girl for me. There never was such a girl. Moves like a spring-bok, and what an eye, what a form, and she can do as much work as any three. Now, if I were a young man, I would have Bess, even if I had to run off with her."

"Dangerous advice, Uncle Croft, I might do that myself."

"All right, my dear fellow, I will give my consent, for the girl who gets Allan Quatermain for a husband is a lucky one."

Uncle did not know I was in the room.

The day had been very sultry and hot, and as the evening shadows gathered, I felt tired and weary.

The little parlor was empty, and I went in for the purpose of taking a sleep, or, at least, as uncle used to say, "forty winks."

I really did fall asleep, and when I woke, I overheard the conversation I have recorded.

As it was about me, I did not like to let them know that I had heard anything, so I pretended to sleep, and waited for them to go out.

But this they did not seem inclined to do, so I must either lie still and trust to the chapter of accidents for escape, or make my presence known.

That I did not like to do, for my ears were tingling and my cheeks were burning.

The very next sentence made my position still worse.

It was the hunter who was speaking, and he said:

"You won't keep Bessie long."

"What makes you think so?"

"That half-breed, Muller, is after her."

"He won't get her," answered my uncle, very emphatically.

"Well, for her sake, I hope not."

"Do you know anything about him?"

"A little, and I think you ought to know. You see, the old man, Jacob Muller, father of Frank, had considerable property down at Lydenberg. On the property there were quite a number of bijwoners (authorized squatters), and some of them had very nice girls.

"Young Frank was rattling fond of the girls, and when he was about sixteen, he wasn't particular about the color. Well, there was one girl, a Zulu, that was a beauty. Her form would have done for a Venus, and she was just about as perfect as they are made.

"Of course, her color was against her, but had she been white, she'd have been the handsomest woman on earth. You can easily see what Frank would think about her. He set to work to make love to her, but she wouldn't listen to him. He even offered to marry her, but she wouldn't have anything to do with him. Now, he wasn't to be beaten by a Zulu girl, so he waited and watched.

"He had a bit of a hut out on the veldt, about three miles away from the nearest house, and one day the Zulu girl was noticed about a mile on that road, going most likely on an errand. That was the last time she was seen, but some Hottentots declared that Baas Muller's hut was haunted, for they had heard screams coming from it several times. About a month after the Zulu girl was missed, her body was found—it had been cut into quarters and thrown out to the aasvogels, but by some miracle it was never touched by the birds. Of course no one can say that Frank Muller had anything to do with the murder, but he kept away for some time, and when in Lyndenberg, prior to the murder, had bought a new hunter's knife.

"The body was found near his hut." The old hunter paused, and I thought of the murdered Mary, and in my own mind the opinion that Muller had murdered her was stronger.

"That is a strange story, and the funniest part about it is that one of my men, Jantje, corroborates a part of it," said my uncle.

"Indeed! in what way?"

"Jantje says his father was a bijwoner on old Jacob Muller's place, and that the place was a bush veldt farm, and old Jacob used to come there with his cattle from the High Veldt in the winter when there was no grass in the High Veldt. Now, once old Jacob accused Jantje's father of stealing some oxen, or at least of allowing a Basutu to take them off. Young Frank Muller was with the old folks, and, says Jantje, 'Baas Frank hated my father about a Zulu girl.' And so they got to a quarrel, and Frank killed Jantje's father and mother. Afterward the cattle were found all right."

"The story is true," said Mr. Quatermain. "I knew all about it at the time, and if I could have got some half dozen to join me, we should have lynched Frank Muller the next day."

"I wish you had done so—from the bottom of my heart I do."

"There is another story about Frank Muller at the same place. This time it was a white girl, and after he had decoyed her away, he murdered her in a most horribly brutal manner, and then set about the report that she was killed by the Bakatla for worship."

"I have heard something about the Bakatla tribe," said my uncle, "but don't know much. Can you tell me of them?"

"Of course I can: The Basutus are divided into three distinct races or tribes, and each race takes for its name that of some animal which they worship, and from which they say they are descended.

"The Bakatla hold the idea that their great ancestor was a monkey; and up to quite recently they held a great religious festival every three years, in which a white girl who was a virgin was offered up, with most disgusting barbarities, to the great ancestor, who was supposed to be pleased with the sacrifice. Then came the Bakuenas, who hold strongly that they are the offspring of, in the first place, an alligator. The other great race is called the Batapi, or they of the fish. Now, if you are fond of deep subjects, Croft, these three races give you one of the deepest and most abstruse."

"What is it?"

"The origin of man."

"Tell it, for I feel deep interest in such a subject."

They did not know that there was another listener who also felt considerable desire to know more of the origin of species. So I listened, and Quatermain continued:

"The Batapi tell us that the fish was the first animal, and that the Batapis were specially allowed to become human, so that they could keep alive the memory of the first fish which had life; then the fish developed into the alligator, which the Bakuenas worship; the alligator went a step higher and became a monkey. Now the Bakatlas say that the monkey developed into something superior, but what it is they have no idea; but they tell many stories of the wonderful animal which was superior to the monkey and yet not equal to man. One Bakatla has told me such stories that I am going to get up a party to find this mysterious creature."*

"You astonish me," said my uncle, "for, long as I have lived in South Africa, I never knew before the origin of the peculiar names of the Basutu tribes."

They lighted their pipes, and I saw I should have very little chance to escape, so I contented myself with the ignoble *role* of eavesdropper for awhile longer.

"Do you think Frank Muller guilty?" asked my uncle.

"I do; he is just the man to do any wickedness of the kind, and if I were in your place I would keep him as far away from Mooifontein as I could."

"I am glad you have told me. I wish you could find me a partner."

"I think I know of one."

"You do?"

"Yes. He is what you would call here a rooibaatje, a captain in her majesty's army, but, poor devil, he is penniless."

"I would want some money for a share."

"Of course you would. Now, what would you take for a third interest in the place?"

Uncle sat considering for some time, and as he watched the smoke from his pipe, it appeared that the greatest interest attached to the cloud, and the distance it traveled before it scattered itself through the atmosphere.

* The curious are referred to the marvellous adventures of Quatermain and others in search of this wonderful animal or creature, as recorded in "IT."

"I don't think a thousand pounds would be too much."

"What for, a third?"

"Yes."

"I should say not; why, Captain John Niel will jump at the chance. I will see him as soon as I return."

"Now, Quatermain, mind, I won't have any kind of fellow here; he must be a gentleman, and must like the place, or I won't have him, not if he gave me ten thousand."

"All right, Croft. I shall have him here in less than ten days; and you will thank me for finding him. John Niel has a good, strong frame, healthy, but as I said before, he is too poor to stay in the army, so he wishes to clear out and invest what little money he still possesses in some kind of good business."

"Is this captain married?"

"No; and what is more, he is not a marrying sort, he won't trouble you about the girls one bit."

"Could you not write to him?"

"No, uncle, I must leave here in the morning, and I will talk to him, and that will be best."

"As you like, but don't stay away from Mooifontein so long again."

"No, that I won't; I want to see the bright sparkling eyes of Jess and Bessie again before I take that long journey from which there is no return."

"Don't talk of death, Allan; you are young yet, and have many years before you."

"I hope so; and now, uncle, I reckon I will have a turn up and down outside a bit, and you will want to go to 'blanket fair,' as my old mother used to say when she wanted to tempt us youngsters to bed."

The jolly hunter left, and very soon after uncle followed his example and retired to rest.

I was getting cramped with my uncomfortable position.

Yet, though I detested eavesdroppers, I was glad I had overheard the conversation.

I had learned from Mr. Quatermain more about Frank Muller, and knew that he was one of the vilest of men.

I could not help letting my thoughts dwell on the idea of Jess marrying our guest.

It would suit her I know, for Mr. Quatermain is a deep, thoughtful, intelligent man, and has some money. I wonder if Jess has ever given it a thought?

It was early yet. Uncle usually retired about seven o'clock; I wondered what had become of Jess, and determined to find out.

CHAPTER XXVI.
UNDER THE BLUE GUMS.

"Jess!"

"Jess! where are you?"

There was no answer. I went to her room. It was empty. I searched the house, but no Jess could be found. How silly of me, I thought; surely this fine evening she has gone to the Blue Gum Walk, for it is a favorite resort of hers in the evening hours.

Perhaps she has gone there expecting to find me.

I threw a loose gauzy shawl over my head, and walked across the garden, and into the Blue Gum Avenue.

No better place for an evening walk could be found.

The trees were high, and their foliage formed a complete archway over the path.

On either side the long grass grew, forming a hedge which effectually shielded the walkers from intrusion.

Jess and I had often called it the "Lovers' Walk," but we had neither of us experienced any of the pleasures of a ramble along its shady path with a lover.

Jess had always declared that she should never marry, and had no desire for lovers.

I—yes, I will confess it—wanted love. It seemed to me that life was almost a failure to an unmarried woman. I yearned for the strong, protecting arm of a husband; but I was equally certain that I would rather remain single than marry one I did not love.

I should want to feel that the whole world was as so much dross compared with the one I had chosen.

He must be a king among men. Yes, I had formed my ideal, and like many other girls I would not marry— so I said—until I had found him.

As I walked down that Blue Gum Avenue, I began wondering whether I had ever found or seen my ideal.

It was not Baas Muller. No, I would rather die than

be compelled to spend a life with him. It was certainly not William Hardy, for, apart from his attempted crimes, he was cowardly, and a poltroon I detested.

"Heigho!" I sighed, and then threw myself on the green sward, a trick I had acquired when I wanted to be quiet and think.

If you have never tried it, do so; get away from the crowded city, far away from houses and men, and then lie down on the soft mossy grass. Thoughts will come to you quicker than at any other time.

I was stretched at full length on the grass. Now, dear reader, don't begin to say I was unladylike; I know all you could say, but don't want to hear it; I was Farmer Bess and a South African at that; we were free out there.

Society, uncle used to say, was in its shirt sleeves.

Mother Grundy had not the stamina to stand the heat, so we boys and girls, men and women, were just natural. Don't be alarmed.

Nature is always right, and the nearer we get to it the happier we shall be.

It is the constant restraint of society, that great sham which mars so many and stunts their growth, which is wrong.

Well, I was happy and free, and cared not for the strict rules of the very polite society.

I had not been on the grass long before I found I was once again eavesdropping. I heard two voices—one I knew instantly to be that of my dear sister, the other, I was for a few moments unable to recognize it, was soft and tender, yet there was a strength and firmness about it which showed to my mind that its owner was to be trusted.

"But, my dear, all you say, has been said before, and is really no reason why you should refuse me."

Then it was that I knew the voice to be that of Allan Quatermain. He had taken uncle's hint and had actually proposed to Jess.

Now, what should I do?

They were standing close to me, in fact Jess could have fanned my face with her dress skirt so near was I to her. If I moved it would spoil a love proposal, and oh, I loved Jess so much that I wanted her to be happy, and it seemed to me she would be so as the wife of Allan Quatermain.

I must lie still and not spoil the *tete-a-tete*.

"But, Mr. Quatermain, I have never thought of such a thing."

"Very likely, Jess, dear, and I know all my disadvantages. I am old——"

"No, no, don't say so."

"Well, then, I will put it that I am much older than you are. I have a son nearly as old as you are, and I am compelled to think I am getting old. I have had a hard, rough life as a hunter, but I have enjoyed it, and now I feel inclined to settle down, if you will share my life with me."

"I cannot, indeed, I cannot. Don't blame me, Mr. Quatermain, but I shall never marry. I don't think there is any one living I could really love, and until I feel that great and absorbing passion I shall never marry."

"But you would learn to love me, or, if not, I would teach you to respect me——"

"Respect, yes, I do that now, better than I respect any man, but——"

"Is not that enough?"

"No, it is a poor basis for marriage. There must be love, deep, lasting love, or there can be no happiness. You find out all the faults and failings, the imperfections and bad tempers, and the thousand and one little inconsistencies after marriage, and respect would see them and shudder; love would see them and draw a curtain over them, and by gentle, loving means try to cure them."

It was a long speech for Jess, and I had never heard her speak so earnestly before.

"Then can you give me no hope?"

"No, Mr. Quatermain; you don't love me; you respect me, I know, but you do not feel that absorbing passion which would lead to the blighting of your life if I refuse you, and therefore I can say to you I love you as a friend. I trust you more than I do any one except uncle, and if I were to be in trouble you would be the first I would appeal to, but I can never be your wife."

"If that is your resolve I must submit to it, but, believe me, Jessie, your happiness will ever be my first thought, and I will ever be ready to do whatever I can to make you happy."

"I know it."

The couple walked on a few yards, and I rose quietly from my resting-place and commenced to walk rapidly, as though I had been hurrying from the house.

Jess was walking quite close to our guest, and I knew that though they would never be man and wife, they would always be friends.

"Jess!"

They both turned.

"Oh! you naughty people, no wonder I could not find you in the house," I said, as I overtook them.

Jess colored. The remembrance of that love proposal which she had but just refused was sufficient to account for it, but there was something more which I could not understand.

We walked back to the house together, and after a pleasant chat we all retired to bed.

Jess came to my room door.

"Bess, may I come in?"

"You silly goose, of course you may."

When Jess came into my room I saw she was deeply agitated. Could it be, I thought, that she had repented of her refusal of Allan Quatermain's proposal?

No, that I did not believe, for Jess was always too earnest and too practical to say a thing at one time and then change her mind immediately.

She sat down at my feet, a position I was fond of taking by her, but which I had never seen occupied by Jess.

"Bess, dear, have I always been a good sister to you?" she asked.

"Good? Why, Jess, you have been both mother, sister, and friend."

"Then, dear, I fear me that we shall be separated."

"What mean you, Jess?"

"I don't know, but oh! there is a weight of woe on me. I feel as if something dreadful was about to happen."

"Nonsense, dear, it is the reaction."

I had spoken unthinkingly, and knew I must now make confession.

"Reaction?" she repeated.

"Yes, dear, forgive me, it was quite unavoidable, but I heard it all."

"All what?" And though she asked, I knew she guessed what I meant, for her face flushed and I could feel her trembling as she leaned against my knees.

"I heard what Mr. Quatermain said to you."

"All?"

"I think so."

"Did you hear him ask me to be——"

"His wife; of course I did. He is a good man, Jess, and I wish you loved him."

"So do I."

"And can't you?"

"No!"

"Why?"

"Now you ask me a strange question. I cannot answer you. I know nothing of him but what is good and honorable, I respect him more than any man I ever knew, except uncle, but when he asked me to be his wife I shuddered."

"You are a strange girl."

"I know it; but, Bessie, marriage is a very serious thing. It is wrong to live with any one you do not love, but it is not wrong to love. It is a crime, the greatest of crimes, for a man and woman to live together when love is not the connecting link, when their thoughts, pursuits, and aims are opposite. Oh, Bess! I have been thinking how many men the world has lost through marriage, how many hopes and ambitions have been blighted through ill-assorted unions, and I have wondered whether we should not be staggered if we knew of the number of women whose hearts have been broken by the ceaseless drudgery of married life when all has not been sanctified by love."

"Jess, dear, you think too much, more than is good for you. Why don't you come out on the farm more and help me?"

"I wish I could. But did you hear what Mr. Quatermain said about uncle?"

"No."

"He thinks he will not last long."

"Oh, Jess!"

"Of course uncle is getting very old. I had never

given it a thought. We have just grown up here forgetful of the fact that he was increasing in age as well as us."

"Jess, it is awful! What should we do if uncle were to die?"

"I don't know. Perhaps it was thinking of that which made me feel so miserable."

"Uncle is trying to get a partner."

"Yes, so I heard."

"It will be a change."

"Yes, but I dread his coming."

"Why?"

"That I cannot say; but, Bess, I feel that he will influence my life or yours, and that we may, one or both, wish we had never seen him."

"I shall begin to believe you have a fit of the miserables soon. Jump into my bed and we will sleep together to-night."

My sister was pleased to do so.

I was soon asleep, but my slumber was disturbed by dreams.

I thought I saw uncle dying and a stranger holding his hand, then a wild delirium seized me as I beheld Jess in the hands of Frank Muller, and being tortured to death as he had tortured the Zulu girl and the white bijwoner.

All we had talked about, all we had seen and heard formed into shapes and passed before my vision in the night. And then, I also dreamt that the new comer would influence my life for good or evil, and before morning dawned I had made up my mind to hate my uncle's partner, whoever he might be. When morning came I was more fit for sleep than the duties of the day, for my eyes were red and heavy, and I felt borne down with headache and nervous excitement.

Jess was bright and lively, and I have never seen her so jolly as she was that day.

She had drawn a life-stream of magnetism from me, and while she had gained, I had lost vitality in the slumber of the night.

CHAPTER XXVII.

JOHN NIEL RESUMES.

I, JOHN NIEL, was the most miserable man, I verily believe, in her majesty's service.

True I had got promotion and was now captain, but a captain's pay was not enough to live upon in the army.

It is all very well talking about living within your income, but when your pay is only £212 a year, and your expenses, all rendered obligatory by the rules of the service, are equal to £200, I ask, how can a captain, who is expected to mix in the very best society, find clothes— apart from regimentals—wines, cigars, not to mention flowers, and luxuries on £12 a year?*

I can't live, and that is a fact.

My aunt did allow me £120 a year; but she, dear, good soul, has gone the way of all flesh, and as her income was derived from an annuity, it did not survive her.

She did the best she could for me, for I was her sole heir. The lawyer writes that I have—after all expenses paid—a clear sum of £1115. And the same legal luminary says he can invest that amount so that I may draw £50 a year.

That is a good income truly!

Well, what is the use of grumbling?

One commander-in-chief, who never faces the music on the battle-field, draws about £23,000 a year; and what does he care about us poor devils; who have to go just wherever we are ordered, and fight against everybody, killing no end of innocent people, all for the glory of those at home?

I'm sick of it, and that's all there is to it.

I was, as you see, very discontented.

After fighting in Africa, murdering women and children in cold blood, my regiment was ordered to India, and from thence to the Mauritius.

After we had endured the serenity of that climate for a time, we were ordered to Africa; and here we are at Durban, awaiting orders.

---

* At the time John Niel became captain, the pay in the British army for captain of foot soldiers was 11s. 7d. per day, and the expenses footed up to 11s.

The general impression is that we are wanted to fight some of the natives, another that we are going home; but if we go to England I shall have to clear out, for I can not live in the army on my income at home.

"Confound it," I exclaimed aloud. "I hate myself."

"Better that than to hate any one else,"

I turned and saw the speaker was my friend, Allan Quatermain.

"Why, old fellow, where did you come from?" I asked.

"Home!"

"Very likely; but where have you been hanging out these last few weeks."

"In the Transvaal."

"Hunting?"

"No."

"What attraction was there then for you?"

"Come to my diggings and I will tell you, for you are the very man I wanted to see."

"I have nothing to do now."

"Come along, then, and we will dine together."

I was glad of the rencounter, for Allan Quatermain was the man I liked above all others I had met in Africa. I knew he was honest and true, and had I pluck enough I would throw up my commission and join him in a hunting expedition.

"Well, old fellow, now for the yarn," I said, after we had partaken of a very good dinner, and had each lighted our pipes.

"Niel, old chap, I actually proposed to marry a girl."

"You did?"

"Fact."

"And she?"

"Refused me."

"She did not know you, then."

"That was the trouble, she knew me too well. You see I was visiting at her uncle's—she lives with him—and we got talking of adventures twenty years ago; made me look kind of old, you see."

"But that was not the reason she refused you?"

"No; she said she valued me as a friend, and all that, but she did not love me."

"Were you badly hit?"

"No. I got over it. I say it was all for the best, but she is a stunner."

"In what way?"

"Now, don't. I tell you there is not another girl in the whole world like Jess, unless it is her sister Bess."

"There are two. You didn't propose to both, did you?"

"Not likely, though I tell you, my boy, they make a good pair, and while Jess can paint and sketch, play.and sing divinely, Bess can milk a cow, shoot a vilderbeeste, fight an ostrich, or thrash a Hottentot with the best of them. Now with these two a man's house is well furnished."

"But you cannot marry both."

"I am not going to marry either. But that is not what I was going to talk about. You want to leave the army?"

"I do."

"And you want a good all-round, knock-about life, which is healthy and not ungentlemanly."

"That is it."

"Then, if you are willing, I can suit you to a T."

"My good fellow, don't keep me in suspense."

"Well, the uncle of these girls has a good ostrich run, a good farm, and besides all this he is 'a rale old English gentleman: one of the olden time.'"

The latter clause Allan Quatermain sang.

"Well, what has that to do with it? does he want a farm laborer or a husband for one of his nieces?"

"Perhaps both," was the reply.

And then my friend continued, between the puffs of his pipe:

"The facts are, my old friend wants to sell a third interest in his farm to a good active fellow who won't object to work, and at the same time is a gentleman."

"But where can I raise the money to purchase a third interest in a voortrekker's place?"

"If you haven't enough I'll loan it. He asks a thousand; but I would give double that myself if I wanted to settle down."

"A thousand pounds! Well, I could raise that amount."

"I am sure you would like Silas Croft; and if you talk

of England and its glories, quote Shakespeare, and praise Dickens he will like you."

"He is literary, then!"

"Yes, but he believes so much in England, that I verily think if you were to quote the finest passages in Goethe or Hugo he would call them trash, but the meanest thing ever written must be good if English."

"Then he is pleased that the British flag floats over the country."

"Glad! I should say so. By the way, you must have heard of the Crofts. Were you not here when that sensational will case was before the courts—Croft *versus* Hardy?"

"No. I heard the name, though, but not the details. What Hardy was it?"

"William Hardy."

"What! lawyer, notary, and English agent, as he called himself?"

"The same one."

"Oh, the coward! He ran after me once, and with tears steaming down his face, begged me to save him."

"That was when you had the brush with the Betjuans in the Transvaal."

"Yes; so William Hardy got his deserts?"

"He did. And the poor girl he abducted died. She was shamefully treated."

"Well, what about the ostrich farm?"

"My boy, that is for you to say."

"I will go."

"But remember, you can only go on trial, for Croft is particular, and he might not like you, or you might not cotton to the work."

"I will get a year's leave of absence, and then, if we don't suit each other, I can come back to the army again."

I left Quatermain's feeling better than I had done for some time.

The prospect of a change, of a wild, free life away from the red tape of the barracks, and the chance of being my own master, made me so elated that I felt inclined to hop, skip, and jump, instead of walking like an English captain should.

I put things to motion at once for leave of absence. I wrote my lawyer in England to immediately transfer my entire fortune to the Royal Colonial Bank at Durban, and then I got a book from the officers' library, and read a long article on ostriches, feeling just as ignorant of the bird after I had finished as I did before.

I could not sleep. I laid in that half unconscious state which is neither sleeping nor waking, and all sorts of visions came before my eyes.

I cannot tell what caused it, but my mind would continually revert to that short brush I had with Boers and Betjuans when we were so well whipped, and in our madness fired the village.

I saw again—not once, but a score of times, before the bugle called me to duty in the morning—that hut in which was a beautiful girl tied to the center post.

I again went through the act of cutting the cords which bound her, and over and over again I felt myself running away, but still thinking of that girl.

I expect she is dead long before this; but why should I think and dream about her so much?

I fell asleep just when I should have been preparing to get up, and was aroused by a heavy hand on my shoulder.

I put my hand impulsively under my pillow for my revolver, but, fortunately, before I seized it my senses were awakened, and as I opened my eyes I saw my major standing by my side.

"Niel, my boy, I've good news for you."

"For me?"

"Yes; You can withdraw your request for leave of absence now."

"How is that?"

"We are ordered home."

"Oh, is that all?"

"Is not that what you wanted?"

"No; ten thousand times no!"

"Why, my boy, I thought you had got home-sick and wanted to see the white cliffs of Dover again."

"No, major; I want to stay here another year."

"The devil!"

"It is a fact."

"Going to get spliced?"

I laughed, and then answered, jocularly: "Yes, to a

Hottentot Venus. But really, major, I am too poor to live in the army at home, and I want a rest here."

"Oh! why, I thought I had brought you good news."

"I am glad, for the sake of the boys, for they have had a long foreign service; but as for me, it is very doubtful if I ever see England again."

"You have a fit of the blues."

"No, I have got over that complaint. I feel better; but, major, get me that leave of absence at once, will you?"

"Certainly, though I shall be sorry to lose you. I tell you, Niel, if the English were not the most contented people in the world, they would never stand the treatment we do."

"You are right."

"Look at me; I get sixteen shillings a day—the pay of a mayor; and if I divided up a year's expenses there is never a day but I have to spend a sovereign. So I am not paid for fighting for my queen and country, but actually pay four shillings a day for the pleasure."

"That's a fact, but why do we submit?"

"Because we can't help ourselves. It is considered 'the thing' to belong to the military, and so, poor fools, we are caught by the red coat fever just as the moth is by the candle's glare."

It was all true, and none knew it better than I did, for was I not leaving the only profession I understood because I could not live?

The days passed along very tediously. All my spare time was spent with the old hunter, and he told me such glowing stories of vilderbeestes, ostriches, and spring-bok in the Transvaal, that I longed to go. When I got the big official blue envelope announcing that Captain John Neil, of the —th Foot, stood relieved from duty for the space of one year, I wanted to stand on my head or turn a summersault, I was so delighted.

CHAPTER XXVIII.
FIRST SIGHT OF MOOIFONTEIN.

THE preliminaries were all arranged, and I was to start at once for Mooifontein.

Allan Quatermain was to have accompanied me, but at

the last moment he backed out. He said his back was paining him, and his thigh, which had once been torn by a lion, was again causing him trouble, but I really think that the heart affection was the reason.

I think he was smitten with a love-dart, and did not like to face the fair Jessie Croft again.

Be that as it may, I started alone, yet not quite alone, for my old war-horse, Blesbok, accompanied me.

It was hot.

I wish there was some other word in the English language which would emphasize my meaning.

Hot! yes, we say so if the thermometer crawls up over seventy; when it mounts to eighty, all we can say is, "It is hot." Then, when old Sol looks down, with one of his glances so full of humor, and sees the grass all shriveled up, notes how the skin has pared off our faces and hands, and blistered us from head to feet, all our language will allow is the one word—"hot."

It was hot.

The thermometer in the shade—that is, if such a thing as shade could be found—would have stood at a clear one hundred; but what of that?

As I rode across the veldt there was no shade; but there was a hurricane, not of cool-tempered breezes—not even a sharp, biting, cutting wind, which penetrates to the spinal marrow, but a blast as from a volcano's crater, hot and sulphury. It burnt like fire; and as it blew up the red dust, which was made to cover all vegetation, the very leaves seemed to hiss and scorch under its terrible burning. But, thank Heaven, the sun was going down, and with it the hot wind.

I had kept on for four hours without off-saddling, and I felt dirty and limpid; and poor Blesbok felt, I am sure, worse than I did.

I was traversing what was called in those days the Wakkerstroom Main Road.

Why it was called a road I never could understand. There were the marks and ruts made by wagon-wheels, but that was the only sign of a road visible.

What sort of a welcome shall I have, I wondered.

I hope it will be a warm one—no, I'm blest if I do. Even ice would be preferable after the heat of the day.

I was deeply immersed in thought, and let Blesbok

amble along as he liked, when I heard the unmistakable
noise of a horse's hoofs, followed by a sound which was
strange to me.

I looked round, and there, just in front of me, about four
hundred yards or so off, I saw a lady mounted on a pony
and riding at breakneck speed.

My first thought was that the pony had run away with
her, but my eyes at once took in the whole scene, and
there was a great cock ostrich putting forth its strength
to chase the pony.

The ostrich is the fastest thing on earth, and now it
had overtaken the pony.

I watched with interest, for was I not going to be an
ostrich farmer?

The great bird raised its thick leg high in the air, and
then brought it down like a bludgeon on the horse's
back.

The animal fell all of a heap, and the lady was thrown
violently forward.

I expected she was stunned, perhaps killed, and I
urged Blesbok forward as much as I could.

The girl was up in an instant, and I thought she spoke
to the bird, but the great leg was raised again, and this
time would have hit the girl and killed her, but she fell
flat on her face, and the great bird, in an instant, was on
the top of her, kicking at her, rolling over and over, and
was fast crushing the life out of the poor girl.

What should I do?

My first impulse was to fire at the ostrich, but I was
afraid I might hurt the lady.

At that moment Blesbok began to neigh, and the bird
looked at us with defiance.

My horse was frightened, and so was I.

I would rather have faced a dozen Kafirs than that
one bird, but I wasn't going to show the white feather,
so, as I had lost control of my horse, I slipped from its
back, and, taking my sjambock, I faced the enemy.

Now, my sjambock happened to be an extraordinary
good piece of hide, and the first cut I gave with it made
the savage bird wince and stagger.

The bird backed, and I was about to follow up my advantage, as I thought, when of a sudden it spread out
its wings and made for me with a speed excelling that of

a whirlwind, and only to be compared to a lightning flash. I sprung on one side, and the wings scraped my face as they passed.

I was not quick enough, for the very next instant I felt a heavy thud in the middle of my back, and down I went.

I thought my spine was broken, but to lie there was certain death, so I struggled to my feet, and had just time to send a crashing blow with my sjambock across the slim neck of the bird.

I got hold of a wing, and then——

Oh, my! didn't I dance round.

The ostrich whirled round at the rate of five hundred revolutions a minute—so it seemed to me.

Round and round we went until I had but one feeling, and that was, I should die if I stood still.

Nature could stand it no more, and I fell with giddiness. Then such a shower of blows on my back; I began to think my ostrich farming would only last an hour, when I saw a vision.

It is before my eyes as I write.

Never, in the whole creation, was there anything so lovely, and yet, it was only a pair of white arms, flung round the legs of the bird, and then I heard a sweet voice saying:

"Break his neck, while I hold his legs, or you will be killed!"

I got hold of the long neck with both hands, and was at once pulled to the ground.

For a few minutes the three of us rolled over and over.

At one moment I would be on the back of the ostrich and the girl underneath all, then our positions would be reversed.

Never before was there such a strange jumble of legs and arms, wings and long feathers, petticoats and coats, all mixed together in inextricable confusion.

Then I heard a snap. I had broken the bird's neck, and in a few minutes the girl and myself were alive, but the great foe was still and quiet.

The girl had fainted—no wonder—and as her head rested on the body of the dead bird, I looked at the face.

It was beautiful.

Low, broad brow, crowned with soft, yellow hair, a

round and white chin, a sweet mouth, just verging on a large one, but lips, never did cherry rival them in color. Oh, how luscious they looked.

I wanted to kiss them. I was badly knocked about and very stiff, but my duty was to try and rouse my companion.

When I did so, her first thought was of the bird.

"Poor Billy!" she said; "poor Billy!"

Then she looked at her clothes, and I must confess they needed some attention, for they were well torn, and had got so mixed that it was difficult to say which belonged to the upper and which to the lower part of the body.

These rags adjusted as well as possible, she turned to me:

"I am afraid you are hurt. You did right to kill the Skellum.* He ought to have been killed before. But you saved my life. What is your name?"

"John Niel."

"And mine is Bessie Croft."

"The niece of Mr. Silas Croft?"

"One of them. And so you have started ostrich farming very early."

She laughed, and so did I.

I had seen her face before. Where could it be?

It seemed familiar to me, and yet I could not think we had ever met before.

I am not impressionable, but I fell in love with Miss Bessie's arms, and then with her lips.

The arms I felt to be models for a sculptor, and I knew that earth could have no greater pleasure for me than to kiss those ruby lips.

"Can you walk?"

"I will try," was my answer; "but how far is it?"

"Nearly a mile."

She took my arm, but speedily changed, and let me take hers, for I was the weakest; and in this way we walked a quarter of the distance, when we fell to the ground thoroughly exhausted.

"We shall have to stay here until assistance comes," she said.

Well, it was pleasant. I felt happy as her head rested

* Vicious animal.

against my shoulder, and her fluffy hair swept over my face.

We had been seated there about ten minutes when we espied a Hottentot coming with our two horses.

They had kept company together, and reached Mooifontein.

Jantje felt there must be something wrong, so he took the horses' bridles, and speaking to Romola—Miss Bessie's horse—he allowed the animal to lead the way.

We were soon mounted, and though very sore and bruised, we reached Mooifontein at last, and never did father bestow a warmer welcome on a son than I received from old Farmer Croft as I entered his house.

I was a hero already, and before supper was over the old gentleman had declared that the man who had saved Bessie for him ought to be treated, not as a partner, but a loved son.

So my first impression of Mr. Croft was a good one, though my first experience in ostrich farming was not very pleasant.

CHAPTER XXIX.
THE CROFT FAMILY.

WHAT a peculiar family was that of Mooifontein.

How can I describe its members? Yet I must do so, for my narrative would be incomplete unless I did.

Word pictures give but a poor idea of a person, but they have to suffice.

First, let me introduce Mr. Croft. He was one of the most remarkable men in the Transvaal, and was possessed of those rugged characteristics which had made the people of that section so brave and independent.

In addition to that, there was the dogged determination and persistence of the Englishman.

As I saw him first, I was impressed with the manifest nobility of his character.

His dress partook of the character of his surroundings. The clothes were made of rough tweed, not cut in the most fashionable style, but made so that the limbs could have full play. His feet and legs were covered with tall riding-boots, and in his hand he held a broad-brimmed Boer hunting-hat.

Such was the outward appearance of Silas Croft, as shown by his apparel.

He had been very tall, but his body was bent with age and rheumatism. The top of his head was as bald as a Catholic bishop's tonsure, but it was fringed with long white hair, which hung on his shoulders, and added to the bright clearness of his prominent brow.

His face showed the wrinkles and marks of age, for it was shriveled, but as rosy as an apple. The eyebrows were black and bushy, and beneath them shone a pair of gray eyes as sharp as an eagle's. There was, however, a twinkle in the eye and an occasional twitching of the lips, which denoted a good temper and love of fun.

Now you have Silas Croft as I saw him first.

He was a patriarch in appearance, and no one could see him without feeling that he was a man to be trusted and loved.

By his side stood a most remarkable-looking girl or woman. This I learned was Jess. She was never called Jessie at home, and when I addressed her as Miss Jessie, and her sister Miss Bessie, old Silas looked at me and with a smile on his face said:

"John Niel, if you want to *miss* this and *miss* the other, you had better board somewhere else. That girl's name is Jess, the other answers to Bess, and I am Silas Croft, or, as most call me, 'Om Silas' (Uncle Silas). Do you understand?"

I laughed, and henceforth the formal miss was dropped, and I fell into the habit of speaking of Jess and Bess.

Jess, I have said, was remarkable looking. She was *petite* and rather thin, with quantities of curling brown hair. She was not handsome—far from it; but she did possess two very remarkable characteristics—her eyes were the most beautiful I had ever seen. What color? Ah! now you puzzle me, for sometimes I would say they were black, and at others dark brown would answer better. Yet again I looked, and hesitated as to whether they were not purple. But they were remarkable and very beautiful, and presented a vivid contrast to her complexion, which was of extraordinary and uniform pallor.

She was, as I have already said, small, but once seen she would never be forgotten.

As for Bess, the more I looked at her, the more was I troubled, for I felt I had known her before.

I was fifteen years older than she. Could it be that I had known her mother?

I asked Jess about their mother, and was told that Bess was not like any member of her family, the mother having dark hair and eyes like Jess', and the same pallid complexion.

I wondered more than ever about Bessie, for I felt she was an old acquaintance, and yet as I mentioned places where I had mixed in society I found it could not have been there where I had seen her.

"I stayed with Marion Delorme in Durban," she said, and mentioned the date.

"I was in the Mauritius at the time," was my reply.

"Now, if it had been Jess," said Uncle Croft, "you might have seen her at Pretoria, Newcastle, Durban, or Cape Town, for she has visited all those places, and spent more time away from home than Bess."

But it was not Jess, for she recalled no remembrance.

One evening, after I had been at Mooifontein a week, I was sitting reading "Zanoni," a book which always possessed a weird fascination for me, when Jess came in.

"Do you like 'Zanoni?'" she asked.

"The man or the story, which do you mean?"

"Well, perhaps, to be explicit," she answered, "I should say do you like the ideas underlying the story?"

"Yes."

"I am so glad, for so do I."

There was a brightness about the eyes which I had never seen there before, and I felt that if Mesmer was correct in his theory, she possessed that occult power to a great extent, and that I should be weak and helpless before the glances of her dark eyes.

"Have you ever thought about pre-existence of the soul?" she asked.

"I have never given it much consideration," was my reply.

"I have," she said; "but I have read no books on the subject, so my ideas are necessarily very crude."

"Won't you give them to me, for I must confess at times I feel that there has been an existence before our present one, as well as that there will be one after death."

"That is it; we feel it, we experience at times an idea that we have a prior knowledge of things and of people."

"Why, Jessie, ever since I have been here I have had the haunting thought that I have seen your sister before. Could it have been in that pre-existence?"

"It may have been so. To me such a thing is not strange."

"Will you say why you believe in pre-existence?"

"Oh, Mr. Niel, I did not mean you to think I believed in it, my thoughts and reasons are too crude; but I have thought—as I have gone about my work—much, and it seems reasonable that it should be so."

"Enlighten me, my dear Jess."

"Then—— Don't laugh at me."

"That I shall never be guilty of doing," I answered, with emphasis.

"If we take the Biblical account as true, how many thousands of millions of people must have lived, that is, if each one had a separate soul? And yet how horrible it is if only twelve thousand people from each tribe of Israel are to be saved, and a proportionate number from the Gentile nations. I would rather think that there have been only perhaps as many souls created as there are on the earth to-day, and that they will keep entering into new existences until purified and the end of the world."

I was astonished to hear Jess, or in fact any woman, talk and argue on such a subject.

Where could she have got her ideas from? Not from books certainly, neither could it have been from contact with philosophers who held these ideas, for very few visitors reached Mooifontein.

I could not argue the subject, so I hedged the matter, and asked if she believed in the Rosicrucian idea of an elixir of life.

"To a certain extent, yes," she replied. "But I believe that, if we had such an elixir, only one in a million or so would ever be able to test its power."

"Why?"

"A variety of reasons, but you are laughing at me."

"No, indeed; I am too deeply interested to do that. Please give me the reasons."

"Then there are not many who would like to test it.

and others would delay until death overtook them, for the majority are too careless."

"I don't agree with you there."

"Take drunkenness," said Jess, "and did you ever find one who intended dying a drunkard's death? No, they are always going to stop, forever going to reform. They know that it is shortening their lives, but they will persist in 'putting an enemy into their mouths to steal away their brains.'"

Jess was called away, and our conversation had to cease.

I had come to the Transvaal to talk for the first time about such deep questions, and I was more than ever astonished. Bess was quite a different creature.

She never troubled about such things. It was her aim always to take life just as it came, never to get ruffled, but always to be calm, ready for any emergency, but at the same time she was full of love.

Affection seemed to her to be not a part of her life, but life itself.

After supper I pressed Jess to sing.

She sat down at the piano and sang one verse of Robert Nicol's "Thought Spirit":

> "Whence comest thou? Far, far away
> I have chased the shadows of morning gray;
> Up through the mists where the stars are shining,
> Like the blest, in their homes of light, reclining.
> Away through the wilds of immensity,
> Where man is afar, and where God is nigh.
> I have looked at the things which thou shalt see,
> Where the earth-bound spirit is soaring free!"

We could not induce her to sing another line.

"I never heard that before, Jess, where did you learn it?" asked her uncle.

"I picked it up in Cape Town," was her reply, and not another word did Jess speak to either of us that night.

It will be seen that the family I had entered was in many ways a remarkable one.

The life I led was enjoyable. There was a freedom about it which just suited me, and I felt I should be quite content to spend my whole life there.

I understood now what Quatermain meant when he

said a man would be happy if he could have both girls with him.

They made one complete whole. Philosophy and sentiment; matter of fact thought and poetry; facts and fiction were represented there.

The two sisters made up the light and shade, the positive and negative, and therefore the one was a completion of the other.

That idea about the pre-existence haunted me, and I wondered whether it was a key to the enigma of my fancied knowledge of sweet Bessie.

CHAPTER XXX.
"SHE IS MY PROMISED WIFE."

My life was a very active one, and I was constantly coming in contact with Bessie.

I only saw her sister in the evening; for, as my work was all outside, I naturally was with Bess a great deal.

She cleaned all the ostrich feathers; and those beautifully modeled arms, that had come to me like a vision when they clasped the legs of the vicious bird, seemed even more beautiful as I saw them in the water opposite to me on feather-cleaning days.

I never talked philosophy to her, but our thoughts drifted more to sentiment.

Who could be thrown into hourly contact with such a girl and not love her?

I have said I was not at all impressionable: but, reader, picture to yourself how you would feel if, every day, from sunrise to sunset, you were constantly meeting, talking to, and assisting a girl, not only remarkably intelligent, but pretty as well. Bessie's form was perfection, and it was natural. No corset-maker's art developed the symmetry of her figure, for, as she said, ostrich farming required plenty of lung power, freedom of the arms, and suppleness of the figure: therefore she wore all her clothes as loosely as possible.

I have said that her arms were perfectly modeled, but had you seen her ankle and classic-shaped foot, you would have been reminded of some fleet racer, for it was, as sporting men would say, clean.

It was a small ankle and equally small foot, but so exquisite that I often longed to copy it in plaster—for I dabbled a little in modeling. I had got to that state of mind when I felt an hour was wasted, that everything had gone wrong, unless I saw Bessie.

Not that I was in love with her. That I would not for a moment admit. I had many opportunities of falling in love, but fortunately had kept clear. Nay, I even laughed at "*la grande passion*," and said that a man was a great simpleton who was tied down to married life.

I was a free man. I loved freedom as much as any could do, and it seemed to me that marriage was a slavery.

Yet with these ideas I was actually miserable if Bess was absent from my side longer than usual.

Now what is this love, this perfection of happiness? I often asked this question.

I knew some of my friends who had been so full of ecstasy that they felt themselves to be in the heaven of perfect delight, and in a few years, or it may be only a few months, they were wishing themselves free.

Ay, and I know others who have told me that to them heaven had opened, and that their daily life was one continued anthem of joy, that it was but a step from earth to the perfection of joy in the presence of the Great Eternal. They experienced that sublimity of affection which is in reality a type of what heaven really is.

It is sweet when such happiness is reached on earth.

Every one arrives at it some time, for Nature has not done its work in vain, and happiness was intended to be the lot of man.

"Male and female created He them," and it is true that for every male there is the proper mate. It may be that years may pass, experiments be tried, and failures recorded. It may so happen that the affinity is not perfected on earth, but it will be in the life to come.

For then, free from all earthly trammels, customs and fetters, the souls will come together and Nature's plan be perfected.

I did not feel that Bess was my special affinity at that time. I liked her, but I also liked Jess. Out among the ostriches, in the plantation or on the farm, I wanted Bess; but in the evening, when I had laid aside my sjambock and my farming thoughts, I wanted Jess.

If then, reader, I loved at that time, I was quite a Mormon, for I wanted both sisters to make my happiness complete.

That was how I felt after I had been a month at Mooifontein, but I felt too secure. My armor was not so invulnerable as I thought, and every day I was getting nearer to liking Bessie best.

She was so even tempered, so jolly, so thoroughly pleasant as a companion that I felt I would have no objection to spending my life with her.

Yet I did not propose.

Why should I? I was under the same roof and saw Bess nearly all day.

There was time enough for making a change.

I was a fixture at Mooifontein, for Uncle Silas liked me, and I liked the life as well as the family, so I transferred one thousand pounds of my money from the Royal Colonial Bank at Durban to Silas Croft at the Standard Bank, Newcastle.

I did not know anything then about the girls' money at Pretoria and the small patch of land at Basta Marica, with its wealth of diamonds. I am glad I did not.

There was one visitor at the place I cordially hated.

That was Frank Muller.

I verily think I never knew what spontaneous feeling was until I first saw him, and then on the very instant an intense, and I felt an abiding, hatred took possession of my soul.

I was led to propose to Bess, though that scoundrel Muller——

Propose—no, let me be correct. I never did "pop the question," I merely appropriated Bess, and she never even consented to be mine.

This is how it came about.

She was out in the Blue Gum plantation, and I was felling a tree a little distance away. Frank Muller rode up on his coal-black horse, and when he saw Bess, dismounted.

I thought nothing of this, for I knew Muller was a friend, or at least an acquaintance, of Uncle Croft.

But the fellow had not been in conversation with Bess long before I heard her say in rather excited tones:

"I have given you your answer, Meinheer Muller, so please leave me."

It was no business of mine, but as I saw he had no intention of leaving I put down my ax—I am glad in one way that I did—and walked quietly across to where the two were standing.

As I neared them, quite unperceived, I heard Muller say:

"As sure as I am here now, you shall be my wife."

"Never!"

"Ha, ha, ha! I like that. I would have you keep up that spirit all the time. All the girls I ever met were always so ready to say yes, that I got tired of them soon. Now, Bess, my dear, keep up that spirit, and nothing would please me better than to have to tie you hand and foot and carry you to the priest and force you to be my wife."

"You will never have the opportunity."

Bessie's face was as white as mountain snow, and I wanted to interfere, but thought I would wait to hear what further he had to say.

"You are as good as mine already," he said, "and to prove it, I will have a kiss just now."

He put his arm round her waist, and as she struggled to free herself I quietly stepped round, and as Muller put down his head to kiss the unwilling girl, his mouth met my fist, and with such force, that not only did he relinquish his hold of Bessie, but he fell to the ground and the red stream of blood from his cut lip dyed the grass.

Muller rose to his feet and faced me.

I had my left arm round Bessie and my right was ready, either to defend myself or to strike, whichever might be necessary.

"I'll make you pay for this, you d—d rooibaatje," he cried or rather hissed through his teeth.

"Whenever you like, you coward," was my reply.

"What right had you to interfere?"

"Every right; the right of a man to protect any insulted woman, and besides Miss Bessie is my promised wife."

"The devil! She shall never be yours."

"You cannot prevent it."

"We shall see." And Frank Muller strode away like a maddened bull.

I had said Bessie was my promised wife. She looked at me, the color returned to her face even more rapidly than it had gone, then it grew a brighter crimson, she pressed close to me, and whispered, "Oh, thank you. I am so happy."

That was all, but it got to be understood that we were engaged.

I did not wish to draw back, so I fell into that sweet and yet uneasy feeling which an engaged man must always experience.

I was very glad I had left my sharp ax behind, for I feel sure I should have been tempted to use it, and rid the world of such a monster as I felt Frank Muller to be.

I did not want to commit murder, but I have often thought that under such provocation it would have been justifiable.

I did not go back to my tree-felling, but insisted on accompanying Bess back to the house.

On the way she pressed close to me, and I could see she had taken me to be in earnest when I said she was to be my wife.

"Do be careful, John, for Muller is a most dangerous man."

"I know that, Bessie, but I am equal to such a scoundrel any time."

"In a fair fight, I know it; but he will use treachery, and perhaps, when you least expect it, he will set a trap for you."

"Would you be sorry in that case?"

"Oh, how can you ask? John, I am so happy."

I looked down at the beautiful face, and I saw a shining at the corner of the eyes which I knew was not there a little time back.

I felt rather than saw the pearl-drop of a tear standing there.

I was a man, so I took her face between my hands, raised it slightly, and then kissed away the sparkling drops.

What would you have done in my place?

If you were at all susceptible to beauty, **you would** have done the same.

Shall I say I stopped there? No, you would not believe me, so I will acknowledge that I kissed those lips so beautiful and luscious, whose sweetness had tempted me the very first time I saw them.

When we reached the house Bessie ran in, and I saw her no more until supper, and then her face was of a darker crimson than usual.

As the color gradually lessened, I knew she was blushing as she caught my eye fixed upon her.

Sweet, dear Bessie! I will make you as happy as I can. Your life shall be free from care, if my power can keep it away from you; and if I don't love you with the fond enthusiasm of youth, and the fervid passion which I had so often imagined should be felt by the man who asks a woman to share his life, at least you shall never know it.

To you I will be as loving as you can wish, and pray Heaven we neither may ever repent the step my few words, uttered unthinkingly, has led us into taking.

CHAPTER XXXI.
BESSIE'S CONFESSIONAL.

My journal is my confessional. To it I tell all; in its pages I record my thoughts and feelings. It is sweet to do so. Oh! how nice to feel that here I can speak without being misunderstood. A change has taken place in my life.

I am no longer myself. My whole being has become transformed. He has come!

The one whose face I have seen in my dreams is under the same roof.

How happy I am to know that only a few inches of wall separates me from my fate.

I love him!

Is it unmaidenly? I have only known him a few hours. How bravely he attacked that skellum. He stood a king among men to do combat with an infuriated bird. Did he know the danger?

Perhaps not. But it would have been the same if he had.

For John Niel would have faced a lion for my sake.

Allan Quatermain, I would give you a kiss if you were here, for sending Captain Niel to us.

I do hope uncle will like him. Of course he will. But will the stranger like us? Will he like me? Of a certainty he will, for he is my fate.

I, Bessie Croft, had written that in my journal before I retired to rest on the very day that John Niel had entered Mooifontein.

I cannot account for my feelings, but the very moment I saw his face I felt that he would influence my life for all time.

And yet, what gave me such an idea? That I cannot tell.

I had not spoken to him, but there was a something which seemed to whisper in my ear, "Bess, there stands your fate."

I could scarcely sleep that night. Whenever I closed my eyes I saw his face. Where have I seen it before?

I strove to think; but not until my brain was freed from the trouble of the body, and was able to see clearer in sleep, did I know.

In my dream I saw again the Hardys taking me away across the Vaal.

I heard their daring plans to abduct me and secure my fortune for themselves.

Then came the capture by the hideous tribe of the Betjuanas, the tortures and practical jokes, all culminating in my being secured and tied up in that hut to die, or submit to a fate worse than death itself.

All came back to me with startling vividness, and I once more felt the cords cutting into my arms and ankles. I saw the flesh swelling and the cord gradually getting embedded in my flesh.

I had given up all hope, and resigned myself to my fate, when a face appeared, and I was liberated, only to fall stifled with smoke on the floor of the hut.

That face!

It haunted me in my sleep for months.

Years had passed, and the events faded from my waking memory only to be recalled in my dreams.

That face!

Once before I had seen it, long, long ago, and then it vanished into the mist. It was only an intangible visionary figure then, but became a reality as it cut the fetters which bound me.

Again there was nothing left but a memory. But now, suddenly as the thunderbolt strikes through a house, shattering it to the very foundations; now, with a vividness which appeared like the strong light of the sun thrown on the darkness, I saw the face, and knew it.

It was that of Captain John Niel.

There was no doubt, no shadow of doubt on my mind. The morrow shall solve it. I will ask him, and if I am right, then I shall rejoice to think he is an inmate of our house.

* * * * * *

Two days later.—Yes, I was right. Captain Niel was helping me wash some ostrich feathers.

We were seated on the open space in the center of the clump of Naatche orange trees, and John—they all call him John, then why should I not write it?—John was asking what everything was for, and I was giving him a lesson. The wash-tub was about half full of warm water, and John was scrubbing the feathers vigorously with soap, prior to immersing them in cold water, over which department I officiated as chief. As I turned up my sleeves, there was a slight red mark round one wrist.

John noticed it, and in a half-shy, half-sheepish way, said:

"Bessie, is that a scratch or a scar on your wrist?"

"Neither, Captain Niel," I answered; "but it is just the mark made by the cord which you once cut for me."

"Cord which I cut."

"Yes. I was once a prisoner, and tied very securely to a post in a hut near the Vaal, and you came in and liberated me; but you were not gallant enough to take me away, but left me to be burned to death or fall again into the hands of the Betjuanas."

"Do you refer to the time when the English annexed the Republic?"

"I do."

"And were you in the same camp as William Hardy?"

"I was. Do you remember the circumstances?"

"Can I ever forget? I have dreamed about it, and often wished to see that face again."

"Did you not know who it was?"

"No."

"Then it was not the desire to see me again which brought you to Mooifontein?"

"I wish I could say yes, but I had no idea you were the one. Did you know me?"

"Not until two nights ago, and then I dreamt it all over again, and as I saw your face in my dream I traced the resemblance."

"You have made me very happy."

"Have I?"

"Indeed you have. And as for old Quatermain, why, I shall not know how to thank him."

There was a pause, and then I exclaimed:

"Dear old Allan! I love him—oh, so much!"

No sooner had I said it than I was almost drenched with hot soap-suds, for John had thrown a batch of feathers so suddenly and with such force into the tub, that it had caused the water to splash all over me.

"I beg your pardon," he said, and then he scrubbed away at the feathers as though he desired to get done with them. I laughed to myself, for I really believe he was getting jealous because I said I loved Allan.

"Do you know, Captain Niel," I said, "that Mr. Quatermain proposed to Jess?"

"Yes."

"And of course he told you her answer?"

"He did, but he said more; he told me"—and John laughed—"that he wanted you both, and that if he could have you both he would be a happy man."

"Thank you, but I don't want half a man. If ever I get a husband—and I don't want one" (that was a fib)—"I shall want him all to myself."

"I should think so, but Allan is a rare good fellow."

"He is so, and I wish Jess had accepted him."

So we talked, and all the time I was feeling a greater interest in handsome John Niel, but I was fully determined I would not lose my heart to him, for had not Allan Quatermain said that John was not a marrying man?

* * * * *

Another day has passed, and to my confessional I again pour out my thoughts.

Don't whisper it to any one—oh, I should go wild if I thought this journal would be seen by any one—I blush even as I write it, but I think I like, no, I mean I—yes, it is true. I love John Niel, but he does not care for me.

His heart is hardened, and, poor fellow, I am not surprised.

He told me how, years ago, soon after he went into the army, he fell in love with the daughter of one of the officers. He says she was beautiful and fair. She led him on to believe she loved him.

He went with her everywhere, took her to parties, and was looked upon as her suitor. Her father gave his consent, and the day for the wedding was fixed.

One morning he found a letter from her, saying she had eloped with a former lover, who was richer than John; and as she could not endure the thought of poverty, even with the man she loved, she had taken that course of ending the engagement.

Poor John! I thought his voice was sad and melancholy as he told me, but I don't wonder that he declares he can never love again.

But, oh! I love him so that life without him would be wretched indeed.

Every day seemed to make him dearer to me.

If he but smiles upon me it seems that the daylight was only made for my own benefit. Wherever I look the world seems full of him; in every ray that trembles on the waters of the fountain, that sparkles in the dewdrops on the leaves, I behold his dear image.

What is this change which has come over me? It has altered me, has changed my whole life, and even the universe itself wears a different aspect.

If all else frowned on me I should care not if I had but thy smile.

Often when I have been asleep I have seen thee, have felt thy hand pressed into mine, have seen thy eyes, and thy soft smile which has haunted me. Oh! John, what is it? Thou art my heart's ideal, my own love.

Once the thought of thee was oppressive, and weighed me down. I had an ideal, and like the child which cries for the moon, I thought that nothing else would satisfy me. I knew not that the ideal was so near.

I feel my littleness; why have I not read and studied like Jess? She can talk to him, and I have to sit by and listen. How little have I read! how little have I learned!

I heard Jess talk to him of "Zanoni"—I had never read the book; then they conversed about Darwin. Oh! how dry I thought the "Origin of Species" was until I heard John talk, and then it had all the fascination of a story.

If thou canst not love me—if our lives are separate and apart—thou canst not deny me thy presence in my dreams. In sleep, I will wander with thee, not through the paths of earth, but in the realms of impalpable air. Till I knew thee, I was a slave to earth. Thou hast freed me, and no sooner do my eyes close in sleep than I am transported to thy side. The cares of earth are forgotten, the trials of the day are of no account—I am with thee! I feel thy hand in mine, thy lips press sweet kisses on my mouth, and thy voice, low and sweet, comforts me, until the morning ushers in the troubles and trials of another day.

The days passed along; but, oh, how quickly. Never before did time pass as rapidly. Why was it?

I scarcely started my work in the morning, so it seemed, before the evening came. And that was a time I dreaded, for then John would talk to Jess, and they lived in a world which I could not enter.

I am getting nervous, for every day I see Frank Muller driving near; and he has several times declared I shall be his wife.

I dislike him more than I ever disliked any one.

I am afraid, whenever I stir away from home, for fear of some trap into which I might be lured, and there is no crime too awful for Muller.

He knows about the diamonds, and if he could force me, by his violence and crimes, to marry him, he would secure all.

My poor father! I wish he had never acquired that little bit of property. But who would ever have thought that half an acre of land would be worth so much.

No one would have dreamt it.

I wish Jess and I were of age, for then there would be no need to be always on our guard against abduction.

We have a strange visitor at Mooifontein.

No one can understand him, but he acknowledges himself such a bad character that, if he is one-half as wicked as he represents, he ought to be in jail.

He brought a letter of introduction to uncle, but we none of us know the man who wrote it.

CHAPTER XXXII.

THE STRANGE VISITOR.

I AM too much afraid to sleep, so I am going to keep myself awake by writing in my journal as near as possible the conversation this evening with our strange visitor.

We were resting during the heat of the day, and it was hot—hotter than I ever remember—when we heard a very decided sound of a horse approaching the house.

Captain Niel went to the door, and saw a fine bay horse, as strong as a lion, and yet evidently swift as regards speed.

On its back sat a man dressed in a variety of colors. He had high hunting boots, from the leg of each hung a gold tassel. His lower limbs were covered with leather trousers, while the upper part was encased in a very old and faded blue velvet jacket, plentifully supplied with yellow braid trimmings. On his head was a wide-brimmed Boer hat or sombrero.

"Are you Meinheer Silas Croft?"

"No," we heard John answer. "Do you wish to see Mr. Croft?"

"What else should I come for? Here, stranger, just look after my horse while I go in and talk to the meinheer."

What a piece of impudence we all thought it was, for no one could mistake the captain for a servant, and besides, all such work had been done for many years by the Kafirs or Betjuans.

"Jantje, hold the gentleman's horse for him," said John as the Hottentot came up.

"Look here, you black imp, take the steed to the stable, take his saddle off, and give him some oats, for he has had a long journey, and he is like me—in want of rest."

"All right, Baas," answered Jantje, at the same time winking at Captain Niel, as much as to say that he would keep his eye on the horse and its owner.

The stranger pushed past John and entered the house, his hat still on his head.

As soon as he saw Jess and me he took off his hat, and said in a very gallant manner:

"Ah, ladies, I see! I beg pardon. It is an unexpected pleasure. All the better; for I like the ladies, and it will help to make my stay the pleasanter. Ah, I see you play and sing. So much the nicer for me! Do you shoot, young ladies? No? Well, that is a pity; but I must rig you up a target and make you some bows, and we will practice archery. So this is your father, eh? Ah, my dear sir, I am glad to see you. Jolly time we can have here; but you are getting old; don't let my visit put you out at all. I can sleep anywhere; and as for food, why, if I get plenty of it, and seasoned by the wit and graced by the beauty of these ladies, I am sure it will be good—— Ah!" as John re-entered; "so, my young buck, you are the son here? and quite as good-looking as could be expected, but not near so handsome as your sisters."

The man rattled on in this style as rapidly as the words could flow from his mouth, and apparently made himself at home.

Uncle looked at him, half afraid and half amazed at his impudence. The stranger's flow of words was cut short by Captain Niel, who put his hand on his shoulder, and said:

"Now, pause a bit. I have a question to ask: Who are you?"

"Who am I? Well, that is rich! Now, if you would change the question, and say, 'Tell me who you are not?' I would answer freely—I am not the king of the Cannibal Islands, though he is a friend of mine; I am not Silas Croft, for there he sits; I am——"

"Who are you?"

"I am—yes, my name; just so; I would give you my card only I haven't one with me—but I am Jacob Browne—mind it is spelled with a final 'e,' and I come from—no matter where. That is of no interest. Meinheer Croft will read that."

The stranger, whom we had begun to believe to be a lunatic, handed a piece of dirty paper to uncle, on which was written the lines:

"'The man who presents this to you is very eccentric; but, for my sake, entertain him as you only know how.
"THOMAS WILKINSON.'

"I don't know any one of the name of Wilkinson," said my uncle. "Where does he live?"

"Ah, that is no matter. What time do you take supper?"

John went out, and I noticed when he returned that he had a revolver in his pocket.

I felt safer then, for the man was evidently insane.

"Do you know Hans Coetzee?" he asked.

"Yes!"

"Good! I will call on him. And does Meinheer Frank Muller ever visit here?"

"Occasionally."

"Good! Send for him often during my stay. Tell me, Meinheer Croft, is there much life in this section of the Wakkerstroom?"

"Yes," answered John, "there are plenty of vilderbeestes, spring-bok and ostriches, with an occasional polecat and aasvogel."

"Ah, you are funny. But, never mind."

"Will you tell us who you are?"

"That I will, with pleasure. I am the worst man that ever lived. I have been everything. Slave catcher in the good old days; pirate on the bounding main; school-teacher when I wanted to know a district thoroughly; government agent; and now, if you like, a corsair, or gentleman of leisure, whichever you like to call it."

"Where are you bound for to-night?" asked John.

"To-night, why my dear young friend, I shall stay here as long as it suits me, and then I will take my letter of introduction somewhere else. Perhaps you would like to hear my story."

"Tell it, by all means," said uncle, who dearly loved a good yarn.

"All right, but haven't you got a drop of good beer or something of the kind, for talking is dry work."

After he had taken a good deep draught, he rattled along with his story. I will try to write it as nearly as possible in the way he told it, though I was too much afraid to notice much what he said:

"I was born in England—a fair country, is it not, meinheer? My father was one of the olden time—my mother—well, god bless her, she is dead, so I won't say anything about her. My father and I soon had a quarrel, for he wanted me to be a lawyer, and then he said I should soon enter parliament, and rise most likely to be prime minister; but I thought I would rather be a pirate —there's not much difference, for you know what Byron said:

> "Let not a pirate's mode of raising cash seem strange,
>   Altho' he fleeced the flags of every nation,
> For into a prime minister but change
>   His title, and 'tis nothing but taxation;
> But the pirate, more modest, took an humbler range
>   Of life, and an honester vocation."

Ha, ha, ha! that is just the truth, and I thought with Byron; so I told my dad I would rather be pirate than prime minister. They couldn't do anything with me in England, so father gave me fifty pounds and a free passage to the Cape. I took a girl with me and that made a big whole in the fifty, but alas, she died before she reached land, so I wasted my money. Life at the Cape was slow, so I set out to seek my fortune in another way. I went on board a merchantman, got attacked by a pirate, half our crew got sent to Davy Jones' locker, I didn't, I always fall on my feet I do, and I was made a prisoner. The captain of the pirate craft liked me and I cottoned to him. 'Serve with me, by boy, and I'll put gold lace on your cap.' 'Agreed,' said I, and pirate I became. I passed a year in that profession, but I ran away and joined a slaver. What fun we had then. We used to go ashore and gather in a hundred or so niggers and then wait about a bit to make sure, and off we'd go to New Orleans. Didn't it pay? We each got a share and I was rich. I wanted to be captain, so I got the crew together and offered them a bigger share if I ever became master; bless me if they didn't mutiny that blessed night; the old captain fed the fishes, and I was elected captain; we made two voyages, and they turned in a lot of money; but I heard my first officer say he would like to have my place, and they all agreed he was worthy, so not wanting to be the food of lobsters or sharks, I went ashore and left them the ship; I changed my profession.

"I was at Port Natal—they call it Durban now—and I fell in love with a pretty girl. Bless me, but she was as nice a one as you would have any desire to meet—saving your presence, ladies—well, I had some money—I always had, for as long as there is any in the world Jacob Browne is going to get a share of it. So I proposed I would go partners with her father, and I would marry and settle down.

"The day was fixed for our wedding, when who should turn up but one of my old messmates.

"I was out walking with Amanda and up comes an old sailor.

"'Shiver my timbers!' he exclaimed, 'but it's old Browne. Tip us yer flipper.'

"I professed not to know him, so I said to Amanda: 'Come on, my dear, the man is drunk.'

"'Drunk, am I?' he exclaimed, 'not a bit of it, Pirate Browne, Mutineer Browne—thief and murderer.'

"Amanda set up a scream and ran home. I followed, but found the door locked, and my adored one's father pointing a shot-gun at me.

"I went to my diggings, and on my way the police kindly gave me a hint that they knew me, so I thought I would clear out and sail up-country.

"The fact was, I was not allowed to lead an honest life."

"Well, what are you doing now?" asked Uncle Crofts.

"Doing, my dear sir? Telling you a yarn about my life," he answered, evasively. "But putting all that aside, I am a corsair, a bandit, brigand, gentleman of leisure, soldier of fortune, or anything you please to call me. I, however, am just now hoping to be of use to the Transvaal."

"In what way?"

"Why, my dear young friend"—looking at John Niel —"there will be war here very soon, and all the rooi baatjes will be driven out, and the Boer Republic be again proclaimed."

"Never, sir!" exclaimed uncle, jumping to his feet.

"Yes, within not many months."

"No, sir, you are mistaken. You are my guest, and

entitled to your opinion; but did I not hear Sir Garnet Wolseley say at Potchefstroom the other day that England would lose the last man before it gave up the Transvaal? Didn't Shepstone, when he raised the British flag, declare it was to float there forever?"

"Yes, Om Croft, I guess he did; but what of that? The English can't fight, and if the Boers rose, why the redcoats would run rather than stand and fight."

"Stranger Jacob Browne, or whatever your name may be, I have a commission in the British army, and——"

"You have?" interrupted Browne. "Well, let me finish your sentence. 'And,' you would say, 'fearing there was to be some fighting, I tried ostrich farming.'"

"John Niel is no coward," said John, angrily.

"A coward, no, but a wise man; for in the Zulu war—lor! wasn't it fun to see the rooibaatjes running away! As soon as a Zulu showed himself, the rule was to see which could run the fastest. It was a regular go-as-you-please scramble for escape."

"I admit our arms were not very successful in some of the engagements."

"I should say your legs were. But the fact is, good folks, England only uses natives like this just as you would chessmen on a board. She will slaughter or not, just as it suits the game, and England's promise was never worth much, and most of the treaties were like the famous one of Limerick:

"Broken, ere the ink wherewith 'twas
Writ could dry."

This so enraged my uncle that he rose from his chair and paced the room uneasily for a few minutes, and then standing more erect than I had seen him for years, he said:

"Mr. Browne, I am an Englishman, and never refused hospitality to any. But there is a limit. I was loyal to the republic when it was in existence, but now that peace exists under the English flag, I will never allow any one in my house to libel the government of my native land."

There was a dignity about this speech which was of that old-fashioned kind which I often imagined must have characterized the courtiers of the fifteenth and sixteenth century.

Our strange guest apologized, and as he retired for the night said that he should leave us on the morrow, but would doubtless return.

No invitation was given, because uncle was far too honest to utter vague society platitudes. If he wanted any one he let them know it, if their presence was not welcome, they soon felt it if he did not tell them.

I feel so uneasy that I don't think I shall attempt to go to sleep.

Jess laughs at my fears, but I cannot shake off the feeling that our visitor has some motive which does not show on the surface of his visit.

Twice since I have been writing I have thought I heard his footsteps moving along the corridor.

Fortunately we all sleep with our doors well locked, and John is always armed.

I shall be glad when morning comes.

CHAPTER XXXIII.
LOVE'S YOUNG DREAM.

I am so happy!

Is it possible for any one to experience greater happiness than I do?

Oh! my journal, as I write on thy clear, white pages and tell of my joy, it is a relief to me.

A load is lifted from my heart, every step seems to be on the air, I want to sing, nay, I would like to shout for very joy.

What happiness it is to love.

But what greater joy to be beloved.

To know that the loved one is worthy, to feel that reason as well as passion, the head as well as the heart, approves the choice, is to experience the greatest of ecstasy.

He loved me all along, and he loves me now!

He has told me so! But let me reflect. What was it he said? I have but an indistinct remembrance, but I do know that as he put his arm round my waist he uttered the momentous words: "She is my promised wife."

How grand and noble he looked, and with what courage he faced Muller and told him what a coward he was.

Oh, my loved one, thou hast made me happy!
But what has come over Jess?
She is strange. Very strange!
I went to her room to-night and she was weeping. What could it be about?
I told her all about Frank Muller's proposal, and she listened attentively, and then said, in such a strange voice:

"Will you marry him?"

"No, Jess, how could I? You know I hate him."

"But you say he threatened."

"Yes; but, Jess, dearest, that is only his way."

"I know it, but Frank Muller is a dangerous man. He has always been uncle's enemy, and I really believe he would betray his own father if it was to his interest to do so. Do you know, Bessie, that two years before the annexation, Muller denounced uncle as a 'Verdomde Engelsmann,' and actually asked the Landdrost to declare uncle a law-breaker, and so get our little property confiscated."

"So I have heard; but now we are English, and he is powerless."

"We are English to-day, but I think we shall soon go back to the old style government, and as for the English courts, there is no justice there."

"You frighten me, Jess. Would you have me marry Muller?"

"No."

"What then?"

"I only fear his power."

"I don't."

"Why?"

"Because—oh, can't you guess?"

"No, Bess, I cannot."

"He loves me."

"And do you think that love would prevent him from wreaking his vengeance on you and uncle and all of us? No, Bess, the more he says he loves, the greater the danger."

"I don't mean Muller."

"Who then?"

"John—Captain Niel."

"Bess, Bess! Explain yourself, for you are very

mixed. You first tell me that Muller has threatened you, and then in the next breath say it does not mean anything because he loves you."

"You, dear, old Jess, you misunderstand me. Muller has threatened, but John has proposed."

I thought I saw the color—what little there was—leave Jess, and her face became corpse-like.

Could it be that she loved John?

No; dear, old Jess, she never will love.

If she did love him, what should I do?

Could I give him up for her sake?

She has been like a mother to me as well as sister; and did she love him? Oh, I believe she would give him up for me.

Dear, darling Jess. She has been so good to me that I know not what to say.

I looked up, and there was Jess sitting immovable—her face rigid and cold, her lips firmly pressed together, and her hands clinched.

The wind might blow, the storm rage, but she would be oblivious to all.

I felt for her, but in the greatness of my love for John Niel, I was nearly heartless.

"Oh, Jess," I cried, "I love him so much! When he came here, that very day I felt that I could die for him. To see how he attacked that vicious bird, brave, noble fellow, was enough to make any girl almost worship him. And every day I have learned to love him more, until now—— Jess, what is the matter?" I cried, as I crossed to where Jess was seated.

Her eyes were strained, and she looked as rigid as a corpse.

I put my arms round her, and kissed her face. It was cold and stiff.

Could it be she was dead?

No; I felt the heart-throbs, and therefore I knew she was alive; but what could I do?

I was about to call for assistance when she opened her eyes, and a sweet smile spread over her face, and she gradually regained control over herself.

I then began to cry.

That seemed to rouse her, and she kissed me, but her lips were cold.

"Bess, dear, why do you cry? You love John Niel, and you say he loves you. What, then, troubles you?"

"Jess, dear," I answered, "I thought you were sick."

"I felt faint; that was all."

"I was so anxious; and, oh, Jess, suppose I should lose John!"

"That you will not do, for if he loves you, he is true, and nothing would shake his allegiance. Good-night, dearest sister."

That was a hint for me to go, and so I kissed her again and left her.

Nearly an hour afterward I felt uneasy about Jess, and I went again to her room.

As I got near the door I heard her weeping as though her heart would break.

I knocked at the door, and it was some time before it was opened, and then I saw a specter.

It could not be Jess! If it was she was transformed so that I scarcely knew her.

With eyes red and bloodshot, her face as pale as that of the dead, her body trembling with intense excitement. I started back as much alarmed as I should have been had a veritable ghost appeared before me.

"Jess, dearest, you will break my heart. What troubles you so much?"

"Nothing. I shall be sorry to lose you, that is all."

I coaxed her to go to bed, and offered to stay with her; but she declined my proposal, and declared she should be better alone.

It was with a strange feeling that I returned to my room. I was sure now that Jess loved John, and——

A new terror almost palsied me.

Jess was strong-willed. What if she used her will-power against me?

I had confidence in the strength of her power, for I had known her face a savage Kafir, and although he had his spear uplifted to throw at her, she merely looked him straight in the face, and he lowered the weapon and crept on his hands and knees to her, vowing he would be her faithful slave.

I also remembered the time when a band of savages surrounded uncle, and were about to kill him.

Jess rushed out of the house, and at once they turned

to secure her as well as uncle; but she raised her hand, gave a piercing look at the howling savages, and they fell back before her, crying, "Tagati! tagati!" (A witch! a witch!) They ran away, and then Jess fell in a faint across the body of Uncle Croft.

I found them there, both in a swoon—uncle from the effects of his ill-treatment and Jess from excitement. With the aid of Jantje and Hebe, who was alive then and helped us with the work of the house, we got the cords loosened from uncle's limbs, and soon had both in the house.

What if Jess should use the same potent power on John Niel?

She could win him to her side, and then I——

Oh, I feel I should kill myself. John, I love you. What a sweet pleasure it is to feel that now, at least, you love me.

I will not doubt you, my own, my beloved.

I had closed my journal for the night, and felt that I would try to sleep; but a book lay on the table. It had been given me by John.

He had been reading it lately. I opened it carelessly, and found a marker in at a certain page.

Curiosity led me to see what piece had taken the fancy of my bonny lover, when I found a verse of poetry marked.

I read it, and then I kissed the lines, for John must have marked it, and as it came before me it seemed like my first love-letter. It gave me happiness, for it read:

> " It is not because your heart is mine—mine only,
>   Mine alone!
> It is not because you chose me, weak and lonely,
>   For your own!
> Not because the earth is fairer and the skies
>   Spread above you
> Are more brilliant for the shining of your eyes
>   That I love you;
> But because this human love, tho' true and sweet,
>   Yours and mine—
> Has been sent by love more tender, more complete,
>   More divine.
> That it leads our hearts to rest in heaven,
>   Far above you,
> Do I take you as a gift that God has given,
>   And I love you."

I kissed the lines again and again. And then—don't
laugh at me—it was love's young dream with me—I put
the book under my pillow, and fell asleep.

All the night my dreams were of him who loved me so
completely, and I thanked Heaven for the gift I had received.

At the breakfast-table Jess complained of a severe
headache, and she looked most wretched and ill.

The great black eyes looked darker than ever, and her
cheeks were pale.

Uncle was much concerned about her, and I am sorry
to say I felt a pang of jealousy when I saw the evident
anxiety which was plainly visible on John's face.

Oh, my dear, I dare not lose you, for you are my all—
my hope—my very life.

CHAPTER XXXIV.

JOHN NIEL'S SURPRISE.

I AM not often surprised, but I have to write in my
journal, for the first time in my life, adventures which
owe their origin to a genuine surprise.

When Frank Muller threatened me I looked upon it as
a piece of bombastic folly, which his sober senses would
repudiate.

I knew the man was mean and cruel.

I had seen him strike Jantje and Billy more than once
through pure deviltry, and I hated the man with an intensity which sometimes fairly astonished me.

I was annoyed with the bandit pirate who called himself Jacob Browne, and who was ever impressing upon us
the desirability and necessity of remembering the final
"e" of his patronymic.

I expected to find him turn up again, like a bad shilling,
long before he was wanted.

A week had passed, and I was settling down into quietude and pleasure at being engaged. I now found delight in walking at night with Bessie, and I even got sentimental.

One evening, about eight days or so after Muller had
threatened me, I was down in the Blue Gum Walk with
Bessie,

Under the shadow of a tree we sat, and Bessie's head was resting on my shoulder.

I was toying with her hair, and I suddenly recalled a pastoral which I had met with in my early days. It was apropos of the scene, and I sang it in a low voice for the benefit of Bessie. It ran:

> " O meadow flowers, primrose and violet,
> Ye touch her slender ankle as she moves;
> But I that worship may not kiss her feet.
>
> " O mountain airs, where unconfined float
> Her locks ambrosial, would that I were you,
> To wanton with the tangles of her hair!
>
> " O leaping waves, that press and lip and lave
> Her thousand beauties, when shall it be mine
> To touch and kiss and clasp her even as you?
>
> " But she more loves the blossom and the breeze
> Than lip or hand of mine, and thy cold clasp,
> O barren sea, than these impassioned arms."

This I sang in a tenor voice, and as I did so, Bessie pressed closer to me.

The last words of the song scarcely died on the air before I continued with descriptive recitative:

> " So ran the song, and even as he sang
> Her head lay on his shoulder, and her hands
> Wove him the prize, a crown of meadow flowers,
> Primrose and violet; and with amorous touch
> He wooed her neck and wantoned with her hair,
> And marked the tell-tale color flush and fail;
> Thrilled with a touch, and felt the counter-thrill
> Through all the passionate pulses of the blood,
> Nor envied in his heart the barren sea."

This recitative described so thoroughly our occupation that Bess thought I must have improvised it on the spot.

I had just finished it when I felt something fall on my head. I looked up, and there was Jantje perched on a branch of a tree just above us, and evidently an interested listener to all we had been saying and I had been singing.

" You infernal young scamp! What are you doing there?" I called out.

" Baas! See! Look!" and he pointed to the north.

I saw nothing to warrant his excitement.

Jantje, seeing that I was not going to take any notice of his warning, slid down the tree and whispered in a hoarse voice:

"Baas, Meinheer Muller is with a bad man, and take care."

The Hottentot had only just sidled away in the long grass before a man approached me.

He was the most hideous-looking creature I had ever seen.

He had but one eye, and his clothes consisted only of a pair of ragged trousers, fastened round the waist with a greasy leather strap. In the wool on his head he had several small distended bladders, such as are worn by medicine men and the lowest kind of witch-doctors.

He had a long stick in his hand, and on the end of the stick was a letter.

As soon as he got near enough to me, he pushed out the stick for me to take the letter.

It read:

"If the rooibaatje is not a coward he will bring his revolver and meet Frank Muller in half an hour."

I was indignant, and I raised my hand to strike the bearer, but Bess drew my arm away and said:

"He is only the messenger, don't harm him."

I turned to the Kafir.

"Go tell thy master that I am no coward, but I will not meet him to either murder or be murdered."

The man turned away, and when he had got a little distance, he threw his long stick up in the air.

I proposed to Bessie that we go back to the house.

We had reached the top of a little hill, where we stood for a moment looking round at the grandeur of a late sunset.

We could see for many miles, and could be seen for quite a distance.

I took Bessie's hand in mine, and was in the act of raising it to my lips, when I heard the unmistakable whiz of a bullet pass unpleasantly near my cheek.

I had just time to push Bessie to the ground, when another bullet passed so close to my shoulder that it tore a hole in my coat.

Had Bessie been standing near me it must have killed her!

This was a surprise with a vengeance, and I could not for the life of me see who was firing.

Jantje wriggled through the grass, and crawling on his belly, got close to me.

"Stoop down, Baas!"

I did so, and then he said that he had overheard Baas Muller plan to kill me.

If I accepted the challenge to fight a duel, I was to be shot from behind. If I declined, then the Kafir messenger was to throw up his stick, and I was to be riddled with bullets as soon as my body was exposed. It seemed that Muller had been able to find out just how I was spending the evening, and the opportunity was a good one. He was safely intrenched.

Jantje had learned all this, and had tried to give me warning, but could not get an opportunity.

While I was singing to Bessie, he had noiselessly climbed the tree, and was able to give me early intimation of the approach of the Kafir.

I suppose Muller must have thought he had killed both of us, for the firing ceased, and we were able to get to the house without any further molestation.

When we reached the house, however, we saw the Kafir witch-doctor hiding among the trees.

When he saw us he set up a yell, and ran at the greatest speed he could command.

That was surprise number one. I now was firmly convinced that Muller meant treachery, and I was also aware that it could only be met by cunning.

He was so careful that evidence against him could not possibly be obtained.

I knew that, although Jantje and Muller's familiar, the witch-doctor, both swore that my murder was planned by the half-breed, their evidence would not be believed.

Strange as it may appear, during the South African Republic, a black, whether Hottentot, Kafir, or Betjuan, could give evidence to a court of law, and it would be accepted, provided there were circumstances or evidence which in any way corroborated it; but after the annexation to Great Britain a colored native's evidence would not be received against a white man.

So that I could get no redress in a court of law.

I sat on the veranda, thinking over all this, when I saw Hans Coetzee coming, and presenting a most ludicrous spectacle.

He was fat and big, and at any time looked comical in his leather breeches and coat and broad-brimmed Boer hat, but now he was mounted on a pony very short but exceedingly fat. The burly Boer's legs nearly touched the ground.

I went forward to meet him, for I had quite a liking for our neighbor.

He reached out his hand and gave mine a hearty shake, bidding me a fair "gooden daag," and then he slipped off his pony and took me by the arm.

"Well, captain, and how like you the Transvaal?"

"Exceeding well, meinheer," I answered.

"Yah, and Mooifontein is a fine place, and there are many mooi (pretty) things there. Let me see, there is the fountain; ah, that is mooi indeed, but I know a pair of eyes prettier than the waters, eh, captain? We are not blind like moles, and we reckon you 'opsit' (sit up at night) often with the pretty Bess. Isn't it so?"

Hans had spoken rapidly and in his usual good-natured way, but I saw he was troubled about something. I liked to listen to the good-tempered, jolly fellow, so I let him run on.

"And you will be marrying soon, I'm thinking, and then the captain will be going back to England, eh?"

"I have no desire or intention of leaving Mooifontein," I answered.

"You haven't? that's good, but——"

"Well, out with it, man."

Coetzee looked round, waddled across to the long grass and listened, and then, when assured that no one was spying, he came up to me, and putting his hand on my shoulder, said:

"I like you, Nef, though Muller does say you are a 'verdomde Engelsmann,' so I thought I would make bold and tell you, that you had better get out, you verdomde Engelsmann," and old Coetzee laughed as he uttered the words.

I perceived he had something to tell me but was afraid

of being overheard, so I invited him to my room to drink a glass of beer.

When he was sure that no spy could hear his conversation, he told me that his vrou had heard Frank Muller plan my death. And that there was to be a bymakaar (by meeting) at which war was to be declared against England: the declaration made a pretext for killing every Englishman in the country.

It was part of the policy to arm the Betjuans as well as the Boers. "And then," said Om Coetzee, "won't the rooibaatjes run?"

Hans laughed again until the ponderous mass of flesh which formed his anatomy shook with the excitement.

"But you can prevent it all," said Coetzee, when he had finished laughing.

"I can?"

"Yes."

"Let me understand—you say I can stop all this threatened disaster?"

"Yah!"

"How?"

"By going away."

"Explain."

"Meinheer Muller can influence the bymakaar for war or peace."

"What of that?"

"If you stay it is war."

"And if I leave?"

"Peace."

"Om Coetzee, you know more than you admit; now, be a man, and out with it all."

The Boer fidgeted about for some time, drank another glass of beer, and filled his big pipe.

When all this was satisfactorily accomplished, he commenced:

"You love Bessie Croft?"

"I do."

"And no wonder."

"What of that?"

"Muller loves her too."

"The scoundrel, I hate him."

"Of course, and he hates you, and will kill you rather than you should marry Bessie."

"But how will war help him?"

"Don't you see? If there is war, Muller will kill you as a 'verdomde Engelsmann,' and then he will kill Om Silas and pretty Jess—they are all English—and he will keep Bess for himself."

"But she won't have him."

"Tut, tut; you don't know the women. If all her friends are dead, and Muller carries her off to Lydenburg or Wakkerstroom, and keeps her there a few weeks, she will cry her eyes out, but as she will be as good as a wife, she may as well be one. You understand?"

"I do! My God! to think such a villain can live. He will destroy her good name, and he thinks by that means she will prefer to be his to going out in the world with a blighted name."

"Yah, that is just so."

"But if Muller gets killed?"

"He has the tagati, and nothing can hurt him."

"That is all nonsense. All the tagati in the world would not prevent a bullet going into his carcass."

"Think as you will; but, if you take my advice, clear out. The girl is a beauty, but she won't be much good if you are dead; so save your own skin, and perhaps you can save Om Silas and Jess as well."

"I shall not leave."

"Just as you will. I have no blood on my soul. But, oh, lor'! wouldn't my vrou make it hot for me if she knew I had split on the wretches? but I am English now. When we were a republic, I was a republican, but when I saw the English flag I said to myself, says I: ' I shall be an Engelsmann now.'"

Although I did not take much notice of Hans Coetzee's advice, I thanked him for the exposure of Muller's villainy, and the old fellow was again mounted on his pony, and went back to his sharp-tongued vrou.

Reduced to plain English, it meant that Frank Muller, on purpose to force a girl into an unwelcome marriage, would plunge a country into war, and slaughter a number of innocent people in cold blood, so that he might coerce and have his way with one.

Alas! Frank Muller was a type of a class I had found in all the colonies, men with an ambition, but destitute of honor and truth.

CHAPTER XXXV.

JESS ON LOVE AND MISERY.

I CANNOT understand Jess. Yesterday I was out with her in a storm, and we talked quite seriously. She was looking so miserable, and her eyes seemed so unnaturally large, that I could not help saying to her:

"Jess, are you as miserable as you look?"

She smiled faintly, and answered by asking me a question:

"Why should we be anything but miserable?"

"Why, Jess, what an odd question! I think every one ought to be happy."

"Ought to be! Yes; but how can they?"

"What is to hinder, except their own doings?"

"John Niel, I am surprised at your question. Look round and you will find some strange reasons for happiness. Last year there was a poor family, who had but one pride, and that was a flock of sheep. 'Blue tongue' seized every one, and in a few weeks that family was ruined. Could they be happy? Then there is a talk of war; hundreds will be killed, and for every man slain, there will be a home made desolate. How can any one be happy?"

"But war is only an occasional evil."

"I know that, but when there is no war there is sickness, and oh, John Niel, how it grieves me to see a strong, hearty man suddenly stricken down, to see him grow pale and thin, to know that his mind is disturbed by the thought of his little ones who will be left, perhaps, desolate, and then to watch the weeping procession which follows the body to the grave; my heart gets so sad that I cannot be very happy."

"But, Jess, there are people who are happy, very happy."

"Oh, yes, I admit that. They are made up of two classes: the intensely egotistic and the intense lovers."

"Are these the only people who are happy?" I asked.

"I think so. The egotist is so well satisfied with himself that the sufferings of others never trouble him. He has but one object in life, one aim, one ambition—a love and gratification of self."

"But what of the lover?"

"I can imagine some who can love with such an intensity that they lose sight of everything but the loved object. That is the only true happiness."

"Then, if that is so, love constitutes the highest source of happiness."

"Yes. Read of the martyrs of olden times, who went into the arena singing psalms of joy, even as the wild beasts sprung upon them. They loved their faith, and gave themselves as a sacrifice on the altar of devotion. Then there are those who have such an earnest love of country that they will endure imprisonment, torture, and death for the cause of patriotism."

"But this is not the only love."

"No. There is that perfect love which unites man and woman. The chain which connects them may be a long one, but while the man is at one end of it, there is a woman at the other, predestined, foreordained to be the perfection of his being. Every day the chain gets shorter, as its links coil round those who are holding it; at times there may be stoppages; some woman may clasp the chain nearer the man, some male may hold its links nearer the woman, but only for a time, they drop out, and the coiling continues, until at last—if not in this world, then beyond the grave—the two meet, and a perfect union is consummated. Now, such a love as would be then felt would be the greatest happiness which the mind of mankind could endure. Beyond that would be insanity and mental death. My ideas are very crude, and perhaps almost unintelligible, but they seem to me to be right."

I was deeply interested, and knew Jess well enough to feel that she wanted no compliment, but would rather have argument.

She had broken through the ice of her nature, and I could see that, while she liked the freedom of the boundless prairie, while I knew that the sublimity and grandeur of the mountain ranges appealed to her and gave her a divine inspiration, yet in the city she would be drawn nearer to congenial minds, and her ideas would get broadened and developed.

"Have you ever loved in that way?" I asked, after quite a lengthy pause.

"I? Oh, no! But every one will love like that before his destiny is filled. Love is the source of all happiness. It fills the soul with ineffable pleasure; and love is the one thing which distinguishes the human from the animal. Love transforms human brutes into men, and makes man capable of the highest excellence."

"You speak with enthusiasm."

"I feel so. I have always admired that old story of Quentin Matsys, the Antwerp blacksmith, who, when he had fallen in love with an artist's daughter, was told by the indignant father: 'Never shalt thou wed a daughter of mine till thou hast copied, with exactness, yon painting.' Quentin loved, and he threw off his blacksmith's apron, left the anvil and took the brush. In one year he had copied the painting so exactly that the critics were unable to say which was the original. That was what love will do. It overpowers and overmasters everything, and therefore I have always thought that love is the most powerful motive-power in the world."

As I looked at Jess there was a fascination from her eyes which seemed to hold me spell-bound.

I trembled beneath her glance, and for the first time I began to believe that there might be some truth in Mesmer's theory.

As her eyes looked into mine, my whole frame was subject to spasmodic thrills, such as I had never before experienced.

"To be loved like you say would be worth living for," I said.

"Worth living for, ay, and worth dying for! Oh, John Niel, when a woman loves like that, earth, heaven, life, all narrows down to the one small object, and the whole universe becomes a single being; but that being is dilated until it reaches the very Deity. Love is a portion of the soul. It is eternal, indivisible—the divine essence. Like the soul, it is from everlasting. Love is life, and life without love is but a negation of being. Did you ever think," continued this strange woman, "that love is, in reality, the manifestation of God on earth?—that as God is the perfection of heaven, so love is the only perfection on earth?"

Her words flowed like honey, sweet and pure, and I was entranced by their eloquence.

I knew not what to say, and yet felt that, to break the spell, I must speak.

"Yet bad men love," was the only thing I could find an utterance for.

"Bad men love! They may be bad in everything else, but in their love they are angelic. No bad or evil thought can enter in the domain of true love; as well expect a thistle to grow in a field of ice. As easy to gather grapes from a hawthorn bush as to find unworthy thoughts and feelings germinate where true love reigns. No, John Niel, the fact is that love ennobles. The lofty and serene soul, inaccessible to emotion, and only in passions soaring above the shadows and dark clouds of the earth, with all the follies, hatreds, vanities, dwells in the sky, and looks down upon this small speck of the universe with pitying eye."

She had finished. The spell which caused her to talk had been broken, and all the way home I could only find the Jess I had known at Mooifontein. She seemed possessed of a dual existence; and the Jess of the house was a plain, uninteresting creature compared to that other Jess with whom I had just conversed.

She was a human riddle, and hard to read.

In one thing she was so plain that there was no possibility for misunderstanding, and that was her love for Bess.

I was ill at ease. I was pledged to Bess, but there was a feeling rising to my heart that there was depth of love in Jess which would be worth a man's seeking.

Was I wavering?

No, but while I loved Bess, or thought I did, there was a mysterious something which seemed to whisper to my soul that Jess and I were destined for each other.

Why did I not realize that earlier?

What misery would have been averted, and what an amount of innocent deceit avoided.

I dreaded meeting Bess, but when I reached the house and saw her happy face, her bright, sparkling eyes, and felt her arms twine round my neck, I felt I loved her. Yet——

Why will these doubts come to me?

Why cannot I love in peace? My love is beset with dangers, and to add to them all is the terrible knowledge that Jess could fill a position which my affianced could not. I was racked with doubt, and sat almost moping in an arm-chair, my mind far from easy, when the clear voice of Bessie broke upon my ear, as she sang:

> "But love is such a mystery,
> I cannot find it out;
> For when I think I'm best resolved
> I then am most in doubt.
> Then farewell care, and farewell woe,
> I will no longer pine,
> For I'll believe I have his heart
> As much as he has mine."

I thought the hint would be very applicable to me, and it seemed to banish many of my doubts and fears, and gave me greater confidence in the future.

I sank into a delightful dream of future happiness, when Bessie wished me good-night.

As Jess looked in to pass the evening wish, she gave me a glance which once again unsettled me.

Ah, me! What a terrible thing it is to love, especially when the soul finds congeniality in the company of one who is an only sister to the affianced.

I am afraid I shall get to love Jess even yet. I hope not.

CHAPTER XXXVI.
A SHORT EXPLANATION BY THE EDITOR.

I FOUND the journals of both Bess and Captain Niel filled for many pages with all sorts of ideas concerning love and its doubts.

I have not thought it interesting enough to print all that these love-sick people had to say about their passion for each other at that time, but waited to see what they thought and felt when many miles separated them.

Between the date of the last chapter and the place where we resume our reading of the journals of these two people, many important events had taken place.

In the first place, Jess found she loved John Niel with a deep and lasting love, and every affectionate word he addressed to Bess seemed, as she expressed it, "to scorch her brain."

To be under the same roof became torture to her, so

she resolved to pay a promised visit to an old school friend, who was living with her parents at Pretoria.

This was a great surprise to her uncle and to Bessie, for Jane Neville was not a favorite with Jess.

However, she insisted, and Silas Croft thought the change would do her good.

She had only just reached Pretoria, where she was warmly welcomed by the Nevilles, when the bymkaar was held, and by Frank Muller's advice, war was declared against England and the South African Republic proclaimed, under a triumvirate.

Then Uncle Silas got uneasy about Jess, and desired to get her home.

He therefore got John Niel to ride over to Pretoria and bring Jess back with him.

It was easy starting, but when the captain got past Wakkerstroom he found he was expected to have a pass.

After several narrow escapes, and once passing through the lines in the wake of the bishop and as one of his aids, he reached Pretoria to find the city deserted, and the residents encamped on the hills.

He found Jess, but instead of being able to return with her, he had to remain in the camp.

In the meantime stirring events were taking place at Mooifontein, and Bess will tell of them in her journal.

CHAPTER XXXVII.
ALONE!

I AM alone. I never knew what that word meant before. It seems even now strange that though there is uncle in the house, I feel as if I was entirely alone.

Jess is with Jane Neville at Pretoria, and writes such strange letters. I cannot understand her. For two days before she went she was so quiet that the day would pass without our hearing her voice once.

It was hard to part with her, for we had grown to understand each other more the last year or two, and she was gone.

Why did she go when I was so happy?

Could it be that my happiness made her wretched.

No, that I will not believe, for she loves me with a holy and true love.

Then that horrid lot of men must go and proclaim the republic, and so bring down upon them the vengeance of the English.

There will be a fearful war, I am sure, and perhaps John—my John—will have to fight. Oh, I hope not!

And now he has gone.

What shall I do while he is away?

John has gone to fetch Jess home.

He has not been gone many hours, but I have learned now how deeply and truly I love him.

His love is my life. I feel that without it I should go mad.

While he is away I shall not be able to write to him on account of this possible war, but we can cheat absence by a thousand things. When he sees the sun shining he will know it is a message from me. The songs of birds, the rustling of the trees, the twinkling of the stars, and the shining of the moon will all be as so many reminders of my love for him, and all the universe will be but my love tokens.

But it is hard to be alone. So hard that all nature seems to mock me in my sorrow.

* * * * * *

A day has gone by, and though it has been one of adventures, it seemed that it would never come to an end.

The dinner had just been finished, when we saw through the open window the form of Frank Muller.

"See what the skellum wants," said my uncle, who had conceived a great dislike for the Boer half-breed.

I went to the door, and was at once accosted by Muller.

"Ah! Miss Bessie. Ever charming you always are."

"Gooden daag," I said, in the language I knew he disliked.

It was silly of me, but I was foolhardy and did not care whether I offended him or not.

For a wonder Muller only laughed at my fun, as he called it.

"Are you coming in to see uncle?" I asked, as I saw no evident intention of dismounting.

"Yes, Miss Bessie, but I would like a few words with you first. Will you walk with me to the Blue Gum Avenue?"

"Really, meinheer, it is an utter impossibility. I never leave uncle alone now."

"Ah, the rooibaatje has left, so he has, and the Om Silas Croft will be lonely. Then I will speak to you here."

He dismounted and gave his horse into the care of Jantje.

As he came near me, I felt that a crisis in my life had arrived.

I don't know what gave me such an idea, neither did I find a reason for the uncomfortable feeling I undoubtedly experienced.

"Miss Bessie," he said, "war is a terrible thing."

"Indeed it is."

"But it will be awful for the English this time."

"Why?"

"Because all will be killed. Not one will be allowed to remain when the war is over."

I could not help feeling a little bit of defiance, so I asked:

"But suppose, now, that the English should triumph?"

"There is no ground for such a supposition. The rooibaatjes will run, like ice melts beneath the summer sun. But I wanted to ask you whether you valued your uncle's life."

"What a question to ask."

"But I want an answer."

I laughed, and then replied, "Of course I do."

"It would pain you to see your aged uncle brought out of his house and placed with his back to that flag staff, while a score of men sent as many bullets into his body."

"Spare him, and spare me the thought of such a thing."

"Oh, you don't like to contemplate it. Well, I am not surprised, but do you think John Niel, your lover redcoat, will ever get back?"

I trembled as he asked the question, for I already was beginning to fear that John and Jess would perish at Pretoria.

"I will be plain with you, Bessie Croft," he continued. "It was my voice which decided for war, and I am powerful enough to save such English alive as I please. Now,

I have taken a fancy to you, and I want you for my wife. What say you?"

"I don't love you, Meinheer Muller."

"I know that, I didn't ask for your love. I shall put it plainer. You have got to be my wife. That is the law of the land, for my voice is that of authority."

"I will obey the laws; but marry you, never!"

"Indeed, then I will tell you what shall be done. A messenger shall be sent to Pretoria for the head of John Niel. You wouldn't believe the story of his death without such evidence."

Frank Muller looked like a fiend as he uttered the words, and, I knew he would execute his threat if he had the power. I, however, determined to defy him.

"Captain Niel's fate is in the hands of a higher power than you, meinheer."

"Indeed. I suppose you speak of that God which I never believed in, of that God who looks so well after his own, that oftentimes they all die of plague or pestilence or else starve. Don't talk of any such fables—there's a sensible girl."

"They are not fables, and Captain Niel is protected——"

"Not by his red coat."

"Perhaps not, but your threats are powerless to influence me."

"Then, hark ye, Bessie Croft, I will kill that redcoat lover; and if you still refuse to be my wife, the same messenger shall fetch the dead body of Jess—the saintly Jess; and if that does not satisfy you, but you want a feast of blood, the old man, your uncle, shall be buried in the plot yonder, his body riddled like a sieve."

"Are you a man, Frank Muller?"

"Oh, I don't care by what name you call me or how you think of me, whether I am a thug or a vampire. I tell you, Bessie Croft, you will be my wife before you are a month older."

"Never!"

"Well," and he laughed a most horrid, demoniac laugh—"well, perhaps not my wife, but you shall live with me, and will go on your knees and beg of me to make you my wife: but if I have to work so hard and shed so much blood to get you, I shall cast you off when I am tired of you."

"Or kill me like you did the Zulu at Lydenburg, or the Boer maiden, or Mary, whose grave is yonder," I said, with slow and deliberate emphasis.

Muller's face turned purple with rage, and he raised his sjambock as if he would strike me, but suddenly let it fall.

"Who has been telling you the tales of the past?" he asked, in a very unsteady voice.

"Thy conscience needs no accuser," I answered; "in thy sleep at night the specters of thy murdered victims haunt thee, and they are well avenged."

"Peace, woman!"

"I care not for thee and thy threats. The air may be black with thy victims if we could but see the invisibles; and see here, meinheer, when thou diest, thy soul shall be escorted to the regions of the damned by the souls of those thou hast ruined and killed on earth."

He was frantic, and again raised his sjambock.

"Strike, meinheer," I said, "for thou art a veritable coward. If thou wishest to rid thee of a fancied rival, instead of meeting him like a man, the brave Meinheer Muller skulks behind a tree and fires at his victim; and then, if a woman's tongue utters unpleasant truths, the same brave warrior would use his sjambock."

"Damnation!" he hissed between his set teeth.

"Yes, Mr. Muller, you have rightly uttered your own future."

"Will you be mine?"

"No! not if there was not another man on earth; not if my soul's salvation depended on it, for I hate you; your very look contaminates; your touch would be a curse."

"Ha, ha, ha!" but what a forced laugh it was! "Then, mark me, my dear Bessie—you shall have my looks day and night, and my touch shall be as gentle as a lover's."

At this moment uncle, getting uneasy at our long conversation, came out and asked what we were engaged in doing.

"Meinheer Croft, I have proposed to the fair Bessie, and asked her to be my wife."

"And what answer did she give?"

"Oh, uncle, you know! I hate him!"

"Then, Frank Muller, let me tell you, I would rather see my niece dead than that she should become your wife."

"Thank you, Om Croft, you will not have the pleasure; but you shall see the dead bodies of John Niel and Jess, and then if Bess refuses to be my wife, your own body will pay the forfeit: but that will not save her, for she shall be mine, even if I have to drag her with chains to her bridal couch."

"You are a fiend, Meinheer Muller, and I bid thee leave my premises, or the dogs shall give a good account of thee."

"Gooden daag, meinheer."

Muller had uttered the parting salutation with as much suavity as if he and uncle were the best of friends.

"Bess, my dear," said my uncle, "that man is going to cause us a deal of trouble unless the English forces are here soon."

"Will they come?"

"Of course they will. England never yet broke faith with the colonies."

"But, uncle, Jess says differently, and she reads the papers carefully."

"Yes, yes, dear, but the papers don't always speak the truth. I tell you, my dear, we shall soon hear the English drum and the march of the soldiers, and then Frank Muller shall be exposed, and his nefarious conduct punished."

I was not so sanguine as uncle, for I did not believe England would interfere effectually, for a change of government had taken place in the old country, and Gladstone had always denounced the annexation.

If we were handed over to the tender mercies of Frank Muller we were undone.

Joubert was one of the triumvirate, and I had far more confidence in his protection than I had in the whole strength of the British Government.

CHAPTER XXXVIII.

JACOB BROWNE REDIVIVUS.

Two days have passed and we have had no news from Pretoria, nor have I seen anything of Frank Muller.

We were just getting ready for supper; our family seems very small now, only uncle and me, when, without any invitation, Jacob Browne walked in.

"Ah! good!" he exclaimed. "Put an extra plate for me. I am always alighting on my feet, you see, or I should not have arrived at supper-time. My dear sir, I am as hungry as a half-starved lion's cub, and my dear Miss Bessie or Jessie—which is it?—put plenty on the table, for I shall be very ravenous."

"To what am I indebted for this——"

"Honor," interrupted Browne. "Ah! I knew you would ask that, but I never forget old acquaintances."

"How is it you are not with the troops? Would they not give you enough for your sword?" I asked.

"Sarcastic as ever, my dear Miss Bessie. Yes, I am engaged by the most glorious South African Republic, and hope soon to spit a few Englishmen on the point of my sword. I have applied for the command of this district. Do you know why? No? Well, then I will tell you. Should I get the command, I will make this my headquarters; and as your hospitality is so very warm, I know I could not do better. Besides, I could not resist the charming eyes, the bonny eyes of Bessie, the pride of Mooifontein."

I am not usually susceptible to flattery, but perhaps I ought to admit the soft impeachment, for there was something about this eccentric visitor I could not help liking.

Uncle was hardly civil to him at first, but under the genial influence of the tea, I suppose, he gradually warmed up, and as soon as the table was cleared, uncle and our uninvited guest were thoroughly enjoying themselves.

The stranger told many yarns of his eventful life.

"I think, Om Croft, that the most comical adventure I ever had was when I was in Abyssinia. We had an orderly sergeant who stuttered and stammered so much that a battle was generally fought before Jack Mayo could finish a sentence. You see, I was in the great English army then——"

"And you would fight against it now?"

"Now, Om Croft, don't spoil my story. In one of the battles Jack Mayo was struck by a spent ball, and partially stunned.

"When he recovered his full senses, he realized that the command to which he belonged had been compelled to change their position, and were then on the retreat, while Mayo was far behind, stuttering and stammering, and determined not to fall into the hands of the enemy.

"Mayo was making every effort to avoid flying bullets and escape capture, when a riderless horse met him.

"Catching and mounting the beast, he was galloping over the bodies of the dead and wounded, when an Irish soldier who had been wounded rose up before Mayo, on his bended knees, and begged that he would allow him to ride behind until he could be left where certain death was not so imminent, as he had been shot in the ankle and was unable to walk.

"Mayo was not the boy to leave another in such distress, so he took the crippled soldier up behind him, bade the Irish boy to clasp him tightly round the waist, and cling firmly to the animal.

"Mayo leaned forward close to the horse's neck to dodge the whizzing bullets, and made the animal dash along at its fullest speed.

"It was getting dark, and what with the clouds and smoke, it was not easy traveling.

"On he dashed, and at last saw the welcome sight of a squad of British troops, of which I was one, and some ambulance wagons.

"Pulling up his horse as he neared us, he called out to me: 'Browne,' says he, 't-t-take this man b-b-behind me in the wagon; he—he n-n-needs a surgeon.'

"We all laughed, and Major Farquhar yelled out at the top of his loud voice:

"'Surgeon, all the doctors in Africa couldn't put a head on that man.'

"Then there was another laugh, and Mayo got almost mad.

"It appears, that as they were riding along, a bursting

shell or a stray ball had carried off the Irishman's head, but had failed to unseat him. Clutching Mayo with a firm grasp, the body finished the journey.

"When Mayo recovered his temper a bit, he unclasped the encircling arm of his companion and hurled the headless trunk as far away as he could, and exclaimed in his usual stuttering way:

"'Get—off—here. Why, why d-d-didn't you—t-t-tell me—you—had—no—head?'

"We could not refrain from another laugh at our comrade's expense, and Mayo got so mad that he wanted to fight a duel with each one of us in turns."

Uncle Croft laughed more heartily over this ghastly story than I had known him to do for many years, but Browne had such an excellent way of telling a story that we could not avoid being amused.

When the effect of the story had worn off, uncle asked how it was that our guest could at one time fight with the English and another time against them.

"You see," he answered, "it is this way. I am fond of fighting; when England wanted men to fight in Abyssinia I joined. I did not know what the quarrel was about, so I merely did the best I could for those who paid me. Now the Boers want men and the English don't, so I go where I am wanted. I don't know what the war is about or which side is right. Very few soldiers do, they are paid to fight, that is all."

"But patriotism, Mr. Browne——" interposed my uncle.

"Is a very good thing for poets to write about, such as:

> "Breathes there a man with soul so dead,
> Who never to himself hath said
> This is my own, my native land,"

etc., etc. And patriotism sounds well from the lips of a stump speaker: but I can't for the life of me see how an Englishman can be more patriotic for killing a lot of poor Africans who never heard the name of England, neither do I see where the patriotism comes in just now, in fighting against a people who are only submissive to England because they are the weaker. No, Om Croft, there is such a thing as patriotism, but you don't find it in the English army."

"But there is the consciousness that you are fighting for the English flag."

"There's no great honor in that. Why, Om Croft, I have seen things done under the English flag which would have made me blush if they had been done under the black flag, with the skull and cross-bones upon it."

"I am English, Mr. Browne, and must doubt you."

"Let me give you one instance?"

"Certainly."

"Then, a few months back, down in the Basutoland colony, the English troops induced all the women and children to leave the village because they were going to fire it. Out came all the poor creatures, and what a wretched lot they looked. They got frightened and sought refuge in a great cave. When what does my English soldiers do, but get a lot of dynamite, put it in the cave, and blow up the whole lot. That was under the English flag, and the soldiers laughed at the shower of legs, arms, and headless trunks which fell all round after the explosion." *

"It was awful, I admit, but——"

"Patriotic, I suppose you would say."

Uncle Silas was unable to cope with the subtle, ingenious arguments of the voluble Jacob Browne; and so, as it was getting late, we all retired to rest.

I don't understand this strange man, but somehow I feel that in case of need he would be very useful, and I don't think he is as bad as he paints himself.

How miserable I feel without John.

If I were to lose him, I should die. Does Jess love him? If so, then I shall never wed John Niel, for he will see how much superior Jess is to me, and though she cannot love him more than I do, yet she is better educated and accomplished, while I, poor Bess, will be nothing but a farmer lass all my life.

* This was made the subject of a question in the English House of Commons, and the War Secretary said it was true, but a great latitude must be allowed to officers in command in savage lands.

CHAPTER XXXIX.

MULLER'S VILLAINY.

Ten days have passed since I wrote anything in my journal, but yet it has not been for want of matter, but rather lack of opportunity.

I will try and remember the events which have happened, and write them down, for I know Jess will like to read about my adventures, and John will get raving mad when he knows all the indignities we have suffered.

It was the night of the second visit of Jacob Browne, and we had all been in bed for three or four hours, when I thought I heard some one walking about in the lower part of the house.

Since John went away I have always had a revolver close to me, so that I might defend myself if necessity arose. I listened, and was now sure that some one was moving stealthily along the corridor. It might be one of the servants, I thought; but I got close to the door, and put my ear as near the keyhole as was safe.

There were two or three persons. Who could they be?

Had Browne been only an advance guard, and opened the door to some enemy?

A sudden fear took possession of me, for I remembered that Jacob Browne admitted himself to be unscrupulous, and also that he was a friend of Frank Muller.

My imagination at once conceived a plan against my happiness.

It occurred to me that Browne was to admit into the house Muller and his gang, and then my abduction would be easy.

I listened, and was perplexed, for no sounds of approaching footsteps could be heard.

What should I do?

Perhaps the whole thing had been but imagination!

Everything was silent, and I was about to return to bed when I heard some whispers.

I felt sure one of the voices was that of Frank Muller; the other was strange to me.

I could not distinguish any words.

Another moment and a terrific crash at my door burst it open.

I had just moved from behind it.

In came two or three men, but it was too dark to see who they were.

"Knock her on the head if she resists, but only stun her," I heard, in the unmistakable voice of Muller.

I slipped out of the room and hurried along the corridor in my night-clothes, just as I had got out of bed.

I had reached the door of the room occupied by Jacob Browne, when it suddenly opened, and before I was able to remonstrate, I was pulled inside.

"Get into my bed there," said Browne, "and I will protect you, even if it costs me my life."

"I would rather be by your side," I answered.

He pointed to my scanty apparel, and said:

"Thought perhaps you'd like to be covered up best."

I showed him my revolver, and he seemed pleased.

"Can you shoot?"

"Yes."

"Good—hit bull's-eye, eh?"

"Five times out of six," I answered, proud of my record as a pistol shot.

"Good again. Now, Bess, don't spare any. Aim for the heart, and make every shot tell."

"What do they want?" I asked.

"You!"

"How do you know it?"

"Heard it to-day, and thinks I to myself, they ain't going to hurt my pretty Bess if Jacob Browne can prevent it; so I came on to your house and have been waiting for the skunks ever since."

"Do you know them?"

"Every mother's son. I'd have told you, only I didn't want you to get alarmed. Wish I had, for you would have been dressed."

"What about uncle?"

"He's safe; at least I reckon so; but keep quiet, they are coming this way."

I tried to refrain from breathing, but how loud every respiration sounded.

The footsteps were nearer.

"She is in here," I heard Muller say.

"How do you know?"

"All the other rooms are locked on the outside."

"Open the door!" commanded Muller.

"What for?" asked Browne.

"The devil!" ejaculated Muller.

"Oh, certainly, the devil will be welcome, but why can't you let me sleep, and what do you want."

"I want Bess Croft."

"Great goodness! this is a strange time to go visiting, but isn't she in the sit-kamie waiting for her company!"

"How the deuce did you get here, Browne?"

"Rode over; this is to be my headquarters—quartered on the enemy, you know."

"Open the door."

"I will not."

"I'll break it open."

"Do so."

Crash went the door, and, no sooner was it down than Browne, pistol in hand, confronted Muller, another Boer and two Kafirs. Four against one man and a feeble girl.

The odds were against us.

Browne had motioned me to a corner behind the curtain of the bed, where I could see to take aim if I had to shoot, but could not be seen.

My strange protector stood defiant, and again asked Muller what he wanted.

"Bessie Croft," was the answer.

"See here, Meinheer Muller, you have command in the Wakkerstroom district. I have command here, and if you interfere in my district by —— I'll shoot you down like a dog. Military law now, you know."

"Come now, Browne. What is Bess Croft to you?"

"Nothing."

"Then give her up."

"I'll see you hanged first."

"You old pirate, I'll report you to the triumvirate."

"I'll report you, if you don't clear out."

"Where is Bess Croft?"

"I won't say."

"Then take that."

"Crack," went the pistol, and a bullet whizzed past Browne's head.

Taking advantage of the cloud of smoke, Browne

struck Muller such a rattling blow on the mouth that, as I heard later, two teeth went down his throat.

Muller fell on the floor.

I thought it time to act, and as I saw the Boer about to fire at Browne I took aim, and a bullet went crunching into his shoulder.

With a shriek of pain he ran from the house, and I thought that it was strange uncle had not come to our assistance.

I fired again, and then Browne's pistol added to the smoke and confusion.

All was still, and as the smoke cleared away I saw that my protector had been shot and was lying on the floor bleeding.

The others had gone.

Forgetting my caution, I stepped from my hiding-place and was on my knees stanching the blood, which was flowing from a bullet wound in Browne's forehead.

I had just commenced my work when Muller sprung into the room and seized me in his arms, and by sheer brute force carried me back to my room.

Throwing me on the bed, he pointed to my clothes which were hanging across the back of a chair, and said:

"Dress!"

"Leave the room, then."

"I will not."

"Then I shall not dress," and I rolled myself very securely in the bed clothes and waited.

"Unless you are dressed in five minutes I shall take you as you are."

"You are a brute, Frank Muller. Where is uncle?"

"Safe."

"But where?"

"Tied to the flag-staff he loves so well."

"Merciful Heaven! Is it possible?"

"It is true."

"What is he there for?"

"Treason to the government."

"Treason?"

"Yes, he kept the English flag flying after the republic was proclaimed, and he dies."

"You would not murder an old man?"

"I don't call it murder. It is an execution, but I

would even murder him or any one else rather than not have my own way. Dress!"

"I will dress if you leave the room."

Muller, finding me obstinate, left, and I dressed more rapidly than I had ever done before, for I was afraid of his return.

When I was dressed I managed to reload the revolver I carried, and secreted the weapon in the bosom of my dress.

The door opened, and Muller looked in.

"Come," he said.

"I will not."

He lifted me in his arms as if I had been but a child, and carried me out of the house to the green.

There, sure enough, I saw poor old uncle standing with his back to the flagstaff, and cords securely fastening him round the waist.

When he saw me, he tried to raise his hands, but he had lost all strength.

Muller, in a loud voice, addressed uncle pretty much in the following words:

"I love Bess, and I am going to marry her. If you will advise her to accept me, your life shall be spared. If, on the other hand, you reject my offers, you shall die, and I will carry Bess away with me."

The old man, with his long white hair hanging on his shoulders, wet with dew, tried to articulate distinctly, but his voice was feeble:

"If I could save my life by asking Bess to marry you, I should refuse to do so, for I hate and detest you, Frank Muller."

Whiz! Crack!

Muller had fired two shots at Uncle Croft, and before I was able to make any resistance, I was seized by the one-eyed witch-doctor and another Kafir, and carried to a tented wagon which stood just outside our grounds.

I was lifted in, and a great, fat, dirty Kafir bound me hand and foot, and then sat on my chest, as an additional precaution to prevent my escape.

He nearly squeezed the breath out of me, but I was determined I would not complain. I was ready to act as soon as free, but not a word would I utter if I could avoid it.

Frank Muller looked inside the wagon, and gave the Kafir a kick, which caused him to fall across my face.

Muller pulled him off and apologized, but I took no heed of what he said.

CHAPTER XL.

BROWNE TO THE RESCUE.

WE drove some distance before I was released from my very unpleasant position.

When I was allowed to sit up I could see we were nearing Wakkerstroom, and I dreaded going there, for Muller held supreme command, and of course all would gladly obey their leader.

"Now, Bessie, you see I am a man of my word. I said I would have you, even if I had to carry you as a prisoner. Your uncle is dead, and John Niel is dead also."

"Dead?" I gasped.

"Ay, dead. I heard it from one who has just left Pretoria."

"When was he killed?"

"Two days ago, and your sister Jess was wounded accidentally, and is dying."

"Take me to them."

"Them?"

"To Jess."

"And then——"

"I'll do anything you wish."

My spirit was broken, and as I believed both uncle and John were dead, I had no desire to live. I had formulated a plan, which was simply this:

Muller was to take me to see Jess, and then I would marry him, but at the altar I would shoot myself.

"If I take you to Jess, you will marry me?"

"Yes!"

"Good; then I will change the plan. We will call at the first dominie's, and he shall marry us, and we will go to Jess as man and wife."

"No, Frank Muller. I will not marry you until I have seen Jess."

"Yes, you will."

"I would rather die first."

"That I cannot help. My wife you shall be before you ever see Jess again."

That evening we camped in a beautiful valley, and quite a sumptuous repast was provided. Evidently all had been prepared with a view to this journey.

I refused to eat, for I was afraid of treachery.

A man, riding rapidly, came in sight, and, after giving the military salute to Muller, he handed him a letter.

"I was on the way to your residence," he said, "and luckily I saw you here."

Muller read the letter.

"D——n seize it!" he exclaimed, as he finished it, and then turning to the man, asked:

"How long will it take?"

"You can be back in two hours, or three at the furthest."

"Good; I will join you."

Frank Muller gave orders to the Kafirs that they were to remain with the wagon until he returned, and that on no account was I to be allowed to escape.

This instruction given, I had the satisfaction of seeing my great enemy ride away with the mounted messenger.

I began to speculate as to whether I could not bribe the Kafirs to aid me in my escape.

There was one of them that had several times tried to make me understand him, but as he could not speak English and I did not know the Batapi dialect, which was the only one he could speak, I was unable to understand what he wanted.

The other fellow was the one who had sat on my body when I was placed in the wagon, and I did not think he would be friendly.

If I could get my arms free, so that my revolver might be of use, it would be something gained, so I set my wits to work to devise some way of bribing these Kafirs.

Half an hour had gone by, when I heard the sound of horses.

They were galloping fast, and my last hope was gone, for I fully believed that it was Muller and the messenger returning.

My heart sank within me and I gave up all hope. I was doomed to die, for I would face death rather than live as Muller's wife.

The horses came nearer. The steady, regular sound of their feet could be heard now very distinctly, and I was getting very nervous.

The Kafirs, however, showed signs of uneasiness, and that rather gave me hope.

They jumped out of the wagon, and started the horses at a gallop.

"Halt!"

The voice sounded familiar, but still I did not recognize it.

A bullet whizzed over the wagon and struck one of the horses, making it plunge and rear.

Another bullet tore through the tented covering unpleasantly near my head.

I threw myself into the bottom of the wagon and prayed to Heaven for deliverance.

A third bullet crunched into the skull of the Kafir whose heavy body had nearly squeezed the life out of mine; and then the other thought his life was worth saving, so the horses were stopped.

In another minute I saw the bandaged face of Jacob Browne looking at me; and as that was withdrawn, I saw the still more welcome one of my uncle.

I was soon liberated, and the extra horses were hitched to the wagon, and we made tracks home again as quick as we could.

The excitement was almost too much for me, for I was prostrated with fever for a week, and still am very low.

Browne's wound was only a flesh one, and when he recovered from his swoon he searched for me.

He found one servant dead, another gagged, and the third—an old woman—so frightened that she declared she was dead, and was only waiting for the angels to fetch her to heaven.

Browne found uncle fastened to the flagstaff, defiant but uninjured, neither of Frank Muller's shots having taken effect.

Browne had overheard sufficient the day before to know which way I was to be taken, so he determined to follow and seize the first opportunity to attack my abductors and rescue me.

So this strange guest, who boasted of having been

pirate, bandit, and thief, has proved to be my best friend in the absence of John Niel!

I wonder if it is true that John is dead?

I am very doubtful, and my doubt gives me hope.

CHAPTER XLI.

LETTERS.

I HAVE had two letters from Pretoria.

John is not dead, but he is wounded. There is no danger, he says.

The other letter is from Jess, and is a very strange one. I cannot understand her at all.

She tells me all about the siege of Pretoria, and how, in a sortie, John had got wounded, and then she goes on:

"You must know, Bess, dear, that John Niel ought to have lived five hundred years ago. He is an ideal knight and is out of place in the nineteenth century. When you are his wife I want you to think of me sometimes, for I shall be far from you; we shall live in different worlds. I may never see you again, so I want to 'preach,' as you used to call it. John Niel is an exceptional man, and needs strange treatment. Don't let all your love be shown before marriage. Let him feel that you love him so much that you will put aside your own thoughts, inclinations, and desires for him.

"He has different thoughts to you, but always let his be the right ones on matters which you do not fully comprehend; and, above all, don't be jealous. John would die rather than wrong you, but if he is misjudged his nature may rebel. You know, Bess, you have often called me a witch; and as I can see clearer sometimes than others, I write you this, because I know both of you love, and I can see your failings."

I don't like the letter Jess has written. There is something uncanny about it. What does she mean, I wonder, by saying she will not see me again?

I wish she hadn't written. Yes, Jess can see clearly, and I know there is truth in what she says: I like to have my own way, and always think I am right.

Still it is not pleasant to be told of one's failings.

Now, John's letter is sweet, but not so satisfactory.

Is he dissatisfied with our engagement?

If so—— but no; he says he loves me, and he would never say so if it was not true.

In that letter he begins most coldly.

Fancy a love-letter commencing "Dear Bess."

Where is the love in that? I could cry with vexation.

Then he goes on:

"I have an opportunity to send a letter by a friend, who is the bearer of dispatches to that eccentric Jacob Browne——"

That's a nice way to write a love-letter. What do I care how he sends the letters as long as I get them.

Ah, now, but this is better:

"My dearest, I would never have come here had I known I should be so long separated; but when next I see you, I shall contrive to have a clergyman with me, and an hour after I arrive your visitors must say: 'How do you do, Mrs. Niel?'"

That part is so nice that I kissed it several times; but the next sentence makes me feel that I would like to slap his face.

He says:

"I am glad I have been so long away from you."

Glad is he? He had better stay away, but the next part is a little better, "for every hour I have been thinking of you."

So have I of you, John: but I don't like you to say, "I have learnt to know Jess thoroughly, and she is the dearest, best and most loving creature on earth——"

You are a mean, good-for-nothing thing, John Niel. I said, my eyes full of tears; but I look at the letter again, and see that he adds, "always understanding that my Bess is far and away above compare with any one."

Then comes some bad news.

"I don't think we shall be able to leave here for a month yet. Our commandant will not surrender, and our position is impregnable; but we can be starved out in about that time. The English government seems to have abandoned us to our fate. Beware of Frank Muller."

The letters are a great event in our lives, but I am far

from pleased with them. I wish I could send a letter to John, but I cannot. It would never reach him; but I would show him what a love-letter ought to be like.

Love is such a strange thing, and sometimes I wonder whether men like John Niel really can love, or whether they marry because there is something wanting in their lives—a need of a companionship which only a woman can fill.

It would be horrible to marry John, and then find that I was not everything to him. I should go mad.

Jacob Browne has been made commander of this district, and has converted our house into his headquarters.

He is a nice fellow, even if he has been a pirate.

This afternoon he actually asked me to marry him.

I could not refrain from laughing, though I was sorry for him.

He came to me, and I thought he had a headache, he looked so heavy about the eyes, and so sheepish.

I asked him if it was so, and he answered:

"Yes, Miss Bessie; I have headache, heartache, and aches all over me, and I want you to cure me."

"How?"

"By being my wife."

"Mr. Browne!"

"I mean it. Ever since that night when you came to my room, like a sheeted ghost, my heart has gone pit-a-pat whenever I have seen you. I can endure it no longer. A girl who can hit a bull's-eye five times out of six would stride a horse—I mean ride a horse by my side, and we would soon be rich. Say the word, and I will be again a brigand bold or a pirate chief. I will be honest or a rogue, just whichever pleases you best; only, Bess, you must be my wife. If you refuse, I wish, instead of saying it, you would think my heart a bull's-eye, and put five out of six bullets into it. Do, there's a dear. Kill me or love me, whichever suits you best."

"Mr. Browne, I am sorry to pain you," I said, "but I am engaged to be married, and I don't love you."

"But I love you."

"Very likely. So does Frank Muller."

"I would like to kill him."

"So would I."

His face brightened, and he put his arm round my waist, and looking very comical, said:

"I will kill him if you will marry me. I will bring his head on a dish as a wedding present. Oh! don't refuse me or I shall die."

"No, Mr. Browne, men don't die from such a cause. There are others better than I am, and you will yet find one to make you happy."

"Very well, Bessie. You hit a man straight from the shoulder, so I know you mean it. Forget all I have said, but when you want to stand on anything to increase your height, call on me and my body shall be your footstool; and, Bessie, I've got some money saved. I reckon I shall get killed in this war. It is in the chest up-stairs, and on the pocket-book is your name. It is all yours."

"But, Mr. Browne——" I was about to remonstrate, but he had disappeared.

It was a strange declaration of love, but a girl who was loved by Jacob Browne might easily fare worse, for he was good and brave, and I began to think all his tales about his piracy and brigandage were only yarns.

I saw no more of him that evening. The next day he met me as if he had never been in love.

He was just the same—jolly, talkative, and witty, fond of a yarn, and enjoying a good hearty laugh.

I learned to respect Jacob Browne.

CHAPTER XLII.
WHAT MIGHT HAVE BEEN.

I, JOHN NIEL, of Canford, England, instead of being able to chronicle myself a hero, must write down my character as that of a thoroughly despicable man.

I am engaged to be married to one of the sweetest girls in creation, and I love another.

Is it, as Allan Quatermain said, that one wants both sisters to make life perfectly happy?

I sit and reflect for hours, and this is the result:

I am engaged to Bessie—sweet, charming Bessie Croft. I love her to a certain extent. So much that if one other was removed my love for Bess would be greater than it could be for any living creature.

When I am with her I feel that there is a charm which

none other can possess, and I hate myself for being false even in thought to her, but——

There are two words in the English language fraught with more meaning than any others—"If" and "But."

Everywhere they obtrude their significance, and on every hand their power is felt.

Just now as I write I stop at the one word—but.

There it is; I hate myself, for in thought I am false to Bess; but who could help it, for I love Jess with that warmth of affection which is something more than can be expressed in words.

I have found out what love is, and what it means.

It is not friendship—it is not affection. It is as far above friendship as the sun is above the earth.

What is it? It is the soul of the world.

"God is love."

Ay, and love is godlike. It lifts the soul above all that is earthly and groveling, and they who love live in an ideal world of their own.

The earth has no attractions for them. No trials or troubles can ever destroy the love they feel.

The man who originated the falsehood which has passed into a proverb, "That when poverty comes in at the door, love flies out of the window," should be held up to eternal execration.

It is false, the very quintessence of a lie.

Poverty will, and often does, destroy friendship. Affection can be, and is, dimmed at times by poverty; but love, never.

Where there is true love, the more bitter the trial, the greater the trouble, the more love asserts itself. It is sweet to feel and know that though the frame may be reduced by hunger until the bones pierce through the skin, though the eyes start from their sockets like coals of fire, glassy and hot, through the fever of famine, yet love lives; and as the soul itself takes flight, and leaves behind the poor, sunken, starved body, the last words are words of love; and when the tie is broken, the love of angels bears the released soul to a heaven which is all love. That is true love.

And that love which is soul-absorbing—which will outlive life itself—that love I felt for Jess.

It was pure, holy, and godlike.

Is it wrong to love?

No. And I felt that even life itself was but a poor thing to offer in place of love.

And Jess loves me.

Never shall I forget that one time when, at Pretoria, I was wounded, but not seriously. The rumor reached her I was dead.

When I returned, able to totter into the temporary residence, I saw her, and as she stood, her breast heaving with emotion as the sea heaves when the fierce and angry scowl of the tempest has passed, she appeared a very incarnation of woman's love—of that intense, earnest depth of affection which is stronger than the grave—of that love which can say that when the sun has ceased to shine, when the heavens and earth shall be gathered together and hurled into oblivion, when ten thousand times ten thousand years have passed, it will live.

I looked at her, and as my eyes met hers, as she saw the lovelight in mine and I beheld her whole face transformed, every wrinkle was gone, and a face beaming with a youthful beauty, eyes sparkling with the fire of passion, I looked into those eyes with a spiritual intensity and I forgot Bessie, my engagement to her, honor, all———— I knew but one thing, and that was that I loved Jess as I had never loved any living creature—that I loved her as she loved me—that for her sake I would sacrifice all I held dear—that I would rather die than lose her. I felt all this, and I was fascinated, absorbed in the one loved being. Our heads were drawn closer by a strange magnetic power until our lips met in one long, earnest, burning kiss.

> "A long, long kiss, a kiss of youth and love
> And beauty, all concentrating like rays
> Into one focus, kindled from above;
> Such kisses as belong to early days,
> Where heart, and soul, and sense in concert move,
> And the blood's lava, and the pulse ablaze,
> Each kiss a heart-quake—for a kiss' strength,
> I think it must be reckon'd by its *length*.
>   Theirs endured
> Heaven knows how long— no doubt they never reckon'd;
> And if they had, they could not have secured
> The sum of their sensations to a second.
> They had not spoken; but they felt allured,
> As if their souls and lips each other beckon'd."

For a time we gave ourselves up to the madness of our passion.

I forgot everything save that I clasped in my arms the one being that I loved with an eternity of intense passion. My eyes shone and sparkled, and flashed; I saw their reflection in hers.

Love had done for us both what Mephistopheles did for Faust, had rejuvenated us.

We were young once more, and in our youth we rejoiced, until gradually Jess regained the consciousness due to our position, and she said:

"Oh, John, John, it is wrong, very wrong; you belong to another. You are engaged to Bessie."

My brain whirled with delirium, my pulse was fevered, my heart beat tempestuously, and my blood flowed like a lava tide through my veins.

I would have given my soul to have retained Jess in my arms. Such was love's delirium, but Jess—God bless her—was noble and true.

She saved us.

'Saved us by the strength of her will. Saved us by keeping honor ever before her eyes, and though she loved me, though she confessed that her life would know no happiness away from me, she never lost control of herself, and by the strength of her will declared:

"I give you up—I give up all for my sister Bessie. Make her happy, John, and Heaven will bless you."

The words were burned into my brain. I was mad. The loss of blood from my wound added to the intensity of my feeling, and I exclaimed:

"Jess, my own dear Jess, do not leave me—I can never know another moment of happiness away from you."

"You must not talk so, compose yourself for Bessie's sake; she loves you, and will make you a good wife."

"I would rather die than give you up."

"Perhaps 'twould be better so."

"Should you grieve, Jess, if I were to die?" I asked.

"No. I should breathe a sigh of relief if I heard of your death," she said, with a strange expression on her face. It staggered me, and I asked why?

In the same tone of voice, with the same far-off expression, as though her soul was away from earth, she answered:

"Because I should know you would be mine, then, mine only, and in Heaven we should be united, for I should soon join you."

Her face changed its expression, and Jess was herself again.

"John—John Niel," she said, almost harshly. "We are both guilty, both in the wrong—never must we speak again as we have done. We must forget the delirium through which we have passed, and you must devote yourself to Bess."

The dream was gone for the time, and I chafed over it, for I could not reconcile my mind to the loss of the one being I loved so much.

The events of the next week left us no chance for love episodes. Several sorties had taken place, and in every case the Boers had been successful.

At last Jess had obtained a pass from Hans Coetzee for us to return to Mooifontein.

It was a mystery to me how she obtained it, but she did, and we started on our homeward journey.

Alas! we soon found that our pass was a delusive one, for Frank Muller had planned that we should be murdered on our way.

The perils we underwent have all been told elsewhere, so my task is but a light one in recording the events of the journey home.

Muller, under pretense of shooting at vilderbeestes, had twice tried to kill me, but his last daring undertaking was skillfully planned.

Pleading that we must avoid an encampment of the English, he ordered our cavalcade to move to the right and cross the river at a ford of which he claimed a knowledge.

It was dark when we reached the river, but we were ordered to make the crossing.

We were but prisoners, and had to obey.

The moment the horses stepped into the water they began to rear and plunge, for they were getting out of their depth.

There was no ford there at all. I seized the reins, and tried to turn the horses round, but a shower of bullets rattled over our heads, and Frank Muller shouted:

"You cannot escape me now. You shall both die; and I will marry Bess!"

We couldn't hear whether he said anything more, for the roar of the water as it dashed over the rocks drowned his voice. We were carried down the stream by the force of the current, and certain death was before us.

"Have we a chance of life?" asked Jess.

"I don't think so," I answered.

"I am not sorry."

And then she got close to me, and I put my arms round her and clasped her to my bosom.

"John!" she whispered. "Fate has ordained we are not to live together. Are you afraid to die with me?"

"No, dearest Jess. It is sweet to die with you in my arms."

"You are all my own. Oh, John, I don't know how I could live without you."

"You shall not try. If we get safe out of this adventure, I will make a clean breast of it to Bessie——"

"No, no, no!" she almost shrieked.

"Pray Heaven we die together, but if we live you must never breathe a word of this to Bess. On your honor swear it. You must marry her, and love and cherish her as if you had never seen me."

"I cannot."

"You must."

"I don't think we shall escape," I said, as the wagon began to rock to and fro on the angry waters.

"I hope not. Kiss me, John, for the last time."

I kissed her, not once, but many times, and then the wagon stopped. It had got wedged in between some rocks, and was held fast until morning.

Jess was asleep in my arms.

Our clothes were wet, and we looked miserable objects, but on Jess' face was a look of such calm happiness that I disliked waking her; but it must be done.

"Jess!"

"Yes, love."

How sweet it was to hear her speak to me in that way.

She opened her eyes and looked round, astonished at finding herself lying in my arms, in that wagon, half filled with water.

"We are saved."

"I am sorry."

"But, Jess, my own, my darling——"

She would not let me finish, but with a strong control of her feelings, said:

"No more of that. I should have liked to die in your arms, but since fate has ordered that we are to live, we must endure. Love must never be mentioned by you again to me. We are brother and sister, but no more. John Niel, remember! Never again must you breathe one word of that—let it be but as a dream of the past."

And that was the last we ever said of that blissful vision of the "might be" which we were not destined to enjoy together.

It was a glimpse of what might have been, and one which opened the gates of Heaven to us for a few hours.

CHAPTER XLIII.

A VICTIM'S SACRIFICE.

"BESSIE! Bessie Croft!"

I heard my name called several times, and in different tones of voice.

What was it? Who wanted me?"

I hurried down-stairs, and found Jacob Browne anxious for me.

"What is it, Mr. Browne?" I asked.

"My dear Bessie, forgive me calling you so, but I am dying."

"Dying?"

"Yes, Bess, dying; but I could not die until I had seen you."

"What makes you say you are dying?" I asked, almost incredulously.

"See!" and he pulled open his shirt and showed me a wound in his chest, made evidently with a poisoned arrow.

"Who did it?"

"I think it was Hendrick, the one-eyed witch doctor."

"Oh, Mr. Browne, what could be his motive? Can nothing be done? Can I not get you anything?"

"No, Bessie. I am dying gradually; the poison is in my blood, and in a few hours all will be over; but there will be no pain. Muller will now be the commandant of this district; and it is his hand which planned it."

"I see it all."

"Bessie, all I have will be yours, there is a pretty good pile in the old chest. It is all honest money, lass, so don't scruple to take it. Kiss me once, won't you?"

I bent over the dying man and pressed my lips to his. He smiled, and the smile gradually died away, and I knew that with that kiss of mine on his lips his soul was wafted into the great unknown.

Since that hour only a few days have passed, but what I have suffered. Words can but feebly express the agonies I have endured, and now I am the promised wife of Frank Muller. It all came about through torture and pain.

Frank Muller, Hans Coetzee, and sixteen others besieged our house, and on the pretense that uncle was a rebel and an aider of the English cause, seized him, and held a court-martial, at which he was sentenced to death.

To add to their villainy they set fire to the house, and in a few hours nothing but two barns, set apart as our prisons, remained of the place which had been an ornament to the whole country, and which had taken uncle nearly twelve years to build.

Then it was that Muller came to me.

"Miss Bessie," he said, "you see I am a man of my word. I declared war because I saw no other way to get you. I could have saved all your friends alive if you had but consented, but you refused, and John Niel is dead and the aasvogels have long since devoured his body. Jess is buried at Pretoria, or on the way from there, for I hear she was shot down when attempting to escape; and now in a few hours your uncle will be shot——"

"Spare him!"

"On one condition. Marry me, and I will not only destroy the warrant for your uncle's death, but I will rebuild Mooifontein. Marry me, and you shall have the diamond lands at Basta Marica——"

"What of them?"

"They are confiscated, as also is your money in the Pretoria Bank."

"And you ca. that justice?" I asked, almost stunned

with the recital of the accumulated misfortunes which had befallen us.

"Justice, my dear Bessie; don't you know that in love and war all things are fair?"

"Love, Meinheer Muller! Never mention such a word, for it is blasphemy as it falls from your lips."

"No, Bessie, you wrong me. I have not been a good man, but I swore you should be my wife, and all the powers of the other world and this could not stop me. I love you so much that I would kill my best friend if he was in the way. I love you so that there is no crime I would not commit, if by that means I could win you for my wife. Now you are mine."

"No, no—never!"

"Then your uncle dies, but that won't save you, for you shall be mine, even then."

"But how do I know you will save my uncle?"

"I will give this warrant into the parson's hands, who shall have orders to destroy it the very moment he declares you to be my wife."

I hesitated. What mattered it now whether I lived or died. If I could save my dear old uncle, I should be content.

No sacrifice would be too great for that.

Muller saw his advantage and seized me in his arms, and pressed his hateful kisses on my lips.

How they seemed to burn me!

If I had possessed a weapon I would have killed him.

"You will be mine?" he asked.

"I suppose so, but I hate you, I loath and detest you more than ever, and, if I am your wife, every day I will plot and plan to accomplish your ruin."

He only laughed, and said he would take the risk.

And so I am Frank Muller's promised wife.

To-morrow I shall be no longer free.

To-morrow I shall be a slave, but out of my degradation, through my sacrifice, uncle's life will be saved.

Dear old uncle! He would have given his life for me. I am giving even more for him.

CHAPTER XLIV.

DELIVERANCE—BUT AT WHAT A COST!

The day has gone, and I am free.
But at what a cost!
The unexpected always happens, but sometimes the mind is so overwrought that even the most horrible certainty is better than the suspense of uncertainty.
I did not sleep all last night.
The thought of my sacrifice preyed upon my mind.
I had planned all sorts of ways of escape.
Should I kill myself as soon as uncle's death warrant was destroyed?
If I did, would not Muller at once find means of avenging himself by killing poor feeble old uncle?
The most effectual way would be to kill Muller.
But could I do it?
No!
I could not stain my hands with blood unless I could kill him in defense of my honor; but as his wife I should be his slave.
"Great Father in heaven," I prayed, "send me deliverance!"
My prayer was answered.
The morning dawned, and my prison door was opened by Hans Coetzee.
"You are free," he said.
I looked at him, not understanding what he meant.
The next moment I was clasped in uncle's arms.
He was standing on the greensward. There was a bright gleam in his eye, even though it dwelt on the charred ruins of our home.
The Boers and Kafirs stood about in groups.
"They are discussing my wedding," I thought.
I was nerved for the ordeal, for uncle's brightness more than recompensed me for my impending sacrifice.
After a good, long embrace, uncle said, with a sigh of relief:
"Muller is dead."
"What?" I cannot say that I asked the question, for I shouted or shrieked out the one word, so loud and

shrill that it seemed to echo in the hills away beyond the river.

"What?" I repeated.

"Frank Muller is dead."

"Thank Heaven!"

"You are right, Miss Bessie, we all say the same," put in old Hans Coetzee.

"He was stabbed to the heart, last night," said uncle.

"Stabbed?"

"Yes!"

"Who by?"

"That we don't know, but no one wants to find out, for, if found, the murderer would have to be shot, and all are glad the bad man is dead."

It was true. Frank Muller lay in his tent on the eve of his wedding, dreaming bright dreams of the bride he had won by fraud, crime and murder.

In the midst of his joyous dreams, when a smile of triumph was on his face, some one had driven a sharp knife through his evil heart.

I was sorry for the crime, but I thanked Heaven for my deliverance.

The warrant for uncle's death was torn up, and Frank Muller was buried in the grave he had prepared for my dear old uncle.

The evening was drawing in, and the neighbors had all gone away, for uncle and I had declared that we would sleep in the barns which had been our prison house the night before.

We were just retiring for the night, when we saw in the distance a man struggling along under a heavy burden.

He got nearer. His appearance seemed familiar, but he was gaunt and thin; a long, thick beard covered the cheeks and chin; his clothes were ragged and dirty, but as he got close to us we recognized in that poor, miserable-looking object—John Niel!

In his arms he carried poor Jess.

Alas! she had gone home. Her prayer was granted, for John told us, as he wiped the tears from his eyes, that she had desired death.

It was not for long afterward that I learned from Jane

Neville, who had heard the deathbed confession of the Hottentot Jantje, that Jess was the murderer of Muller.

She had arrived at Mooifontein and heard me promise to be the wife of Muller.

She heard me say how much I hated him, and then she remembered the promise she had given mother long years before, that she would always think first of Bess.

She tried to induce Jantje to avenge the murder of his own father and mother, but failed, and then as the hours were rolling by, she did the deed herself.

Her great love for me had saved me from a living death.

Poor dear Jess! If thy pure spirit can see into my heart as I write, thou knowest how grateful I am, and yet thou canst see that I would rather have died in thy place, if thou by that means couldst have been free from the stain of blood.

"Greater love hath no man than this, that he lay down his life for his friends." And Jess, my darling, loving sister had given her life for me. I blame thee not! I cannot judge thee, neither can I think that the great Eternal could deal harshly with one who loved so much.

John told me how they had been hunted since they left Pretoria, and how he had been taken prisoner and Jess allowed to return home.

He knew no more until, two days later, faint and weary, he had managed to escape, and had reached the cave which was so well known to us all.

He was so exhausted that he laid down to rest.

When he awoke, he found a head resting on his breast. He roused up and saw to his horror that it was Jess—cold and stiff.

She had died in his arms, and her last breath had been breathed out on his manly bosom.

For weeks John was delirious with fever, and we expected he would have to be laid in the grave beside our beloved Jess, but his youth and strength triumphed, and he recovered.

The Transvaal had no attraction for us now.

England had withdrawn its army, and the republic again existed.

The accumulated wealth from the sales of diamonds from the Basta Marica property left by our father, as well as the land itself, was confiscated to the government; and England had, in its terms and conditions of withdrawal, sanctioned and guaranteed such confiscation.

We were ruined.

Mooifontein was a wreck, and all that remained was John's thousand pounds, which was safe in the bank at Newcastle. With this money we returned to England; and left our Jess in the far-off grave.

I married my heart's love; but often I have seen a dreamy far-away expression on John's face; and I wonder did he love Jess? I think he did, and I feel sure she loved him.

But John has been honest and true, and there is not a woman in all God's universe that has a better husband than I have.

"Jess" is a sacred word to us, and when they placed in my arms a tiny babe, I kissed it, and named it by the most holy name I knew—Jess.

It has been a blessing and comfort to us both, and little Jess shall be taught to love and honor her aunt, who looks down from Heaven on her little namesake, and I feel sure protects her and guards her from many dangers.

Dear, good Jess, more than sister, I love thee with a love which is greater than sister ever had before for one of her own sex.

John Niel is honored and respected, and there is a talk of sending him to Parliament; but if he goes, he says he will denounce any ministry that sanctions or approves such terrible crimes as the wars in Africa, in which England has been engaged.

CHAPTER XLV.

END OF JOHN NIEL'S JOURNAL.

Jess is dead!

I stood beside her grave out there at Mooifontein, and saw the earth cover her remains.

She is dead!

Oh, my heart, be still! I feel that my brain must go mad, my heart must burst.

Jess, my only love, my true wife! She was never

mine; but yet, if marriages are made in heaven, she was my destined bride.

Cruel fate separated us, and honor made me appear a scamp; for I must marry Bessie, even though my heart was in the grave beside the darling whose eyes had pierced my very soul, and whose love was far above rubies in value to me.

She is dead!

But what is death?

'Tis but the opening of the full-blown flower.

'Tis but the getting rid of the incubus and weariness of earth, and reveling in the grandeur and sublimity of the world of truth. The world where no sham or subterfuge can enter, but all is joy and purity.

Her last words to me will be stamped on my memory forever.

She confessed her love, but bade me act with honor, and marry Bessie.

Jess is dead! But I feel that her spirit will keep watch over me, and help me do my duty. I can fancy her singing now, as I have heard her sing on earth:

> "Oh! friends of mortal years—
> The trusted and the true—
> Ye are watching yet in the vale of tears,
> But I wait to welcome you.
>
> "Do I forget? Oh, no!
> For memory's golden chain
> Shall bind my heart to the heart below
> Till they meet to touch again.
>
> "Each link is strong and bright,
> And love's electric flame
> Flows freely down, like a river of light,
> To the world from whence it came."

There is comfort in the thought, and, dear Jess, I will be brave for thy sweet sake.

* * * * * *

The months have rolled away.

There is a pleasure in doing one's duty and acting with honor.

I conclude my journal, for I have but few things to record.

I have a good, bright, loving wife and a greater treasure still.

Yes, I am free to confess that earth does not contain a greater treasure than my little Jess.

She is my joy, my pride. Her winning ways, her pleasant prattle, her inquisitive questioning, her merry laughing face, her deep thoughtfulness, all make her the brightest, dearest and best of earthly angels.

Some day I will take her to South Africa, and she shall place a garland on the grave of her angel aunt—the dear Jess of the past. But not yet. Bessie knows of my love. I have told her of it, and she sympathizes with me.

Bessie, dearest, there is a pleasure in thy company which I knew not before, and though the love of that Jess who was mine, and yet not my own—that Jess who was brought into my life too late—though that love will live as a holy sentiment in my heart, yet I am happy, for I love my Bessie.

> "She is a flower, a lovely flower.
>   Gently nurtured, nobly bred;
> All that's rich or sweet or rare
>   At her dainty feet I spread,
>   My love, my own sweet love.
>
> "You boast your 'teeth of shining pearl,'
>   Your 'coral lips' and 'glossy curl;'
> But my love has all and more,
>   I cannot count her beauties o'er,
>   My love, my own sweet love.
>
> "My Bessie is the loveliest far,
>   Pure as spotless angels are;
> Her eyes are bright as ocean deep.
>   They shine upon me e'en in sleep.
>   Bessie! my own sweet love."

And at Mooifontein, in England, we pass our time, as happily as any can.

But we are not jealous of that dear loved one who gave her life to secure our happiness. Some day we shall join her, and in the realms of eternal life make one great and happy harmonious family.

EPILOGUE.

BY THE EDITOR.

My labor of love is over. I have given to the world the story of Bess, just a little before the same world was made acquainted with her sister, the brave, devoted, thoughtful Jess.

When I had got the book nearly ready for the press, I had some doubts.

Would Bess be jealous?

John Niel, ex-captain and now member of Parliament (for he was returned at the last general election), has gone into such rhapsodies about his love for Jess that I thought Bess would not like it to go before the public, so I wrote to Niel, and here is his—or rather, I should say—their answer:

"Mooifontein, Rutland, ——, 188—

"MY DEAR ADAIR,—I have read your letter several times, and have also pondered over the proof slips you sent me. Bess knows all, and I can lay my hand on my heart and honestly say, that my love for Jess is a sacred memory, but my deep attachment and lasting love for my darling Bessie is a living reality. Yes, I love her, and have no sighs of regret.

"As for being jealous, my Bess is too true a woman, and loves me with too deep a love to be jealous. She knows I am true to her in thought and word, and therefore she does not understand what jealousy means. Jealousy, she says, is a disease which should disqualify any one from marrying. So you see, dear Adair, you need have no hesitation in publishing. The story of Bess is, I think, interesting, because it is the innocent outpouring of our souls, written without any thought of publication. If you like, you can tear up the journals (you are at full liberty to do so), and whatever course you decide on, you will always find a warm welcome awaiting you when you care to visit your old and true friend,

"JOHN NIEL."

POSTSCRIPT BY BESSIE.

"I HAVE read the above, dear Captain Adair, and also your letter to John. You ought to be ashamed of yourself for thinking I should be jealous. Dear old John loves me and I love him, and I am proud of him because he still loves the dear spirit of self-sacrificing Jess.

"BESSIE."

So the last obstacle was removed, and I sent the last copy to the printers.

I have been deeply interested in the story, and can only wish that all its readers could take a trip to Mooifontein and see the billing and cooing which goes on there between those lovers, whose honeymoon never seems likely to end, for John Niel and Bessie grow more loving every day, and are proving that love can grow even after marriage.

I must not forget to say that I have just received a telegram which informs me that the coming generation will number among its heroines a Bess as well as a Jess; and John Niel declares he is the happiest man in the world, for he is the proud possessor of a darling Jess and a tiny Bess, whose entrance into this world of adventures dates back only a day or two from this writing. As I lay down my editorial pen I do so with the hope and prayer that the baby Bess may never have to endure the horrors and adventures of mamma Bess; but that in the future she may, like her mother, find the love of some man as honest and true as John Niel.

And now I have finished, and bid you a pleasant future even as you read the story of Bess.

[THE END.]

www.ingramcontent.com/pod-product-compliance
Lightning Source LLC
Chambersburg PA
CBHW020344170426
43200CB00005B/43